Solar System
Astrophysics

John C. Brandt

Assistant Astronomer, Space Division
Kitt Peak National Observatory
Tucson, Arizona

Paul W. Hodge

Assistant Professor, Department of Astronomy
University of California
Berkeley, California

McGraw-Hill Book Company, Inc.

New York
San Francisco
Toronto
London

Solar System

Astrophysics

SOLAR SYSTEM ASTROPHYSICS

Dedicated to
OUR PARENTS

Preface

This book has a twofold purpose. First, it is intended to be used as a text in advanced undergraduate or graduate courses in solar system astronomy and space physics. During the course of lecturing in such classes at the University of California, Berkeley, we became aware of the difficulties students experienced because of the lack of a suitable text. This discovery prompted us to prepare the present volume.

Second, we hope this book will be of some value to the growing band of men working in various fields of space research as a fairly high-level introduction to the astrophysics of the solar system. We have observed that many of these scientists, working in industry and government laboratories, often have a hard time in getting urgently needed information about or descriptions of various astronomical techniques. We hope that this volume will be a helpful guide to the principles, the facts, and the literature.

We assume that the reader is acquainted with the astronomical terminology given in elementary astronomy courses, although he need not be an alumnus of such a course. Any simple astronomy text will quickly familiarize him with the terms he needs to know. We assume further that he has completed a course in elementary and atomic physics and is familiar with use of the calculus. Although a large portion of the book can be read without recourse to higher mathematics, in certain sections we have given important derivations that require use of ordinary and vector calculus. The mathematical sections of these derivations could be omitted by classes or individuals without the necessary background.

During the preparation of this volume, the counsel and suggestions of the following individuals were most helpful: J. W. Chamberlain, D. Cudaback, G. Herbig, D. M. Hunten, W. Liller, H. Spinrad, and J. H. Waddell. We are also grateful to the many others who assisted with the preparation of the manuscript and to the individuals and organizations who supplied us with illustrations and other copyrighted material. Our task was made materially lighter through the efficient and conscientious help of Mrs. B. E. Denham, Miss C. Calhoon, Miss P. Minteer, Mrs. Rose Sullivan, M. L. Stephens, E. Hedemann, and W. Wewer.

John C. Brandt

Paul W. Hodge

Contents

Introduction

Science often appears to be a vast collection of unrelated data, specific experiments, and limited conclusions. In actual fact, these are steps in the solution of larger and more vital questions. A physicist who develops an instrument that can accelerate particles to 10^{10} ev does not merely want to see if the machine will perform as planned; he has in mind the potential of such an instrument to penetrate the structure of the nucleus and provide information on the nature of matter. Similarly, an astronomer who measures the distance to a certain distant galaxy is motivated by more than the intrinsic interest of such an observation; he also has in mind the greater problem of the nature of the cosmos, and his measurement is normally directed by his desire to answer the larger question. In the case of solar system research, the questions that appear to motivate and underlie a great number of the individual projects are the origin and the development of the solar system.

The detailed manner in which the solar system began and developed is still unknown, in spite of the fact that the solar system is one of the oldest and most hotly pursued problems of astronomy and astrophysics. A truly workable theory of the origin of the solar system, a cosmogony,

1

must be capable of explaining every known feature. It is unacceptable if it explains the motions but fails to account for the physical properties of the planets. It must be comprehensively successful and therefore intricately detailed.

No such theory exists. There are too many data and there is too little understanding. So far, astronomers tackling the problem have been content to deal only with certain gross features of the solar system, especially those which seem to be the most stable features and which are not likely to have been altered and confused by intervening events.

First among these data are certain strange regularities that are conspicuous because of their very nonrandom nature and that openly invite speculation on their cause. These are primarily concerned with the motions of solar system bodies. In particular, they are:

1. The planets' orbits are nearly coplanar.
2. The planets' orbits are nearly in the plane of the Sun's rotation.
3. The planets' orbits are nearly circular.
4. The direction of revolution of all planets in their orbits is the same, and it corresponds with the direction of solar rotation.
5. The direction of rotation of the planets is in the same sense as that of revolution.
6. The distances of the planets from the Sun follow a simple function, called Bode's law:

$$a_n = c + 2^n$$

where a_n is the semimajor axis of the orbit of the nth planet and c is a constant.

7. Each satellite system mimics the solar system in all of the above respects.
8. The planets contain far more angular momentum than does the Sun.

Of course, there are a few exceptions, but the above rules generally hold so well that the exceptions can normally be explained as due to some more recent event. For instance, Jupiter's outer satellites are flagrant violators of the rules, but they are believed to be asteroids that have been captured more recently by Jupiter because of its dominating mass and thus are unrelated to the original beginnings of the solar system.

Many of the early cosmogonies dealt only with the above data, but recent attempts have dealt more realistically with the physical properties of solar system bodies also. The mass, density, structure, and composition of each planet provide evidence which must be considered. Why, for instance, are the four inner planets so different in these respects from the outer ones? Also, why has Mercury an appreciably higher density than the Moon, although their sizes are nearly the same?

Table 1-1   Brief summary of theories of solar system origin

Author	Date	Features of theory	Does explain (chief points)
Descartes	1644	Vortex motion is the only stable type; primary and secondary vortices	Near circularity of orbits
Buffon	1745	A giant comet collided with the sun and tore off the planetary material	Coplanar orbits, rotations
Kant	1755	A rotating nebula condensed from interstellar gas	Coplanar orbits, rotations
Laplace	1796	A rotating nebula contracted, giving off rings of gas each time the centrifugal force became too large	Coplanar orbits, rotations
Bickerton	1878	Star-Sun encounter with explosive eruption forming the planets	Coplanar orbits, rotations
Chamberlin	1901	Star-Sun encounter with tidal eruption	Coplanar orbits, rotations
Moulton	1905	Star-Sun encounter with tidal eruption, planetesimal accretion	Coplanar orbits, rotations
Birkeland	1912	Ions from Sun formed rings in Sun's magnetic field	Discrete orbits
Arrhenius	1913	Head-on star-Sun collision leaving Sun and long filament	Coplanar orbits, angular momentum
Jeffreys	1916	Grazing star-Sun encounter caused long filament which fragmented	Coplanar orbits, angular momentum
Jeans	1917	Close star-Sun encounter caused tidal filament	Coplanar orbits, angular momentum
Berlage	1930	Gaseous disk or rings formed from solar particle emission	Bode's law
Russell	1935	The Sun was a binary which a star disrupted, forming filament	Coplanar orbits, angular momentum
Lyttleton	1936	Sun was a triple system; the other two bodies coalesced, were unstable, and left the system; a filament was formed	Coplanar orbits, angular momentum
Alfvèn	1942	Sun encountered a gas cloud briefly; atoms fell into toward the Sun, became ionized, and then went into orbits dictated by magnetic field	Coplanar orbits, Bode's law
Schmidt	1943	Sun encountered and captured a swarm of interstellar bodies, became planets by collisional accretion	Coplanar orbits, Bode's law
Von Weizäcker	1944	Turbulent eddies formed in contracting envelope of proto-Sun, forming planets and satellites	Coplanar orbits, Bode's law
Hoyle	1944	Sun was a binary, the other star became a supernova, expelling gaseous shells and leaving the system	Angular momentum, coplanar orbits
Whipple	1947	Proto-Sun captured dust or smoke cloud of large relative angular momentum	Angular momentum, rotations, coplanar orbits
Ter Haar	1938	Planets formed in turbulent contracting solar envelope	Angular momentum, rotations, coplanar orbits
Kuiper	1949	Planets formed due to gravitational instabilities in proto-Sun's surrounding envelope	Angular momentum, rotations, coplanar orbits

The smaller bodies of the solar system also must be explained. Recently, meteorites have been especially rich sources of evidence on the early history of the solar system. Isotopes of xenon in meteorites may actually provide an accurate time schedule for certain cosmogonic events. Also, it may be that meteors, comets, and interplanetary dust are the last leftover fragments of the pre-solar-system material.

Undoubtedly, most of what we know about the solar system is relevant to the question of origin. Probably, success in solving this puzzle will come only when the most important data are clearly isolated and the whole of our relevant knowledge is at the same time taken into account. Surely, solar system cosmogony is one of astronomy's most challenging future tasks.

Several of the many published theories on the origin of the solar system are summarized in Table 1-1. Most of these have dealt primarily with the motions and positions of solar system objects. Few of them have been worked out extensively in a quantitative way, and all fall far short of giving a truly workable theory that encompasses all relevant evidence.

There are two common types of theory: those that call upon an unusual and cataclysmic event to produce planets for a once-planetless Sun and those that propose that the planets were formed as normal by-products in the process of formation of the Sun itself. The latter view is most commonly held at present, but probably the choice will finally be made only when an accurate age for the Sun is determined astrophysically and accurate ages for the planets are obtained by isotope studies. Through such future evidence and a thorough understanding of the data discussed and explored in the following chapters, an acceptable cosmogonical theory will surely emerge.

BIBLIOGRAPHICAL NOTES

Jastrow, R., and A. G. W. Cameron (eds.): "Origin of the Solar System," proceedings of a 1962 conference at the Goddard Institute for Space Studies, Academic Press Inc., New York, 1963.

As a good general reference for the classical problems of solar system research and as an excellent introduction to the terminology used in astronomy, we recommend the following book:

Russell, H. N., R. S. Dugan, and J. Q. Stewart: "Astronomy. I. The Solar System," Ginn and Company, Boston, 1945 (rev. ed.).

Users of the present text should also refer to the current literature on solar system research. Recent review articles are frequently published in the following journals and review publications:

Icarus, Academic Press Inc., New York. Frequent bibliographies are published on various solar system subjects.

Space Science Reviews, Reidel Publishing Co., Dordrecht, Holland.

Annual Review of Astronomy and Astrophysics, Stanford University Press, Palo Alto, Calif.

Advances in Astronomy and Astrophysics, Academic Press Inc., New York.

Advances in Space Science and Technology, Academic Press Inc., New York.

Celestial mechanics

The application of Newton's law of gravity to the planets and other bodies of the solar system is a specialized discipline called *celestial mechanics*. In recent years the interest in celestial mechanics has experienced a tremendous increase because of the needs of the space effort, and numerous recent excellent texts and treatises have been published (see end-of-chapter lists). Because the detailed methods of celestial mechanics are so well treated in other books and because the emphasis of this volume is on astrophysics (which traditionally excludes celestial mechanics), this chapter is limited to basic principles and a few applications that are appropriate to other solar system problems.

2.1 PLANETARY MOTIONS AND THE LAW OF GRAVITATION

The basic facts concerning the motions of planets were inferred by Kepler in the seventeenth century in the process of reducing the observations of Tycho Brahe. Kepler's three empirical laws are:

1. The orbit of each planet relative to the Sun is an ellipse lying in a fixed plane; the Sun occupies one focus of the ellipse. The law can be written mathematically as

$$r = \frac{a(1 - e^2)}{1 + e \cos \eta} \tag{1}$$

where r is the distance from the Sun to the planet, a is the semimajor axis of the ellipse, e is the eccentricity (distance from center to focus divided by a), and η is the polar angle measured from the point of closest approach, called the *perihelion*.

2. The radius vector joining the Sun to each planet sweeps out equal areas of its ellipse in equal times. This implies

$$\frac{dA}{dt} = \frac{1}{2} r^2 \dot{\eta} = \frac{h}{2} \tag{2}$$

and the areal constant h is thus defined.

3. The squares of the orbital periods P of the planets are proportional to the cubes of the semimajor axes of the orbital ellipses. This law is here expressed in terms of the mean motion n, which equals $2\pi/P$, thus

$$n^2 a^3 = \text{const} \tag{3}$$

Kepler's second law, Eq. (2.1-2), implies that the angular momentum **J** is conserved since

$$\mathbf{J} = \mathbf{r} \times m\mathbf{v} = m\mathbf{r} \times (\dot{\mathbf{n}} \times \mathbf{r}) \tag{4}$$

The absolute magnitude is equal to $mr^2\dot{\eta}$, where m is the planet's mass. From Newton's second law we know that

$$\frac{d\mathbf{J}}{dt} = \mathbf{r} \times \mathbf{F} \tag{5}$$

Since $d\mathbf{J}/dt$ is zero and since **r** and **F** are not, we have the result that the force acts along the radius vector (central force). Thus, considering symmetry,

$$\mathbf{F} = \mathbf{r}\mathfrak{G}(r) \tag{6}$$

From the equation of motion

$$\mathbf{F} = m\mathbf{a} \tag{7}$$

and the radial acceleration in a rotating coordinate system, notice the appearance of the "centrifugal acceleration"

$$a_r = \ddot{r} - r\dot{\eta}^2 \tag{8}$$

we obtain the following equation for the force law,

$$F(r) = m\ddot{r} - mr\dot{\eta}^2 \tag{9}$$

Equation (2.1-9) can be rewritten in terms of the angular momentum [Eq. (2.1-4)] as

$$F(r) = m\ddot{r} - \frac{J^2}{mr^3} \tag{10}$$

or in terms of the areal constant as

$$F(r) = m\ddot{r} - \frac{mh^2}{r^3} \tag{11}$$

We may differentiate the equation of the orbit (2.1-1) to obtain

$$\ddot{r} = \frac{h^2}{r^3}\left[1 - \frac{r}{a(1 - e^2)}\right] \tag{12}$$

Equation (2.1-12) can be substituted into Eq. (2.1-11) to yield

$$F(r) = \frac{-mh^2}{a(1 - e^2)r^2} \tag{13}$$

Since h, a, and e are constants of the orbit, we find that the force is attractive and that it varies as the *inverse square*.

We do not, as yet, know that the constant in Eq. (2.1-13) is the same for all planets. This follows from Kepler's third law. Since the area of an ellipse is $\pi a^2(1 - e^2)^{\frac{1}{2}}$ and since the rate of sweeping out area is $h/2$, the period can be written as

$$P = \frac{2\pi a^2(1 - e^2)^{\frac{1}{2}}}{h} \tag{14}$$

The mean motion has been defined as $2\pi/P$ or

$$n = \frac{h}{a^2(1 - e^2)^{\frac{1}{2}}} \tag{15}$$

Thus,

$$n^2a^3 = \frac{h^2}{a(1 - e^2)} = \mu \tag{16}$$

Hence, the constant in Eq. (2.1-13) is the same for all planets, and

$$F(r) = \frac{-m\mu}{r^2} \tag{17}$$

From Newton's third law and Eq. (2.1-17), we know that a planet's attraction for the Sun is proportional to the planet's mass. Hence, the Sun's attraction for the planet must be proportional to the Sun's mass; thus,

$$F(r) = \frac{-mMG}{r^2} \tag{18}$$

where M is the mass of the Sun and G is a universal constant which must be determined experimentally and which has the approximate value of 6.67×10^{-8} cm^3/(g)(sec^2).

As is readily verified, the force law given by Eq. (2.1-6) or Eq. (2.1-18) has the property that

$$\nabla \times \mathbf{F}(r) = 0 \tag{19}$$

Since the force law has zero curl, we may introduce the gravitational potential such that

$$\mathbf{F}(r) = -\nabla V(r) \tag{20}$$

Such force fields (force a function of position only) are termed conservative because they lead to Eq. (2.1-24).

For a spherical mass or point mass,

$$V(r) = \frac{-mMG}{r} \tag{21}$$

The change in the potential energy in moving a point mass from r_1 to r_2 is

$$\int_{r_1}^{r_2} \mathbf{F} \cdot d\mathbf{r} = V(r_1) - V(r_2) \tag{22}$$

This is really a line integral, but because $\nabla \times \mathbf{F} = 0$, it is independent of the path. The potential is usually defined as the work done on the particle by the force as the particle is moved from some arbitrary point to a chosen reference point; for gravitational potentials, the reference point is usually chosen as $r = \infty$. If we denote the kinetic energy at a time t by T, a standard derivation yields

$$T_2 - T_1 = \int_{t_1}^{t_2} \mathbf{F} \cdot \mathbf{v} \, dt = \int_{r_1}^{r_2} \mathbf{F} \cdot d\mathbf{r} \tag{23}$$

Comparison of Eqs. (2.1-23) and (2.1-22) yields the equation of the conservation of energy,

$$T(r) + V(r) = E \tag{24}$$

2.2 THE ONE- AND TWO-BODY PROBLEMS

The motion of a body of negligible mass about a fixed mass point is the one-body problem. The equation of motion is derivable from Eqs. (2.1-11) and (2.1-13):

$$m\ddot{r} - \frac{mh^2}{r^3} = \frac{-mh^2}{a(1 - e^2)r^2} \tag{1}$$

The solution of this equation is just the inverse of the primary discussion in Sec. 2.1. It may be achieved formally by making the substitution $r = 1/u$. The solution is readily found to be

$$\frac{1}{u} = r = \frac{a(1 - e^2)}{1 + e \cos \eta} \tag{2}$$

The conservation of energy for the problem at hand (see Eq. 2.1-24) gives us

$$E = \frac{mv^2}{2} - \frac{mMG}{r} \tag{3}$$

From Eqs. (2.2-2) and (2.2-3) we can construct (after some manipulation) Table 2.2-1 concerning the type of orbit, eccentricity, and total energy. Since the parabola requires the least energy of any unbounded orbit, we may obtain an expression for the escape velocity by setting $E = 0$ in Eq. (2.2-3). This gives us

$$v_{esc} = \left(\frac{2MG}{r}\right)^{1/2} \tag{4}$$

Table 2.2-1

Orbit	e	E
Ellipse	$0 \le e < 1$	$E < 0$
Parabola	$e = 1$	$E = 0$
Hyperbola	$e > 1$	$E > 0$

The two-body problem is concerned with the motion of two bodies around their common center of gravity. It is readily reduced to the one-body problem. We set up a coordinate system relative to the center of mass. Let p be the distance from the center of mass to the primary or Sun and let q be the distance from the center of mass to the other body; then the center of mass is defined by

$$Mp = mq \tag{5}$$

The equations of motion are

$$\ddot{p} - p\dot{\theta}^2 = -\frac{mG}{r^2} \tag{6}$$

and

$$\ddot{q} - q\dot{\theta}^2 = -\frac{MG}{r^2} \tag{7}$$

where $p + q = r$. Adding the last two equations gives us

$$\ddot{r} - r\dot{\theta}^2 = -\frac{G}{r^2}(m + M) \tag{8}$$

Since the forces are still central, the areal velocity is still a constant and the equation is formally the same as in the one-body problem [Eq. (2.2-1)] with

$$\frac{h^2}{a(1 - e^2)} = G(m + M) \tag{9}$$

2.3   THREE–BODY PROBLEM: LAGRANGIAN POINTS

We shall have need for some information concerning the lagrangian points later in this book. The general problem of three bodies does not have a solution in closed form, but there do exist five stationary solutions or lagrangian points. At these points there are no net forces on a particle. An algebraic demonstration of the five lagrangian points is possible, but the details are too lengthy to be given here.

For the case of circular motion in the two-body problem, the gravitational attraction is equal to the centrifugal force. We seek the similar situation in the three-body problem, but here the condition of gravitational attraction balancing centrifugal acceleration occurs only in discrete points, the lagrangian points. The solutions are of two distinct types.

Consider for the purpose of illustration the system composed of the Earth, the Moon, and a body of small mass such as an artificial satellite. Solutions of the first class lie on a straight line joining the Earth and the Moon. They are called the straight-line solutions. Since the three straight-

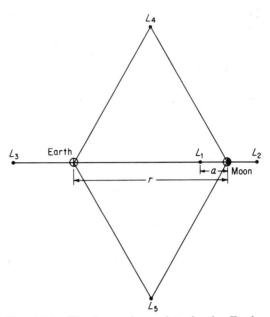

Fig. 2.3-1 The lagrangian points in the Earth-Moon system. See the text for discussion.

line points denoted by L_1, L_2, and L_3 rotate about the Earth with the same period as the Moon, the solutions are also said to be synodic. As an example, let us compute the position of the lagrangian point L_1 between the Earth and the Moon.

The geometry appropriate to this problem is shown in Fig. 2.3-1. For the Earth-Moon system, we can write down an equation for the distance a of the lagrangian point L_1 from the Moon. In our first degree of approximation, the quantity a is also the distance from the moon to L_2. This equation (balancing gravitational forces and centrifugal force) is

$$\frac{M_E G}{(r-a)^2} - \frac{M_M G}{a^2} = (r-a)\dot{\theta}_M^2 \tag{1}$$

where r and a are shown in the figure, G is the constant of gravitation, M_E and M_M are the masses of the Earth and Moon respectively, and $\dot{\theta}_M$ is the angular velocity of the Moon. Now,

$$h_M = r^2 \dot{\theta}_M \tag{2}$$

and Eq. (2.3-1) can be rewritten as

$$M_E G \left[\frac{1}{(r-a)^2} - \frac{M_M}{M_E a^2} \right] = \frac{(r-a)h_M^2}{r^4} \tag{3}$$

Let $\eta = M_M/M_E$ and let $y = a/r$. Inserting these abbreviations in Eq. (2.3-3) gives

$$\frac{1}{(1-y)^2} - \frac{\eta}{y^2} = \frac{(1-y)h_M^2}{M_E Gr} \tag{4}$$

If $M_E \gg M_M$, we would expect that y is small. Hence, we may use the expansion

$$\frac{1}{(1-y)^2} \approx 1 + 2y + 3y^2 + \cdots \tag{5}$$

Here we keep only two terms. We note that

$$P = \frac{2\pi r^2}{h_M} \qquad \text{taking } e = 0 \tag{6}$$

and from Kepler's third law, we also note that

$$P^2 = \frac{4\pi^2 r^3}{M_E G} \tag{7}$$

Thus, by squaring Eq. (2.3-6) and equating it to the above, it can be shown that $h_M^2/M_E Gr$ equals unity. Now by utilizing the series expansion of Eq. (2.3-5), we can rewrite Eq. (2.3-4) as

$$y^3 - \frac{\eta}{3} = 0 \tag{8}$$

Hence,

$$\frac{a}{r} = y \approx \left(\frac{\eta}{3}\right)^{1/3} \tag{9}$$

Here, we take a as positive, remembering that there is one lagrangian point on each side of the Moon. For the Earth-Moon system, $\eta = \frac{1}{82}$ and we find $a = 61,000$ km. We can correct this value by considering the term in $3y^2$ neglected in the expansion given by Eq. (2.3-5). With this term included, we have

$$y^3 = \frac{\eta}{3(1+y)} \tag{10}$$

Since y appears in an insensitive manner on the right-hand side of this equation, we can use the value of y obtained from Eq. (2.3-9), which we now call y_1, to obtain an improved value y_2. Hence,

$$y_2(L_1) = +\left[\frac{\eta}{3(1+y_1)}\right]^{1/3} = y_1\left(\frac{1}{1+y_1}\right)^{1/3} \tag{11}$$

Since y_1 is small compared to 1, we may use the series expansion again to obtain

$$y_2(L_1) = +y_1(1 - y_1)^{1/3} = +y_1\left(1 - \frac{y_1}{3}\right) \tag{12}$$

Likewise,

$$y_2(L_2) = -y_1\left(1 + \frac{y_1}{3}\right) \tag{13}$$

For the case of the Moon, this gives

$$\begin{aligned} a_2(L_1) &= 58{,}000 \text{ km} \\ a_2(L_2) &= -64{,}000 \text{ km} \end{aligned} \tag{14}$$

It should be noted explicitly that L_1 does not occur at the neutral gravity point in the Earth-Moon system.

The other two lagrangian points, L_4 and L_5, are found at the apex of an equilateral triangle whose base is the Earth-Moon line. The most interesting examples of natural bodies that occupy points L_4 and L_5 are the Trojan asteroids, which are in the Sun-Jupiter system (Sec. 12.1).

In the foregoing discussion, we have said nothing concerning the stability of objects in the various lagrangian points. In other words, if an object is displaced slightly from one of the lagrangian points, does it tend to return to the point or does it tend to go farther away? In the case of the straight-line solutions L_1, L_2, L_3, instability occurs in any event. However, the equilateral triangle solutions can be stable (depending on the mass ratios involved), and they are stable for the case of the Trojan asteroids, for example.

2.4 THREE-BODY PROBLEM: COMET TAILS

To consider this problem, we introduce the coordinate system shown in Fig. 2.4-1. We adopt the convention (as shown) that primed coordinates x', y' refer to the tail particle and unprimed coordinates x, y refer to the head of the comet (see Chap. 9 for comet nomenclature). The two coordinate systems shown are related by

$$r\xi = xx' + yy' - r^2 \tag{1a}$$

and

$$r\eta = yx' - xy' \tag{1b}$$

The physical situation considered is this: The force on the comet head is the gravitational attraction of the Sun; the mass of the head is considered to be so small that the motion of the tail particle is unaffected by the mass of the comet. However, it is clear that forces other than solar

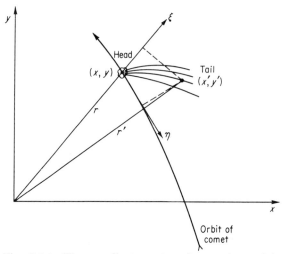

Fig. 2.4-1 The coordinate system for use in studying comet tails. The ξ-η system has the origin in the head of the comet with ξ in the radial direction and η in the direction opposed to the motion of the comet.

gravitation act on the tail particles, and an additional parameter must be introduced. The equations of motion for the head are

$$\ddot{x} + \frac{x}{r^3} = 0 \tag{2a}$$

and

$$\ddot{y} + \frac{y}{r^3} = 0 \tag{2b}$$

Note the use of a rectangular coordinate system (no centrifugal force). Also note that we are working the problem in two dimensions, i.e., the z coordinate is neglected. The unit of length in Eqs. (2.4-2) is the astronomical unit (1 AU = 1.5×10^{13} cm), and the unit of time is the reciprocal of Gauss's constant, $1/k = 58.1$ days. The equations of motion for the tail particles are

$$\ddot{x}' + \frac{\mu x'}{r^3} = 0 \tag{3a}$$

$$\ddot{y}' + \frac{\mu y'}{r^3} = 0 \tag{3b}$$

Here we have introduced the parameter μ, which is equal to the ratio of the actual force on the tail particle to the gravitational force. The nongravitational force is invariably repulsive, and its magnitude is given by $1 - \mu$; this is the total repulsive force in units of the gravitational force, but it is undiminished by gravity. The parameter $1 - \mu$ determines the form of the tail particle orbit. For $1 - \mu < 1$, the solar gravitation is diminished and the particle moves in a hyperbola concave to the Sun. For $1 - \mu = 1$, the effective gravity is zero and the particle moves in a straight line. For $1 - \mu > 1$, the net force is repulsive and the orbit is a hyperbola convex to the Sun.

The solution we desire is

$$x'(t) = x'(x,y, \text{ initial conditions, } t - t_0) \tag{4}$$

The Bessel-Bredichin method is to expand each coordinate in a Taylor series in $T = t - t_0$:

$$x' = x'\Big]_{t_0} + \frac{dx'}{dt}\Big]_{t_0} T + \frac{d^2x'}{dt^2}\Big]_{t_0} \frac{T^2}{2} + \cdots \tag{5}$$

The required coefficients in Eq. (2.4-5) are determined from the equation of motion. The procedure for determining $\xi(t)$ and $\eta(t)$ from the equations given above is straightforward in principle, but lengthy. We do not reproduce the details here. The results can be written as

$$
\begin{aligned}
\xi = -gT \cos G &+ \left[\frac{1 - \mu}{r^2} - 2g \sin G \frac{p^{1/2}}{r^2} \right] \frac{T^2}{2} \\
&+ \left[\frac{1 - \mu}{r^3} \frac{4e \sin v}{p^{1/2}} - g \cos G \left(\frac{2\mu}{r^3} - \frac{3p}{r^4} \right) \right. \\
&\left. \qquad - g \sin G \frac{6e \sin v}{r^3} \right] \frac{T^3}{6} + \cdots
\end{aligned} \tag{6}
$$

and

$$
\begin{aligned}
\eta = +gT \sin G &- g \cos G \left(\frac{2p^{1/2}}{r^2} \right) \frac{T^2}{2} + \left[\frac{1 - \mu}{r^4} 2p^{1/2} \right. \\
&\left. - g \sin G \left(\frac{\mu}{r^3} + \frac{3p}{r^4} \right) - g \cos G \frac{6e \sin v}{r^3} \right] \frac{T^3}{6} + \cdots
\end{aligned} \tag{7}
$$

Here we have kept terms up to the cubic; it must always be remembered that the expression obtained is only a series expansion valid for times which are sufficiently small. The various symbols used are as follows: g is the velocity of ejection from the head; G is the angle the direction of ejection makes with the radius vector; $p = a(1 - e^2)$ is called the parameter of the orbit; e is the eccentricity; and v is the true anomaly, the angle of the comet with respect to perihelion as seen from the Sun. This bears the same physical significance as the angle η in Secs. 2.1 and 2.2.

If g is constant and G is allowed to assume all values, Eqs. (2.4-6) and (2.4-7) give a drifting and expanding form for the comet head if it is formed from particles ejected at one instant (halos). If the ejection is continuous, the equations can be used to show that the envelope of the head is parabolic. Finally, the general shape of the tail can be obtained by assuming that $\langle g \rangle = 0$. Then,

$$\xi = \frac{1 - \mu}{r^2} \frac{T^2}{2} + \frac{1 - \mu}{r^3} \frac{4e \sin v}{p^{\frac{1}{2}}} \frac{T^3}{6} + \cdots \tag{8}$$

and

$$\eta = \frac{1 - \mu}{r^4} 2p^{\frac{1}{2}} \frac{T^3}{6} + \cdots \tag{9}$$

The time may be eliminated from the last two equations to give the syndyname of the tail axis, viz.,

$$\xi = \left[\frac{9r^2(1 - \mu)}{8p}\right]^{\frac{1}{3}} \eta^{\frac{2}{3}} + \frac{2re \sin v}{p} \eta \tag{10}$$

Equation (2.4-10) does not represent the path taken by the tail particles; it does represent the curve describing the location (at a given time) of particles continuously emitted from the head. Notice that the tail is tangent to the radius vector at the head of the comet. This completes our brief introduction to the Bessel-Bredichin theory of comet tail motions.

2.5 A SIMPLE APSE PROBLEM

The closed, elliptical orbits found for the two-body problem in Sec. 2.2 occur when there are no additional forces in the problem and when the attracting body can be considered a point source. If the force law is not the inverse-square law, then the orbit is not, in general, a closed one. However, if the departures from the inverse-square law are small, the orbit approximates an ellipse. In that case, the orbit may be considered as being an ellipse which is slowly rotating. The major axis of the ellipse determines the line of apsides, or simply the apse line. We now consider the case of a satellite in an approximately elliptical orbit in the equatorial plane of a planet which can be represented as a slightly oblate spheroid.

The potential of a slightly oblate spheroid can be written as

$$V(r) = -Gm\left(\frac{M}{r} + \frac{C - A}{2r^3}\right) \tag{1}$$

or, setting $u = 1/r$,

$$V(u) = -Gm[Mu + \tfrac{1}{2}(C - A)u^3] \tag{2}$$

where M is the mass of the planet, m is the mass of the satellite, and the moments of inertia C and A are defined, for example, by

$$C = \iiint_{\text{planet}} \rho\tilde{\omega}^2 \, dx \, dy \, dz \tag{3}$$

Here C is the moment of inertia about the axis of rotation and $\bar{\omega}$ is the distance from the axis. A is the analogous integral about an axis lying in the equatorial plane.

The equation necessary for this problem can be derived from the equation of conservation of energy

$$E = \tfrac{1}{2}m\dot{r}^2 + \tfrac{1}{2}mr^2\dot{\theta}^2 + V(r) \tag{4}$$

In terms of u and θ, $\dot{r}$ can be written as

$$\dot{r} = -r^2\dot{\theta}\,\frac{du}{d\theta} \tag{5}$$

and Eq. (2.5-4) becomes

$$E = \tfrac{1}{2}mr^2\dot{\theta}^2\left[r^2\left(\frac{du}{d\theta}\right)^2 + 1\right] + V(r) \tag{6}$$

Since the force is still central, θ can be eliminated through a relation analogous to Eq. (2.1-4). Thus

$$E = \frac{1}{2}\frac{J^2}{mr^2}\left[r^2\left(\frac{du}{d\theta}\right)^2 + 1\right] + V(r) \tag{7}$$

or finally,

$$\frac{du}{d\theta} = \left\{\frac{[E - V(u)]2m}{J^2} - u^2\right\}^{\frac{1}{2}} \tag{8}$$

This can be written as

$$\theta - \theta_0 = \int \frac{du}{(\{[E - V(u)]2m/J^2\} - u^2)^{\frac{1}{2}}} \tag{9}$$

or with the potential inserted explicitly,

$$\theta - \theta_0 = \int \frac{du}{\{[E + GmMu + Gm(C - A)u^3/2](2m/J^2) - u^2\}^{\frac{1}{2}}} \tag{10}$$

The integration is possible if we can find the roots of the cubic. Approximate solutions can be obtained by considering that the graph of the cubic $f(u)$ resembles the curve shown in Fig. 2.5-1. Thus, we may obtain an approximate solution for γ by neglecting the constant term, and α and β can be approximated by neglecting the term in u^3. The procedure is straightforward, and Eq. (2.5-10) becomes

$$\theta - \theta_0 = 2\int_\alpha^\beta \frac{du}{[Gm^2(C - A)/J^2]^{\frac{1}{2}}[(u - \alpha)(u - \beta)(u - \gamma)]^{\frac{1}{2}}} \tag{11}$$

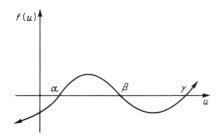

Fig. 2.5-1   A sketch of the cubic $f(u)$ [Eq. (2.5-10)] showing the solutions α, β, and γ which appear in Eq. (2.5-11).

Notice that we have written the indefinite integral as twice the definite integral between α and β, because this clearly corresponds to the region of bounded motion.

The integration is straightforward, and the answer is 2π plus a quantity θ_A, which we identify as the angular rotation of the apse per revolution:

$$\theta_A = \frac{3\pi G^2 M(C - A)m^4}{J^4} \tag{12}$$

This formula relates the rotation of the apse to the value of $C - A$ for the particular planet. This approximation is sufficient to give meaningful values for the ratios of the apsidal motion around Mars of Deimos and Phobos; it also gives a reasonable value for the Jovian $C - A$ from the apsidal motion of Jupiter's satellites. Such information is of value in the study of planetary interiors (Sec. 15.1).

2.6 EXPERIMENTAL CELESTIAL MECHANICS

Now that artificial satellites and planets are available, there are many experiments that can be performed besides the straightforward data-gathering type. An obvious one would obtain information concerning the internal structure of the Earth (for example, in the spirit of Sec. 2.5). However, it appears that the most interesting aspects of experimental celestial mechanics are those which could yield information concerning the nature of the gravitational interaction or serve as checks on general relativity.

One entertaining problem in the theory of gravitation concerns the gravitational constant G. There is no a priori reason why G could not, for example, vary with time. In fact, some geological evidence can be interpreted in terms of a G which varies as the inverse of the age of the universe. This is also a feature of a cosmology due to Dirac. A suitably placed satellite would provide a gravitational standard of time which could be compared with an atomic standard on the Earth's surface; this experiment would be suitable for detecting a secular variation in G. Many other experiments are available to investigate possible aspects of gravitational interaction.

The only established astronomical test of general relativity is the well-known advance of the perihelion of the orbit of the planet Mercury. The solar gravitational red shift (due to the prediction that the frequency of light varies with the gravitational potential) is not considered definite, because the effect appears to be masked by spurious frequency shifts caused, for example, by turbulence in the solar atmosphere. The gravitational red shift has been measured in the laboratory via the Mössbauer effect, but an independent astronomical check would be most desirable. This could be secured by comparing a rocket-borne atomic time standard with a ground-based one. A technical problem is which type of atomic clock would retain sufficient stability to be useful in a satellite environment; note that allowance must be made for the special relativistic time dilation.

The experiments described and others like them promise substantial contributions to our understanding of the basic physical processes. It is to be hoped that they will be vigorously pursued.

2.7 STABILITY OF THE SOLAR SYSTEM

One of the most difficult problems in celestial mechanics is that of the stability of the planetary orbits over very long periods of time. If one asks how many years will elapse before the orbit of the Earth, for instance, is appreciably different, one must consider many things. In addition to a rigorous solution to the planetary equations of motion and perturbation, which are not yet within our mathematical capabilities, one must also consider relativistic, tidal, and electromagnetic effects, as well as possible encounters with stars or interstellar clouds.

The problem remains unsolved. Only certain statements can presently be made concerning such individual subproblems as the secular variation of the orbital elements of a planet assuming newtonian gravitation as the only force involved. For instance, Table 2.7-1 results from

Table 2.7-1   Yearly secular variation in mean yearly motion

Planet	Secular variation,
Mercury	$+0.''00000495$
Venus	$+0.''00000096$
Earth	$-0.''00000403$
Mars	$+0.''00000169$

Newcomb's computation of the secular changes in the mean motion of four planets. From this we see that for the Earth the mean yearly motion decreases by $0.''000004$ per year, neglecting all effects but newtonian per-

turbations. Since the yearly motion of the Earth is $360°/\text{yr} \times 3600''/$
deg $= 1,296,000''/\text{yr}$, this secular decrease is one part in 3×10^{11}. Thus
the tropical year (365.24 days) decreases by the amount of about 10^{-9}
days or 10^{-4} sec every year.

In 10^{10} years only a relatively small difference in the Earth's orbit
would be noticeable if other effects are neglected. We feel assured that
the solar system is stable over a very long period of time; just how long
is yet to be rigorously calculated.

BIBLIOGRAPHICAL NOTES

An excellent source of references covering most branches of celestial
mechanics is:

R 2-1. Blitzer, L.: *Am. J. Phy.*, **31**: 233 (1963).

Section 2.1. This material is covered, for example, in:

R 2.1-1. Sterne, T. E.: "An Introduction to Celestial Mechanics,"
chap. 1, Interscience Publishers, Inc., New York, 1960.

R 2.1-2. Symon, K. R.: "Mechanics," chap. 3, Addison-Wesley
Publishing Company, Inc., Reading, Mass., 1953.

Section 2.2. See R 2-1, R 2.1-1, R 2.1–2, and:

R 2.2-1. Smart, W. M.: "Textbook on Spherical Astronomy," 4th
ed., chap. 5, Cambridge University Press, London, 1944.

Section 2.3. The three-body problem and stability considerations are
discussed in:

R 2.3-1. Moulton, F. R.: "An Introduction to Celestial Mechanics,"
chap. 8, The Macmillan Company, New York, 1953.

An algebraic demonstration of the five lagrangian points has been given
by:

R 2.3-2. Vertregt, M.: "Principles of Astronautics," pp. 83–95,
Elsevier Publishing Company, Amsterdam, 1960.

Section 2.4. The pertinent material is outlined in the following references.
Additional detailed references are given in these review articles.

R 2.4-1. Bobrovnikoff, N. T.: In "Astrophysics," ed. J. A. Hynek,
pp. 302–356, McGraw-Hill Book Company, New York, 1951.

R 2.4-2. Wurm, K.: In "Handbuch der Physik," vol. 52, ed. S. Flügge,
pp. 465–518, Springer-Verlag OHG, Berlin, 1959.

Section 2.5. The application of the observation of satellite orbits to the
study of planets is thoroughly covered in:

R 2.5-1. Brouwer, D., and G. M. Clemence: In "Planets and Satellites," eds. G. P. Kuiper and B. M. Middlehurst, pp. 31–94, The
University of Chicago Press, Chicago, 1961.

Section 2.6. The general topic of experimental celestial mechanics and the feasibility of various satellite experiments is covered in:

R 2.6-1. Dicke, R. H.: In "Science in Space," eds. L. V. Berkner and H. Odishaw, pp. 91–118, McGraw-Hill Book Company, New York, 1961.

Section 2.7. The stability of the solar system is discussed by:

R 2.7-1. Hagihara, Y.: In "Planets and Satellites," eds. G. P. Kuiper and B. M. Middlehurst, pp. 95–158, The University of Chicago Press, Chicago, 1961.

Basic solar data and the solar interior

3

The Sun is of great importance in astronomy not only because it is dominant in the solar system but also because it is the only star near enough for detailed scrutiny of its surface, its atmosphere, and its activity. Solar physics is therefore a foundation for the study of both solar system astronomy and general stellar astrophysics. Most of the discussion in the chapters comprising solar physics can be applied, with certain modifications, to the majority of other stars in the Sun's neighborhood. But in the case of the Sun, the scientist is able to see and measure features which for more distant stars can only be inferred. After a review of basic solar data, we outline the methods of determining the internal structure of the Sun, as well as the state of present knowledge of its formation and evolution. The physical conditions in its atmosphere will be discussed in Chapters 4 and 5. The wide variety of solar activity will be discussed in Chapter 6.

3.1 BASIC DATA

Location

The Sun lies near the plane of a spiral galaxy at a distance of some 10 kpc (1 kpc = kiloparsec = 3.1×10^{21} cm) from the central nucleus. It is at the inner edge of a spiral arm and has the chemical composition and kinematical properties typical of the stars which make up the flat, fast-rotating disk of the galaxy. The rotational velocity of the Sun, though not easy to determine, is of the order of 250 km/sec. A peculiar motion of 20 km/sec is detected by comparison with the nearest stars.

Mass

The mass of the Sun can immediately be determined from the orbital parameters of the planets, together with the experimental determination of the gravitational constant G. The value is found to be 1.99×10^{33} g, and this mass, designated by $M_\odot$, is often used as a unit in astronomical reckoning. The escape velocity from the Sun is 617 km/sec; any neutral particle must exceed this velocity to escape from the solar surface.

Distance and radius

The mean distance to the Sun can be determined by celestial mechanics, once some differential distance is independently known. The most accurate means so far is to use the distance of the planet Venus that is found by radar range measures. The resulting mean solar distance from the Earth is 1.496×10^{13} cm. The mean angular diameter is $31'59''$, so that the linear solar radius is 6.96×10^{10} cm. No departure from a perfectly spherical shape has ever been detected. The solar radius $R_\odot$ is often used as a unit of distance, especially in work on the interplanetary medium. The Sun-Earth distance, for example, is $215 R_\odot$.

Rotation

The fact that the Sun rotates can be easily demonstrated by observations of a sunspot or other marking on two successive days. The mean sidereal

Table 3.1-1   Daily rate of solar rotation*

Latitude, deg	Spots, deg	Doppler effect, deg
0	14.37	14.70
35	13.51	13.15
65	12.23	12.00
80	11.85	11.73

* After Pettit, see R 3.1-1.

period (referred to the "fixed" stars) is found to be 25.36 days. This can be measured by the motion of markings across the solar disk or by the radial velocity of the edge of the disk (the solar "limb"), which is about 2 km/sec. Both methods show a striking variation of the rotational motion with latitude. Although the mean sidereal angular motion is $14°.20$ daily, this value is greater at the equator and considerably less near the poles (Table 3.1-1).

Luminosity

The amount of energy given off by the Sun per second can be determined by first measuring the *solar constant*, which is the amount of energy received by a square centimeter surface in space held perpendicular to the Sun's rays at the Earth's mean distance from the Sun. Exceedingly careful measures made by rockets and mountain-top observatories have determined the solar constant to be approximately 1.95 cal/(cm²)(min). From this a total luminosity of the Sun of 3.9×10^{33} ergs/sec is computed by integration over a sphere of 1 AU radius. The flux at the surface, designated as (πF), is

$$(\pi F) = \frac{L_\odot}{4\pi R_\odot{}^2} \tag{1}$$

Temperature

Assuming the Sun to radiate like a black body allows the computation of its temperature from the measured flux. The Stefan-Boltzmann law states that

$$\pi F = \sigma T^4 \tag{2}$$

where $\sigma = 5.7 \times 10^{-5}$ erg/(cm²)(sec)(deg⁴). This gives an effective temperature for the Sun's surface of 5750°K, in reasonable agreement with other types of temperatures measured in other ways (Secs. 4.2, 4.4, and 7.4).

3.2 THE FORMATION OF THE SUN

It is thought that the formation of stars begins with a condensation of interstellar gas. The physical properties of the condensation depend on position in the galaxy and the time, taken as an indicator of the evolutionary state of the galaxy. The interstellar material from which the Sun was once thought to have originated was not pure hydrogen. It is now believed probable that all elements were made in stars with hydrogen as the starting material. Various mechanisms (violent and nonviolent ejection of material from stars) serve to place material which has undergone nuclear processing back into the interstellar medium. Thus, interstellar space is constantly being supplied with material rich in heavy elements.

It is known that mixing between the surface layers and the interior of the Sun is not important. Hence, the composition of the outer solar envelopes should reflect the composition of the Sun's original interstellar condensation; it is found that this implies that the Sun is at least a third-generation star. There are stars in the galaxy that are younger than the Sun and many that are older. In fact, evidence suggests that star formation is going on at present. Certain photographs appear to show the birth of young stars in the form of the so-called Herbig-Haro objects.

The problem of the formation of condensations of interstellar material is not trivial, because the influences of turbulent motions and magnetic fields must be taken into account. A satisfactory theory of protostar formation has not yet been developed. Given a protostar, the next step in its evolution is the gravitational contraction. This proceeds to a stage of near-stability called the *main sequence*, which is the region in a luminosity-effective temperature diagram (called a Hertzsprung-Russell, or H-R, diagram) near which a star spends the major portion of its life (Fig. 3.2-1).

Even if conditions are suitable for contraction, there are theoretical difficulties here also. For example, the protostar is usually considered to have come from a gas cloud with a characteristic dimension of a few parsecs, or $\sim 10^{19}$ cm. A cloud of this size would have rotational velocities on the surface of $\sim 10^{-1}$ km/sec caused by differential galactic motions. If such a cloud were to contract to a body of stellar dimensions with angular momentum conserved, the velocity on the surface of the star would exceed the velocity of light. Since this result is clearly absurd, an efficient braking mechanism (such as magnetic coupling to the interstellar gas) must be invoked.

The contraction onto the main sequence involves the conversion of gravitational energy into thermal energy and into the luminosity of the star. The thermal or internal energy of a star is

$$U = \int_0^R \left[\frac{3}{2} \frac{kT(r)}{m} \right] 4\pi\rho(r)r^2 \, dr \tag{1}$$

where m is the mean mass per particle ($\approx m_p/2$), and the gravitational energy is

$$\Omega = - \int_0^R \left[\frac{M(r)G}{r} \right] 4\pi\rho(r)r^2 \, dr \tag{2}$$

where the temperature $T(r)$ and the density $\rho(r)$ are dependent on the radius and $M(r)$ is the mass interior to r. The gravitational energy is computed as if the star were assembled piece by piece; the work done on a

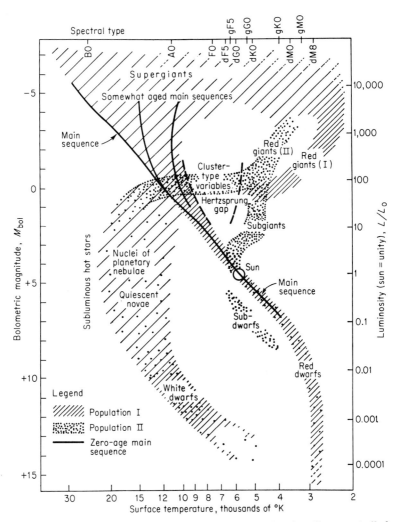

Fig. 3.2-1 Hertzsprung-Russell, or temperature-luminosity, diagram (called H-R diagram), showing the regions occupied by stars of various kinds or populations, the main sequence, and the position of the Sun. (*From Goldberg and Dyer, see R* 3.1-2.)

particle is computed relative to the mass left, i.e., interior to the r in question. See the appropriate definition of the potential energy [Eq. (2.1-21)]. For a star in equilibrium, we have (the virial theorem)

$$2U + \Omega = 0 \qquad\qquad (3)$$

Numerical integrations have shown that the contraction in the Kelvin-Helmholtz stage, where the star is opaque to radiation, is a homologous

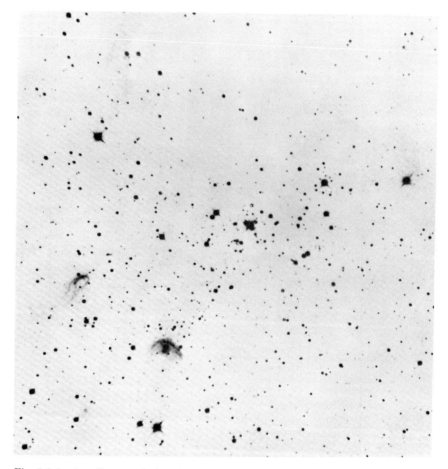

Fig. 3.2-2 A stellar association, in the nebula IC 410, of newly formed stars in our galaxy and the associated nebulosity. (*Courtesy of Stewart Sharpless, U.S. Naval Observatory.*)

one; this means that the star's radius reduces, but the mass distribution does not change. Thus, if we imagine that a star undergoes a contraction through a series of equilibrium configurations, it is clear [Eq. (3.2-3)] that half of this energy goes into the internal energy and half into the luminosity of the star.

Since the internal energy must increase and since the mass distribution does not change, the temperature must increase. This process continues until the central temperature of the star is $\sim 10^7$ °K when nuclear reactions become sufficiently efficient to provide the energy source for the star's luminosity. When this balance occurs, the contraction ceases and the star settles down to a relatively quiet life on the main sequence. Stars (for example, T Tauri stars) which appear to be contracting toward the main sequence are found in associations (loose groups of $\sim 10^2$ stars, see Fig. 3.2-2). Thus, the evolutionary sequence could be [Herbig-Haro object] → [T Tauri star] → [Sun]. The fact that both Herbig-Haro objects and T Tauri stars are found in regions with appreciable gas and dust (i.e., regions which we may suppose are suitable for star formation) gives some support to this view. It may be that all star formation at present occurs in stellar associations. We shall not trace the evolution of the Sun beyond its present state.

3.3 THE SOLAR INTERIOR

It is not possible to obtain any direct observational evidence relevant to the interior of the Sun. The solar material is opaque to all usable wavelengths only a short distance below its relatively cool outer layers. All of our knowledge of solar structure comes from theoretical considerations of the conditions which must exist assuming the Sun's state of equilibrium, its known mass, radius, composition, its source of energy, and the observed boundary conditions at its surface. This limitation may soon be removed when the observation of neutrinos produced by nuclear reactions becomes possible. Neutrinos readily escape from the solar interior.

Hydrostatic equilibrium

In constructing a theoretical model of the Sun, it is usually assumed for simplicity that the Sun is a nonrotating, nonvariable star in hydrostatic equilibrium. This last condition is simply a statement that the outward force of pressure is just balanced by the inward force of gravity at any point in the Sun. Since the pressure on any small volume dV is

$$-\frac{dP}{dr} \, dV$$

and the gravitational force on it is

$$\frac{GM(r)}{r^2} \, \rho \, dV$$

it is possible to state the condition of hydrostatic equilibrium by the equation

$$\frac{dP}{dr} = -\rho \, \frac{GM(r)}{r^2} \tag{1}$$

which gives us an expression for the variation of the pressure throughout the Sun.

The mass equation

The specification of the variation of mass with radius in the Sun is readily found by considering the mass in any spherical shell:

$$\frac{dM(r)}{dr} = 4\pi r^2 \rho \tag{2}$$

The energy balance equation

If we consider that energy is conserved, then the net flux of energy through any volume of the Sun must exactly balance the amount of energy produced in that volume. This is specified by the equation

$$\frac{dL(r)}{dr} = 4\pi r^2 \rho \epsilon \tag{3}$$

where $L(r)$ is the energy flux due to the layers interior to r, and ϵ is the rate of energy generation, in ergs per second per gram.

Radiative transfer of energy

The next equations relate to the energy transport in the Sun, which may be by either radiation or convection. For stellar interiors, the radiation field is nearly isotropic (equal in all directions), so that radiative transfer is relatively easy to handle mathematically. Because of its importance, especially in relation to the photosphere (Sec. 4.2), the problem of radiative transfer is treated in a section especially devoted to it (Sec. 4.1). There the following relation is derived:

$$\left[\frac{dT}{dr}\right]_{\text{rad}} = -\frac{3K\rho L(r)}{4\sigma c T^3 4\pi r^2} = -\frac{1}{\lambda_r}\frac{L(r)}{4\pi r^2} \tag{4}$$

where K is a coefficient of the opacity of the material (suitably defined below), σ is the Stefan-Boltzmann constant, and c is the velocity of light.

Convective transfer of energy

In addition to radiative transfer, convection occurs in certain parts of the solar interior. Let us first examine convective stability, in order to establish under what conditions convection occurs. Consider a perturbation in the form of a bubble of material in the Sun which moves upward a small distance δr. The change in T of the bubble is just the product of this distance and the temperature gradient $\left(\dfrac{dT}{dr}\right)_{\text{ad}}$, called the adiabatic temperature gradient, for which the bubble would suffer no loss or gain of energy.

Similarly, the surrounding material at the new location has a difference in temperature of $\delta r \left(\dfrac{dT}{dr}\right)_{\text{str}}$, where $\left(\dfrac{dT}{dr}\right)_{\text{str}}$ is the actual or structural temperature gradient. If $\left|\dfrac{dT}{dr}\right|_{\text{str}} > \left|\dfrac{dT}{dr}\right|_{\text{ad}}$, then the bubble becomes hotter than the surroundings in moving upward. Because the bubble must be in pressure equilibrium with the surroundings, we have ρ (bubble) $< \rho$ (surroundings). Because of the buoyancy force, the bubble continues to rise and the situation is unstable. Under the same conditions, a bubble traveling downward continues to sink, and we again have instability. The condition for convection,

$$\left|\frac{dT}{dr}\right|_{\text{str}} > \left|\frac{dT}{dr}\right|_{\text{ad}} \tag{5}$$

is often referred to as the Schwarzschild condition for convective instability. Note that the opposite condition favors stability, because a rising bubble would then find itself heavier than the surroundings and would stop.

Since equilibrium is maintained, we can use the equation of hydrostatic equilibrium (3.3-1) written as

$$dP = -g\rho\, dr \tag{6}$$

Now the equation of state appropriate to stellar interiors is the perfect-gas equation,

$$P = \frac{k\rho T}{\mu m_{\text{H}}} = NkT \tag{7}$$

where k is the Boltzmann constant ($= 1.38 \times 10^{-16}$ erg/deg), m_{H} is the mass of the hydrogen atom ($= 1.67 \times 10^{-24}$ g), N is the particle density, and μ is the mean molecular weight. This use of the perfect-gas equation at the densities encountered in stellar interiors is permissible because the particles involved are nearly all bare nuclei for which any corrections to the perfect-gas equation are unimportant. In writing the equation of state, we have assumed that radiation pressure is unimportant. This is a good approximation in the Sun and was implicit in our writing of the equation of hydrostatic equilibrium. Equations (3.3-6) and (3.3-7) give

$$-\frac{dP}{dr} = \frac{gPm_{\text{H}}\mu}{kT} \tag{8}$$

If Eq. (3.3-8) is multiplied by dT/dP, we find

$$-\frac{dT}{dr} = \frac{gm_{\text{H}}\mu}{k}\frac{d\log T}{d\log P} \tag{9}$$

Thus the Schwarzschild condition can be written as

$$\left(\frac{d \log T}{d \log P}\right)_{str} > \left(\frac{d \log T}{d \log P}\right)_{ad} \tag{10}$$

The effect of convection is always to reduce the structural gradient and to attempt to bring it close to the adiabatic value. This process is very efficient in stellar interiors, and the difference between the structural gradient and adiabatic gradient is so small that the latter is a good approximation in layers which are in convective equilibrium. The adiabatic relation can be written as

$$\rho = \text{const } P^{1/\gamma} \tag{11}$$

where $\gamma = c_p/c_v$, the ratio of specific heats. Note that $\gamma = \frac{5}{3}$ for a highly ionized gas. The density ρ may be eliminated with the aid of Eq. (3.3-7), and logarithmic differentiation then yields

$$\left[\frac{d \log T}{d \log P}\right]_{ad} = 1 - \frac{1}{\gamma} \tag{12}$$

When Eqs. (3.3-12), (3.3-9), and (3.3-8) are combined, we find

$$\left[\frac{dT}{dr}\right]_{ad} = \frac{dP}{dr}\frac{T}{P}\left(1 - \frac{1}{\gamma}\right) \tag{13}$$

This is the analogue of Eqs. (3.3-4) for the case of convective equilibrium. In constructing a model stellar interior, we must apply the stability criterion [Eq. (3.3-10)] at each point to determine whether Eq. (3.3-4) or Eq. (3.3-13) is to be used.

Energy sources

We now consider the source of solar energy and the specification of ϵ in Eq. (3.3-3). It has been well established that gravitational energy sources cannot provide the Sun's luminosity for a sizable fraction of a star's life. This follows from the fact that one-half of the total gravitational energy is available for radiation; dividing the energy by the rate of energy loss (= the Sun's luminosity), we obtain the so-called Kelvin contraction time, which is 3×10^7 years for the Sun. This time scale is about a hundred times shorter than the age of the crust of the Earth as determined from geological evidence.

Nuclear energy sources in the Sun are far more promising. If the entire mass of the Sun were hydrogen, the conversion to helium would yield $0.007c^2 M_\odot$ ergs, where 0.007 is the mass defect for the transmutation of hydrogen into helium. This nuclear energy source would be sufficient to run the Sun for some 10^{11} years. This appears to be a time scale which is sufficiently long, because the age of the universe as estimated from the ages of the oldest known stars in the galaxy and from cosmological considerations appears to be 1 to 3×10^{10} years.

Applications of nuclear physics to conditions appropriate to stellar interiors have shown that we need consider only two types of sequences of nuclear reactions in the Sun. The first series, suggested by H. Bethe, is called the carbon cycle. In it C^{12} acts as a catalyst in the conversion of hydrogen to helium. The appropriate reactions are

$$C^{12} + H^1 \rightarrow N^{13} + \gamma \tag{14}$$
$$N^{13} \rightarrow C^{13} + e^+ + \text{neutrino} \tag{15}$$
$$C^{13} + H^1 \rightarrow N^{14} + \gamma \tag{16}$$
$$N^{14} + H^1 \rightarrow O^{15} + \gamma \tag{17}$$
$$O^{15} \rightarrow N^{15} + e^+ + \text{neutrino} \tag{18}$$
$$N^{15} + H^1 \rightarrow C^{12} + He^4 \tag{19}$$

The net effect is simply to change $4\ H^1$ into $1\ He^4$; note however, that the neutrinos escape from the star, and hence this loss must be taken into account in computing the total energy $(4.0 \times 10^{-5}$ ergs) liberated per helium atom formed in the carbon cycle.

The other process, the proton-proton reaction, is given by

$$H^1 + H^1 \rightarrow D^2 + e^+ + \text{neutrino} \tag{20}$$
$$D^2 + H^1 \rightarrow He^3 + \gamma \tag{21}$$

This may be completed through

$$He^3 + He^3 \rightarrow He^4 + H^1 + H^1 \tag{22}$$

or through

$$He^3 + He^4 \rightarrow Be^7 + \gamma \tag{23}$$

This last reaction may, in turn, be completed through

$$Be^7 + e^- \rightarrow Li^7 + \text{neutrino} \tag{24}$$
$$Li^7 + H^1 \rightarrow He^4 + He^4 \tag{25}$$

or through

$$Be^7 + H^1 \rightarrow B^8 + \gamma \tag{26}$$
$$B^8 \rightarrow Be^8 + e^+ + \text{neutrino} \tag{27}$$
$$Be^8 \rightarrow He^4 + He^4 \tag{28}$$

The total energy available in making one helium atom is 4.3×10^{-5} erg. Because the neutrinos carry away some energy, the proton-proton reaction as completed by Eqs. (3.3-22), (3.3-25), and (3.3-28) have losses relative to this figure of 2, 4, and 29 per cent, respectively. There is still some question of the relative importance of the three variants of the proton-proton reaction. Consequently, we shall give below some estimates of the energy production rates based on the first method of completion of the proton-proton reaction. These estimates should be regarded as merely illustrative; the exact numerical values are uncertain.

Table 3.3-1   Parameters for interpolation formulas (3.3-29) and (3.3-30)*

Proton-proton			Carbon cycle		
$T/10^6 °K$	$\log \epsilon_1$	ν	$T/10^6 °K$	$\log \epsilon_1$	ν
4–6	−6.84	6	12–16	−22.2	20
6–10	−6.04	5	16–24	−19.8	18
9–13	−5.56	4.5	21–31	−17.1	16
11–17	−5.02	4	24–36	−15.6	15
16–24	−4.40	3.5	36–50	−12.5	13

* Courtesy Bosman-Crespin, Fowler, and Humblet, see R 3.3-4.

The detailed expressions for the reaction rates of the carbon cycle and the proton-proton reaction are rather complicated. However, the temperature range in a star over which energy generation is important is usually not large. Hence, interpolation formulas may be used without serious loss of accuracy. The energy loss per cubic centimeter per second can then be approximated by

$$\rho \epsilon_{pp} = \epsilon_1 \rho^2 \, X^2 \left(\frac{T}{10^6} \right)^{\nu} \tag{29}$$

$$\rho \epsilon_{cc} = \epsilon_1 \rho^2 X X_{\mathrm{CN}} \left(\frac{T}{10^6} \right)^{\nu} \tag{30}$$

where X is the fraction of hydrogen by mass and X_{CN} is the similar abundance of all nitrogens and carbons together. The parameters in Eqs. (3.3-29) and (3.3-30) are given in Table 3.3-1.

Opacity

The three important processes contributing to the opacity of solar material are bound-free transitions, free-free transitions, and Thompson scattering. The opacity is a widely varying function of the frequency ν of the radiation. The opacity for a particular frequency is designated K_ν, the monochromatic opacity. One may add the monochromatic opacities in the following manner:

$$K_\nu \text{ (total)} = K_\nu \text{ (b-f)} + K_\nu \text{ (f-f)} + K_\nu \text{ (}e\text{)} \tag{31}$$

The actual computation of detailed opacities is very difficult. It requires the specification of the abundance and stage of ionization of many elements. For the Sun, the bound-free transitions of the heavy elements are the most important. Note that the opacity used in Eq. (3.3-4) is a mean taken over frequency, and only for an appropriately defined mean opacity is Eq. (3.3-4) valid. We show in Sec. 4.1 that the correct mean (Rosseland mean absorption coefficient) is defined by

$$\frac{1}{K} = \frac{\int_0^\infty \frac{1}{K_\nu (1 - e^{-h\nu/kT})} \frac{dB_\nu}{dT} d\nu}{\int_0^\infty \frac{dB_\nu}{dT} d\nu} \tag{32}$$

where B_ν, the specific intensity, is given by Planck's law,

$$B_\nu(T) = \frac{2h\nu^3}{c^2} \frac{1}{e^{h\nu/kT} - 1} \tag{33}$$

and the factor $1 - e^{-h\nu/kT}$ in Eq. (3.3-32) allows for stimulated emissions. An approximation to the opacity in the Sun is given by Kramers' law of opacity,

$$K \text{ (b-f)} = 4 \times 10^{25} \frac{\bar{g}}{t} Z(1 + X) \frac{\rho}{T^{3.5}} \tag{34}$$

where Z is the heavy element mass fraction, $\bar{g}$ is a constant called the mean Gaunt factor, and t is the so-called guillotine factor. Generally $t \approx 1$ to 10 and $\bar{g} \approx 1$; for example, $t/\bar{g} \approx 3$ for the Sun. For future reference, we note that Y is the mass fraction for helium and that $X + Y + Z = 1$.

Ionization

The stage of ionization in stellar interiors is given by the Saha equation

$$\frac{N(r - 1)N_e}{N(r)} = 2 \frac{g(r - 1)}{g(r)} \frac{(2\pi m_e kT)^{3/2}}{h^3} e^{-\chi(r)/kT} \tag{35}$$

where $N(r)$ is the number density of the ion which has r remaining electrons, $\chi(r)$ is the corresponding ionization potential, and $g(r)$ is the appropriate statistical weight. Detailed calculations give the following information (Table 3.3-2) concerning the ionization of elements in the solar interior for $T = 10^7 \, °\text{K}$ and $\log [2(2\pi m_e kT)^{3/2}/N_e h^3] = 5$. Thus, we see that we may consider as a good approximation the supposition that all elements in the interior are completely ionized. Hence, the number of particles per cubic centimeter can be computed as follows: hydrogen contributes $2X\rho/m_H$; helium contributes $\frac{3}{4}Y\rho/m_H$; and the heavy elements contribute $(A/2) Z\rho/Am_H = Z\rho/2m_H$, which is almost entirely due to elec-

Table 3.3-2   Ionization conditions in the solar interior*

Element	A	Number of bound electrons	Number of free electrons	Total number of free particles per nucleus
O	16	0.24	7.76	8.76
Mg	24.3	0.3	11.7	12.7
Si	28.1	0.5	13.5	14.5
Ca	40.1	1.9	18.1	19.1
Fe	55.8	3.0	23.0	24.0

* After Strömgren, quoted in R 3.3-1.

trons. Then,

$$N = (2X + \tfrac{3}{4}Y + \tfrac{1}{2}Z)\,\frac{\rho}{m_H} \tag{36}$$

Comparing Eqs. (3.3-36) and (3.3-7) yields the following expression for the mean molecular weight

$$\mu = \frac{1}{2X + \tfrac{3}{4}Y + \tfrac{1}{2}Z} \tag{37}$$

Chemical composition

The determination of the chemical composition can be obtained (at least in principle) from studies of absorption lines in the photospheric spectrum. At best, however, this gives the chemical composition of the initial Sun, the Sun when nuclear reactions just began to be important. Nuclear reactions have continuously depleted the central regions of the Sun of hydrogen, and thus the chemical composition is a function of time and r. Hence, one must construct an initial model of the Sun and analytically follow the evolution until a model of approximately the solar luminosity is obtained. The time changes can be computed from the known nuclear reaction rates.

Solar models

With the above information it is possible to consider the problem of the solar interior. Four basic equations are available:

1. Hydrostatic equilibrium

$$\frac{dP}{dr} = -\rho\,\frac{GM(r)}{r^2}$$

2. Mass distribution

$$\frac{dM(r)}{dr} = 4\pi r^2 \rho$$

3. Energy balance

$$\frac{dL(r)}{dr} = 4\pi r^2 \rho \epsilon$$

4. Energy transfer

$$\left[\frac{dT}{dr}\right]_{\text{rad}} = -\frac{1}{\lambda_r}\frac{L(r)}{4\pi r^2}$$

$$\text{or} \quad \left[\frac{dT}{dr}\right]_{\text{conv}} = \frac{dP}{dr}\cdot\frac{T}{P}\left(1 - \frac{1}{\gamma}\right)$$

We also have three relations describing the properties of the gas:

1. The perfect-gas law

$$P = \frac{k\rho T}{\mu m_{\text{H}}}$$

2. The law of opacity

$$K \text{ (b-f)} = 4 \times 10^{25} \frac{\bar{g}}{t} Z(1 + X) \frac{\rho}{T^{3.5}}$$

3. The energy generation rates

$$\rho\epsilon_{pp} = \epsilon_1 \rho^2 X^2 \left(\frac{T}{10^6}\right)^{\nu}$$

and

$$\rho\epsilon_{cc} = \epsilon_1 \rho^2 X X_{\text{CN}} \left(\frac{T}{10^6}\right)^{\nu}$$

With these equations and with the specification of appropriate boundary conditions (the boundary is the solar atmosphere, discussed in later sections), the conditions in the solar interior can be found, since we have sufficient equations to solve the problem. Unfortunately, there is no suitable analytical solution, so that numerical methods are used to build up a model of the interior, layer by layer. One tests at each point whether the material is in convective or radiative equilibrium and then chooses the appropriate equations.

A model for the present Sun is shown in Figs. 3.3-1 and 3.3-2. The chemical inhomogeneity and the central depletion of hydrogen are clearly shown in Fig. 3.3-2. The model is in convective equilibrium from $r/R_\odot = 0.86$ outward to just beneath the surface; the layer above the convective layer, called the photosphere, is in radiative equilibrium. We consider the photosphere in Sec. 4.2 after we equip ourselves with the elements of radiative transfer in Sec. 4.1.

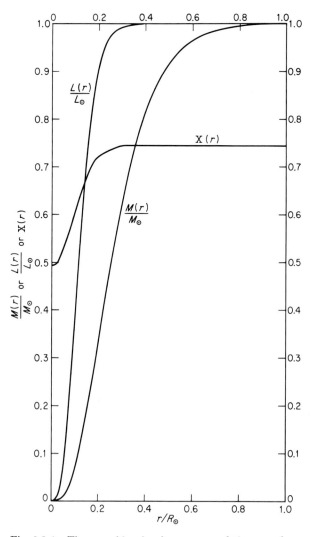

Fig. 3.3-1   The run of luminosity, mass, and the mass fraction of hydrogen (X) on the basis of Weymann's model (*see* R 3.3-5) of the Sun. The central depletion of hydrogen is clearly shown.

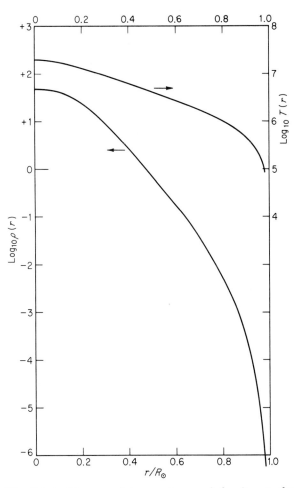

Fig. 3.3-2   The run of temperature and density on the basis of Weymann's solar model. (*See R* 3.3-5.)

BIBLIOGRAPHICAL NOTES

Papers covering the history of solar physics and the development of our knowledge of the physics of stars are:

R 3-1. Strömgren, B.: In "Astrophysics," ed. J. A. Hynek, pp. 1–11 and 172–258, McGraw-Hill Book Company, New York, 1951.
R 3-2. Goldberg, L.: In "The Sun," ed. G. P. Kuiper, pp. 1–35, The University of Chicago Press, Chicago, 1953.

A standard text covering most aspects of solar physics is:

R 3-3. Ambartsumyan, V. A. (ed.): "Theoretical Astrophysics," Pergamon Press, New York, 1958.

Also see references and summary material given in:

R 3-4. Allen, C. W.: "Astrophysical Quantities," The Athlone Press, London, 1955.

Section 3.1. See R 3-2, R 3-3, R 3-4, and:

R 3.1-1. Pettit, E.: In "Astrophysics," ed. J. A. Hynek, pp. 259–301, McGraw-Hill Book Company, New York, 1951.

For an introduction to the problems of galactic structure see (and see also references given there):

R 3.1-2. Goldberg, L., and E. R. Dyer: In "Science in Space," eds. L. V. Berkner and H. Odishaw, pp. 341–399, McGraw-Hill Book Company, New York, 1961.

Section 3.2. See R 3.1-2 and:

R 3.2-1. Burbidge, G. R., and E. M. Burbidge: In "Handbuch der Physik," vol. 51, ed. S. Flügge, pp. 134–295, Springer-Verlag OHG, Berlin, 1958.

R 3.2-2. Schwarzschild, M.: "Structure and Evolution of the Stars," Princeton University Press, Princeton, N.J., 1958.

Section 3.3. The definitive text covering this material is R 3.2-2. The early work is discussed in:

R 3.3-1. Chandrasekhar, S.: "An Introduction to the Study of Stellar Structure," Dover Publications, Inc., New York, 1957.

R 3.3-2. Chandrasekhar, S.: In "Astrophysics," ed. J. A. Hynek, pp. 598–674, McGraw-Hill Book Company, New York, 1951.

R 3.3-3. Strömgren, B.: In "The Sun," ed. G. P. Kuiper, pp. 36–87, The University of Chicago Press, Chicago, 1953.

The nuclear reaction rates are from:

R 3.3-4 Bosman-Crespin, D., W. A. Fowler, and J. Humblet: *Bull. Soc. Roy. Sci. Liege*, (9/10): 327 (1954). (See Figs. 1 and 2 and R 3.2-2.)

The solar model discussed here is given in:

R 3.3-5. Weymann, R.: *Astrophys. J.*, **126:** 208 (1957), and p. 259 of R 3.2-2.

The solar neutrino flux is the topic of:

R 3.3-6. Bahcall, J. N., W. A. Fowler, I. Iben, and R. L. Sears: *Astrophys. J.*, **137:** 344 (1963).

Radiative transfer and the photosphere

The photosphere comprises the portion of the solar atmosphere from which we receive the major portion of the Sun's optical radiation. This region of the Sun is generally considered to be in radiative equilibrium, and hence we must equip ourselves with the principles of radiative transfer.

4.1 RADIATIVE TRANSFER

A knowledge of the principles of radiative transfer is of great importance, because most astronomical data come to us in the form of radiation. The properties of the transfer of radiation are necessary to the study of solar physics, but they are also involved in many other astrophysical problems.

Definitions

Consider the radiant energy dE_ν (per frequency interval $d\nu$) in a cone of solid angle $d\omega$ passing through a surface of area $d\sigma$ in time dt. If the axis of the cone makes an angle θ with the normal to the surface, the specific intensity or intensity I_ν is defined by the equation

$$dE_\nu = I_\nu \cos \theta \, d\omega \, d\nu \, dt \, d\sigma \tag{1}$$

The intensity integrated over frequency is denoted simply by I. The net flux is defined by

$$[\pi F_\nu] = \int_{4\pi} I_\nu \cos \theta \, d\omega \tag{2}$$

Many situations in radiative transfer problems are characterized by plane-parallel layers and axial symmetry. If we consider a coordinate system whose z axis coincides with the outward normal, then

$$d\omega = \sin \theta \, d\theta \, d\phi \tag{3}$$

where θ is the polar angle and ϕ is the azimuthal angle. Then, the flux along the axis of symmetry is

$$[\pi F_\nu] = 2\pi \int_0^\pi I_\nu(\theta) \sin \theta \cos \theta \, d\theta \tag{4}$$

The mean intensity is defined by

$$J_\nu = \frac{1}{4\pi} \int_{4\pi} I_\nu \, d\omega \tag{5}$$

which becomes

$$J_\nu = \tfrac{1}{2} \int_0^\pi I_\nu(\theta) \sin \theta \, d\theta \tag{6}$$

for the case of axial symmetry.

A pencil of radiation of intensity I_ν is changed by the amount dI_ν on passing normally through a slab of material of density ρ and thickness ds. The mass absorption coefficient K_ν is defined by

$$dI_\nu = -K_\nu \rho I_\nu \, ds \tag{7}$$

We must distinguish between true absorption and scattering. If we think of the absorbing material as a blackbox, then true absorption occurs when the absorbed photons do not reappear at all or have their frequency significantly changed. Scattering occurs when the blackbox does nothing but keep the photon for a short time and then sends it off in another direction with essentially its initial frequency. The amount of radiation scattered from a pencil beam is $K_\nu \rho \, ds \, I_\nu \cos \theta \, d\nu \, d\sigma \, d\omega \, dt$. Since $dm = \rho \cos \theta \, d\sigma \, ds$, this is

$$K_\nu I_\nu \, dm \, d\nu \, d\omega \, dt \tag{8}$$

The phase function $p(\cos \Theta)$, where Θ is the scattering angle, is defined by the expression for the amount of radiation scattered into the solid angle $d\omega'$, namely,

$$K_\nu I_\nu \, dm \, d\nu \, d\omega \, dt \, p(\cos \Theta) \frac{d\omega'}{4\pi} \tag{9}$$

This expression can be integrated over the solid angle. For Eq. (4.1-9) to agree with Eq. (4.1-8), we must have

$$\int_{4\pi} p(\cos \Theta) \frac{d\omega'}{4\pi} = 1 \tag{10}$$

In other words, the phase function is normalized to unity for pure scattering. In general, only a fraction of the absorbed radiation is scattered. In this case, the left-hand side is set equal to $\bar{\omega}_0$, the albedo for single scattering. Thus, in an absorbing process, a fraction $\bar{\omega}_0$ is simply scattered, while a fraction $1 - \bar{\omega}_0$ is lost from the radiation field. It is clear that $0 \leq \bar{\omega}_0 \leq 1$. The simplest phase function is $p(\cos \Theta) = \bar{\omega}_0$.

The energy scattered or emitted into the solid angle $d\omega$ is given by

$$j_\nu \, dm \, d\omega \, d\nu \, dt \tag{11}$$

The emission coefficient j_ν is defined by this expression.

Equation of transfer

We may obtain the equation of transfer by noting that the change in intensity along a cylinder of surface area $d\sigma$ and length ds, that is,

$$\frac{dI_\nu}{ds} \, ds \, d\omega \, d\nu \, d\sigma \, dt \tag{12}$$

must be caused by a difference in the emission and absorption processes in the cylinder. We express this fact by setting Eq. (4.1-12) equal to Eq. (4.1-11) minus Eq. (4.1-8). When common factors are canceled, we have the equation of transfer,

$$\frac{dI_\nu}{ds} = -\rho K_\nu I_\nu + j_\nu \rho \tag{13}$$

A most useful quantity is the source function, defined by

$$\mathcal{I}_\nu = \frac{j_\nu}{K_\nu} \tag{14}$$

In terms of the source function, the equation of transfer can be written as

$$-\frac{dI_\nu}{K_\nu \rho\, ds} = I_\nu - \mathcal{J}_\nu \tag{15}$$

For problems with axial symmetry and plane-parallel layers, we define the optical thickness by

$$\tau_\nu = \int_z^\infty K_\nu \rho\, dz \tag{16}$$

Note that the opacity increases as we move inward from the boundary of the layer. We often deal with problems with semi-infinite atmospheres, i.e., atmospheres which are infinitely deep but which have an upper boundary.

If we denote the angle between the cone of radiation and the outward normal by θ and let $\mu = \cos\theta$, the equation of transfer can be written as

$$\mu \frac{dI_\nu}{d\tau_\nu} = I_\nu - \mathcal{J}_\nu \tag{17}$$

This is the standard form of the transfer equation. There are two special cases of interest in the expression for $\mathcal{J}_\nu$. If at each point in an atmosphere we may assign a temperature such that Kirchhoff's law applies, that is,

$$j_\nu = K_\nu B_\nu(T) \tag{18}$$

where $B_\nu(T)$ is given by Planck's law [Eq. (3.3-33)], then the atmosphere is in local thermodynamic equilibrium (LTE). For LTE,

$$\mathcal{J}_\nu = B_\nu(T) \tag{19}$$

On the other hand, the emission coefficient may be completely due to scattered radiation. Then for isotropic pure scattering [compare Eqs. (4.1-14), (4.1-11), (4.1-9), and (4.1-5)],

$$\mathcal{J}_\nu = J_\nu \tag{20}$$

It is important to note the significance of the source function. Equation (4.1-17) is a first-order differential equation with a known solution that can be written down. The solution for the radiation emerging from the top of an atmosphere (a case of obvious interest) is

$$I(0,+\mu) = \int_0^\infty \mathcal{J}(t,+\mu) e^{-t/\mu}\, \frac{dt}{\mu} \tag{21}$$

This equation shows that the emergent radiation is simply the radiation emitted at each point diminished by the intervening opacity. Thus, a determination of the source function is essentially a complete solution to a radiative transfer problem.

Methods of solution

We now sketch three common techniques for the solution of the transfer equation, namely, the method of discrete streams, the principles of invariance, and the method of moments. Consider the problem in which a constant net flux flows through an isotropically scattering atmosphere with $\bar{\omega}_0 = 1$ (called conservative scattering). If the radiation field is caused by scattering only, then $\bar{\omega}_0$ must equal 1 to keep the flux constant. For this case, Eq. (4.1-20) applies, and the transfer equation is

$$\frac{\mu \, dI(\tau,\mu)}{d\tau} = I(\tau,\mu) - J(\tau) \tag{22}$$

where we note explicitly that $J(\tau)$ is not a function of direction; this is a consequence of the assumption of isotropic scattering. Since we have used μ in the left-hand side of the above equation, we can write the integral for $J(\tau)$ in terms of μ also, and we find

$$\mu \frac{dI}{d\tau} = I - \frac{1}{2} \int_{-1}^{+1} I \, d\mu \tag{23}$$

Thus, the problem consists of the solution of an integro-differential equation

The ideas involved in the method of discrete streams were originally due to Schuster and Schwarzschild, who divided the radiation field into an inbound and an outbound stream composed of intensities I_- and I_+. This idea replaces the one equation above with the following *two* equations:

$$+ \frac{1}{2} \frac{dI_+}{d\tau} = I_+ - \tfrac{1}{2}(I_+ + I_-) \tag{24}$$

$$- \frac{1}{2} \frac{dI_-}{d\tau} = I_- - \tfrac{1}{2}(I_+ + I_-) \tag{25}$$

The μ in the left-hand side has been replaced by a representative average value. The solution to the equations is straightforward and can be obtained subject to the condition that $I_- = 0$ at $\tau = 0$, since there is no radiation incident on the top of the atmosphere. While this method as contained in Eqs. (4.1-24) and (4.1-25) is crude, it can be developed and refined into a powerful technique, as it has been by Chandrasekhar.

We can replace the equation of transfer by a system of $2n$ linear equations,

$$\mu_i \frac{dI(\tau,\mu_i)}{d\tau} = I(\tau,\mu_i) - \frac{1}{2} \sum_j a_j I(\tau,\mu_j)$$

$$i = \pm 1, \pm 2, \ldots, \pm n \quad (26)$$

where there is no $j = 0$ term in the summation. This method is powerful if the summation can be made in such a way that the lower-order solutions ($n \approx 2$ or 3) contain the essential features of the problem.

It is necessary to consider the problem of the integral

$$\int_{-1}^{+1} f(\mu)\, d\mu \cong \sum_{j=1}^{m} a_j f(\mu_j) \quad (27)$$

It appears that the use of the Gauss formula is advantageous, because m terms evaluate the integral exactly for all polynomials of degree $2m$ or less. The gaussian weights a_j and divisions μ_j can be found in tabulated form. For applications to the transfer equation, we note that $a_j = a_{-j}$, $\mu_{-j} = -\mu_j$, and $\sum_1^m a_j = 1$. Using these weights and divisions, we wish to solve Eq. (4.1-26) subject to the condition

$$I(\tau = 0, -\mu) = 0 \quad (28)$$

and subject to the condition that none of the various integrals over the source function diverge. This last condition implies that

$$J(\tau)e^{-\tau} \to 0 \quad \text{as} \quad \tau \to \infty \quad (29)$$

In abbreviated notation, we write Eqs. (4.1-26) as

$$\mu_i \frac{dI_i}{d\tau} = I_i - \frac{1}{2} \sum_j a_j I_j \quad i = \pm 1, \ldots, \pm n \quad (30)$$

Let us try a solution of the form

$$I_i = g_i e^{-k\tau} \quad (31)$$

where g_i and k are unspecified constants. Substituting Eq. (4.1-31) in Eq. (4.1-30) gives us

$$g_i(1 + \mu_i k) = \tfrac{1}{2} \sum_j a_j g_j = \text{const} \quad (32)$$

or

$$g_i = \frac{\text{const}}{1 + \mu_i k} \quad (33)$$

The combination of Eqs. (4.1-32) and (4.1-33) gives us the characteristic equation

$$1 = \frac{1}{2} \sum_j \frac{a_j}{1 + \mu_j k} \tag{34a}$$

$$= \sum_{j=1}^{n} \frac{a_j}{1 - \mu_j^2 k^2} \tag{34b}$$

where the second equality comes from the properties of the gaussian roots and divisions. The solution of the characteristic equation gives us $2n - 2$ of the $2n$ solutions that we must have for our problem. We lose two solutions because $k = 0$ is a root of Eq. (4.1-34b) since

$$\sum_{j=1}^{n} a_j = 1$$

We try another solution of the form

$$I_i = b(\tau + q_i) \qquad i = \pm 1, \ldots, \pm n \tag{35}$$

which (as above) can be written as

$$I_i = b(\tau + Q + \mu_i) \tag{36}$$

where b and Q are constants. We collect our results [Eqs. (4.1-31), (4.1-33), and (4.1-36)] to write down the general solution,

$$I_i = b \left(\sum_{\alpha=1}^{n-1} \frac{L_\alpha e^{-k_\alpha \tau}}{1 + \mu_i k_\alpha} + \sum_{\alpha=1}^{n-1} \frac{L_{-\alpha} e^{+k_\alpha \tau}}{1 - \mu_i k_\alpha} + \tau + \mu_i + Q \right) \tag{37}$$

Here, b, Q, and the $L_{\pm\alpha}$'s are the $2n$ constants to be determined from the boundary conditions. The $L_{-\alpha}$'s must all be zero to satisfy Eq. (4.1-29). Clearly, b is related to the flux, and it can be computed by quadratures using the gaussian weights. The result is $F = \frac{4}{3}b$ and our solution is now

$$I_i = \frac{3}{4} F \left(\sum_{\alpha=1}^{n-1} \frac{L_\alpha e^{-k_\alpha \tau}}{1 + \mu_i k_\alpha} + \tau + \mu_i + Q \right) \tag{38}$$

The L_α's and Q are determined from the fact that

$$I_{-i}(\tau = 0) = 0 \tag{39}$$

from Eq. (4.1-28). The emergent intensity or the law of darkening is given by setting $\tau = 0$ in Eq. (4.1-38), which gives us

$$I(0,+\mu) = \frac{3}{4} F \left(\sum_{\alpha=1}^{n-1} \frac{L_\alpha}{1 + \mu k_\alpha} + \mu + Q \right) \tag{40}$$

Here we have dropped the subscripts because we use this form of the solution for all μ.

The expression for the source function can be obtained from the quadrature formulas; it is

$$J(\tau) = \tfrac{3}{4}F[\tau + q(\tau)] \tag{41}$$

where $q(\tau)$ is a slowly varying function defined by

$$q(\tau) = Q + \sum_{\alpha=1}^{n-1} L_\alpha e^{-k_\alpha \tau} \tag{42}$$

This completes our introduction to the method of discrete streams. We note that the general methods are applicable to other problems, such as the diffuse reflection of a semi-infinite layer illuminated by a parallel beam. We shall mention this problem in the discussion of the principles of invariance.

The principles of invariance are due to Ambartsumyan and have been extensively developed by Chandrasekhar. The first principle of invariance states that the emergent radiation from a semi-infinite plane-parallel atmosphere is invariant to the addition or subtraction of layers of arbitrary optical thickness to or from the atmosphere. We now introduce the scattering function. Let a parallel beam of radiation of net flux (πF) per unit area normal to itself be incident on a plane-parallel atmosphere. Then we define the scattering function, $S(\mu,\mu_0)$, in terms of the diffusely reflected intensity through

$$I(0,\mu) = \frac{F}{4\mu} S(\mu,\mu_0) \tag{43}$$

where μ_0 refers to the incident beam and where we consider the case of axial symmetry.

A diagram illustrating the principles of invariance in connection with the law of darkening in the constant net flux problem is shown in Fig. (4.1-1). From the principle stated, $I(\tau,+\mu)$ would become equal to $I(0,+\mu)$ if the top layer were completely removed. Hence, the difference between $I(0,+\mu)$ and $I(\tau,+\mu)$ must come about because of the top layer that makes itself known through the radiation $I(\tau,-\mu)$, which is zero when the top layer is removed. It is clear that $I(\tau,+\mu)$ is greater than $I(0,+\mu)$, and the increase is due to the radiation $I(\tau,-\mu)$ from the top layer, which is

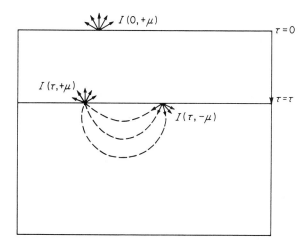

Fig. 4.1-1   The principles of invariance in the constant net flux problem. See the text for discussion.

incident on and diffusely reflected by the atmosphere below τ. In terms of the scattering function, this becomes

$$I(\tau,+\mu) = I(0,+\mu) + \frac{1}{2\mu} \int_0^1 S(\mu,\mu')I(\tau,-\mu')\,d\mu' \tag{44}$$

To continue, we differentiate this equation with respect to τ and then set $\tau = 0$; that is,

$$\left[\frac{dI(\tau,+\mu)}{d\tau}\right]_{\tau=0} = \frac{1}{2\mu} \int_0^1 S(\mu,\mu') \left[\frac{dI(\tau,-\mu')}{d\tau}\right]_{\tau=0} d\mu' \tag{45}$$

The derivatives needed can be obtained from the equation of transfer; they are

$$\left[\frac{dI(\tau,+\mu)}{d\tau}\right]_{\tau=0} = \frac{1}{\mu}[I(0,+\mu) - J(0)] \tag{46}$$

$$\left[\frac{dI(\tau,-\mu')}{d\tau}\right]_{\tau=0} = \frac{1}{\mu'}J(0) \tag{47}$$

Remember that $I(0,-\mu) = 0$. When these derivatives are inserted in Eq. (4.1-45), we obtain

$$I(0,+\mu) = J(0)\left[1 + \frac{1}{2}\int_0^1 S(\mu,\mu')\frac{d\mu'}{\mu'}\right] \tag{48}$$

If we had carried out a similar procedure with the law of diffuse reflection, we would find that

$$\left(\frac{1}{\mu} + \frac{1}{\mu_0}\right) S(\mu,\mu_0) = \tilde{\omega}_0 H(\mu)H(\mu_0) \tag{49}$$

where

$$H(\mu) = 1 + \frac{1}{2}\tilde{\omega}_0\mu H(\mu) \int_0^1 \frac{H(\mu')\,d\mu'}{\mu + \mu'} \tag{50}$$

Substituting for the scattering function gives us

$$I(0,+\mu) = J(0)\left[1 + \frac{1}{2}\mu H(\mu)\int_0^1 \frac{H(\mu')\,d\mu'}{\mu + \mu'}\right] \tag{51}$$

or simply,

$$I(0,+\mu) = J(0)H(\mu) \tag{52}$$

where by $H(\mu)$ we mean the functions defined by Eq. (4.1-50) with $\tilde{\omega}_0 = 1$. We may write the definitions of $J(0)$ and the flux πF in terms of μ and substitute for $I(0,+\mu)$ from Eq. (4.1-52) to obtain

$$4\,\frac{J(0)}{F} = \frac{\displaystyle\int_0^1 H(\mu)\,d\mu}{\displaystyle\int_0^1 H(\mu)\mu\,d\mu} = \frac{\alpha_0}{\alpha_1} \tag{53}$$

The moments of the H functions are known and we find that

$$J(0) = \frac{3^{\frac{1}{2}}}{4}F \tag{54}$$

This last equation is called the Hopf-Bronstein relation. Our final result for the emergent intensity in the constant net flux problem is

$$I(0,\mu) = \frac{3^{\frac{1}{2}}}{4}FH(\mu) \tag{55}$$

We note that the reflected intensity from a semi-infinite atmosphere illuminated by a parallel beam of flux πF, where the scattering is isotropic with single scattering albedo $\tilde{\omega}_0$ is

$$I(0;\mu,\mu_0) = \frac{\tilde{\omega}_0}{4}\frac{\mu_0}{\mu + \mu_0}H(\mu)H(\mu_0)F \tag{56}$$

It is important to note that these are the same H functions involved in the solutions to these two problems. Hence, the H functions are the basic tabulated functions of radiative transfer in problems involving semi-infinite atmospheres. Tables of H functions bear the relationship to these transfer problems that tables of sine and cosine bear to trigonometry.

The principles of invariance can also be applied to problems in finite atmospheres, i.e., atmospheres of finite optical thickness. Here the scattering function is a function of the optical thickness of the atmosphere τ_1.

the center of the Sun. Using Eqs. (4.1-69) and (4.1-16), we can rewrite our result as

$$\frac{c}{K_\nu \rho} \frac{d}{dr} [P_r]_\nu = \pi F_\nu \tag{71}$$

We shall want to integrate this equation over frequency to relate it to the total flux. The integration is best done in this form, because it is just those frequencies for which K_ν is small that contribute most to the net flow of radiation. Integrating over frequency and using Eq. (3.1-1), we find

$$\frac{L(r)}{4\pi r^2} = \frac{c}{\rho} \int_0^\infty \frac{1}{K_\nu} \frac{d}{dr} [P_r]_\nu \, d\nu = \frac{c}{\rho K} \frac{dP_r}{dr} \tag{72}$$

where the Rosseland mean opacity used here is defined by Eq. (3.3-32). We have noted before that the mean free path in stellar interiors is very short; this implies that the radiation interacts strongly with the matter, which ensures near isotropy of the radiation field and a close approach to thermodynamic equilibrium. For near isotropy, the basic definition [Eq. (4.1-69)] shows that the radiation pressure is proportional to the intensity, and for thermodynamic equilibrium, the intensity is given by Planck's law [Eq. (3.3-33)]. These remarks show how the transition from the first to the second equality in Eq. 4.1-72 is made with the aid of the Rosseland mean opacity [Eq. 3.3-32], where the factor of $1 - e^{-h\nu/kT}$ in the definition of the mean opacity includes the effects of stimulated emission.

The radiation pressure for thermodynamic equilibrium is given by

$$P_r = \tfrac{1}{3}aT^4 \tag{73}$$

where $a = 4\sigma/c = 7.6 \times 10^{-15}$ erg/(cm^3)(deg^4). Substituting Eq. (4.1-73) into Eq. (4.1-72) gives us Eq. (3.3-4), which we quoted earlier for the temperature gradient in a layer in radiative equilibrium.

This brief digression completes our introduction to radiative transfer. These developments have applications especially to the physics of the photosphere, which we shall consider next.

4.2 THE SOLAR PHOTOSPHERE

The objective of the study of the solar photosphere is to obtain the dependence of various physical properties, such as temperature, pressure, and density, on depth in the atmosphere and to use these properties to predict the emergent radiation field.

The T-τ relation

We shall begin by discussing some approaches which illustrate the general principles involved, but which must be regarded as historical as far as numerical accuracy is concerned. Consider an atmosphere in local thermo-dynamic equilibrium where the equation of transfer is [see Eqs. (4.1-17) and (4.1-19)]

$$-\mu \frac{dI_\nu(z,\mu)}{\rho \, dz} = K_\nu I_\nu(z,\mu) - K_\nu B_\nu(T_z) \tag{1}$$

In such an atmosphere, the problem is relatively simple, because the determination of T as a function of z completely determines the solution, i.e., through Eq. (4.1-21). We consider that the photosphere is in radiative equilibrium. This means that there are no mechanisms other than radiation for transporting energy and that there are no sources or sinks. If we take a layer which has a thickness small compared to the radius of the Sun, we must have (see Fig. 3.3-2)

$$\pi F = \pi \int_0^\infty F_\nu(z) \, d\nu = \text{const} \tag{2}$$

The equation of transfer (4.2-1) can be integrated over μ to obtain

$$-\frac{d}{\rho \, dz} \int_{-1}^{+1} \mu I_\nu(z,\mu) \, d\mu$$
$$= K_\nu \int_{-1}^{+1} I_\nu(z,\mu) \, d\mu - K_\nu B_\nu(T_z) \int_{-1}^{+1} d\mu \tag{3}$$

With the basic definitions, this becomes

$$-\frac{dF_\nu}{4\rho \, dz} = K_\nu J_\nu - K_\nu B_\nu \tag{4}$$

An integration over frequency gives

$$-\frac{dF}{4\rho \, dz} = \int_0^\infty (J_\nu - B_\nu) K_\nu \, d\nu \tag{5}$$

Since the net flux is constant with z, we have the result that

$$\int_0^\infty J_\nu K_\nu \, d\nu = \int_0^\infty B_\nu K_\nu \, d\nu \tag{6}$$

which is valid for atmospheres in local thermodynamic and radiative equilibrium. Physically, this result shows that every mass element must absorb as much energy as it emits.

This leads to an idealized problem of interest, the gray atmosphere, where the absorption coefficient is independent of frequency. The optical thickness is given by

$$\tau = \int_z^\infty \bar{K} \rho \, dz \tag{7}$$

where the method of obtaining $\bar{K}$ is left unspecified. The equation of transfer (4.2-1) can, after an integration over ν, be written as

$$\mu \frac{dI}{d\tau} = I - B \tag{8}$$

Proceeding as above, we immediately find that $B = J$, and hence the integrated intensity distribution in a gray atmosphere is given by a solution of the constant net flux problem which we considered in Sec. 4.1. This problem has an emergent flux given by Eq. (4.1-55),

$$I_{\text{gray}}(0,\mu) = \frac{3^{1/2}}{4} FH(\mu) \tag{9}$$

where also we have the Hopf-Bronstein relation [Eq. (4.1-54)]

$$J_{\text{gray}}(0) = \frac{3^{1/2}}{4} F \tag{10}$$

The integrated Planck intensity is related to the local temperature through

$$\pi B(T) = \pi \int_0^\infty B_\nu(T) \, d\nu = \sigma T^4 \tag{11}$$

This equation, along with Eq. (3.1-2), allows us to obtain a relation between the effective temperature and the boundary temperature for a gray atmosphere:

$$T_0{}^4 = \frac{3^{1/2}}{4} T_e{}^4 \tag{12}$$

where T_0 denotes the boundary temperature. Numerically, this relation implies $T_0 = 0.81 T_e$.

The temperature distribution in a gray atmosphere can be obtained from the source function for the constant net flux problem [Eq. (4.1-41)],

$$J(\tau) = \tfrac{3}{4} F[\tau + q(\tau)] \tag{13}$$

The function $q(\tau)$ is very slowly varying; it varies monotonically from 0.58 at $\tau = 0$ to 0.71 as $\tau \to \infty$. For simplicity we adopt $q(\tau) = \tfrac{2}{3}$, and we use Eqs. (3.1-2) and (4.2-11) to write

$$T^4 = \tfrac{1}{2} T_e{}^4(1 + \tfrac{3}{2}\tau) \tag{14}$$

This is the standard result for the temperature distribution in a gray atmosphere.

It is a simple matter to compute the limb darkening in white light on this simple picture as [see Eqs. (4.2-14), (4.2-11), and (4.1-21)]

$$I(\mu,0) = \int_{t=0}^{\infty} B(t)e^{-t/\mu}\,\frac{dt}{\mu} \tag{15a}$$

$$= \int_{t=0}^{\infty} B_0(1 + \tfrac{3}{2}t)e^{-t/\mu}\,\frac{dt}{\mu} \tag{15b}$$

$$= B_0(1 + \tfrac{3}{2}\mu) \tag{15c}$$

With this result, the limb darkening can be written as

$$\frac{I(\mu,0)}{I(1,0)} = 1 - u + u\mu \tag{16}$$

where $u = \tfrac{3}{5}$. This is a reasonably accurate representation for the Sun where the observational value is $u \approx 0.56$. The limb darkening can be easily computed as a function of wavelength, and again there is reasonable agreement with the observations. We note that the limb darkening is a direct consequence of the temperature gradient in the solar atmosphere. An observation effectively penetrates to unit slant opacity, which carries observations near the center of the disk to deeper, hotter, and hence brighter regions.

Departures from grayness can be considered by writing the opacity as

$$K_{\nu} = \bar{K}(1 + \delta_{\nu}) \tag{17}$$

and considering that δ_{ν} does not vary with depth. Again we leave the definition of $\bar{K}$ unspecified. The equation of transfer becomes

$$\mu\,\frac{dI_{\nu}}{d\tau} = I_{\nu} - B_{\nu} + \delta_{\nu}(I_{\nu} - B_{\nu}) \tag{18}$$

Since we expect—or hope—that the departures from grayness are small, we can adopt an iterative procedure and evaluate the term $\delta_{\nu}(I_{\nu} - B_{\nu})$ from the gray solution. Using the equation of transfer, we write

$$\mu\,\frac{dI'_{\nu}}{d\tau} = I'_{\nu} - B'_{\nu} + \delta_{\nu}\mu\,\frac{dI_{\nu}}{d\tau} \tag{19}$$

where the primes denote nongray or improved quantities. Integrating this equation over μ and ν gives (as above)

$$B' = J' + \frac{1}{2}\int_{0}^{\infty}\int_{-1}^{+1} \mu\delta_{\nu}\,\frac{dI_{\nu}}{d\tau}\,d\mu\,d\nu \tag{20a}$$

$$= J' + \frac{d}{4d\tau}\int_{0}^{\infty} \delta_{\nu}F_{\nu}\,d\nu \tag{20b}$$

If we introduce the Chandrasekhar mean, defined by

$$\bar{K} \int_0^\infty F_\nu \, d\nu = \int_0^\infty K_\nu F_\nu \, d\nu \tag{21}$$

it is clear that this straight mean over the flux makes the integral in Eq. (4.2-20b) equal to zero; thus we again have the gray atmosphere with the opacity defined through Eq. (4.2-21). This fact is the advantage of the Chandrasekhar mean. However, it is clear from our discussion of interiors that the Rosseland mean is to be preferred for interiors, and we may expect some difficulty in attempting to join an atmosphere solution to an interior solution if two different mean opacities are used. The fact seems to be that recourse must be made to numerical methods if accuracy is desired in the solution of the equation of transfer for the T versus τ relation.

We illustrate two methods of handling the nongray problem numerically. The formal solution of the equation of transfer can be inserted into the definition of the mean intensity, and, for the case of local thermodynamic equilibrium, we find

$$J_\nu = \int_0^\infty B_\nu(t_\nu) E_1(|\tau_\nu - t_\nu|) \, dt_\nu \tag{22}$$

Thus, we can compute J_ν from an initial model. The net flux must be constant, however, and we can insert our first attempt at J_ν into the equation [see Eq. (4.2-6)]

$$\int_0^\infty B'_\nu K_\nu \, d\nu = \int_0^\infty J_\nu K_\nu \, d\nu \tag{23}$$

to obtain an improved value B'_ν by trial and error. This process may be regarded as an iterative procedure; it appears to converge rapidly for small optical depths.

A procedure useful in the deeper layers utilizes Eddington's approximation (valid only in deeper layers). The radiation field is taken to be nearly isotropic, and the basic definitions give [see Eqs. (4.1-68) and (4.1-5)] $J = 3K$

Thus, Eq. (4.1-69) gives, in Eddington's approximation,

$$\frac{dJ}{d\tau} = \frac{3}{4} F \tag{24}$$

Equation (4.2-24) can be integrated and written in the form

$$J(\tau) = \tfrac{1}{2} F(0) + \tfrac{3}{4} \int_0^\tau F \, d\tau \tag{25}$$

where we have applied the condition $2J(0) = F(0)$, which is appropriate to the approximation of a nearly isotropic radiation field. We also have the equation of conservation of energy for a gray atmosphere,

$$B(\tau) = J(\tau) - \frac{1}{4}\frac{dF}{d\tau} \tag{26}$$

If we eliminate $J(\tau)$ from these two equations, we can write the variation in $B(\tau)$ in terms of the variation in the flux πF as

$$-\Delta B(\tau) = +\frac{1}{2}\,\Delta F(0) + \frac{3}{4}\int_0^\tau \Delta F(\tau)\,d\tau - \frac{1}{4}\frac{d}{d\tau}[\Delta F(\tau)] \tag{27}$$

Thus, for a given temperature distribution versus τ, we can evaluate the monochromatic flux using

$$F_\nu = 2\int_{\tau_\nu}^\infty B_\nu(t_\nu)E_2(t_\nu - \tau_\nu)\,dt_\nu - 2\int_0^{\tau_\nu} B_\nu(t_\nu)E_2(\tau_\nu - t_\nu)\,dt_\nu \tag{28}$$

This equation is derived in a manner similar to that used to derive Eq. (4.2-22). At every depth, we can integrate Eq. (4.2-28) over frequency to obtain F and compare it with the required value. This allows us to compute ΔF and hence ΔB, where the Rosseland mean opacity is normally used. If we then compute the temperature from Eq. (4.2-11) by using $B'(\tau) = B(\tau) \doteq \Delta B(\tau)$, the constant net flux condition should be more

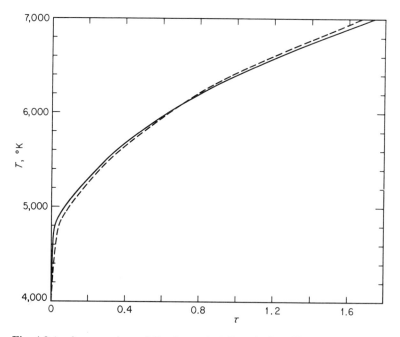

Fig. 4.2-1   A comparison of the theoretical T-τ relation (K. H. Böhm) with the empirical T-τ relation (E. Böhm–Vitense). The agreement is good except for rather small optical depths. (*See R* 4.2-9 *and R* 4.2-10.)

closely satisfied than on the basis of the original temperature distribution, *if* the assumptions involved in this iteration procedure are valid. It should be noted that considerable labor is involved in such iterations.

Models based on refined, iterative procedures such as those described in the preceding paragraphs have been constructed. One begins with an empirical model and takes into account nongrayness arising from the continuous and line absorption coefficients. Such models are in reasonably good agreement with the empirical models; comparison of these models is shown in Fig. 4.2-1. The empirical models are generally based on limb-darkening observations. Thus, Eq. (4.2-15*a*) can be used to predict the limb darkening if the T-τ relation is known. Or, if the limb darkening is known, the T-τ relation can be derived. It is important to note that this T-τ relation does not rest on the assumption of radiative equilibrium. The central intensities of the Fraunhofer lines (formed very high in the atmosphere) are useful for determining T-τ for τ very small.

Structural equations and model

Given the T-τ relationship, we need additional equations to determine the structure of the photosphere. We have the equation of hydrostatic equilibrium,

$$dP = -g\rho \, dz \tag{29}$$

Also, the mean optical depth is related to the geometrical depth through

$$d\tau = -\bar{K}\rho \, dz \tag{30}$$

and the last two equations yield

$$\frac{dP}{d\tau} = \frac{g}{\bar{K}} \tag{31}$$

To evaluate $\bar{K}$, we need to know the physical conditions and the most important absorption mechanism at each point, that is,

$$\bar{K} = \bar{K}(T,P,P_e,A_i) \tag{32}$$

where we denote the composition by the A_i's. The composition is taken as given, and we know T through the T-τ relationship. We shall find that the absorption coefficient per neutral hydrogen atom can be written as $\bar{K}(\tau,P_e)$, and hence we need a P-P_e relation to integrate Eq. (4.2-31). It is easily seen that this relation can be written as

$$\frac{P_e}{P} = \frac{x_H}{1 + x_H} + \frac{1}{A}\frac{x_M}{1 + x_H} \tag{33}$$

where x_H and x_M denote the mean degree of ionization of hydrogen and the metals, respectively, and A is the ratio of hydrogen to metals by number. Metals include the elements Mg, Si, Fe, Ca, Al, and Na. Sometimes the metals can all be taken as singly ionized ($x_M = 1$) and the hydrogen as all neutral ($x_H = 0$); then Eq. (4.2-33) reduces to $P_e/P = 1/A$, which would give $P_e \approx 10^{-4}P$ for the Sun, a reasonable result. With the Saha equation, it is possible to construct tables of x_H and x_M as a function of temperature and electron pressure only, since we can write

$$\frac{x}{1-x} P_e = K_r(T) \tag{34}$$

where

$$K_r(T) = \frac{u_{r+1}}{u_r} \frac{2(2\pi m_e)^{3/2}(kT)^{5/2}}{h^3} e^{-\chi_r/kT} \tag{35}$$

Here x is the fraction of the element $r + 1$ times ionized and $1 - x$ is the fraction r times ionized. The function u_r is the partition function defined by

$$u_r(T) = \sum_{j=1}^{\infty} g_{r,j} e^{-\epsilon_{r,j}/kT} \tag{36}$$

where the various states are denoted by the subscript j. The ionization energy and the excitation energy are denoted by χ_r and $\epsilon_{r,j}$, respectively, and $g_{r,j}$ is the statistical weight. In most cases, the factor $2u_{r+1}/u_r \approx 1$. With these developments, we can regard a P-P_e relation as established, and thus the mean absorption coefficient is known as a function of P and τ, when the source of the opacity is known (see below).

With $\bar{K}(P,\tau)$ we may integrate Eq. (4.2-31) to establish a P-τ relation. Then, using the perfect-gas law, we may establish the relation between optical and geometrical depth by integrating Eq. (4.2-30). This completes the specification of a model solar photosphere. A model solar atmosphere due to Unsöld is given in Table 4.2-1.

The opacity

The source of the continuous opacity in the Sun had been somewhat of a mystery prior to Wildt's suggestion in 1939 that it was due to bound-free absorption of the negative hydrogen ion H$^-$. The ionization limit is about 16,500 A and H$^-$ appears to dominate the absorption in the visible portion of the solar spectrum. The various quantum-mechanical problems associated with the determination of the absorption coefficient for H$^-$ are not trivial (owing to weak binding of the outer electron), and considerable effort has been exerted in this direction. It seems that the principal fea-

Table 4.2-1 A model solar atmosphere constructed by Unsöld*

Height z, km	Solar radii / Opt. depth τ_{5000}	Temperature T, °K	Gas pressure, dynes/cm², log P	Electron pressure, dynes/cm², log P_e	Electrons/cm³, log N_e	Turbulent velocity V_t or ΔV, km/sec	Layer	Main energy transfer
1,400,000	3.0	$2\cdot10^6$	-3.8	-4.1	5.5		Corona	Thermal conduction
700,000	2.0	$2\cdot10^6$	-2.8	-3.1	6.4			
350,000	1.50	$2\cdot10^6$	-2.1	-2.4	7.2			
42,000	1.06	$2\cdot10^6$	-0.9	-1.2	8.4			
20,000	1.03	$2\cdot10^6$	-0.8	-1.1	8.5	~15	Transition layer	Mechanical energy
3,000		~4-6000	0.2	-1.7	10.5			
2,000	***	~4-6000	0.5	-1.4	10.8	12	Chromosphere	Radiation
1,000		~4-6000	1.2	-0.9	11.3	7		
0	0.005	4090	4.1	-0.5	11.7	1-2		
	0.01	4295	4.3	-0.3	12.0			
	0.05	4855	4.6	+0.2	12.4		Photosphere	Radiation
	0.1	5030	4.8	+0.4	12.6			
	0.5	5805	5.1	1.2	13.3	2		
	1.0	6400	5.2	1.8	13.8			
	2.0	7180	5.3	2.4	14.4			
-260		10^4	5.3	4.0	15.86	2	Hydrogen Convection zone	Convection
-280	***							
-16,000	-0.02	10^5	9.4	9.1	20.0	0.3		Radiation
-140,000	-0.2	10^6	12.3	12.0	21.9	0.0		

(Temperature in the chromosphere rows is noted as "Very inhomogeneous.")

* Courtesy of Academic Press Inc.; see R. 4.2-11.

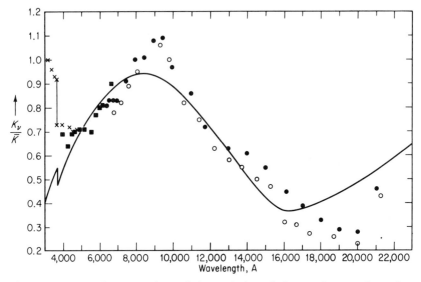

Fig. 4.2-2 An early comparison of the variation of the continuous absorption coefficient of H⁻ calculated for $T = 5740°K$ (solid line) with the observations (crosses, circles, and squares). (*From S. Chandrasekhar, "Radiative Transfer,"* published by Dover Publications, Inc. See R 4.1-1.)

tures are now understood, however. This can be shown in the following way. The emergent intensity can be written as

$$I_\nu(0,\mu) = \int_0^\infty B_\nu(T) \exp\left(-\frac{K_\nu}{\bar{K}}\frac{\tau}{\mu}\right) d\left(\frac{K_\nu}{\bar{K}}\frac{\tau}{\mu}\right) \qquad (37)$$

Since we have a T-τ relationship, we can evaluate this integral with $K_\nu/\bar{K}$ as the parameter, under the assumption that we can assign a meaningful $K_\nu/\bar{K}$ averaged over depth. Since we can observe $I_\nu(0,\mu)$, we can determine $K_\nu/\bar{K}$ and compare it with the values computed from the theory for H⁻. This comparison is made in Fig. 4.2-2, where $K_\nu/\bar{K}$ is assumed constant and the atmosphere is taken to have the gray temperature distribution with τ given in terms of the Chandrasekhar mean. The agreement appears to be satisfactory.

Other absorbers, of course, make some contribution to the solar opacity. The bound-free absorption of neutral hydrogen is important near and shortward of the various continua limits such as the Balmer limit at 3,645 A. Absorption due to metals continua amounts to some 20 per cent of the value for (H⁻ + H) at the Balmer limit; absorption by metals becomes more important as one goes into the ultraviolet from the Balmer limit. Absorption due to bound-free transitions of the H_2^+ molecule may contribute a few per cent in the solar ultraviolet; electron scattering is negligible in the solar photosphere. We note that extensive tables of

$K_\nu(P_e,T)$ are available. We also note that absorption lines can contribute appreciably to $\bar{K}$; this is called the "blanketing effect."

4.3 ABSORPTION LINES

The solar optical spectrum contains many regions of localized wavelength where relatively less energy is contained (per unit wavelength) than in the continuum on either side. These are called absorption lines or the Fraunhofer spectrum (Fig. 5.2-2).

The formation of absorption lines in the photosphere is, in principle, relatively simple. We introduce the pure absorption coefficients per unit mass, K_ν and l_ν, for the continuum and the line, respectively. The scattering coefficients are denoted by i_ν and σ_ν for noncoherent and coherent scattering, respectively. Thus, the equation of transfer can be written as

$$\mu \frac{dI_\nu(x_\nu,\mu)}{dx_\nu} = I_\nu(x_\nu,\mu) - \mathcal{I}_\nu(x_\nu,\mu) \tag{1}$$

where

$$dx_\nu = (K_\nu + l_\nu + i_\nu + \sigma_\nu)\rho \, dr \tag{2}$$

The specification of the various coefficients and the source function is necessary to complete the specification of the problem. In an obvious way, the source function can be written as

$$\mathcal{I}_\nu = \frac{K_\nu + l_\nu}{K_\nu + l_\nu + \sigma_\nu + i_\nu} B_\nu + \frac{\sigma_\nu}{K_\nu + l_\nu + \sigma_\nu + i_\nu} J_\nu$$
$$+ \frac{i_\nu}{K_\nu + l_\nu + \sigma_\nu + i_\nu} \cdot \frac{\int i_\nu J_\nu \, d\nu}{\int i_\nu \, d\nu} \tag{3}$$

The assumption used to handle the noncoherent scattering is one of complete redistribution; the noncoherent portion of the emitted radiation does not depend on the frequency distribution of the incident intensity, but is simply taken as proportional to i_ν. The importance of noncoherent scattering in the Sun is not completely understood; it could influence the centers of strong absorption lines.

We consider, as illustrations, two simple cases of line formation. First, consider that there is no scattering, but only pure absorption. Then $\sigma_\nu = i_\nu = 0$. Also let $\mathcal{I}_\nu = B_\nu$; in this case, we say that the line is formed in local thermodynamic equilibrium, and the solution can be immediately written down as

$$I_\nu(0,\mu) = \int_0^\infty B_\nu(x_\nu)e^{-x_\nu/\mu} \frac{dx_\nu}{\mu} \tag{4}$$

The general scheme of calculation of line profiles for lines formed in local thermodynamic equilibrium is shown in Fig. 4.3-1. The physical

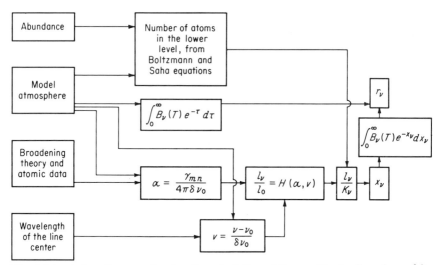

Fig. 4.3-1   A flow diagram showing the calculation of line profiles for lines formed in local thermodynamic equilibrium. (*After A. M. Heiser, see R 4.3-1 and R 4.2-6.*)

meaning of line formation on the basis of Eq. (4.3-4) is as follows. The atoms of an absorbing constituent increase the monochromatic opacity near the absorbing frequency of the atom. Thus, we can see to a depth in the line which is somewhat higher up in the photosphere than in the continuum. For a photosphere with the temperature increasing inward, we see to hotter regions in the continuum than in the line, with the obvious result. Note that there would be no absorption line in an isothermal atmosphere.

The other simple case of interest is line formation by continuous absorption and line scattering. In Eq. (4.3-3), $i_\nu = l_\nu = 0$, and

$$g_\nu = \frac{K_\nu}{K_\nu + \sigma_\nu} B_\nu + \frac{\sigma_\nu}{K_\nu + \sigma_\nu} J_\nu \tag{5}$$

For this case, the equation of transfer can be written as

$$-\mu \frac{dI_\nu}{\rho\, dr} = (K_\nu + \sigma_\nu)I_\nu - \tfrac{1}{2}\sigma_\nu \int_{-1}^{+1} I_\nu\, d\mu' - K_\nu B_\nu \tag{6}$$

In terms of x_ν [see Eq. (4.3-2)] we have

$$+\mu \frac{dI_\nu}{dx_\nu} = I_\nu - \tfrac{1}{2}(1 - \lambda_\nu) \int_{-1}^{+1} I_\nu(x_\nu, \mu')\, d\mu' - \lambda B_\nu(x_\nu) \tag{7}$$

where

$$\lambda_\nu = \frac{K_\nu}{K_\nu + \sigma_\nu} \tag{8}$$

An exact solution to this problem can be obtained if we assume that λ_ν is independent of depth and that B_ν increases linearly with the optical depth in the continuum, that is, $B_\nu = a + b\tau_\nu$ (called the Eddington-Barbier approximation). With these two assumptions, the equation of transfer becomes

$$\mu \frac{dI_\nu}{dx_\nu} = I_\nu - \tfrac{1}{2}(1 - \lambda_\nu) \int_{-1}^{+1} I_\nu(x_\nu, \mu') \, d\mu' - \lambda[a + \lambda b x_\nu] \tag{9}$$

This equation can be solved in a straightforward manner by using the method of discrete ordinates with the usual boundary condition, namely, that there be no radiation incident on the upper surface. It is possible to pass to the limit of infinite approximation and express the solution in terms of the H functions and their moments. The emergent intensity is

$$I(0,\mu) = \lambda^{3/2} b H(\mu) \left(\mu + \frac{a}{\lambda b} + \frac{1 - \lambda}{2\lambda^{1/2}} \alpha_1 \right) \tag{10}$$

where the H functions and their first moment α_1 [see Eq. (4.1-53)] are defined with respect to a single scattering albedo $\tilde{\omega}_0 = 1 - \lambda$. A convenient quantity is the residual intensity defined by

$$r_\nu = \frac{I_\nu(0,\mu)}{I_c(0,\mu)} \tag{11}$$

These quantities are illustrated in Fig. 4.3-2. The continuum intensity is obtained from Eq. (4.3-10) by letting $\lambda \to 1$ and noting that $H(\lambda = 1) = 1$. Thus, the residual intensity becomes

$$r_\nu = \frac{\lambda^{3/2} H(\mu)}{\mu + a/b} \left[\mu + \frac{a}{\lambda b} + \frac{(1 - \lambda)\alpha_1}{2\lambda^{1/2}} \right] \tag{12}$$

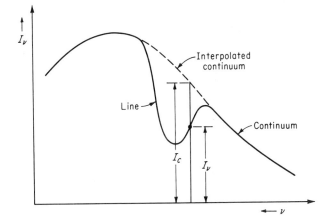

Fig. 4.3-2   A schematic diagram showing quantities used in Eq. (4.3-11).

The centers of strong lines, for which $\lambda \ll 1$, would be almost black, $(r_\nu \ll 1)$ according to Eq. (4.3-12). This is not the case for a line formed in local thermodynamic equilibrium; even for a very strong line, we must have $r_\nu \gtrsim B_\nu(T_0)/B_\nu(Te) \approx \frac{1}{4}$. This same argument also shows that absorption lines formed in local thermodynamic equilibrium should disappear at the limb.

Note that solar absorption lines such as the H and K lines of ionized calcium show only a relatively small center-to-limb variation in their profile. We also note that the formation of an absorption line by scatterers in an absorbing atmosphere does not depend exclusively on a temperature gradient. Equation (4.3-12) in the case $b \to 0$ becomes

$$r_\nu = \lambda^{\frac{1}{2}} H(\mu; 1 - \lambda) \tag{13a}$$

$$\approx 2 \left(\frac{K_\nu}{\sigma_\nu} \right)^{\frac{1}{2}} \qquad K_\nu \ll \sigma_\nu \quad \text{and} \quad \mu = 0.5 \tag{13b}$$

On this picture, the role of the scatterers is to increase the distance traveled by a photon with the characteristic frequency of the scatterers before it leaves the photosphere. This increase in path length increases the probability that a photon of the characteristic frequency will be absorbed (say, by H^-). Thus, we have a random-walk problem. We shall not continue this discussion further except to note that the square-root dependence in Eq. (4.3-13b) is suggestive of a random-walk process.

The line absorption coefficient

To specify the detailed method of line formation, we must specify the atomic processes which contribute to the determination of the line absorption coefficient s_ν. Depending on the physics of the situation, s_ν can be equal to l_ν or σ_ν, that is, we do not specify the future of a photon which is "absorbed" by an atom with absorption coefficient s_ν.

We begin with radiation damping. The energy of a classical, radiating oscillator decreases with time according to

$$W = W_0 e^{-\gamma_c t} \tag{14}$$

where the classical damping constant is given by

$$\gamma_c = \frac{8\pi^2 e^2 \nu_0^2}{3 m_e c^3} \tag{15}$$

In this equation e is the electron charge and ν_0 is the natural frequency of the oscillator. A harmonic analysis of the oscillations yields the frequency dependence

$$s_\nu = \frac{e^2 \gamma_c}{m_e c 4\pi} \frac{1}{(\nu - \nu_0)^2 + (\gamma_0/4\pi)^2} \tag{16}$$

This equation rests on the classical assumptions for one oscillator. The quantum-mechanical broadening of states is a consequence of the Heisenberg uncertainty principle, $\Delta E \, \Delta t \approx \hbar$. It is clear that the inverse of the sum of the various transition probabilities for leaving a particular state is just the mean lifetime of that state, that is,

$$\gamma_m = \frac{1}{\tau_m} = \sum_n A_{mn} + \sum_{n<m} B_{mn} I_\nu(mn) + \sum_{k>m} B_{mk} I_\nu(mk) \tag{17}$$

Here the first term is due to spontaneous emission, the second is due to stimulated emission, and the third is due to absorption, which can be taken to include ionizations if need be. The A_{mn}'s, B_{mn}'s, and B_{mk}'s are the Einstein A and B's (constants of the atom) which describe such processes and which are proportional to the f value or oscillator strength for the transition in question. In many astronomical applications it is necessary to consider only the term $\sum_n A_{mn}$ in Eq. (4.3-17); if this is the case, the radiation field is termed *dilute*. It is known from quantum theory that the damping constant appropriate to a transition between levels m and n is given by $\gamma_{mn} = \gamma_m + \gamma_n$. Thus, the line profile due to radiation damping is given by

$$s_\nu = \frac{e^2 \gamma_{mn}}{m_e c 4\pi} \frac{f}{(\nu - \nu_0)^2 + (\gamma_{mn}/4\pi)^2} \tag{18}$$

Several kinds of line broadening due to collisions (pressure broadening) can be expressed in the same form as Eq. (4.3-18). Some types of line broadening can be described by discrete encounters; the rapid passage of the disturbing particle can be thought of as (slightly) changing the energy of the states in the atom. Classically, we may think of a change $\Delta \nu$ in the frequency of a radiating oscillator caused by the impinging particle. The frequency change can be written as

$$\Delta \nu = \frac{c}{r^k} \tag{19}$$

where k depends on the nature of the interaction. Three cases of interest are known:

    1. Self-broadening $(k = 3)$: here the perturbing particles are the same as the atom of the spectral line under study.

    2. Quadratic Stark effect $(k = 4)$: the perturbing particles are ions and electrons.

    3. Van der Waals broadening $(k = 6)$: the perturbing particles are atoms of neutral hydrogen.

Sufficient information is available to calculate γ_{coll} for these types of line broadening due to collisions; then, these effects can be included in the line profile by replacing γ_{mn} in Eq. (4.3-18) by $\gamma_{mn} + \gamma_{coll}$.

The linear Stark effect cannot be handled in this manner. Here the lines are shifted by the electrostatic fields of ions and electrons. In a given volume element, various atoms have various displacements, and the net result is a statistical broadening of the line. This effect can be handled by assuming that the perturbing ions and electrons are stationary with respect to the particle of interest. Note that this is just the opposite of the procedure necessary to handle the types of line broadening described in the preceding paragraph. The linear Stark effect is important for hydrogen lines and has a frequency dependence in the wings given by

$$s_\nu \propto (\nu - \nu_0)^{-5/2} \tag{20}$$

The Doppler broadening of lines in stellar atmospheres caused by thermal motions and turbulent motions is most important. If we assume that the velocity distribution is maxwellian [see Eq. (4.4-1)], then the distribution of radial velocities is given in terms of the fraction of particles with radial velocities between v and $v + dv$, that is,

$$\frac{dN}{N} = \frac{1}{\pi^{1/2}} e^{-(v/v_0)^2} \frac{dv}{v_0} \tag{21}$$

where

$$v_0^2 = \frac{2kT}{m} + v_t^2 \tag{22}$$

Here we have included the possibility of a maxwellian distribution of small-scale turbulent velocities. We ignore the turbulent motions in the following discussion. By Doppler's principle,

$$\frac{\delta\nu}{\nu} = \frac{v}{c} \tag{23}$$

and the distribution of absorbing atoms in frequency is then given by

$$\frac{dN}{N} = \frac{1}{\pi^{1/2}} e^{-(\delta\nu/\delta\nu_0)^2} \frac{d\nu}{\delta\nu_0} \tag{24}$$

where $\delta\nu_0/\nu_0 = v_0/c$. For our case of pure thermal motion,

$$\delta\nu_0 = \frac{\nu}{c} \left(\frac{2kT}{m} \right)^{1/2} \tag{25}$$

Equation (4.3-24) gives the relative absorption profile for the case of negligible radiation or pressure damping. This expression can be normalized by using the fact that

$$\int_0^\infty s_\nu \, d\nu = \frac{\pi e^2}{m_e c} f \tag{26}$$

This last equation can be derived by integrating Eq. (4.3-18) from $\nu = 0$ to $\nu = \infty$ and noting that the Doppler broadening cannot alter the net absorption. Setting $s_\nu \propto dN/N$ and normalizing according to Eq. (4.3-26) gives us

$$s_\nu = \frac{\pi^{1/2} e^2}{m_e c} \frac{f}{\delta \nu_0} \exp\left[-\frac{(\nu - \nu_0)^2}{(\delta \nu_0)^2} \right] \tag{27}$$

Many absorption profiles can be represented by the combined action of Doppler and natural broadening, called the Voigt profile. A single atom has its natural broadening profile shifted an amount $\delta \nu$ because of its motion. For this atom, the absorption coefficient is just

$$\frac{e^2 \gamma_{mn}}{m_e c 4\pi} \frac{f}{(\nu - \nu_0 - \delta \nu)^2 + (\gamma_{mn}/4\pi)^2} \tag{28}$$

The relative proportion of such atoms is given by Eq. (4.3-24). Now, the absorption coefficient at any frequency is due to the combined action of many profiles, such as that given by Eq. (4.3-28), with different $\delta \nu$'s because of the velocity distribution. The total absorption coefficient is given by

$$s_\nu = \frac{e^2 \gamma_{mn} f}{4\pi^{3/2} m_e c} \int_{-\infty}^{+\infty} \frac{e^{-(\delta \nu/\delta \nu_0)^2}}{(\nu - \nu_0 - \delta \nu)^2 + (\gamma_{mn}/4\pi)^2} \, d\left(\frac{\delta \nu}{\delta \nu_0}\right) \tag{29}$$

This can be rewritten by setting $\alpha = \gamma_{mn}/4\pi \, \delta \nu_0$, $y = \delta \nu/\delta \nu_0$, and $v = (\nu - \nu_0)/\delta \nu_0$, whence

$$H(\alpha, v) = \frac{s_\nu}{s_{\nu_0}} = \frac{\alpha}{\pi} \int_{-\infty}^{+\infty} \frac{e^{-y^2} \, dy}{\alpha^2 + (v - y)^2} \tag{30}$$

Here s_{ν_0} is the absorption coefficient for the center of the line when Doppler broadening alone is considered [see Eq. (4.3-27)]. The function $H(\alpha, v)$ is the Hjerting function, which is handled numerically. Some plots of $H(\alpha, v)$ are given in Fig. 4.3-3. These curves clearly show that for most cases of interest in photospheres (that is, $\alpha \ll 1$), the absorption profile tends to be nearly the same as the Doppler profile near the line center and essentially the natural profile [s_ν proportional to $(\nu - \nu_0)^{-2}$] far from the center. Hyperfine structure and the Zeeman effect are additional factors which can complicate the determination of the absorption coefficient.

When the absorption coefficient is specified, it is necessary to specify the physical nature of the reemission in order to compute the line profile.

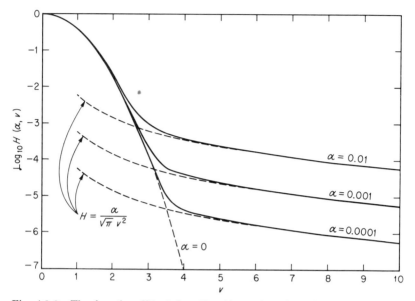

Fig. 4.3-3   The function $H(\alpha,v)$ [see Eq. (4.3-30)] evaluated by using tables given by D. Harris (R 4.3-2). The Doppler broadened core and natural broadened wings are clearly shown.

The photon "absorbed" can be involved in a true absorption, a coherent scattering, or a noncoherent scattering. Each case must be decided after considering the structure of the atom in question, the parameters of the line, and where the line is formed. Such information is used to determine the source function $\mathcal{S}_\nu$. Because the intensity is involved, the determination of $\mathcal{S}_\nu$ may well involve an iteration.

As an example, consider the formation of a weak absorption line or the wings of a strong line. Such lines are formed relatively deep in the photosphere where $\gamma_{\text{coll}} \gg \gamma_{mn}$. It is clear that under these conditions, the scattering is noncoherent, because a classical oscillator would be disrupted many times before it would radiate. It is clear that noncoherent scattering with complete redistribution mimics local thermodynamic equilibrium, because in both cases the reemission is proportional to the absorption coefficient. For lines formed deep, $\mathcal{S}_\nu$ is close to B_ν, and thus we may consider that such (weak) lines are formed in local thermodynamic equilibrium—a well-known fact.

Equivalent widths and weighting functions

When the various considerations discussed above are combined, the contours of absorption lines can be computed. It is often more convenient to compute in terms of W, the equivalent width, which can be determined observationally with greater certainty. We have the definition

$$W_\lambda = \int (1 - r_\lambda)\, d\lambda = \int R_\lambda\, d\lambda \tag{31}$$

For the Sun, the equivalent widths can be determined by using a model atmosphere and the method of weighting functions, which we now illustrate. This method is rather convenient, and it is valid for faint lines and the wings of strong lines where it is permissible to write $\mathcal{I}_\nu = B_\nu$. If we write the separate optical depths for the line and continuum, viz., $d\tau_\nu = \rho l_\nu\, dr$ and $d\tau = \rho K_\nu\, dr$, the emergent intensity can be written as

$$I_\nu(0,\mu) = \int_0^\infty B_\nu(\tau) e^{-\tau/\mu} e^{-\tau_\nu/\mu} \frac{d\tau_\nu}{\mu} + \int_0^\infty B_\nu(\tau) e^{-\tau/\mu} e^{-\tau_\nu/\mu} \frac{d\tau}{\mu} \tag{32}$$

The second term on the right-hand side can be rewritten by using an integration by parts; then we find

$$R_\nu = \int_0^\infty \frac{l_\nu}{K_\nu} g_1(\tau,\mu) e^{-\tau_\nu/\mu}\, d\tau \tag{33}$$

where the weighting function is given by

$$g_1(\tau,\mu) = \frac{\displaystyle\int_\tau^\infty B_\nu(\tau) e^{-\tau/\mu} \frac{d\tau}{\mu} - B_\nu(\tau) e^{-\tau/\mu}}{\displaystyle\int_0^\infty B_\nu(\tau) e^{-\tau/\mu}\, d\tau} \tag{34}$$

If $l_\nu \ll K_\nu$ and $\mu \approx 1$, Eq. (4.3-33) becomes

$$R_\nu = \int_0^\infty \frac{l_\nu}{K_\nu} g_1(\tau,\mu)\, d\tau \tag{35}$$

The weighting function can be reduced by using the identity

$$B_\nu(\tau) e^{-\tau/\mu} = -\int_\tau^\infty \frac{dB_\nu}{d\tau} e^{-\tau/\mu}\, d\tau + \int_\tau^\infty B_\nu e^{-\tau/\mu} \frac{d\tau}{\mu} \tag{36}$$

and becomes

$$g_1(\tau,\mu) = \frac{\displaystyle\int_\tau^\infty \frac{dB_\nu}{d\tau} e^{-\tau/\mu}\, d\tau}{\displaystyle\int_0^\infty B_\nu(\tau) e^{-\tau/\mu}\, d\tau} \tag{37}$$

We note that the weighting function depends on the gradient of B_ν and that it depends only on the continuous opacity (not on l_ν). Thus, it is often possible to use the same weighting function for a number of lines. This method is suitable for handling large quantities of data which we have, for example, in the case of the Sun. An integration of R_λ over wave-

Table 4.3-1   Comparison of solar abundance results*

$$\log (N_{El}/N_H)$$

Atomic number	Element	This investigation (1960)	Claas (1951)	Unsöld (1948)	Goldberg-Aller (1943)	Russell (1929)	Others†
1	H	12.00	12.00	12.00	12.00	11.5	
3	Li	0.96	1.08	.....	.....	2.0	1.26 (G-T); 0.93 (D)
4	Be	2.36	.....	.....	.....	1.8	2.18 (G-T)
6	C	8.72	.....	8.29	7.56	7.4	9.06 (H)
7	N	7.98	.....	8.61	8.09	7.6	9.02 (H)
8	O	8.96	8.65	8.73	8.56	9.0	9.23 (H); 8.20 (B); 8.73 (C-D)
11	Na	6.30	6.33	6.28	6.56	7.2	6.13 (W); 5.96 (S); 6.0 (R)
12	Mg	7.40	7.57	7.51	8.39	7.8	7.28 (W); 7.60 (S); 7.25 (R)
13	Al	6.20	6.17	6.33	6.39	6.4	6.13 (W)
14	Si	7.50	7.12	7.29	7.87	7.3	
15	P	5.34	.....	.....	.....	....	
16	S	7.30	.....	6.92	7.57	5.7	
19	K	4.70	5.01	5.20	5.09	6.8	5.32 (S)
20	Ca	6.15	6.46	6.23	6.57	6.7	6.17 (W); 6.42 (G-T); 6.23 (S)
21	Sc	2.82	.....	3.33	.....	3.6	
22	Ti	4.68	7.56	4.96	4.57	5.2	
23	V	3.70	.....	4.05	4.09	5.0	
24	Cr	5.36	.....	5.58	4.87	5.7	
25	Mn	4.90	.....	5.46	5.09	5.9	
26	Fe	6.57	7.16	7.26	6.99	7.2	6.55 (W)
27	Co	4.64	.....	5.03	4.69	5.6	
28	Ni	5.91	.....	5.95	6.39	6.0	
29	Cu	5.04	4.80	4.23	4.39	5.0	
30	Zn	4.40	4.52	4.78	5.57	4.9	
31	Ga	2.36	.....	.....	.....	2.0	
32	Ge	3.29	.....	.....	.....	3.0	
37	Rb	2.48	.....	.....	.....	1.7	
38	Sr	2.60	2.88	3.35	.....	3.3	
39	Y	2.25	.....	3.21	.....	2.6	
40	Zr	2.23	.....	2.37	.....	2.5	
41	Nb	1.95	.....	.....	.....	1.0	
42	Mo	1.90	.....	1.78	.....	1.4	
44	Ru	1.43	.....	.....	.....	1.7	
45	Rh	0.78	.....	.....	.....	0.5	
46	Pd	1.21	.....	.....	.....	1.1	
47	Ag	0.14	.....	.....	.....	1.0	
48	Cd	1.46	.....	.....	.....	2.2	
49	In	1.16	.....	.....	.....	0.0	
50	Sn	1.54	.....	.....	.....	1.2	
51	Sb	1.94	.....	.....	.....	0.8	
56	Ba	2.10	2.38	2.95	.....	3.3	
70	Yb	1.53	.....	.....	.....	....	
82	Pb	1.33	.....	2.55	.....	1.2	1.24 (K)

* From Goldberg, Müller, and Aller, copyright 1960 by the University of Chicago, published by the University of Chicago Press, from R 4.3-3.
† The code for the abbreviations in this column is: (B) I. S. Bowen (1948); (C-D) J. Cabannes and J. Dufay (1948); (D) E. E. Dubov (1955); (G-T) J. L. Greenstein and E. Tandberg-Hanssen (1954); (H) J. Hunaerts (1947); (K) M. Z. Khokhlov (1958); (R) M. Rudkjøbing (1945); (S) B. Strömgren (1940); (W) V. Weidemann (1955).

length gives the equivalent width. The determination of W_λ leads to the abundances of many elements relative to hydrogen.

The determination of the abundances of the elements is usually made via a particularly useful artifice called the curve of growth, which is a plot of W_λ/λ versus $g_i N_i f_{ij}$, where N_i is the relative number of absorbing atoms, g_i is the statistical weight of the level, and f_{ij} is the oscillator strength. In practice, one plots $\log W_\lambda/\lambda$ versus $\log C$, where C contains all factors (including ionization temperature and excitation temperature) except abundance factors. A comparison of the empirical and theoretical curves of growth yields the abundance relative to hydrogen.

Curve-of-growth analyses are very valuable, and details are given in the texts on stellar atmospheres. Such abundance determinations are given and compared with other determinations in Table 4.3-1. Helium is not listed in this table, because no suitable lines are available. We note and stress that the principal uncertainties in the abundances are not the photospheric model or the assumptions used, but are due to the lack of reliable f values. The f values are difficult to measure experimentally and are difficult to calculate quantum-mechanically; thus f values are usually uncertain by at least a factor of 2.

4.4 THERMODYNAMIC CONSIDERATIONS

The concept of local thermodynamic equilibrium has been used many times in the preceding discussion. We now examine the implications of this assumption, and we also open the question of possible deviations from LTE. The assumption of LTE, $\mathcal{I}_\nu = B_\nu$, implies a maxwellian distribution of speeds

$$f(v)\,dv = 4\pi \left(\frac{m}{2\pi kT}\right)^{3/2} v^2 e^{-mv^2/2kT}\,dv \tag{1}$$

the Boltzmann formula

$$\frac{N_m}{N_n} = \frac{g_m}{g_n} \exp\left(-\frac{h\nu_{mn}}{kT}\right) \tag{2}$$

and the Saha equation [see Eq. (3.3-35)]. The g's in Eq. (4.4-2) are the statistical weights. Note that there is no question of departures from thermodynamic equilibrium. In the photosphere, the radiation temperature is a function of direction and of frequency—a far cry from Hohlraum conditions. Hence, we can, at best, hope that the inevitable deviations from LTE are small. We first consider the question of the velocity distribution.

The velocity distribution of electrons in the photosphere is most important. Electrons are produced by the photoionization of H^- and H, and they are removed by photorecombinations. There is no a priori reason that guarantees a maxwellian velocity distribution for these electrons. The velocity distribution is determined by the electron's history after the electron is injected into the continuum. If it suffers many collisions before it recombines, we expect from the Boltzmann H-theorem that the velocity distribution approaches a maxwellian one.

Thus, we must compare the relaxation time for electrons with the lifetime for recombination to form H^- or H. By using standard formulas, one finds that an electron in the solar photosphere makes some 10^5 to 10^6 collisions before it recombines. Hence, we expect a close approach to a maxwellian velocity distribution for the electrons. The same is true for the ions, because the relaxation time is greater by a factor of $(m/m_e)^{1/2}$. A consideration of energy balances indicates that the kinetic temperatures of the electrons, ions, and atoms are about the same.

The question of the radiation temperature vs. the electron temperature is also important. It can be handled with the standard methods used for the same problem in gaseous nebulae. Two equations may be obtained to express the conservation of continuum energy and numbers equilibrium for the continuum (i.e., the number of recombinations equals the number of ionizations). These two equations may be combined to give the radiation temperature as a function of the electron temperature. The two temperatures are nearly equal for conditions in the photosphere. Every time we write down an expression containing a "T" (Planck formula, Saha equation, etc.) we are in effect introducing another parameter. In thermodynamic equilibrium, all these "temperatures" are equal, and it is fortunate that they are essentially equal for most applications in the photosphere.

It is difficult to test the Boltzmann formula in a simple way. Unless anomalous excitation conditions exist, it is usually a reasonable approximation (but see below for a brief discussion concerning line formation in LTE). The Saha equation can be tested in a more direct fashion. Since the electrons follow a maxwellian distribution, the recombination rate is the same in and out of LTE. Then, we may divide the two equations expressing the steady state to obtain

$$C = \frac{\left(\dfrac{N_{r+1}N_e}{N_r}\right)_{NE}}{\left(\dfrac{N_{r+1}N_e}{N_r}\right)_E} \tag{3a}$$

$$= \frac{\displaystyle\int_0^\infty \frac{J_\nu}{h\nu} K_{\nu,r}\, d\nu}{\displaystyle\int_0^\infty \frac{B_\nu}{h\nu} K_{\nu,r}\, d\nu} \tag{3b}$$

The abbreviations NE and E stand for nonequilibrium and equilibrium (equivalent to Saha equation), respectively. The ionization coefficient $K_{\nu,r}$ includes all continua, and hence we must use the Boltzmann formula to calculate the populations of the various levels. We may then evaluate C to check for consistency as the various conditions corresponding to LTE are coupled. For an approach to LTE, we expect that $C \approx 1$. The Fe I–Fe II equilibrium has been considered, and one finds $C = 2.91$, 1.3, and 1.0 for mean optical depths of 0.01, 0.05, and 0.1, respectively. Similar calculations give $C \approx 1$ for H^-. Thus, we approach LTE for $\tau > 0.05$.

It is always expected that deviations from LTE occur near the boundary, because the situation is far from isotropy in the radiation field. From our discussion of LTE, it appears that, when used with care, the assumption of LTE is a useful one throughout much of the photosphere.

A conceptual difficulty concerning the assumption of local thermodynamic equilibrium in the photosphere is the use of the Planck function as the source function. The Planck function is appropriate for trapped radiation, which is certainly not the case in the photosphere. Perhaps a source function derived on the assumption of escaping photons would be more appropriate.

The assumption of *LTE in line spectra* may be theoretically unwarranted; existing collisional cross sections and f values indicate that the radiation field and not collisions determine the populations of the various atomic levels. However, some solar observations appear to mimic LTE. For example, if lines in the same multiplet are formed in LTE, then observations on the solar disk so that $gf/\mu = $ const (where f is the f value of the line; g is the statistical weight; and $\mu \equiv \cos \theta$, θ being the angle measured from the outward normal to the photosphere) should yield identical line profiles. This is in fact observed. Note that the observations are a necessary condition for LTE, but do not guarantee it.

Temperature fluctuations

In our discussion of the photosphere, we have said nothing concerning density and temperature fluctuations. The most important of these would appear to be the solar granulation and related phenomena, which we discuss in the next chapter under the topic of convective transport of energy in the photosphere. Certain problems in the center-to-limb variations of line profiles seem to point to a nonhomogeneous model of the solar photosphere with temperature fluctuations of several hundred degrees Kelvin.

BIBLIOGRAPHICAL NOTES

Section 4.1. Radiative transfer is covered in most texts on stellar atmospheres. See the references for Sec. 4.2 and R 3-3. The standard texts are:

R 4.1-1. Chandrasekhar, S.: "Radiative Transfer," Dover Publications, Inc., New York, 1960.

R 4.1-2. Kourganoff, V.: "Basic Methods in Transfer Problems," Oxford University Press, London, 1952.

See also:

R 4.1-3. Milne, E. A.: *Handbuch Astrophys.*, **3**: 65 (1930).

Section 4.2. The basic material is covered in R 3-3, R 4.1-1, R 4.1-3, and:

R 4.2-1. Minnaert, M.: In "The Sun," ed. G. P. Kuiper. pp. 88–185, The University of Chicago Press, Chicago, 1953.

R 4.2-2. Aller, L. H.: In "Astrophysics," ed. J. A. Hynek, pp. 29–84, McGraw-Hill Book Company, New York, 1951.

R 4.2-3. Unsöld, A.: "Physik der Sternatmosphären," 2d ed., Springer-Verlag OHG, Berlin, 1955.

R 4.2-4. Aller, L. H.: "Astrophysics. 1. The Atmospheres of the Sun and Stars," The Ronald Press Company, New York, 1953. (See also the second edition, 1963.)

R 4.2-5. Münch, G.: In "Stellar Atmospheres," ed. J. L. Greenstein, pp. 1–49, The University of Chicago Press, Chicago, 1960.

R 4.2-6. Böhm, K-H.: In "Stellar Atmospheres," ed. J. L. Greenstein, pp. 88–155, The University of Chicago Press, Chicago, 1960.

R 4.2-7. Aller, L. H.: In "Stellar Atmospheres," ed. J. L. Greenstein pp. 156–259, The University of Chicago Press, Chicago, 1960.

R 4.2-8. Goldberg, L., and A. K. Pierce: In "Handbuch der Physik," vol. 52, ed. S. Flügge, pp. 1–79, Springer-Verlag OHG, Berlin, 1959.

The theoretical and the empirical T-τ relations discussed are contained in:

R 4.2-9. Böhm, K-H.: *Z. Astrophys.*, **34**: 182 (1954).

R 4.2-10. Böhm-Vitense, E.: *Z. Astrophys.*, **34**: 209 (1954).

The summary solar atmosphere is from:

R 4.2-11. Unsöld, A.: In "Space Age Astronomy," eds. A. J. Deutsch and W. B. Klemperer, pp. 161–170, Academic Press Inc., New York, 1962.

Section 4.3. See many references for Sec. 4.2, especially R 4.2-6, and R 3-1 and R 3-3.

The scheme for the computation of the profiles of lines formed in thermodynamic equilibrium is adapted from:

R 4.3-1. Heiser, A. M.: *Astrophys. J.*, **125**: 470 (1957).

Tables for the calculation of the line absorption coefficients are in:

R 4.3-2. Harris, D. L.: *Astrophys. J.*, **108**: 112 (1948).

The abundances listed are from:

R 4.3-3. Goldberg, L., E. A. Müller, and L. H. Aller: *Astrophys. J. Suppl.*, **V**: 1 (1960).

Section 4.4. See R 3-1, R 3-2, R 3-3, R 4.1-3, and the many books and papers on stellar atmospheres referenced for Sec. 4.2.

The hydrogen convection zone, chromosphere, and corona

chapter

Although the major portion of the solar energy flux is transported through
the photosphere by radiation, a minute but significant amount is transported in the form of mechanical energy; this fact greatly alters the physical situation in the outer solar atmosphere. The temperature in the solar
atmosphere does not monotonically decrease with increasing r (as one
might expect), but passes through a minimum of a few thousand degrees
Kelvin and then increases rapidly to values of $\sim 10^6$ °K. This increase re-

sults from the deposition of mechanical energy. This energy is apparently related to the solar granulation and is probably produced in the hydrogen convection zone, which we now consider.

5.1 THE HYDROGEN CONVECTION ZONE AND NOISE GENERATION

Although there is no satisfactory theory of the physical processes occurring in the convective zone beneath the photosphere, some understanding of this zone is important because of the many observable phenomena it produces. In the convection zone the temperature gradient must be calculated from the equation

$$[\pi F]_\text{total} = [\pi F]_\text{conv} + [\pi F]_\text{rad} \tag{1}$$

Hence, we need an expression for the convective flux.

Convective theory

We recall the Schwarzschild stability criterion [Eq. (3.3-10)]

$$\left(\frac{d \log T}{d \log P}\right)_\text{str} > \left(\frac{d \log T}{d \log P}\right)_\text{ad} \tag{2}$$

In the discussion of this inequality in the regions below the solar photosphere, we need to take into account the ionization of hydrogen in the calculation of the adiabatic gradient. The adiabatic condition can be derived from the first law of thermodynamics. Let E/ρ be the energy per unit mass and $1/\rho$ the volume of the unit mass. Then, the first law of thermodynamics becomes

$$d\left(\frac{E}{\rho}\right) + P\,d\left(\frac{1}{\rho}\right) = dQ = 0 \tag{3}$$

When the differentiation is carried out, the adiabatic condition becomes

$$\frac{dE}{P} = \frac{d\rho}{\rho}\left(1 + \frac{E}{P}\right) \tag{4}$$

Consider first a perfect gas with kinetic energy only. We have the equation of state

$$P = \frac{k\rho T}{m_\text{H}\mu} \tag{5}$$

and

$$E = \frac{3}{2}\frac{k\rho T}{m_\text{H}\mu} = \frac{3}{2}P \tag{6}$$

Using logarithmic and ordinary differentiation, the last two equations become

$$\frac{dP}{P} = \frac{d\rho}{\rho} + \frac{dT}{T} \tag{7}$$

and

$$dE = \tfrac{3}{2}dP \tag{8}$$

Equations (5.1-4) and (5.1-6) to (5.1-8) give the usual relation

$$\frac{dP}{P} = \frac{5}{2}\frac{dT}{T} \tag{9}$$

In general, the energy consists of kinetic, ionization, and excitation energies. In this case $\rho = \rho(T,P)$ and $E = E(T,P)$, or

$$\frac{dE}{P} = c_1\frac{dT}{T} + c_2\frac{dP}{P} \tag{10}$$

$$\frac{d\rho}{\rho} = -c_3\frac{dT}{T} + c_4\frac{dP}{P} \tag{11}$$

These last two equations are the general analogs of Eqs. (5.1-8) and (5.1-7). The last two equations and the adiabatic condition [Eq. (5.1-4)] give

$$\left[\frac{dT/T}{dP/P}\right]_{\text{ad}} = \frac{-c_2 + (1 + E/P)c_4}{c_1 + (1 + E/P)c_3} \tag{12}$$

If we consider the influence of the ionization of hydrogen, the perfect-gas law becomes

$$P = \frac{k}{m_{\text{H}}\mu}(1 + x)\rho T \tag{13}$$

where x is the degree of ionization and μ is taken to have the same value as for $x = 0$. Then, the energy (neglecting excitation energy) becomes

$$E = \frac{3}{2}P + \frac{x\rho}{m_{\text{H}}\mu}I \tag{14}$$

where I is the ionization energy. With these relations and with the Saha equation, we may reduce Eq. (5.1-12) for the case at hand to

$$\left[\frac{d\log T}{d\log P}\right]_{\text{ad}} = \frac{1 + \tfrac{1}{2}x(1 - x)[\tfrac{5}{2} + I/kT]}{\tfrac{5}{2} + \tfrac{1}{2}x(1 - x)[\tfrac{5}{2} + I/kT]^2} \tag{15}$$

Note that the degree of ionization appears only in the combination $x(1 - x)$, and hence the gradient is the same for zero or total ionization.

In the intermediate regions, the value of $(d \log T/d \log P)_{ad}$ is less than the traditional value of $\frac{2}{5}$. Thus, the hydrogen convection zone exists in its present location for two reasons:

1. The adiabatic gradient decreases because of the hydrogen ionization.

2. The structural gradient increases because of an initial increase in the opacity.

The increase in the opacity is most important, because it reduces the "mixing" of photons and allows the existence of the large temperature gradient responsible for the convection. The combination of these two effects places the convection zone below $\tau = 1$. In more detailed studies, the ionization of metals and helium must be considered.

The only available theory for the convective transport of heat is the Prandtl mixing-length theory. Here one imagines that the rising bubbles travel a mixing length l before they merge with the surroundings. Since the bubbles are presumed to be hotter than the surroundings, the process results in the convective transfer of energy. For a rising bubble with volume V the buoyancy force is given by

$$F_b = Vg\,\Delta\rho \tag{16}$$

where g is the acceleration of gravity. Since $\Delta\rho/\rho = \Delta T/T$, this becomes

$$F_b = V\rho g\,\frac{\Delta T}{T} \tag{17}$$

where $\Delta\rho$ and ΔT are the differences between the bubble and the surroundings. Note that we are considering a case of free rise. If we measure the distance a bubble has traveled up by z, then the ΔT can be expressed as the difference between the structural and adiabatic gradients, and the buoyancy force [Eq. (5.1-17)] becomes

$$F_b = V\rho g\,\frac{z}{T}\left[\left.\left|\frac{dT}{dz}\right|\right._{str} - \left.\left|\frac{dT}{dz}\right|\right._{ad}\right] \tag{18}$$

The work done by this force is

$$W = \int_0^z F_b\,dz = \frac{V\rho g}{T}\left[\left.\left|\frac{dT}{dz}\right|\right._{str} - \left.\left|\frac{dT}{dz}\right|\right._{ad}\right]\frac{z^2}{2} \tag{19}$$

If we neglect resistance, the work goes into the kinetic energy of the bubble

$$W = \tfrac{1}{2}V\rho v^2 \tag{20}$$

The velocity, obtained by equating (5.1-19) and (5.1-20), is

$$v = z\left[\left.\left|\frac{dT}{dz}\right|\right._{str} - \left.\left|\frac{dT}{dz}\right|\right._{ad}\right]^{\frac{1}{2}}\left(\frac{g}{T}\right)^{\frac{1}{2}} \tag{21}$$

The mean velocity is obtained by introducing the mixing length l. The appropriate value of z is then $l/2$ and

$$\langle v \rangle = \frac{l}{2} \left[\left| \frac{dT}{dz} \right|_{\mathrm{str}} - \left| \frac{dT}{dz} \right|_{\mathrm{ad}} \right]^{\frac{1}{2}} \left(\frac{g}{T} \right)^{\frac{1}{2}} \tag{22}$$

The introduction of the scale height,

$$H = \frac{kT}{\mu m_{\mathrm{H}} g} \tag{23}$$

which is the distance over which the density changes by a factor of e in an isothermal atmosphere, enables us to rewrite Eq. (3.3-9) as

$$\frac{dT}{dz} = \frac{T}{H} \frac{d \log T}{d \log P} \tag{24}$$

Thus we can write

$$\langle v \rangle^2 = \frac{l^2 g}{4H} \left[\left(\frac{d \log T}{d \log P} \right)_{\mathrm{str}} - \left(\frac{d \log T}{d \log P} \right)_{\mathrm{ad}} \right] \tag{25}$$

This expression is consistent with Doppler observations of rising granules which give rise to velocities of some 2 km/sec. For the Sun, $H \approx l \approx 10^7$ cm, $g \approx 2.5 \times 10^4$ cm/sec^2, and the bracket in Eq. (5. 1-25) is ~ 1 in regions of instability just below the photosphere. These values give $\langle v \rangle \approx 2.5$ km/sec, in essential agreement with the observations. In principle, one may regard the quantity l as a free parameter and determine it from the observations. One expects that $H \approx l$, because the scale height gives a measure of the distance over which the properties of the region do not change appreciably.

A rising element contributes energy in the amount $c_P \rho \, \Delta T$ to its surroundings, where c_P is the specific heat at constant pressure. With these developments, the convective energy flux can be written as

$$(\pi F)_{\mathrm{conv}} = c_P \rho v \frac{l}{2} \left[\left| \frac{dT}{dz} \right|_{\mathrm{str}} - \left| \frac{dT}{dz} \right|_{\mathrm{ad}} \right] \tag{26a}$$

$$= c_P \rho v \frac{Tl}{2H} \left[\left(\frac{d \log T}{d \log P} \right)_{\mathrm{str}} - \left(\frac{d \log T}{d \log P} \right)_{\mathrm{ad}} \right] \tag{26b}$$

$$= \frac{c_P \rho l^2 g^{\frac{1}{2}} T}{4H^{\frac{3}{2}}} \left[\left(\frac{d \log T}{d \log P} \right)_{\mathrm{str}} - \left(\frac{d \log T}{d \log P} \right)_{\mathrm{ad}} \right] \tag{26c}$$

The temperature difference in Eq. (5.1-26a) has been reckoned with the distance $l/2$, because at any point in the convection zone bubbles which have traveled all distances between 0 and l are present. We assume that the effects which we have neglected can be absorbed into the mixing-length parameter l; such effects include photon exchange between the bubble and the surroundings, and the existence of rising *and* falling bubbles.

It is of interest to compare the convective flux with the radiative flux. The convective flux is negligible at $\tau \approx 1$; it is a few tens of per cent of the radiative flux at $\tau \approx 2$ to 3, and it dominates in the deeper layers. We note that serious departures from a radiative model occur only for $\tau > 3$.

Granulation

A fairly direct link between the observations and the theory of the convective zone comes from studies of the solar granulation. Ground studies of solar granulation are seriously hampered by the effects of atmospheric seeing. This difficulty seems to have been overcome through observations of the Sun from balloons at an altitude of 80,000 ft. Figure 5.1-1 is a beautiful photograph of the solar granulation. From detailed studies of

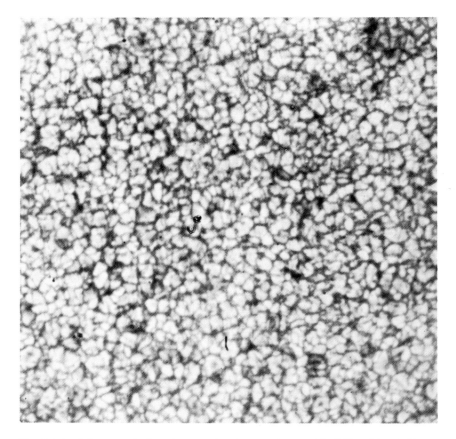

Fig. 5.1-1   Solar granulation photograph taken on August 17, 1959, with a balloon-borne telescope. Scale: 1 cm on print = 4,600 km on Sun. (*Courtesy of Project Stratoscope of Princeton University, sponsored by the Office of Naval Research, the National Science Foundation, and the National Aeronautics and Space Administration.*)

many such pictures one may obtain facts of importance in understanding convection. The mean diameter of the granules is about 700 km; the mean half-life is about 4 min; and the root-mean-square temperature fluctuation is some 100°K. Note that this last result does not necessarily conflict with the somewhat larger temperature fluctuations considered in the nonhomogeneous models, because the fluctuations on a scale smaller than the resolution of the instrument ($\sim$300 km) are not included.

The order of magnitude of the mean half-life is readily explained, because a distance of some few hundred kilometers (i.e., the mixing length) is traversed in a time of the order of a few minutes by an element traveling at a velocity of $\sim$1 km/sec. Other facts concerning granulation which have been known for some time are that the granulation is independent of heliocentric latitude and also of solar cycle. It thus appears to be a basic process which is independent of solar activity. The granulation is obscured near the limb by the increase in the slant optical thickness of the photosphere.

We may wonder if the convective motions penetrate into the relatively thin photosphere above. This would seem to be true intuitively, and it can be verified both theoretically and observationally that penetration does occur. It seems certain that the granules are tops of convection cells which have penetrated some distance into the photosphere; the structures shown in Fig. 5.1-1 are reminiscent of the convection cells studies years ago by Bénard. We may idealize the average cells as being some 700 km wide and 300 km deep with hot gases rising up in the middle and cool gases flowing down around the periphery.

The nature of the cell structure involves the use of the Rayleigh number, defined by

$$\Lambda = \frac{g\alpha|\beta|d^4}{K\nu} \tag{27}$$

where α is the coefficient of volume expansion, K is the coefficient of thermometric conductivity, and ν is the coefficient of kinematic viscosity. The acceleration of gravity is denoted by g; d is the depth of the layer; and β is the adverse temperature gradient which is maintained. For experiments in fluids, the temperature gradient can be slowly increased and one obtains the onset of convection when Λ exceeds a certain critical value. This critical value Λ_0 depends on the nature of the boundaries, but in general $\Lambda_0 \approx 10^3$. When Λ first passes Λ_0 and until Λ passes about 10^5, one has stationary convection (Bénard cells). For Λ above 10^5, the convection becomes nonstationary and, as Λ is further increased, finally becomes random or chaotic.

To apply Eq. (5.1-27) to the Sun, we must identify the adverse temperature gradient β with the excess of the temperature gradient over the adiabatic gradient; d becomes a characteristic dimension, presumably of the order of the scale height. For the subphotospheric layers appropriate values of the various quantities are (cgs units): $d = 3 \times 10^7$, $\alpha = T^{-1}$ (for perfect gas) $= 10^{-4}$, $\beta = 10^{-4}$, $g = 2.7 \times 10^4$, $\nu = 10^3$ (atomic viscosity); and $K = 10^{12}$, a value which is determined by the radiation field. These numbers give $\Lambda \approx 10^{11}$, a value so large that random convection would be expected. This difficulty may be due to the fact (which we show below) that the motions involved are turbulent. In this case, we should use the turbulent viscosity, which is presumed to be somewhat larger than the ordinary atomic viscosity; the needed values are not available.

The physical significance of the Rayleigh number is as follows. The buoyancy force per unit volume is proportional to $\alpha \rho l g \beta$ [see Eq. (5.1-18) and recall that $\alpha = T^{-1}$ for perfect gases]. The friction force per unit volume is

$$\frac{F_v}{l^3} = \frac{\eta l^2 (v/l)}{l^3} = \frac{\eta v}{l^2} = \frac{\rho \nu v}{l^2} \tag{28}$$

where v/l is a characteristic velocity gradient and $\eta = \rho \nu$.

Friction acts over the entire travel of a bubble, and hence the characteristic time is l/v. The buoyancy force may not be effective over the entire length of travel if energy exchange is important. In the layers immediately beneath the photosphere the energy exchange is almost completely radiative. Thus, the rate of energy exchange of a volume element with its surroundings divided by its energy content is just

$$\frac{\text{exchange rate}}{\text{energy content}} = \frac{\lambda_r (\Delta T/l) \cdot l^2}{c_{P\rho} \, \Delta T \cdot l^3} \tag{29a}$$

$$= \frac{\lambda_r}{c_{P\rho} l^2} \tag{29b}$$

where all linear dimensions are denoted by l and λ_r is as defined in Eq. (3.3-4).

The exchange rate times a characteristic time $t = c_{P\rho} l^2 / \lambda_r$ gives a quantity equal to the total energy content. We take this as the characteristic time for the buoyancy force. This time can be written as $t = l^2/K$, where $K = \lambda_r / c_{P\rho}$ is the thermometric conductivity. With these remarks, the Rayleigh number can be written as the ratio of the impulse on a bubble due to buoyancy and viscous forces, viz.,

$$\Lambda = \frac{F_b \cdot t_b}{F_v \cdot t_v} \tag{30a}$$

$$= \frac{\alpha \rho l g \beta}{\rho \nu v / l^2} \cdot \frac{l^2/K}{l/v} \tag{30b}$$

$$= \frac{\alpha l^4 g \beta}{\nu K} \tag{30c}$$

We note that the fact that Λ must exceed a critical value Λ_0 for convection is a more stringent requirement than the Schwarzschild criterion [Eq.

(5.1-2)]. Thus, we see that the Schwarzschild criterion is a necessary but not a sufficient condition for convection. The fact that Λ must exceed a critical value indicates that the buoyancy forces generated must be of sufficient magnitude to overcome the resistance of the system before convection can occur.

Another dimensionless quantity commonly used in studies of convection is the Prandtl number $\sigma = \nu/K$. A representative value for the subphotospheric layers is $\sigma \sim 10^{-9}$ (from the numbers used above). Under most laboratory conditions the Prandtl number is of the order of 1; this fact illustrates the difficulty in applying laboratory results to certain astrophysical situations. Advances using theories of turbulent motions and the method of laminar modes can be expected in the future.

Noise generation and atmospheric heating

The turbulent subphotospheric motions are very important, because they appear to be the source of mechanical energy for the chromosphere and corona. The motions in the hydrogen convection zone are turbulent, as can be seen from the Reynolds number

$$\mathrm{Re} = \frac{vl}{\nu} \tag{31}$$

which is simply the ratio of the force required to produce the acceleration $\rho v^2/l$ to the viscous force $\rho \nu v/l^2$. Thus it appears that viscous forces can keep the flow laminar if the acceleration forces do not exceed a certain limiting value. For larger Reynolds numbers, the flow becomes turbulent. The critical value is $\mathrm{Re} \gtrsim 10^3$.

We note that the kinematical viscosity is approximately $\frac{1}{3}v_{th}\lambda$, where λ is the mean free path and $v_{th} = (8kT/\pi\mu m_{\mathrm{H}})^{1/2}$. In the subphotospheric layers $v \sim v_{th}$ and the Reynolds number is roughly l/λ, or about 10^{10} for the layers in question. These turbulent motions are capable of generating mechanical noise. One generally assumes isotropic turbulence, although there is clearly a preferred direction in the Sun. The rate of generation of acoustic noise per unit volume is

$$j_1 = \alpha\rho\epsilon \left[\frac{\langle v^2 \rangle}{v_s{}^2} \right]^{5/2} \tag{32}$$

where α is a numerical constant, v is the turbulent velocity, and the rate of energy dissipation is

$$\epsilon = \frac{\langle v^2 \rangle^{3/2}}{l} \tag{33}$$

Here l is the scale of the turbulence and the speed of sound is $v_s = (\gamma P/\rho)^{1/2}$. Also, γ is the usual ratio of the specific heats c_P/c_V. Note that the ratio of

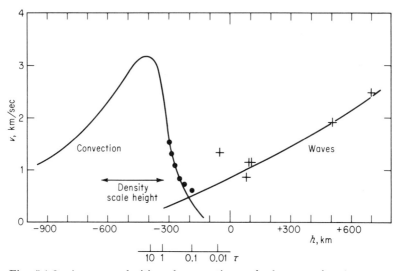

Fig. 5.1-2   Average velocities of convection and of progressive (e.g., acoustic or Alfvén) waves in the photosphere and chromosphere. (*M. Schwarzschild, Copyright 1961 by the University of Chicago, published by The University of Chicago Press, from R* 5.1-1.)

noise production to energy dissipation goes as M^5, where $M = v/v_s$, the Mach number. The total noise production goes as a high power of the turbulent velocity (say, $\sim v^6$); the exact number is somewhat uncertain.

The total noise generation can then be computed, and the upward flux is

$$[\pi F]_{\text{noise}} = \tfrac{1}{2}\textstyle\int j_1\, dz \tag{34}$$

where the integration is carried through the hydrogen convection zone. The turbulent velocities are shown on Fig. 5.1-2. Since the turbulent velocity has a fairly sharp maximum and since the noise generation goes as a high power of the velocity, almost all of the energy is generated in a layer about 100 km thick. This energy goes into acoustic waves which travel at the velocity of sound. The upward flux is then

$$[\pi F]_{\text{noise}} = \tfrac{1}{2}\rho(\Delta v)^2 v_s \tag{35}$$

where Δv is the amplitude of the material velocity.

If there is no dissipation, the $[\pi F]_{\text{noise}}$ remains constant as these longitudinal waves travel upward. As one moves upward from the convection zone, the density decreases very rapidly while the velocity of sound increases only relatively slowly. This implies that the velocity amplitude Δv increases rapidly. Eventually, as Δv increases, the waves become shock waves and dissipation of energy takes place. It is this deposition of energy which provides the energy for the chromosphere and the corona.

Actually, the situation is much more complicated than we have described above, primarily because of the presence of the solar magnetic field. In an incompressible fluid with high electrical conductivity and a magnetic field B, small disturbances propagate along the magnetic field as transverse waves with the Alfvèn velocity

$$V_A = \frac{B}{(4\pi\rho)^{1/2}} \tag{36}$$

For the compressible case, three types of waves are found: the fast mode, the slow mode, and the Alfvèn mode. These different modes result from the coupling through the magnetic field of the longitudinal sound waves, which may propagate in any direction, with the transverse Alfvèn waves, which can propagate only in the direction of the magnetic field. The Alfvèn mode has the same properties as above; the other two are essentially hybrid waves which depend on the relative magnitudes of the Alfvèn and sound velocities and the direction of propagation relative to the magnetic field. The fast mode can propagate in any direction, whereas the propagation of the slow mode is restricted to a relatively small cone of directions about the magnetic field. In principle, the calculation proceeds as described above for the case of acoustical noise generation.

There are many difficulties in carrying out such calculations, and only tentative results are available. We describe briefly the results of a recent calculation. Most of the energy is generated in the fast mode, which is essentially a sound wave in the hydrogen convection zone and photosphere but which becomes a wave more magnetohydrodynamic in character at great heights. The fast mode waves are largely dissipated in the lower chromosphere. The slow mode and the Alfvèn mode do not appear to be produced in sizable quantities in the convection zone, and, moreover, they appear to be strongly absorbed in the photosphere. However, refraction of the shocks occurs and the result is collisions between shocks.

The interaction between shocks in the chromosphere is expected to feed energy into the slow and Alfvèn modes, which then propagate along the magnetic field and carry energy into the corona. These latter modes are also probably responsible for heating the upper chromosphere and the transition region. The order of magnitude of the energy dissipated is equal to the order of magnitude of the radiation losses from the chromosphere and corona, as it must be.

Other photospheric motions

The hydrogen convection zone may also produce other motions of importance in the solar atmosphere. First, vertical velocities of $\approx\frac{1}{2}$ km/sec have been observed in cells with sizes of $\approx 2,000$ to $3,000$ km with time scales of about 5 min. These motions are oscillatory.

Second, horizontal motions of $\frac{1}{2}$ km/sec have been observed in cells with sizes of $\approx 30,000$ km with lifetimes of 10^4 to 10^5 sec. These cells have been called the "supergranulation." The appearance is similar to the chromospheric network in Ca II. These motions may provide a clue to the size of the chromospheric network if the origin of the network is the same as the faculae (Sec. 6.5), as seems likely. Faculae are known to be closely correlated with the presence of magnetic fields (and presumably the resultant enhanced mechanical energy deposition). If the general solar magnetic field is convected to the cell boundary by the motions in supergranulation, the scale and existence of the chromospheric network can be qualitatively understood.

5.2   THE CHROMOSPHERE

The chromosphere is a poorly understood 10,000- to 15,000-km thick layer of the solar atmosphere which lies between the 5000°K photosphere and the 1,000,000°K corona. This region is very inhomogeneous and is clearly not in thermodynamic equilibrium (particularly above 5,000 km) owing to the extreme anisotropy of the radiation field. Besides the lines of hydrogen, helium, and the usual metals, emission of CN is observed in the lower chromosphere and the $\lambda 7,892$ coronal line of Fe XI throughout much of the chromosphere. This contrast serves to illustrate the way quantities change very rapidly in the chromosphere.

The chromosphere can be conveniently divided into three regions:

1. The first 500 km is essentially an extension of the photosphere. This situation comes about because of the fact that the zero level ($h = 0$) is defined as the visible edge of the Sun.

2. The lower chromosphere ($h < 5,000$ km) is composed mostly of neutral hydrogen, and the gas is cool ($T_e \approx 5000°K$).

3. The upper chromosphere is essentially ionized, and the temperature lies between 5000°K and the coronal value.

The chromosphere can be observed at the time of a total solar eclipse. When the seeing is very good, the chromosphere shows a fine, hairlike structure which has been compared to a burning prairie (Fig. 5.2-1). The lower chromosphere appears as an essentially homogeneous layer from which emerge the brilliant streamers called *spicules*. These features extend some 10,000 km above the limb; they flare up and disappear in a time of 2 to 5 min.

Spicules are a property of the quiet Sun. The fact that the spicules appear to be aligned with the solar magnetic field lends support to the suggestion that the spicules are material from the lower chromosphere being carried upward by the slow mode waves discussed in Sec. 5.1. This opens the possibility of the spicules being related to the deposition of energy in the chromosphere. We shall not repeat or continue the discussion

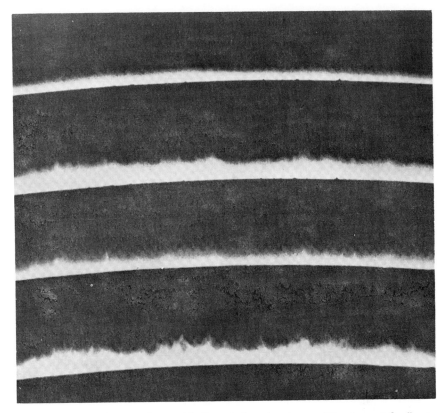

Fig. 5.2-1 The chromosphere with its spicular structure. (*Courtesy of the Sacramento Peak Observatory, Air Force Cambridge Research Laboratories.*)

given in Sec. 5.1. We note, however, that an important source of energy for the upper chromosphere could be the conduction of energy downward from the corona.

In the following subsections we discuss briefly some of the basic problems associated with the chromosphere.

Eclipse data and scale heights

Many of the basic data concerning the chromosphere come from observations of the flash spectrum (Fig. 5.2-2) at solar eclipse. For this reason, we must develop the mathematical treatment of such a circumstance. Consider observations of the chromosphere at a solar eclipse according to the geometry shown in Fig. 5.2-3. The emergent intensity is given simply by

$$I_\nu(x) = \int_{-\infty}^{+\infty} \rho j_\nu(x,y) e^{-\tau_\nu(x,y)} \, dy \qquad (1)$$

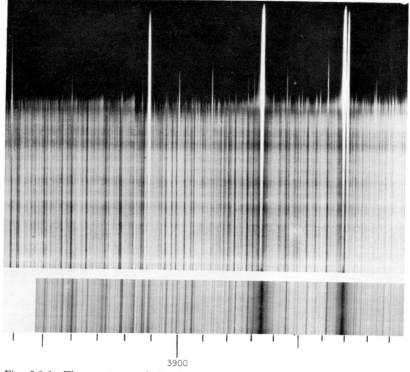

3900

Fig. 5.2-2 The spectrum of the chromosphere or flash spectrum (top) near 3,900 A: the photospheric spectrum is included for comparison (bottom). Notice the reversal (positive print). (*Courtesy of The Lick Observatory.*)

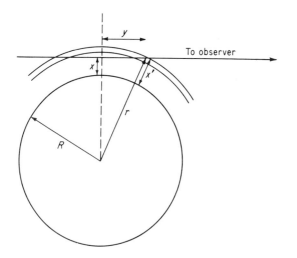

Fig. 5.2-3 The geometry of a solar eclipse, used in Eq. (5.2-1) et sequence.

where $\rho j_\nu(x,y)$ is the emission coefficient for the volume element (x,y) and $\tau_\nu(x,y)$ is the optical thickness between the observer and the point (x,y). Note that

$$y = [r^2 - (R + x)^2]^{\frac{1}{2}} \tag{2}$$

and

$$dy = \frac{r \, dr}{[r^2 - (R + x)^2]^{\frac{1}{2}}} \tag{3}$$

If we neglect self-absorption [the exponential in Eq. (5.2-1)], we can express the intensity in terms of x' and get

$$I_\nu(x) = 2 \int_x^\infty \frac{\rho j_\nu(R + x') \, dx'}{[(R + x')^2 - (R + x)^2]^{\frac{1}{2}}} \tag{4}$$

Now $(R + x)^2 = R^2 + 2xR + x^2 \approx R^2 + 2xR$, because the chromosphere is a narrow region and $x \ll R$. This same approximation holds for x', and Eq. (5.2-4) can be simplified to

$$I_\nu(x) = 2R \int_x^\infty \frac{\rho j_\nu \, dx'}{(2x'R - 2xR)^{\frac{1}{2}}} \tag{5a}$$

$$= (2R)^{\frac{1}{2}} \int_x^\infty \frac{g_\nu \, dx'}{(x' - x)^{\frac{1}{2}}} \tag{5b}$$

where $g_\nu = \rho j_\nu$, that is, g_ν is the emission coefficient per unit volume per unit solid angle. The last equation is simply Abel's integral equation, which has a well-known solution, and for the case at hand we have

$$g_\nu(x) = \frac{-1}{\pi(2R)^{\frac{1}{2}}} \frac{d}{dx} \int_x^\infty \frac{I(x') \, dx'}{(x' - x)^{\frac{1}{2}}} \tag{6}$$

It is customary to represent the height dependence of the observed emission as

$$I_\nu(x) = \sum_i a_i e^{-\beta_i x} \tag{7}$$

where a_i are constants and β_i is the emission gradient of the ith element, defined below. Combining these equations gives

$$g_\nu(x) = \frac{1}{(2\pi R)^{\frac{1}{2}}} \sum_i a_i \beta_i^{\frac{1}{2}} e^{-\beta_i x} \tag{8}$$

The observed quantity is often not $I_\nu(x)$ but is the *total* emission above a certain height given by

$$F_\nu(x) = \int_x^\infty I_\nu(x) \, dx \tag{9}$$

This is convenient for working with solar eclipse observations, because the value of x in $F_\nu(x)$ is determined by the limb of the Moon. It is often found that one term of Eq. (5.2-7) gives an adequate representation of the data. In this case,

$$\frac{d \log I_\nu(x)}{dx} = \frac{d \log g_\nu(x)}{dx} = \frac{d \log F_\nu(x)}{dx} = -\beta \tag{10}$$

We call β the emission gradient; it is the reciprocal of the emission scale height [see Eq. (5.1-23)]. Representative values for the lower chromosphere above 1,000 cm are given in Table 5.2-1. Note that we differentiate the data a number of times in the last few equations; this leads to considerable uncertainty in the final results.

The most striking fact illustrated by the various values given in Table 5.2-1 is the near equality of β for various elements of both large and small atomic weights and of different stages of ionization. The effects of self-absorption and differential excitation have not been included in the numbers given; nevertheless they seem to strongly imply that the chromosphere is not in hydrostatic or diffusive equilibrium. If there were no mix-

Table 5.2-1   Emission gradients in the chromosphere*

λ, A	Identification	β, 10^{-8}/cm	
		HAO	Soviet
4,861	Hβ	1.60	1.20
4,101	Hδ	1.70	1.32
3,835	H9	1.51	1.37
3,750	H12	1.68	1.47
3,712	H15	1.73	1.55
3,692	H18	1.85	2.04
5,876	He I	1.25	0.88
4,713	He I	1.25	1.96
4,472	He I	1.25	1.11
4,026	He I	1.25	0.75
4,227	Ca I	2.16	1.33
4,064	Fe I	2.84	1.28
3,860	Fe I	1.94	1.36
5,018	Fe II	2.90	1.32
4,584	Fe II	3.21	1.23
5,184	Mg I	2.16	1.64
4,076	Sr II	1.47	1.60
4,572	Ti II	2.52	2.60

* Data from R 3-3 and R 5.2-3.

ing and if diffusive equilibrium prevailed (Sec. 18.2), β would be approximately gm/kT, where g is the local acceleration of gravity and m is the mass of the atom of the species under consideration.

On this simple picture, the β for iron would be some 56 times the β for hydrogen. This is clearly not so. If the chromosphere is mixed, then the mean atomic weight is about 1.3, assuming a composition of 0.9 hydrogen and 0.1 helium by number. Then taking $T = 5000°K$,

$$\beta \text{ (mixture)} = 9 \times 10^{-8}$$

some 5 to 6 times the observed value. This result implies that there are velocities other than thermal velocities which contribute to the support of the chromosphere. We expect that the deposition of mechanical energy (discussed above) could lead to the existence of turbulent velocities in the chromosphere. From Eq. (5.1-35) we expect that these velocities are in the range 10 to 20 km/sec. If we then postulate that the x component can be represented by a gaussian distribution (as can the thermal velocities), then

$$\frac{N}{N_0} = \exp\left[-\frac{gx}{(kT/m) + (v_t{}^2/2)} \right] \tag{11}$$

where v_t is the turbulent velocity, N is the number density at x, and N_0 is that at $x = 0$. Then

$$\beta = \frac{g}{(kT/m) + (v_t{}^2/2)} \tag{12}$$

Assuming the same parameters as above in addition to $v_t = 15$ km/sec, we find $\beta = 2 \times 10^{-8}$ cm^{-1}, that is, approximately the observed value. We expect from Eq. (5.1-35) that the v_t ($= \Delta v$) increases with height in the chromosphere. This latter expectation is in agreement with the observations, because turbulent velocities of only 1 to 2 km/sec are shown by the faint lines observed in the lowest 1,000 km of the chromosphere.

This rough sketch of the scale height and support of the chromosphere is consistent with our discussion of the hydrogen convection zone and mechanical energy transport.

The density

Fortunately, the general run of the density of neutral particles in the lower chromosphere can be inferred from the observed gradients and the boundary density taken from models of the photosphere. The metal lines are particularly suited for this purpose, because the excitation conditions for them are essentially constant throughout the lower chromosphere. This means that the observed emission gradients [Eq. (5.2-10)] are essentially the gradients of the material density.

The metal lines have the additional advantage that one can eliminate the effects of self-absorption by using lines in the same multiplet
(i.e., lines which originate from the same upper level). This method can
be used to obtain densities of the chromosphere up to a height of about
4,000 km.

The gradient of $N_e N_p$ can be determined from the high members of
the Balmer series. The conditions in the chromosphere are intermediate
between local thermodynamic equilibrium, which holds approximately in
the photosphere, and the case of strong dilution, which applies to gaseous
nebulae.

The general approach is that used in the traditional theory for gaseous
nebulae, where departures from thermodynamic equilibrium are introduced by inserting a factor b_n, to be determined from the actual conditions, in the combined Saha-Boltzmann equation [see Eqs. (3.3-35) and
(4.4-2)],

$$N_n = b_n N_p N_e n^2 h^3 (2\pi m_e k T_e)^{-3/2} \exp\left(\frac{\chi_n}{kT_e}\right) \tag{13a}$$

$$= b_n N_n \text{ (for thermodynamic equilibrium)} \tag{13b}$$

The notation is standard; we recall that χ_n is the ionization potential of
the nth level. For the higher members of the Balmer series, the quantity
χ_n / kT_e can be made small, and hence the exponential would not be sensitive to changes in the temperature. Also, for large n, $b_n \approx 1$.

Hence, the assumption of a reasonable temperature distribution and
observations of the higher members of the Balmer series enables one to
obtain the gradient of $N_e N_p$. The absolute value is pinned down at $h = 0$
from a photospheric model. We note that $N_e \neq N_p$ for heights up to 500
km because the electrons are supplied by the metals (as in the photosphere); above 500 km, the electrons are supplied by hydrogen and
$N_e = N_p$. Again we note that the entire model is based on observed gradients and the absolute densities determined at $h = 0$ for a photospheric
model.

The absolute densities can be checked in two ways. Recombinations
(which are proportional to $N_e N_p$) to the $n = 2$ level result in the emission
of photons with $\lambda < 3,646$ A (called the Balmer continuum). Observations
of the energy in the Balmer continuum can be used to calculate $N_e N_p$.
Also, the broadening of the Balmer lines can be interpreted as due to the
intermolecular Stark effect; hence, the measurement of widths of the
Balmer lines and other hydrogen lines can provide information concerning
the electron and ion densities. These two methods give results which are
roughly consistent with the results derived by using the methods based
on the observed emission gradients and the photospheric densities.

Very little is known concerning densities in the upper chromosphere,
the region from $1.007R_\odot$ to $1.03R_\odot$. Hydrogen is completely ionized, and

since the temperature rises rapidly to some 10^6 °K at $1.03R_\odot$ (lower boundary of the corona), we expect that the density gradient is very small. Some information concerning models can be inferred from the radio observations; these techniques are discussed in Sec. 5.3.

The temperature and fine structure

The observed neutral-hydrogen densities (taken as proportional to the total density) indicate that the opacity for photoionization in the Lyman continuum, $\lambda < 912$ A (analogous to the Balmer continuum), is such that the lower chromosphere is effectively shielded from the high-temperature radiation of the upper chromosphere and the corona. Thus, the ratio $N_H/N_e N_p$ is probably determined by the local temperature; hence, we may compute the temperature as a function of height from the Saha equation (3.3-35). This procedure gives a temperature of 4600°K at $h = 0$, and it increases slowly to some 6000°K at 4,000 km. The temperature in the upper chromosphere rises steeply to the coronal value.

This type of temperature for the lower chromosphere is supported by a considerable body of evidence, e.g., the excitation and ionization of metals and the intensity distribution in the Balmer continuum. However, there is evidence that hot elements are mixed in with the model described above, which we now refer to as the cold elements. The hot elements appear to be necessary to account for the existence of ionized helium radiation (for example, $\lambda 4,686$, He II) and to account for the radio observations in the millimeter range. The radio observations enable one to specify the function $A(h)$, which gives the fraction of the area occupied by the hot elements.

One might expect the hot and cold elements from photographs of the Sun taken in essentially one wavelength; such photographs are called *spectroheliograms*. The spectroheliograms can be made to refer to different heights in the chromosphere by varying the wavelength as, for example, from the center of a strong line such as Hα or the K line of Ca II to the wing of the same line. It is clear that the spectroheliogram taken in the center of the line refers to a higher layer than the spectroheliogram taken in the wing.

Such photographs show the existence of mottling or chromospheric granulation (Figs. 5.2-4 and 5.2-5). The fine mottling are elements with characteristic dimensions of $\sim 10^3$ km. These appear to cluster together to form the coarse mottles with diameters of $\sim 5 \times 10^3$ km. The coarse mottles seem to be arranged in a coarse network (the chromospheric network) with a characteristic dimension or mesh width of 30,000 to 50,000 km. It may be possible to understand the formation of the chromospheric network on the basis of the theory of faculae and the large-scale motions observed in the photosphere; see the discussion at the end of Sec. 5.1.

The hot elements in the lower chromosphere are identified with the fine bright mottles in the K line Ca II spectroheliograms and with fine dark mottles in Hα. We shall not go into details, but the studies of mottling indicate that the hot elements exist only for heights above 1,000 to 2,000 km. At these heights, $A \approx 0.15$, and it decreases with height. Also of interest is the relative area occupied by the spicules in the upper chromosphere. If A is used to measure the relative area of the hot elements for $h < 5,000$ km and the spicules for $h > 5,000$ km, then $A(h)$ seems to be a continuous function; thus, it may be permissible to assume an intimate connection between the hot elements in the lower chromosphere and the spicules in the upper chromosphere.

A two-element model provides a basis for the interpretation of many phenomena and is not unexpected on the basis of an inhomogeneous model of the photosphere. It is also consistent with some of the ideas involved with the transport of mechanical energy. Such models are rather tentative and are not included in our summary model.

Fig. 5.2-4   An Hα spectroheliogram showing chromospheric fine structure. (*Observatoire de Paris–Meudon photograph.*)

Fig. 5.2-5   A Ca II (K_3 = central emission core of the K line) spectroheliogram clearly showing the mottling and the chromospheric network.   (*Observatoire de Paris–Meudon photograph.*)

Transition zone

A separate name has been advocated for the region comprising the extreme upper chromosphere and the extreme lower corona. This region of extreme change is important, because it seems that many important lines in the solar rocket ultraviolet (for example, $\lambda 1{,}215$, Lyman-α of hydrogen) are formed here.

5.3   THE CORONA

The portion of the solar atmosphere above $1.03R_\odot$ is called the corona. The corona can be arbitrarily divided into the inner corona ($1.03 \leq r/R_\odot \leq 1.3$), medium corona ($1.3 \leq r/R_\odot \leq 2.5$), and the outer corona ($r > 2.5R_\odot$). At many solar radii, the outer corona is called the interplane-

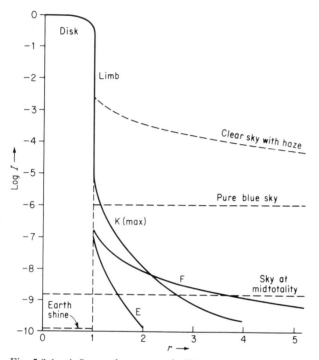

Fig. 5.3-1   A figure, due to van de Hulst, showing the relative intensities of the components of coronal light: K is the
continuous light due to electron scattering; F is the inner
zodiacal light; E is the combined light of emission lines.
(*Copyright* 1953 *by the University of Chicago, from R* 5.2-1.)

tary medium (the subject of Chap. 8). The light of the corona is divided
into three components:

1. The K corona, which is a continuum due to electron scattering.
2. The F corona, or inner zodiacal light, which is solar radiation
diffracted by interplanetary dust. The radiation is not physically connected with the corona and we do not further consider the F corona here.
3. The E or emission corona, which is the total light of the coronal
emission lines.

The variation of the brightness of the various components of the
corona is shown in Fig. 5.3-1. The corona can be studied by radio and
optical techniques. There is general agreement that the corona is a highly
ionized gas with a temperature of $\sim 10^6$ °K. The density is fairly well
known, but there are many details on which agreement is lacking. An
example is the role of fine structure.

Structure

Photographs of the corona can be taken at solar eclipse; they show a fairly
complicated structure (Figs. 5.3-2 to 5.3-4). The word "streamer" has been

used to refer to any long extension of the corona. The streamers can be subdivided as follows:

1. Fans are the large streamers with dimensions of $\sim 1 R_\odot$ or greater; they determine the general form of the corona at any given time. A fan is associated with a quiescent prominence. Coronal arch systems in the fan surround the prominence, and further detail in the fan is visible as fan rays.

2. Rays are the narrow streamers; besides the fan rays, there are the rays over undisturbed regions (e.g., the polar rays) and the rays over faculae (see Sec. 6.5 for a discussion of faculae). The rays above faculae are straight, but the polar rays show the curvature which reminds one of a dipole magnetic field. It is probably significant that the density gradient in the fans and rays is the same as in the surroundings, even though the density in the fans and streamers appears to be some 5 to 10 times higher than the surroundings.

For the polar rays, a simple explanation in terms of the magnetic field is possible. The magnetic field would very effectively inhibit diffusion

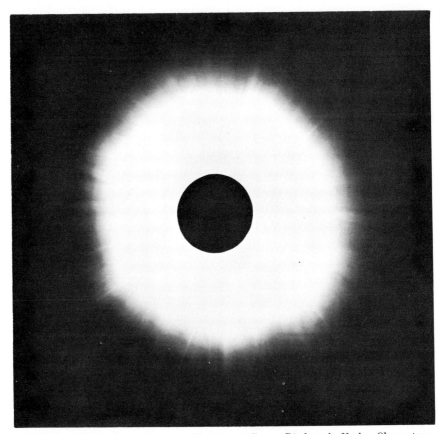

Fig. 5.3-2   The maximum corona. (*Courtesy of G. van Biesbroeck, Yerkes Observatory, see also R 5.3-1.*)

Fig. 5.3-3   The intermediate corona. (*Courtesy of G. van Biesbroeck, Yerkes Observatory, see also R* 5.3-1.)

perpendicular to the lines of force. Along the lines of force, the atmosphere may be in hydrostatic equilibrium. The pressure gradient is balanced by the gradient of the potential, but since the magnetic field does no work on a particle, there is no magnetic term in the potential. Hence, as long as we go along a line of accessibility (i.e., along the lines of force of the magnetic field), the corona is free to maintain itself in hydrostatic equilibrium. The polar rays can therefore be understood in terms of density fluctuations in an atmosphere in hydrostatic equilibrium along the lines of force. On this picture, we would not expect a difference in the density gradients in and out of the rays (as observed).

Besides the arches mentioned in connection with the fans and prominences, there are smaller arch-systems apparently of the same nature but not associated with fans. There is also a wide variety of other structural details. In the light of the emission lines, one finds emission regions (lifetime $\sim$ several days) and coronal condensations (lifetime $\sim$ 10 hr). This emission line detail is associated with solar activity (Chap. 6).

The large-scale changes in the structure of the solar corona can be seen in Figs. 5.3-2 and 5.3-4. These changes occur with the sunspot cycle (Chap. 6). At sunspot maximum the corona is almost spherically symmetrical, whereas appreciable flattening is observed at sunspot minimum.

This fact can be represented quantitatively as follows. Define the flattening of the corona by

$$\epsilon = \frac{d_1}{d_2} - 1 \tag{1}$$

where d_1 is the average of the equatorial diameter and the two diameters which make an angle $22°.5$ with the equator and d_2 is the analogous quantity defined for the polar diameter. One can collect various determinations of ϵ for various distances and determine the constants a and b through the relation

$$\epsilon = a + b(r_{eq} - 1) \tag{2}$$

where r_{eq} is the equatorial radius measured in solar radii. Actually, ϵ starts to decrease beyond $2R_\odot$, but this is probably due to the F corona. The quantity $a + b$ is approximately the flattening of the real corona at $2R_\odot$, and a plot of $a + b$ versus phase of the solar cycle is given in Fig. 5.3-5. The change of the coronal form through the solar cycle is clearly related to the solar activity. At sunspot minimum, there is little activity and it is concentrated toward the equator. At sunspot maximum, there is so much solar activity that the corona is nearly circular.

Fig. 5.3-4 The corona at solar minimum. (*Courtesy of Å. Wallenquist, Uppsala, see R 5.3-2.*)

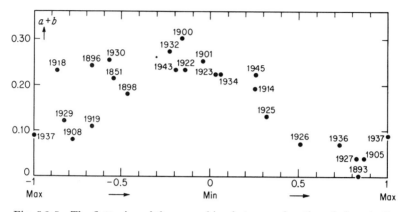

Fig. 5.3-5   The flattening of the coronal isophotes as a function of phase in the solar cycle (after van de Hulst). The flattening is for $2R_\odot$ [the quantity $a + b$ in Eq. (5.3-2)]. (*Copyright 1953 by the University of Chicago Press, from R 5.2-1.*)

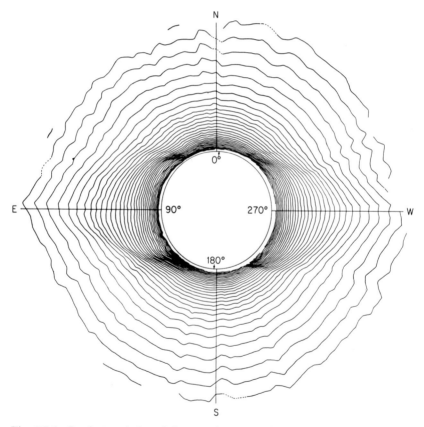

Fig. 5.3-6   Isophotes of the minimum solar corona in the photovisual region at intervals of 0.2 magnitudes.   The solar axis is marked by the small arrow.   (*Courtesy of Å. Wallenquist, Uppsala, see R 5.3-2.*)

Densities

The densities in the corona can be derived from a set of isophotes (e.g., see Fig. 5.3-6). Assume for the present that the corona is spherical and that we have separated the K corona from the F corona. Assume also that the emission per unit volume (in cubic centimeters) can be written as a power series

$$g(r) = \sum_{n} a_n r^{-(n+1)} \tag{3}$$

where r is measured in solar radii. Then each term of this expansion contributes an amount to the surface brightness given by integrating along the line of sight (see Fig. 5.3-2 for geometry), and

$$4\pi I_n = 2a_n R_\odot \int_0^\infty \frac{dy}{r^{+(n+1)}} \tag{4a}$$

$$= 2a_n R_\odot \int_0^\infty \frac{dy}{[(x + R_\odot)^2 + y^2]^{(n+1)/2}} \tag{4b}$$

$$= \frac{2a_n R_\odot}{(x + R_\odot)^n} \int_0^{\pi/2} \cos^{n-1} \phi \, d\phi \tag{4c}$$

Hence

$$4\pi I = \sum_{n} b_n (x + R_\odot)^{-n} \tag{5}$$

where the relation between the a_n's and the b_n's can be determined from Eq. (5.3-4c). The K corona is caused by Thompson scattering of solar photons by the free electrons in the corona. Thus, the source function per unit volume under the assumption of isotropic scattering is just

$$g(r) = \sigma N_e(r) \int \frac{I \, d\omega}{4\pi} \tag{6a}$$

$$= \sigma N_e(r) J(r) \tag{6b}$$

Here σ is the Thompson scattering cross section ($= 6.6 \times 10^{-25}$ cm²) and $J(r)$ is the mean intensity at the distance r. To find $J(r)$, one integrates over the disk of the Sun, and it is found that one must take account of the limb darkening. We recall that the brightness across the solar disk can be written as

$$I(\theta) = I_0(1 - u + u \cos \theta) \tag{7}$$

where for a wavelength of 4,300 A, $u \approx 0.8$. Thus,

$$J(r) = \frac{I_0}{4\pi} \int_{\substack{\text{solar} \\ \text{disk}}} (1 - u + u \cos \theta) \, d\omega \tag{8}$$

Carrying out the integration yields a fairly complicated formula which for $r > 1.2$ can be written as

$$J(r) = \frac{I_0}{2}\left[(1 - u)\left(\frac{1}{2r^2} + \frac{1}{8r^4} + \cdots\right)\right.$$
$$\left. + u\left(\frac{1}{3r^2} + \frac{1}{15r^4} + \cdots\right)\right] \quad (9)$$

For $u = 0.8$, we have

$$\frac{J(r)}{I_0} = \frac{0.183}{r^2} + \frac{0.039}{r^4} \quad (10)$$

Equations (5.3-10) and (5.3-6b) can be combined to give

$$N_e = \frac{1.52 \times 10^{19} g(r)}{1.83/r^2 + 0.39/r^4} \quad (11)$$

where the unit of brightness is taken to be 10^{-6} the brightness of the center of the disk. Hence, one determines the function $g(r)$ through Eqs. (5.3-3), (5.3-4c), and (5.3-5), and then the electron density is determined through Eq. (5.3-11). Sometimes a factor of $R_\odot$ (cm) is included in $g(r)$, in which case the numerical factor in Eq. (5.3-11) becomes 2.18×10^8 instead of 1.52×10^{19}. The extension of the theory to include the effects of nonspherical geometry and the angular dependence of the scattered radiation is straightforward in principle but complicated in practice. Calculations can also be made from the observed polarizations in the corona. The dependence of the electron density on solar latitude can be summarized by noting that although the density at the pole is approximately one-half the equatorial density, the density goes through a minimum (about one-fourth the equatorial density) at a latitude of 70°. These results are strictly true for a corona near minimum at $r = 1.15R_\odot$. The minimum results from the "discontinuity" at 60 to 70° in the isophotes in (for example) Fig. 5.3-6.

As we remarked above, it is necessary to separate the K and F coronas. One method is to use the fact that the Fraunhofer lines appear at normal strength in the F corona whereas they are almost completely washed out in the K corona. If both K and F components of the corona are present in given observations, the central depression of a Fraunhofer line will be less than the photospheric value (Fig. 5.3-7). In this case, the simple formula

$$\frac{I_K}{I_F} = \frac{d_{phot}}{d_{obs}} - 1 \quad (12)$$

enables one to separate the K and F corona. At large distances, it has been customary to take the F corona as unpolarized and to use the polarization measures to separate the K and F coronas. This latter procedure can be risky, because the F corona at large distance, i.e., the zodiacal light,

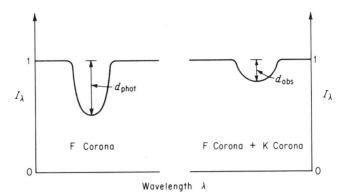

Fig. 5.3-7   Schematic diagram showing the change in the central depression of Fraunhofer lines from the photosphere (same as the F corona) to the observed corona: see the text for discussion.

appears to have a polarized component of radiation caused by dust particles. However, no serious inconsistencies appear to exist between the two methods, at least out to a distance of approximately $5R_\odot$. Some coronal electron densities are given in Table 4.2-1.

The emission lines

The wavelengths of the lines in the emission corona do not coincide with the wavelengths of the Fraunhofer lines. The origin of the lines was unclear for some time, and for some years the emission lines were attributed to a hypothetical element called "coronium". After the periodic table of the elements was completed, this idea was abandoned. This puzzle was unraveled by Grotrian and Edlén, who showed that these lines come from highly ionized atoms.

The intensities, wavelengths, and identifications of some of the stronger coronal lines are given in Table 5.3-1. The lines given in the table are all forbidden lines; they come from states (called metastable states) which have a lifetime that is $\sim 10^6$ times the lifetime of ordinary states. For forbidden lines to appear, one usually requires a low-density medium, and this condition is met by the corona.

If we assume the result that the temperature of the corona is about 10^6 °K, the existence of such highly ionized atoms can be explained as follows. Assume that at each point in the corona a steady-state condition prevails. Then the rate of formation of ions of, say, stage p equals the rate of disappearance of ions from stage p. Ionization can occur through inelastic collisions with electrons or through photo-ionizations. For conditions prevalent in the corona, collisional ionization predominates. For recombinations, we have the normal photoelectric recombination and the three-body collisional recombination. The difference lies in the disposition

Table 5.3-1   Coronal emission lines

Wavelength, A	Intensity	Identity
5,116.03	8	Ni XIII
5,302.86	198	Fe XIV (green line)
5,694.42	3	Ca XV (yellow line)
6,374.51	40	Fe X (red line)
6,701.83	9	Ni XV
7,059.62	5	Fe XV
7,891.94	30	Fe XI
10,746.80	130	Fe XIII
10,797.95	81	Fe XIII

of the excess energy available in recombination. Normally it comes off in a photon of appropriate energy, but in three-body recombination, the third body receives the energy.

Normal photo recombination dominates in the corona. Hence, the equilibrium of a particular stage of ionization can be expressed by considering all of the ways collisional ionization and photo recombination add or subtract ions from the stage in question, that is,

$$N_e N_p [S(p \rightarrow p + 1) + \alpha(p \rightarrow p - 1)]$$
$$= [N_{p-1} S(p - 1 \rightarrow p) + N_{p+1} \alpha(p + 1 \rightarrow p)] N_e \quad (13)$$

where N_e is the electron density, N_p is the ion density of stage p, $S(i \rightarrow j)$ is the collisional ionization coefficient for stage i, and $\alpha(i \rightarrow j)$ is the recombination coefficient onto stage j. If stage p corresponds to a completely ionized atom, Eq. (5.3-13) becomes

$$N_p \alpha(p \rightarrow p - 1) = N_{p-1} S(p - 1 \rightarrow p) \quad (14)$$

Replacing p by $p - 1$ in Eq. (5.3-13) and combining this new equation with Eq. (5.3-14) gives another equation of the same form as (5.3-14). Hence, if there are $N(1 - x)$ ions per unit volume in the pth stage and the remainder Nx in the $p + 1$ stage, we have

$$\frac{x}{1 - x} = \frac{S(p \rightarrow p + 1)}{\alpha(p + 1 \rightarrow p)} \quad (15a)$$

or

$$x = \frac{S(p \rightarrow p + 1)}{S(p \rightarrow p + 1) + \alpha(p + 1 \rightarrow p)} \quad (15b)$$

Note that the degree of ionization is not a function of the electron density. This is to be expected, because both collisional ionizations and recombinations are proportional to N_e and thus N_e cancels out in an equilibrium situation.

The needed rate coefficients are approximately

$$S(p \rightarrow p + 1) = 3 \times 10^{-8} T^{1/2} \chi_i^2 \exp \left[\frac{-11600\chi_i}{T} \right] \tag{16}$$

and

$$\alpha(p + 1 \rightarrow p) = 1.5 \times 10^{-11} Z^2 T^{-1/2} \tag{17}$$

where Z is the ionic charge of stage $p + 1$ and χ_i is the ionization potential of the pth stage in eV the degree of ionization depends only on atomic parameters and the temperature. For temperatures of $\sim 10^6$ °K, we find that the highly ionized species required to explain the emission lines (Table 5.3-1) are present. It is also found that several stages of ionization of the same atomic species can exist simultaneously.

Ratios of the coronal emission lines can be used to study temperature changes in the corona as a function of position. In comparing the green and red coronal lines, we are essentially evaluating the ratio

$$\frac{N \text{ (Fe XIV)}}{N \text{ (Fe X)}} = \frac{N_{\text{XIV}}}{N_{\text{XIII}}} \cdot \frac{N_{\text{XIII}}}{N_{\text{XII}}} \cdot \frac{N_{\text{XII}}}{N_{\text{XI}}} \cdot \frac{N_{\text{XI}}}{N_{\text{X}}} \tag{18}$$

where the contracted notation is obvious. Each factor increases rapidly with increasing temperature, and thus the ratio (green line)/(red line) is very sensitive to changes in the temperature. A 10 per cent change in the temperature would change the ratio (green line)/(red line) by a factor of 10. Since the observed variations are usually smaller, we conclude that the corona is nearly isothermal over the region covered by the observations of the red and green lines.

The ratio of red and green lines is not a very accurate way to determine the temperature because of uncertainties in the cross sections; nonetheless, a temperature of about 1.0×10^6 °K is indicated. The forbidden lines are excited by electron collisions (which go as N_e^2) in the inner corona and by radiation (and hence excitation proportional to N_e/r^2) in the outer corona. These two mechanisms are comparable from $1.5R_\odot$ to $2.0R_\odot$. From the functional dependences mentioned and with the steep gradient in the density, this behavior is expected.

Finally, we should mention that the condition for the appearance of forbidden lines—that the radiative lifetime for the excited level (determined by the Einstein A) be shorter than the lifetime due to collisional de-excitation—is satisfied in the corona. The condition is satisfied because the electron densities are relatively low and because the Einstein A's involved are relatively large, considering that they refer to forbidden transitions.

The temperature

It is well known that the temperature in the corona is $\sim 10^6\,°\mathrm{K}$, as found from the stage of ionization of atoms required to produce the coronal emission lines. We shall show that this result can be inferred a variety of ways.

If we assume that the corona is isothermal and in hydrostatic equilibrium, then its density distribution follows the generalized barometric formula

$$\frac{N_e}{N_{e,0}} = \exp\left[+\frac{GM\mu m_{\mathrm{H}}}{R_\odot kT}\left(\frac{1}{r} - \frac{1}{r_0}\right)\right] \tag{19}$$

where $N_{e,0}$ = electron density at reference level r_0
$\quad\quad r$ = distance from center of Sun, in solar radii $R_\odot$
$\quad\quad G$ = constant of gravitation
$\quad\quad k$ = Boltzmann's constant
$\quad\quad T$ = temperature
$\quad\quad M$ = mass of the Sun
$\quad\quad m_{\mathrm{H}}$ = mass of the hydrogen atom
$\quad\quad \mu$ = mean molecular weight

On this picture a plot of log N_e versus $1/r$ should give a straight line with the slope determined by the temperature. Taking logarithms and differentiating Eq. (5.3-19) gives

$$\frac{d(\log_{10} N_e)}{d(1/r)} = \frac{GM m_{\mathrm{H}}}{2.3026 R_\odot k}\left(\frac{\mu}{T}\right) \tag{20}$$

or

$$T = \frac{1.004 \times 10^7 \mu}{d\log_{10} N_e/d(1/r)} \tag{21}$$

A plot of $\log_{10} N_e$ versus $1/r$ is shown in Fig. 5.3-8 for data referring to the equator at sunspot minimum. The straight line shown gives a good fit out to 3 solar radii, again implying an isothermal corona out to that distance. The temperature derived from this plot by using Eq. (5.3-21) is $1.5 \times 10^6\,°\mathrm{K}$, where $\mu = 0.608$ corresponding to a mixture containing 1 helium atom per 10 hydrogen atoms. Similar determinations from the monochromatic gradients yield much the same answer. The temperature appears to be cooler in the polar regions ($T \approx 1.2 \times 10^6\,°\mathrm{K}$).

The width of the forbidden lines in the coronal spectrum offers another way of determining the temperature. If we assume that the line in question is widened by the thermal Doppler effect alone, the profile is given by

$$I = I_0 e^{-(\lambda-\lambda_0)^2/(\delta\lambda_0)^2} \tag{22}$$

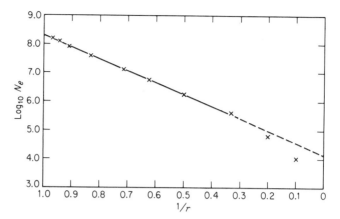

Fig. 5.3-8   The logarithm of the equatorial, minimum, coronal electron densities (*from* R 5.2-2) versus r^{-1}. See Eq. (5.3-20) et sequence.

where

$$\delta\lambda_0 = \frac{\lambda}{c}\left(\frac{2kT}{\mu m_{\mathrm{H}}}\right)^{1/2} \tag{23}$$

If we call h the full width at half intensity (the measured quantity), then $h = 1.67\delta\lambda_0$ and substituting yields

$$T = \left(\frac{h^2}{\lambda^2}\right)\mu \times 1.95 \times 10^{12} \tag{24}$$

where μ is the atomic weight of the atom involved. Typical results (after correction for instrumental effects) are $h = 0.89$ A for the red line (Fe X, $\mu = 55.85$, $\lambda = 6{,}375$ A) which corresponds to a temperature of 2.1×10^6 °K.

We also have the fact that the Fraunhofer lines in the K corona are not detectable, with the possible exception of the H and K lines. A rough estimate of the width expected can be obtained from Eq. (5.3-24) for $T = 10^6$ °K and by using the atomic weight of an electron, $\frac{1}{1836}$. One finds $h \approx 120$ A, which explains why the Fraunhofer lines are not visible in the K corona. The method is not too sensitive and really only establishes that $T > 10^5$ °K.

Nonetheless, the results obtained are consistent with the picture obtained by other methods. The corona emits considerable soft X radiation in the 10- to 100-A wavelength region. Detailed calculations have been made, and the total intensity (made up of many discrete lines) is consistent with a temperature of 0.75×10^6 °K.

Finally, we have the results from the radio observations of the quiet Sun. These observations (discussed below) give a temperature for the lower corona of some 0.7×10^6 °K.

Thus, the status of the temperature of the corona is as follows. As long as we consider factors of 2 to be unimportant, then 1×10^6 °K is a good value for the "temperature of the corona" consistent with all methods. However, temperatures which are strictly *electron temperatures* (given by the obliteration of the Fraunhofer lines, the degree of ionization and the forbidden line intensities, the X-ray intensities, and the radio observations) seem to cluster in the 700,000 to 900,000°K range, while the *kinetic temperatures* (given by the density gradient, monochromatic intensity gradient, and the observed line widths) are some 2 times higher. If this result were well established, it would be of considerable interest. Unfortunately, the uncertainties are rather large. One might ascribe some of this difference to turbulent motions, but extreme velocities would be required. It appears that the source of this discrepancy (if real) could be in a temperature fine structure, a general expansion of the corona, or a depletion in the population of high-velocity electrons.

Radio models

The radio emission from the solar corona is now known to be largely thermal in origin. This radiation is of interest because the physics relating to its formation and the handling of the equation of transfer are somewhat different from those applying to the optical wavelengths. In addition, this radiation gives valuable information concerning models of the corona and chromosphere.

The absorption coefficient per unit length due to free-free transitions by electrons is usually taken as

$$K \doteq \frac{\nu x}{cn} \tag{25}$$

where the index of refraction in the absence of magnetic fields is

$$n = (1 - x)^{1/2} \tag{26}$$

and where

$$x = \left(\frac{f_0}{f}\right)^2 = \left(\frac{e^2 N_e}{\pi m_e}\right)\frac{1}{f^2} \tag{27}$$

one of the dimensionless magnetoionic parameters. Here f_0 is the plasma frequency or critical frequency. Also, c is the velocity of light in vacuum, and the collision frequency is given by

$$\nu = \frac{4}{3} e^4 \left[\frac{\pi}{2m_e(kT)^3}\right]^{1/2} Z^2 N_i A_1 \tag{28}$$

where

$$A_1 = \log_e\left[1 + \left(\frac{4kT}{Ze^2 N_i^{1/3}}\right)^2\right] \tag{29}$$

Here Z is the degree of ionization and N_i is the number of ions. For most coronal conditions it is sufficient to take $N_i = N_e$ and $Z = 1$. Note that the function A_1 is slowly varying. Equation (5.3-25) is valid as long as the refractive index n is not close to zero. The absorption coefficient is more accurately given by

$$K = \frac{8^{1/2} \pi f}{c} \left\{ \left[\frac{(1 - x)^2 + z^2}{1 + z^2} \right]^{1/2} - \frac{1 + z^2 - x}{1 + z^2} \right\}^{1/2} \tag{30}$$

where

$$z = \frac{\nu}{2\pi f} \tag{31}$$

is another of the magnetoionic parameters. It is found from Eq. (5.3-30) that as $n \to 0$ the absorption coefficient rises to a finite value of approximately

$$K(n \to 0) = \frac{8^{1/2} \pi f}{c} z^{1/2} \tag{32}$$

If one considers rays which pass close to the level for which $n \to 0$, it is necessary to consider the complications dictated by Eqs. (5.3-30) and (5.3-32).

The opacity can be computed from Eq. (5.3-26), or its equivalent, where the integration is carried out over the trajectory which is curved in the corona because the index of refraction varies. The trajectory is given (assuming a spherical corona throughout) by Snell's law. All rays lie in planes containing the center of the Sun, and

$$nr \sin i = a \tag{33}$$

where a is a constant for a given ray, r is measured in units of the solar radius, and i is the angle of incidence of the ray on the surface. For any ray in the corona (Fig. 5.3-9), we have

$$\frac{r \, d\theta}{dr} = - \tan i \tag{34}$$

Equations (5.3-33) and (5.3-34) give

$$\frac{d\theta}{dr} = \frac{-a}{r(n^2r^2 - a^2)^{1/2}} \tag{35}$$

and thus the equation of a ray path is

$$\theta = a \int_r^\infty \frac{dr}{r(n^2r^2 - a^2)^{1/2}} \tag{36}$$

If a model corona is chosen, the index of refraction can be computed at each point and the ray path determined from Eq. (5.3-36). Some ray paths

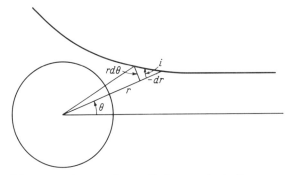

Fig. 5.3-9   A ray path at radio frequencies in the corona.

in the corona for 18 Mc/sec are shown in Fig. 5.3-10. Each ray shows a turning point, and hence the radiation can reach us along a direct or a reflected path. The signal along the reflected path can be strongly absorbed, however. The distance of closest approach r_c can be obtained by setting $i = 90°$ in Eq. (5.3-33), that is, $r_c = a/n$. Notice that the different r_c's determine a volume of the corona from which we receive no radiation.

Thus, in certain radio wavelengths we are able to observe the corona free from the "glare" of the photosphere. The ray which penetrates deepest is the ray for which $a = 0$ and which is reflected at the level where $n = 0$, that is, $x = 1$. For $x > 1$ (that is, $f_0 > f$), n is imaginary and the

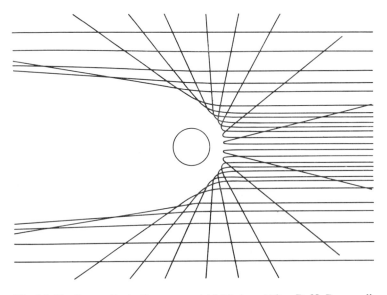

Fig. 5.3-10   Ray paths in the corona at 18 Mc/sec. (After R. N. Bracewell and G. W. Preston.) (*Copyright* 1956 *by the University of Chicago, published by The University of Chicago Press, from R 5.3-5.*)

radiation is absorbed. Thus, at a given frequency, there are two surfaces important for the escape of radiation. For escape in any direction, the surface is the sphere for which $n = 0$. For escape in the direction of the observer, the surfaces are similar to those shown in Fig. 5.3-10 as the lower envelope of the given trajectories. This latter surface is tangent to the surface for which $n = 0$ at the "center of the disk."

In the presence of a magnetic field, the conditions for escape of radio waves are given by the magnetoionic theory and are somewhat more complicated than the simple $x = 1$ condition mentioned above. In the presence of a magnetic field there are two modes of propagation, the ordinary and the extraordinary, and the index of refraction depends on the magnitude of the magnetic field and the direction of propagation relative to the magnetic field. Propagation in rays along the magnetic field is said to be quasi-longitudinal, and that perpendicular to the field, quasi-transverse. If the electron density and the magnetic field decrease monotonically outward, radiation originating below a certain surface does not escape. The escape limits are given by

$$
\begin{array}{lll}
x = 1 & \text{ordinary ray} & \left.\vphantom{\begin{array}{c}a\\b\end{array}}\right\} \text{quasi-transverse} \\
x = 1 - y & \text{extraordinary ray} & \text{propagation}
\end{array}
\tag{37}
$$

and

$$
\begin{array}{lll}
x = 1 - y & \text{extraordinary ray} & \left.\vphantom{\begin{array}{c}a\\b\end{array}}\right\} \text{quasi-longitudinal} \\
x = 1 + y & \text{ordinary ray} & \text{propagation}
\end{array}
\tag{38}
$$

Here y (a magnetoionic parameter)

$$
y = \frac{eB}{2\pi m_e cf} = \frac{f_B}{f}
\tag{39}
$$

where f_B is the gyrofrequency and numerically is $f_B \doteq 2.8B$ Mc/sec. Since the general magnetic field in the corona is some 1 gauss or less, the gyrofrequency is ~ 1 Mc/sec. This is much lower than most frequencies used in solar work, and usually $y \ll 1$. Hence, these complications are normally unimportant for the observations of the quiet Sun; but they can be important over a large sunspot, where the field could be as much as 10^3 gauss or higher.

With the trajectory determined by the considerations discussed above, we return to the specification of the emissivity per unit volume. This can be obtained from the absorption coefficient via Kirchhoff's law, which is valid for local thermodynamic equilibrium. This requires a word of explanation, because the mere mention of the phrase "local thermodynamic equilibrium" usually excludes one from further consideration of the corona. However, here we are dealing with the emission and absorption of radiation by free-free processes, and hence the only property of LTE required is that the electrons have a maxwellian distribution of speeds at temperature T. Since there are sufficient collisions to maintain a maxwellian distribution, it is permissible to assume LTE in this case and write

$$\eta = n^2 K B(T) \tag{40}$$

where η is the emissivity and $B(T)$ is the specific intensity due to a black-body at temperature T. Note the appearance of the factor n^2 in the last equation; normally, $n^2 \doteq 1$ and Kirchhoff's law is written as in Eq. (4.1-18). At radio frequencies, we may use the Rayleigh-Jeans approximation,

$$B(T) = \frac{2kT}{\lambda^2} \tag{41}$$

Combining Eqs. (5.3-40) and (5.3-41)

$$\eta = n^2 K \frac{2k}{\lambda^2} T \tag{42}$$

We now need the equation of transfer for radio wavelengths that contains an additional term because of the convergence or divergence of the rays when $dn/ds \neq 0$. Consider rays propagating through a medium of varying index of refraction. Let θ and θ' be the angles of incidence and refraction of a pencil of radiation incident on an area $d\sigma$ of a surface between media with refractive indices n and n'. The energy passing through this surface must be a constant in both media (assuming no reflection at the interface) and hence,

$$I \, d\sigma \, d\omega \, \cos \theta = I' \, d\sigma \, d\omega' \, \cos \theta' \tag{43}$$

where the solid angle of the pencil of radiation is $d\omega = \sin \theta \, d\theta \, d\phi$, and there is a similar expression for the other medium. The coordinate system can be so chosen that $d\phi = d\phi'$. Then we have Snell's law

$$n \sin \theta = n' \sin \theta' \tag{44}$$

and differentiating gives

$$n \cos \theta \, d\theta = n' \cos \theta' \, d\theta' \tag{45}$$

Equations (5.3-43) to (5.3-45) give

$$\frac{I}{n^2} = \frac{I'}{n'^2} \tag{46}$$

Thus, in a medium of varying index of refraction without emission or absorption, the quantity I/n^2 is a constant. Hence, we may formulate the equation of transfer as usual with an extra term due to the effects of refraction, or we may formulate it in terms of the quantity I/n^2.

By analogy with our previous equation of transfer, the total change of the quantity I/n^2 due to absorption and emission is

$$\frac{d}{ds}\left(\frac{I}{n^2}\right) = \frac{1}{n^2}(-KI + \eta) \tag{47a}$$

or

$$\frac{1}{K}\frac{d}{ds}\left(\frac{I}{n^2}\right) = -\frac{I}{n^2} + \frac{\eta}{Kn^2} \tag{47b}$$

Here the emission and absorption coefficients are related as in thermodynamic equilibrium [see Eq. (5.3-40)]. We then have

$$\frac{1}{K}\frac{d}{ds}\left(\frac{I}{n^2}\right) = -\frac{I}{n^2} + B(T) \tag{48}$$

The solution to Eq. (5.3-48) is obtained exactly as Eq. (4.1-21) is found to be the solution of Eq. (4.1-17); thus, we let

$$\tau = \oint_s^\infty K\,ds \tag{49}$$

and find

$$e^{-\tau}\frac{I}{n^2} = \frac{I_0}{n_0^2}e^{-\tau_0} + \oint_\tau^{\tau_0} e^{-\tau}B(T)\,d\tau \tag{50}$$

where I_0 and n_0 apply to the location $\tau = \tau_0$. Note that the optical thickness is measured from a particular point in the corona to the observer (outside the corona) along the ray path. Since we are interested in the emergent intensity, we take $\tau = 0$ and $n = 1$. It is also convenient to take τ_0 at the point where the trajectory under observation originally enters the corona, where $n_0 = 1$. Then,

$$I = I_0 e^{-\tau_0} + \oint_0^{\tau_0} e^{-\tau}B(T)\,d\tau \tag{51}$$

This equation can be interpreted as giving the emergent radiation as the radiation incident on the corona reduced by the optical thickness along the ray path $(I_0 e^{-\tau_0})$ plus the emission from each point along the trajectory $[B(T)]$ reduced by the intervening opacity. For the case at hand, there is no incident radiation, and

$$I = \oint_0^{\tau_0} e^{-\tau}B(T)\,d\tau \tag{52}$$

Using Eq. (5.3-41), we have

$$I = \frac{2k}{\lambda^2}\oint_0^{\tau_0} Te^{-\tau}\,d\tau \tag{53}$$

In the radio region, the intensity is related to the brightness temperature T_b through

$$I = \frac{2kT_b}{\lambda^2} \tag{54}$$

This is simply the temperature of a blackbody required to produce the same intensity at the same frequency. We may rewrite Eq. (5.3-53) as

$$T_b = \oint_0^{\tau_0} Te^{-\tau}\, d\tau \tag{55}$$

If the temperature of the corona is uniform,

$$T_b = T_c(1 - e^{-\tau_0}) \tag{56}$$

From studies of the corona at meter wavelengths using Eq. (5.3-56) and opacities (i.e., electron densities) from optical models, we find coronal temperatures of $\sim 10^6$ °K.

If the wavelength is sufficiently short, the trajectory may penetrate into the chromosphere. In this case, we may assume the corona and chromosphere to be at their respective, constant temperatures T_c and T_{ch}. If the opacity is large in the chromosphere

$$T_b = T_c[1 - e^{-\tau_0/2}] + T_{ch}e^{-\tau_0/2} \tag{57}$$

This equation follows directly from Eq. (5.3-51), where we understand that $\tau_0/2$ is the opacity in one traverse of the corona. Observations at the appropriate frequencies yield valuable information which is reasonably consistent with the optical studies. By choosing the frequency, the observed brightness can be made to originate entirely in the chromosphere or

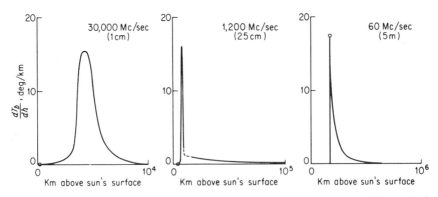

Fig. 5.3-11 Showing the contributions to the brightness temperature of the central ray (dT_b/dh) as function of height and frequency, after Pawsey and Smerd. The turning points of the trajectory are marked with a circle. (*Copyright 1953 by the University of Chicago, from R 5.3-3.*)

the corona (see Fig. 5.3-11). For example, T_b at 30,000 Mc/sec originates entirely in the chromosphere, whereas at 60 Mc/sec it originates entirely in the corona.

Finally, we mention that the corona can be probed by observing a discrete radio source as it passes through the corona. The Crab nebula (= Taurus A radio source) has been used. The principal inference of these observations points to the existence of considerable inhomogeneity or fine structure in the corona. This point is discussed in Sec. 8.3.

BIBLIOGRAPHICAL NOTES

Section 5.1. The problems of the convection zone are discussed in R 3-3, R 3.2-2, R 4.2-3, R 5.2-2, and:

R 5.1-1. Schwarzschild, M.: *Astrophys. J.*, **134**: 1 (1961).

R 5.1-2. Biermann, L., and R. Lüst: In "Stellar Atmospheres," ed. J. L. Greenstein, pp. 260–281, The University of Chicago Press, Chicago, 1960.

R 5.1-3. Woolley, R. v.d. R., and D. W. N. Stibbs: "The Outer Layers of a Star," The Clarendon Press, Oxford, 1953.

The picture of energy generation and heating of the chromosphere and corona follows:

R 5.1-4. Osterbrock, D. E.: *Astrophys. J.*, **134**: 347 (1961).

The supergranulation is described in:

R 5.1-5. Leighton, R. B., R. W. Noyes, and G. W. Simon: *Astrophys. J.*, **135**: 474 (1962).

Section 5.2. The early work and basic concepts are given in:

R 5.2-1. van de Hulst, H. C.: In "The Sun," ed. G. P. Kuiper, pp. 207–321, The University of Chicago Press, Chicago, 1953.

The recent work, including the two-element model, is covered in:

R 5.2-2. de Jager, C.: "Handbuch der Physik," vol. 52, ed. S. Flügge, pp. 80–362, Springer-Verlag OHG, Berlin, 1959.

A recent text on the chromosphere is:

R 5.2-3. Thomas, R. N., and R. G. Athay: "Physics of the Solar Chromosphere," Interscience Publishers, Inc., New York, 1961.

See also R 3-3, R 4.2-3, and:

R 5.2-4. Goldberg, L., and E. R. Dyer: In "Science in Space," eds. L. V. Berkner and H. Odishaw, pp. 307–340, The McGraw-Hill Book Company, New York, 1961.

Section 5.3. The corona is discussed at length in R 5.2-1, R 5.2-2, and R 4.2-3. Coronal photography and isophotes are covered in:

R 5.3-1. van Biesbroeck, G.: In "The Sun," ed. G. P. Kuiper, pp. 601–604, The University of Chicago Press, Chicago, 1953.

R 5.3-2. Wallenquist, Å.: *Uppsala Ann.*, **4**(4): (1957).

Radiophysics and the application to the corona (and chromosphere) are discussed in:

R 5.3-3. Pawsey, J. L., and S. F. Smerd: In "The Sun," ed. G. P. Kuiper, pp. 466–531, The University of Chicago Press, Chicago, 1953.

R 5.3-4. Pawsey, J. L., and R. N. Bracewell: "Radio Astronomy," Clarendon Press, Oxford, 1955.

R 5.3-5. Bracewell, R. N., and G. W. Preston: *Astrophys. J.*, **123**: 14 (1956).

Recent developments in coronal physics are discussed in:

R 5.3-6. Evans, J. W. (ed.): "The Solar Corona," Academic Press Inc., New York, 1963.

The derivation of the equation of transfer given here for radio wavelengths is standard, but it has been questioned in:

R 5.3-7. Oster, L.: *Astrophys. J.*, **138**: 761 (1963).

The discrepancy between coronal temperatures deduced from ionization equilibrium and from line broadening may be removed by considering dielectronic recombination, as reported in:

R 5.3-8. Burgess, A.: *Astrophys. J.*, **139**: 776 (1964).

The solar magnetic field and solar activity

6.1 INTRODUCTION

There is now no reasonable doubt that magnetic fields are of considerable importance in solar physics. They are undoubtedly of importance in the transfer of energy from the hydrogen convection zone to the solar envelope, and they certainly influence the structure of the corona. However, the most spectacular and obvious manifestations of the solar magnetic field are the various aspects of solar activity, particularly sunspots.

Sunspots have been observed since the time of Galileo and have been used, for example, to determine the period of solar rotation. Other forms of solar activity, such as flares, can cause geophysical effects such as radio communication fade-out and auroras. In this chapter, we discuss the possibility of a general solar magnetic field, sunspots, faculae, flares, prominences, and the concept of a "center of activity."

Much of the discussion is, of necessity, descriptive and phenomenological; much of the physical theory involved properly comes under the heading "solar electrodynamics or solar hydromagnetics," an unsettled field. We conclude this introduction by quoting T. G. Cowling, who remarks: "Solar hydromagnetics is a fascinating subject and one which is very imperfectly understood; but it is also one in which the probability of being led astray by seductive theories is very high."

6.2 BASIC HYDROMAGNETICS

We now sketch the basic principles and some illustrative results of magnetohydrodynamics. These concepts are most important in the discussion of solar activity and the solar magnetic field.

Basic equations

It is considered that the solar atmosphere is essentially electrically neutral, that is,

$$N_e = N_i Z \tag{1}$$

where N_e is the electron density, N_i is the ion density, and Z is the absolute value of the ionic charge in units of the electron charge. The condition is valid because the charged particles always tend to restore electrical neutrality, unless a special mechanism is available to maintain very large potential differences. As long as the dimension of the region greatly exceeds the Debye shielding length, Eq. (6.2-1) is a good approximation. Also, in the solar atmosphere as well as in many other applications (except rapid oscillations), neglect of Maxwell's displacement current is a good approximation. Thus, Maxwell's equations become

$$\text{curl } \mathbf{B} = 4\pi \mathbf{j} \tag{2}$$
$$\text{div } \mathbf{B} = 0 \tag{3}$$
$$\text{curl } \mathbf{E} = -\frac{\partial \mathbf{B}}{\partial t} \tag{4}$$
$$\text{div } \mathbf{E} = 0 \tag{5}$$

Here $\mathbf{j}$ is the current density, $\mathbf{B}$ is the magnetic field in gauss (if q is in electromagnetic units and the velocity $\mathbf{w}$ is in centimeters per second, then the magnetic force in dynes is $q\mathbf{w} \times \mathbf{B}$), and $\mathbf{E}$ is the electric field (such that $q\mathbf{E}$ is the electric force, in dynes). We use $\mathbf{B}$ instead of $\mathbf{H}$ in Eq. (6.2-2), since we treat all plasma currents explicitly.

The equations of motion for the ions and electrons can be derived from the Boltzmann equation for a group of identical particles,

$$\frac{\partial f}{\partial t} + \sum_j w_j \frac{\partial f}{\partial x_j} + \sum_j \frac{F_j}{m} \frac{\partial f}{\partial w_j} = \left(\frac{\partial f}{\partial t}\right)_{coll} \tag{6}$$

where w_j is the jth component of the particle velocity, F_j is the jth component of the force, and f is the distribution function which is defined by $f(t;\mathbf{r},\mathbf{w})$ times the spatial volume element $(dx\, dy\, dz)$ times the volume element in velocity space $(dw_x\, dw_y\, dw_z)$, giving the total number of particles in the six-dimensional volume of phase space $(dw_x\, dw_y\, dw_z\, dx\, dy\, dz)$ around $\mathbf{r}$ and $\mathbf{w}$. The right-hand side of Eq. (6.2-6) gives the change of the distribution function due to collisions; with the right-hand side set equal to zero, Eq. (6.2-6) is simply Liouville's theorem, which asserts that f is constant along a dynamical trajectory. We ignore the time dependence of the distribution function. The equations we desire can be obtained by multiplying Eq. (6.2-6) by $m\mathbf{w}$ and integrating over all possible velocities. The force in the third term of Eq. (6.2-6) has parts due to gravitational forces and electromagnetic forces and is

$$\mathbf{F} = q(\mathbf{E} + \mathbf{w} \times \mathbf{B}) + m\mathbf{g} \tag{7}$$

The charge q is in emu (electromagnetic units); the charge on the electron (emu) is e/c, where $e = 4.8 \times 10^{-10}$ esu (electrostatic units). The macroscopic equation of motion for ions is then

$$N_i m_i \left(\frac{\partial \mathbf{v}_i}{\partial t} + \mathbf{v}_i \cdot \nabla \mathbf{v}_i\right) = N_i q_i(\mathbf{E} + \mathbf{v}_i \times \mathbf{B}) - \nabla P_i + N_i m_i \mathbf{g} + \mathbf{P}_i^* \tag{8}$$

Here we have assumed that the random velocities are isotropic to reduce the term involving the stress tensor to the term in the scalar pressure P. This also assumes, in essence, that viscous forces are negligible. The term $\mathbf{P}_i^*$ comes from the collision term in Eq. (6.2-6) and represents the momentum transferred to the ions from the other constituents. Also

$$\mathbf{v}_i = \frac{1}{N_i} \int\!\!\!\int\!\!\!\int_{-\infty}^{+\infty} \mathbf{w} f\, dw_x\, dw_y\, dw_z \tag{9}$$

To derive the linearized equation of motion, we first assume that the gas is composed of electrons and one kind of ion. The various macroscopic quantities are

$$\mathbf{v} = \frac{1}{\rho} [N_i m_i \mathbf{v}_i + N_e m_e \mathbf{v}_e] \tag{10}$$

$$\mathbf{j} = q_i N_i \mathbf{v}_i + q_e N_e \mathbf{v}_e \tag{11}$$

$$\rho = N_i m_i + N_e m_e \tag{12}$$

Then we add Eq. (6.2-8) (for ions) to the analogous equation for electrons assuming electrical neutrality [Eq. (6.2-1)] and neglecting quadratic terms in the velocity and terms in m_e/m_i as compared to 1. The result is

$$\rho \frac{\partial \mathbf{v}}{\partial t} = \mathbf{j} \times \mathbf{B} - \nabla P + \rho \mathbf{g} \tag{13}$$

This equation is simply the mass times the acceleration being set equal to the magnetic force, the pressure force, and the external force (usually gravitation). The interaction terms do not appear in this equation, because $\mathbf{P}_i^* = -\mathbf{P}_e^*$ from Newton's third law.

An additional equation can be derived by considering Eq. (6.2-8) for ions multiplied by Z/m_i and subtracting from it the equation analogous to Eq. (6.2-8) for electrons multiplied by $1/m_e$ (neglecting quadratic terms in $\mathbf{j}$ and its derivatives in addition to the simplifications used above). The same relation can be derived in an illustrative manner by considering the flow of the electrons relative to the ion gas, which essentially moves at a velocity $\mathbf{v}$. If we let $\mathbf{V}$ be the velocity of the electrons relative to the ions, then the current density is simply

$$\mathbf{j} = -N_e q_e \mathbf{V} \tag{14}$$

The various forces per unit volume are the gradient of the electron pressure, the total electric force, and the drag caused by collisions with the positive ions. Because of the small mass and hence large q/m of the electrons, the gravitational force can be neglected. The drag force is computed by assuming that the electrons transfer momentum in the amount $m_e \mathbf{V}$ at each collision. If the collision frequency is denoted by ν, the retarding force per unit volume is $N_e m_e \mathbf{V} \nu$. Thus, the equation for equilibrium (which is reached quite rapidly because of the small electron mass) is

$$\nabla P_e + N_e q_e [\mathbf{E} + (\mathbf{v} + \mathbf{V}) \times \mathbf{B}] + N_e m_e \mathbf{V} \nu = 0 \tag{15}$$

Rearranging Eq. (6.2-15) and using Eq. (6.2-14) gives

$$\nabla P_e + N_e q_e [\mathbf{E} + (\mathbf{v} \times \mathbf{B})] = + \frac{m_e \nu \mathbf{j}}{q_e} + \mathbf{j} \times \mathbf{B} \tag{16}$$

We introduce the scalar conductivity, defined in the absence of a magnetic field by

$$\sigma = \frac{N_e q_e^2}{\nu m_e} \tag{17}$$

Note also that the term $\mathbf{E} + (\mathbf{v} \times \mathbf{B})$ is simply the electric field as seen by an observer moving at the velocity of the fluid $\mathbf{v}$; we set $\mathbf{E} + (\mathbf{v} \times \mathbf{B}) = \mathbf{E}_1$. In addition, we set $\nabla P_e/N_e q_e = \mathbf{E}_2$. Collecting these definitions, we may write Eq. (6.2-16) as

$$j = \sigma \left(E_2 + E_1 - \frac{j \times B}{N_e q_e} \right) \tag{18}$$

Recalling the definition of σ and using the cyclotron frequency,

$$\omega_c = \frac{q_e B}{m_e} \tag{19}$$

$[\omega_c = 2\pi f_B,\ f_B$ from Eq. (5.3-39)] Eq. (6.2-18) can be rewritten as

$$j = \sigma(E_2 + E_1) - \frac{\omega_c}{B\nu} (j \times B) \tag{20}$$

Putting this expression for j [i.e., the *left*-hand-side of Eq. (6.2-20)] in the *right*-hand-side of equation (6.2-20) gives

$$j \left[1 + \left(\frac{\omega_c}{\nu} \right)^2 \right] - \left(\frac{\omega_c}{B\nu} \right)^2 (j \cdot B)B$$
$$= \sigma \left[(E_2 + E_1) - \frac{\omega_c}{B\nu} (E_2 + E_1) \times B \right] \tag{21}$$

We have used the expansion for the triple vector product in obtaining Eq. (6.2-21). If $E_2 + E_1$ is parallel to B, it is clear from the Eq. (6.1-21) that j is parallel to B, and we have

$$j_{\parallel} = \sigma(E_2 + E_1) \tag{22}$$

This is simply Ohm's law, and hence the conduction along the lines of force is not reduced by the magnetic field. This is not the case for other orientations. If $E_2 + E_1$ is perpendicular to B, then the right-hand side of Eq. (6.2-21) is entirely perpendicular to B. Then, the only way the equation can be satisfied is if $j \cdot B = 0$. Hence, the current flows only in the plane perpendicular to B and is

$$j_{\perp} = \frac{\sigma \left[(E_2 + E_1) - \frac{\omega_c}{B\nu} (E_2 + E_1) \times B \right]}{1 + (\omega_c/\nu)^2} \tag{23}$$

The second term in this equation gives the Hall current, which is perpendicular to the effective electric field and to B; the Hall current is directly related to particle drifts (Sec. 18.9). The first term indicates that the conductivity along $E_2 + E_1$ (and hence perpendicular to B) is reduced by a factor of $[1 + (\omega_c/\nu)^2]^{-1}$. This result is physically understandable, because it is collisions that enable the electrons to diffuse across the lines of force instead of just spiraling about them like free particles. A similar result apparently holds for the coefficient of thermal conductivity K, which is unaffected along the magnetic field and reduced by a factor $[1 + (\omega_c/\nu)^2]^{-1}$ perpendicular to the field. The collision drag results in energy dissipation by the electrons in the amount $N_e m_e V^2 \nu = j^2/\sigma$ ergs/cm^3. The effect of neutral particles (such as atomic hydrogen) is to reduce the conductivity due to the additional collisions. Collisions of electrons with neutral hydrogen can be very important because the cross section is high.

The electron collision frequency in a proton-electron gas is roughly

$$\nu = 15 N_e T^{-3/2} \tag{24}$$

and hence the conductivity is approximately

$$\sigma = 2 \times 10^{-14} T^{3/2} \tag{25}$$

Equation (6.2-24) is a simplification of the full expression given by Eq. (5.3-28). From Eqs. (6.2-24) and (6.2-19), and taking account of the effect of neutrals, it appears that $B > 10^3$ gauss is a necessary condition for $\nu \approx \omega_c$ anywhere in the main body of the Sun. Thus, effects of the magnetic field in limiting conduction are important only in the chromosphere and the corona.

Frozen-in fields

As long as $\omega_c/\nu < 1$ and the gradient of the electron pressure is negligible, we see from Eqs. (6.2-23) and (6.2-22) that

$$\mathbf{j} = \sigma(\mathbf{E} + \mathbf{v} \times \mathbf{B}) \tag{26}$$

Equations (6.2-26) and (6.2-4) give

$$\frac{\partial \mathbf{B}}{\partial t} = \mathbf{curl}\ (\mathbf{v} \times \mathbf{B}) - \mathbf{curl}\left(\frac{\mathbf{j}}{\sigma}\right) \tag{27}$$

The current can be eliminated by using Eq. (6.2-2), and

$$\frac{\partial \mathbf{B}}{\partial t} = \mathbf{curl}\ (\mathbf{v} \times \mathbf{B}) - \frac{1}{4\pi\sigma}\ \mathbf{curl\ curl\ B} \tag{28}$$

where we assume that σ is constant. Using the expansion for the last term,

$$\mathbf{curl\ curl\ A} = \nabla(\nabla \cdot \mathbf{A}) - \nabla^2\mathbf{A} \tag{29}$$

we obtain

$$\frac{\partial \mathbf{B}}{\partial t} = \mathbf{curl}\ (\mathbf{v} \times \mathbf{B}) + \frac{1}{4\pi\sigma}\ \nabla^2\mathbf{B} \tag{30}$$

If there are no fluid motions, $\mathbf{v} = 0$ and we have the diffusion equation,

$$\frac{\partial \mathbf{B}}{\partial t} = \frac{1}{4\pi\sigma} \nabla^2 \mathbf{B} \tag{31}$$

This equation is discussed in Sec. 6.3. As to orders of magnitude, the two terms on the right-hand side of equation (6.2-30) are vB/ℓ and $B/4\pi\sigma\ell^2$, respectively, where ℓ is a characteristic dimension. Hence, when $v \ll 1/4\pi\sigma\ell$, Eq. (6.2-31) is applicable. The quantity $4\pi\sigma\ell v$ is called the magnetic Reynolds number; if we introduce the resistivity $\eta = (4\pi\sigma)^{-1}$, the magnetic Reynolds number becomes $\ell v/\eta$ and the analogy with the ordinary Reynolds number [(Eq. (5.1-31)] is exhibited.

On the other hand, if $v \gg 1/4\pi\sigma\ell$, Eq. (6.2-30) becomes

$$\frac{\partial \mathbf{B}}{\partial t} = \mathbf{curl}\ (\mathbf{v} \times \mathbf{B}) \tag{32}$$

Equation (6.2-32) is usually a consequence of the large conductivity and large characteristic dimensions. In this case $\mathbf{E} + \mathbf{v} \times \mathbf{B}$, the electric field as seen by an observer moving with the fluid, must essentially vanish [see Eq. (6.2-26)]. The electric field results from the rate of change of the magnetic flux, which in turn results from the motion of the material across the lines of force. Since the conductivity is extremely large, the effective electric field must vanish, and hence the lines of force must move with the material. In this case the lines are said to be frozen-in.

This concept can be made quantitative by considering the magnetic flux through a surface area $\mathbf{s}$. The condition for the field lines being frozen-in is that

$$\frac{d}{dt} \int_{\text{surf}} \mathbf{B} \cdot \mathbf{ds} = 0 \tag{33}$$

Changes in the flux occur for two reasons: (1) the magnetic field can change with time and (2) the lines of force are cut owing to the motion of the boundary of the area $\mathbf{s}$. The specification of these two terms yields

$$\int_{\text{surf}} \frac{\partial \mathbf{B}}{\partial t} \cdot \mathbf{ds} + \int_{\text{line}} \mathbf{B} \cdot (\mathbf{v} \times \mathbf{ds}) = 0 \tag{34}$$

The second term is obtained by noting that the vector area swept out by the line per unit time is $\mathbf{v} \times \mathbf{ds}$. The second integral can be transformed by using Stokes theorem, and

$$\int_{\text{surf}} \left[\frac{\partial \mathbf{B}}{\partial t} - \mathbf{curl}\ (\mathbf{v} \times \mathbf{B}) \right] \cdot \mathbf{ds} = 0 \tag{35}$$

Since Eq. (6.2-35) must be satisfied regardless of s, Eq. (6.2-32) follows; hence, Eq. (6.2-32) is completely equivalent to Eq. (6.2-33), i.e., frozen-in lines of force.

The application of an external force can cause slippage of the lines of force with respect to the material. The relative velocity is set by the induced force canceling the impressed force.

Magnetic pressure and tension

The concept of the magnetic pressure can be illustrated by considering Eq. (6.2-13) for a steady state

$$0 = \mathbf{j} \times \mathbf{B} - \nabla P + \rho \mathbf{g} \tag{36}$$

The vector product of $\mathbf{B}$ with Eq. (6.2-36) with the acceleration of gravity neglected gives

$$\mathbf{B} \times (\mathbf{j} \times \mathbf{B}) = B^2 \mathbf{j} = \mathbf{B} \times \nabla P \tag{37}$$

or

$$\mathbf{j} = \frac{\mathbf{B} \times \nabla P}{B^2} \tag{38}$$

Thus, the effect of a pressure gradient is to produce a current transverse to the magnetic field. The action of this current can be seen by substituting for $\mathbf{j}$ from Maxwell's equation for the current [Eq. (6.2-2)] in Eq. (6.2-36) for zero gravity to yield

$$\nabla P = \mathbf{j} \times \mathbf{B} \tag{39}$$

$$= \frac{\operatorname{curl} \mathbf{B} \times \mathbf{B}}{4\pi} \tag{40}$$

$$= \frac{\mathbf{B} \cdot \nabla \mathbf{B}}{4\pi} - \frac{\nabla B^2}{8\pi} \tag{41}$$

If the lines of force are such that $\mathbf{B} \cdot \nabla \mathbf{B}$ is zero (e.g., straight and parallel), Eq. (6.2-41) immediately integrates to give

$$P + \frac{B^2}{8\pi} = \operatorname{const} \tag{42}$$

For this case, a simple interpretation of the term $B^2/8\pi$ as a magnetic pressure is possible. The first term on the right-hand side of Eq. (6.2-41) can be interpreted as a tension along the lines of force of magnitude $B^2/4\pi$. Thus, the magnetic force $\mathbf{j} \times \mathbf{B}$ can be interpreted as a hydrostatic pressure of $B^2/8\pi$ plus a tension $B^2/4\pi$ along the lines of force. We find again (below) that the lines of magnetic force can be considered as elastic strings in the propagation of waves. We note that the magnetic pressure $B^2/8\pi$ is equal to the magnetic energy density.

Alfvén waves

There are three elementary types of waves or oscillations which can exist in a plasma:

1. Electromagnetic waves; these are physically the same as ordinary electromagnetic waves propagating through a vacuum. Their propagation through a plasma is not simple, although a simple case is treated in Sec. 5.3 on the corona. We do not consider them further here.

2. Plasma oscillations, discussed in the next subsection. They result from an electrostatic restoring force.

3. Hydromagnetic waves.

Consider a region of infinite extent composed of an infinitely conducting, incompressible fluid in which a uniform magnetic field is embedded. In this region, Eq. (6.2-32) is applicable; since div $\mathbf{v} = 0$ (incompressible fluid) and div $\mathbf{B} = 0$, the standard expression for the curl of a vector can be used to simplify Eq. (6.2-32) to

$$\frac{\partial \mathbf{B}}{\partial t} = (\mathbf{B} \cdot \nabla)\mathbf{v} - (\mathbf{v} \cdot \nabla)\mathbf{B} \tag{43}$$

We now introduce a disturbance into the magnetic field by replacing $\mathbf{B}$ by $\mathbf{B}_0 + \mathbf{b}$ in the last equation. Neglecting second-order quantities in $\mathbf{v}$ and $\mathbf{b}$, we find

$$\frac{\partial \mathbf{b}}{\partial t} = (\mathbf{B}_0 \cdot \nabla)\mathbf{v} \tag{44}$$

If we take the magnetic field lines along the x direction, Eq. (6.2-44) becomes

$$\frac{\partial \mathbf{b}}{\partial t} = B_0 \frac{\partial \mathbf{v}}{\partial x} \tag{45}$$

If we consider that $\mathbf{j}$ is small (since it is the product of a small disturbance) and again neglect the product of small quantities, Eq. (6.2-13) becomes

$$\rho \frac{\partial \mathbf{v}}{\partial t} = \mathbf{j} \times \mathbf{B}_0 - \nabla P + \rho \mathbf{g} \tag{46}$$

This can be written as

$$\rho \frac{\partial \mathbf{v}}{\partial t} = -\nabla \left(P + \frac{\mathbf{B}_0 \cdot \mathbf{b}}{4\pi} \right) + \rho \mathbf{g} + \frac{B_0}{4\pi} \frac{\partial \mathbf{b}}{\partial x} \tag{47}$$

since **curl** $\mathbf{b} = 4\pi\mathbf{j}$. Application of the divergence operator to the last equation leaves only the first two terms on the right-hand side, since div $\mathbf{v} = 0 = $ div $\mathbf{b}$. This result can be written as

$$\nabla^2 \left(P + \frac{\mathbf{B}_0 \cdot \mathbf{b}}{4\pi} \right) = \nabla \cdot \rho \mathbf{g} = \nabla^2 P_0 \tag{48}$$

where P_0 is the pressure away from the disturbance where $b = 0$. The solution can be written as

$$\nabla^2 \left(P - P_0 + \frac{\mathbf{B}_0 \cdot \mathbf{b}}{4\pi} \right) = 0 \tag{49}$$

Thus we have obtained a solution of Laplace's equation. This solution has the property that it vanishes away from the disturbance, and hence, as a solution of Laplace's equation, it vanishes everywhere. This property greatly simplifies Eq. (6.2-47) to

$$\rho \frac{\partial \mathbf{v}}{\partial t} = \frac{B_0}{4\pi} \frac{\partial \mathbf{b}}{\partial x} \tag{50}$$

Differentiating the last equation with respect to t and using Eq. (6.2-45) gives

$$\frac{\partial^2 \mathbf{v}}{\partial t^2} = \left(\frac{B_0^2}{4\pi\rho} \right) \frac{\partial^2 \mathbf{v}}{\partial x^2} \tag{51}$$

Similarly,

$$\frac{\partial^2 \mathbf{b}}{\partial t^2} = \left(\frac{B_0^2}{4\pi\rho} \right) \frac{\partial^2 \mathbf{b}}{\partial x^2} \tag{52}$$

The last two equations are simply wave equations representing waves traveling in opposite directions along the x axis with velocity

$$v_A = \frac{B_0}{(4\pi\rho)^{1/2}} \tag{53}$$

which is called the Alfvén velocity [$= V_A$ of Eq. (5.1-36)]. This is the same result that follows from considering the lines of force as elastic strings with a tension of $B^2/4\pi$.

The velocity and the magnetic disturbance are related through $\mathbf{b} = \pm (4\pi\rho)^{1/2}\mathbf{v}$. In this case, the kinetic energy per unit volume $\frac{1}{2}\rho v^2$ is equal to the magnetic energy per unit volume $b^2/8\pi$.

The foregoing derivation contains several idealizations which must be kept in mind. The fluid was taken to be incompressible; the compressibility is not important as long as the sound velocity v_s is large compared to the Alfvén velocity V_A. When $v_s \approx V_A$, the Alfvén waves interact with sound waves and hybrid waves are produced; the latter are discussed in Sec. 5.1, which concerns the heating of the chromosphere and corona.

When $V_A \gg v_s$, the wave is essentially a sound wave traveling at the velocity of sound along the lines of force.

The fact that we have assumed a constant ρ and B_0 also needs mention. As long as the variations of ρ and B_0 occur slowly, the theory given above applies locally. Under some circumstances, the corrections due to nonuniformity and the finite amplitude of the waves can become very involved. Nonetheless, the picture sketched above is a rather useful one.

Plasma oscillations

We consider the oscillations that occur if, for some reason, a charge separation occurs. If the force sustaining the charge separation is removed, the electric field tends to remove the charge separation and oscillations can occur. We recall the derivation of Eq. (6.2-15) under the assumption that $\partial \mathbf{j}/\partial t = 0$. We now write the appropriate equation with this term remaining, but for the collisionless case (formally, $\sigma = \infty$) and $\mathbf{B} = 0$. This gives

$$\frac{m_e}{N_e q_e^2} \frac{\partial \mathbf{j}}{\partial t} = \mathbf{E} + \frac{\nabla P_e}{N_e q_e} \tag{54}$$

Since we are now admitting the possibility of charge separation, we must write

$$\text{div } \mathbf{E} = 4\pi c^2 \rho_c \tag{55}$$

where the charge density, ρ_c is given by

$$\rho_c = +q_e(N_i Z - N_e) \tag{56}$$

Since charge is conserved, we also have

$$\frac{\partial \rho_c}{\partial t} + \nabla \cdot \mathbf{j} = 0 \tag{57}$$

We now take the divergence of Eq. (6.2-54) and eliminate div $\mathbf{E}$ and div $\mathbf{j}$ with the aid of Eqs. (6.2-55) and (6.2-57) to obtain

$$-\frac{m_e}{N_e q_e^2} \frac{\partial^2 \rho_c}{\partial t^2} = 4\pi c^2 \rho_c + \frac{\text{div } \nabla P_e}{N_e q_e} \tag{58}$$

The gradient of the electron pressure can be found from the assumption that the variations are adiabatic, i.e.,

$$\nabla P_e = \gamma k T_e \nabla N_e \tag{59}$$

Here γ is the ratio of the specific heats, and γ is also approximately $(2 + n)/n$, where n is the number of degrees of freedom. Since we are considering a one-dimensional oscillation, we set $\gamma = 3$. The gradient of the electron density can be evaluated in terms of the charge density ρ_c, where we consider that the ions are uniform and motionless. This gives $\nabla \rho_c = -q_e \nabla N_e$. Notice that we are treating strictly electron oscillations with the positive ions regarded as stationary; hence, $\mathbf{v}$ is nearly zero. Collecting these results gives

$$\frac{\partial^2 \rho_c}{\partial t^2} = -\frac{4\pi c^2 N_e q_e^2}{m_e} \rho_c - \frac{3kT_e}{m_e} \nabla^2 \rho_c \qquad (60a)$$

$$= -\omega_p^2 \rho_c - \frac{3kT_e}{m_e} \nabla^2 \rho_c \qquad (60b)$$

where we have the angular plasma frequency, $\omega_p = (4\pi c^2 N_e q_e^2 / m_e)^{1/2}$. Note that ω_p is related to the plasma frequency f_0 introduced in Eq. (5.3-27) by $\omega_p = 2\pi f_0$. This equation can be solved by assuming a solution of the form $\cos(\ell x + \omega t)$. The frequency is found to be

$$\omega^2 = \omega_p^2 + \ell^2 \frac{3kT_e}{m_e} \qquad (61)$$

At a given point the charge density ρ_c varies periodically with frequency ω. This is clearly a collective oscillation of the electrons. Thus the plasma oscillates at the plasma frequency for very low temperatures, but at higher temperatures, the wavelength of the disturbance needs to be taken into account.

These plasma (that is, electron) oscillations may find application in the explanation of certain solar radio phenomena. However, it is not clear how the oscillations are excited; presumably, a passing disturbance can be the cause.

Radiation from plasmas

There are several ways in which a pure proton-electron plasma can radiate. Here we briefly describe them. In a steady-state plasma, the number of recombinations equals the number of ionizations. Even in a nonequilibrium situation, recombinations occur, and for densities normally encountered the mode is radiative recombination. This means that a photon is given off with a total energy equal to the ionization energy plus the kinetic energy of the recombining electron. The capture cross section has a dependence on the principal quantum number n, which gives approximately 43 per cent of the recombination into the ground state ($n = 1$) at 10^4 °K. Ground-state recombination produces radiation at wavelength $\lambda < 912$ A (the Lyman continuum). Recombinations to other states produce other continua and lines by cascading. Note that the energy loss in any case is as if the recombination occurred to the ground state.

Energy can be emitted by electrons in the presence of positive ions via free-free transitions; these produce free-free radiation or bremsstrahlung. For a maxwellian distribution of speeds at a temperature T, the energy emitted in the wavelength interval from λ to $\lambda + d\lambda$ is approximately proportional to

$$\frac{e^{-(hc/\lambda kT)}}{\lambda^2} \, d\lambda \tag{62}$$

It is readily seen from the Eq. (6.2-62) that the emission per unit wavelength interval has a maximum near the mean particle energy.

Radiation from plasma oscillations at the plasma frequency can occur as discussed above.

When magnetic fields are present, gyro radiation can be produced by electrons spiraling under the influence of the Lorentz force. At low velocities, the electron radiates primarily at the gyrofrequency,

$$\nu_B = f_B = \frac{eB}{2\pi m_e c} = \frac{q_e B}{2\pi m_e} \tag{63}$$

However, when the energies of the electrons become relativistic, that is, $E \gg m_e c^2$, the harmonics become important. These merge into a continuous spectrum with a maximum near

$$\nu_{\max} = \nu_B \left(\frac{E}{m_e c^2}\right)^2 \tag{64}$$

This radiation is called synchrotron radiation or magnetic bremsstrahlung. The physical basis for synchrotron radiation comes from the (Liénard-Wiechert) retarded potentials.

It also follows from the retarded potentials that radiation can occur for the case of uniform motion at velocity v of a charged particle through a medium with index of refraction n such that $v > c/n$. This is Čerenkov radiation, and it may be important at radio wavelengths.

The addition of impurities to a proton-electron plasma can greatly complicate the picture. The heavy ions take part in the recombination and free-free transitions. However, at certain temperatures ($\sim 10^6$ °K) excitation of permitted lines by electron collisions can become very important and completely dominate the energy loss by radiation.

6.3 THE GENERAL MAGNETIC FIELD

For some time, there was considerable doubt of the existence of a general, solar magnetic field, in that attempts to measure it were negative or inconsistent. Indirect evidence did exist, however. A general magnetic field is implied by coronal structural forms (e.g., polar rays, see Fig. 5.3-4), which are very suggestive of a poloidal field. Additional indirect arguments can be given for magnetic fields *outside* sunspots, such as the chromospheric fine structure observed in Hα spectroheliograms of regions near sunspots (Fig. 6.3-1). Unfortunately, one cannot be certain that evidence for magnetic fields near but outside sunspots is evidence for a general solar magnetic field.

Ultimately, the existence of a general magnetic field depends on the direct measurement of the field. Equipment based on the magnetic splitting of spectral lines by the Zeeman effect has been developed for measuring the general field. Modern equipment can detect magnetic fields down to 0.3 gauss, and thus a general magnetic field of approximately 1 gauss at

Fig. 6.3-1 An Hα spectroheliogram (flare) showing chromospheric fine structure suggesting a magnetic field. (*Courtesy of Mount Wilson and Palomar Observatories.*)

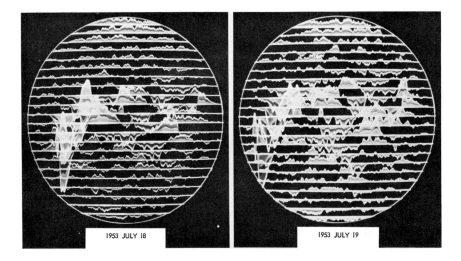

1953 JULY 18   1953 JULY 19

THESE MAGNETIC MAPS OF THE SUN'S DISK SHOW THE LOCATION, FIELD INTENSITY, AND POLARITY OF WEAK MAGNETIC FIELDS IN THE PHOTOSPHERE OF THE SUN, APART FROM SUNSPOTS. THE RECORDS ARE MADE AUTOMATICALLY BY A SCANNING SYSTEM THAT EMPLOYS A POLARIZING ANALYZER, A POWERFUL SPECTROGRAPH, AND A SENSITIVE PHOTOELECTRIC DETECTOR FOR MEASURING THE LONGITUDINAL COMPONENT OF THE MAGNETIC FIELD BY MEANS OF THE ZEEMAN EFFECT. A DEFLECTION OF ONE TRACE INTERVAL CORRESPONDS TO A FIELD OF ABOUT ONE GAUSS. THE SMALL DEFLECTIONS OF OPPOSITE MAGNETIC POLARITY NEAR THE NORTH AND SOUTH POLES ARE INDICATIVE OF THE SUN'S "GENERAL MAGNETIC FIELD". THE EXTENDED FIELDS NEAR THE EQUATOR ARISE FROM CHARACTERISTIC "BM" (BIPOLAR MAGNETIC) REGIONS THAT SOMETIMES PRODUCE SPOTS. NORTH IS AT TOP, EAST AT RIGHT.

Fig. 6.3-2   Solar magnetograms. (*Courtesy of H. W. Babcock, Mount Wilson and Palomar Observatories.*)

solar latitudes of greater than $\pm 55°$ is firmly established. A magnetogram showing the weak field at high latitudes is reproduced in Fig. 6.3-2.

The origin and maintenance of a general solar magnetic field has been a stimulating challenge, and many theories have been proposed:

1. One may suppose that the field is essentially a fossil—a natural product of the Sun's process of formation. A decay time for a magnetic field can be estimated from Eq. (6.2-30) which, for a material at rest, becomes

$$4\pi\sigma \frac{\partial \mathbf{B}}{\partial t} = \nabla^2 \mathbf{B} \tag{1}$$

The conductivity σ may be approximated by

$$\sigma = 2 \times 10^{-14} \frac{T^{3/2}}{Z} \tag{2}$$

where Z is the ionic charge. The conductivity is probably not altered by the effect of magnetic fields in the solar interior. If we seek only orders of

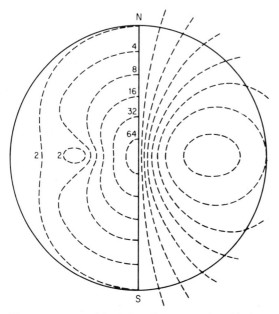

Fig. 6.3-3   A model of the solar magnetic field showing (right half) lines of force and (left half) constant
magnetic intensity given as a multiple of the equatorial
intensity at the surface. (*Courtesy of T. G. Cowling
and The Monthly Notices of the Royal Astronomical
Society, from R* 6.3-1.)

magnitude, Eq. (6.3-1) can be written as

$$\frac{4\pi\sigma B}{t_0} \approx \frac{B}{\ell^2} \qquad (3a)$$

or

$$t_0 = 4\pi\sigma\ell^2 \qquad (3b)$$

Here ℓ is a characteristic linear dimension. Note that the decay time is
independent of the magnitude of the field. The form of Eq. (6.3-1) is that
of a diffusion equation; it indicates that the decay occurs by the field leak-
ing into regions where the field is in the opposite direction, with subsequent
neutralization.

For a general solar field, we adopt a characteristic dimension of $R_\odot/3$
($\ell \approx 2 \times 10^{10}$ cm) and $\sigma \approx 10^{-4}$ emu (for solar interior conditions).
These numbers give a t_0 of 10^{10} yr—greater than the age of the solar system. Detailed calculations confirm this estimate; the configuration giving
the longest decay time is shown in Fig. 6.3-3. The only way to obtain a t_0
much lower than 10^{10} years would be to confine the field to a thin layer near
the surface where the conductivity would be greatly reduced. Such a field

is shown in Fig. 6.3-4. In this case, $\ell \approx R_\odot/10$, and with $T \approx 2 \times 10^5\,°\mathrm{K}$, $\sigma \approx 2 \times 10^{-6}$. This gives $t_0 \approx 10^7$ yr.

Other theories of the general solar magnetic field provide for current production or maintenance. These are briefly:

2. Origin in the solar rotation due to the motion of electric charges. The net charge of solar material is very small and the field resulting from rotation is negligible.

3. Thermal and pressure theories. Gradients of the electron pressure and solar rotation can produce currents flowing in meridianal planes which, in turn, produce an azimuthal magnetic field. However, the solar field is thought to be poloidal. It is more difficult to produce a poloidal field, and pressure theories are probably inadequate.

4. Dynamo theories. Here the motion of solar material across the lines of force of an existing field produces currents, and these currents are thought to maintain the field. Attempts to establish dynamo mechanisms have not met with success; on the other hand, it has not been possible to disprove the dynamo mechanism.

5. Turbulent magnetic fields. One might suppose that the interaction of turbulent motions with the field could produce a turbulent magnetic field by a process roughly analogous to equipartition. The result of such a mechanism is to build up an irregular, small-scale field which probably cannot be identified with the general solar field.

This concludes our brief survey of the problems associated with a general solar magnetic field. We probably do not have even a working

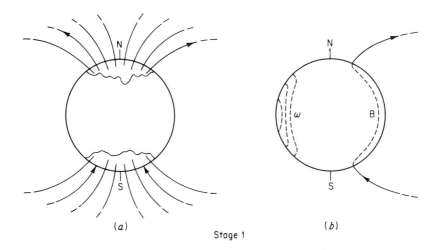

(a)   (b)

Stage 1

Fig. 6.3-4   Babcock's model of the solar magnetic field showing the polar field lines, the submerged field lines in the equatorial regions, and the surfaces of constant angular velocity (labeled ω). (*Copyright 1961 by the University of Chicago, published by the University of Chicago press, from R 6.3-2.*)

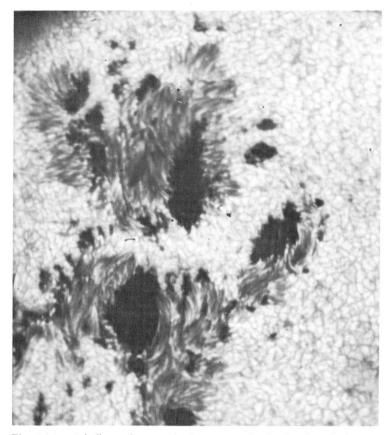

Fig. 6.4-1. A balloon photograph of sunspots clearly showing the features described in the text. (*Courtesy of Project Stratascope of Princeton University, sponsored by the Office of Naval Research, the National Science Foundation, and the National Aeronautics and Space Administration.*)

hypothesis of its origin, but the existence of a general solar magnetic field appears to be established. We note that the general field reverses polarity with the same period as the solar cycle; this is a demanding requirement on any theory of the general solar magnetic field.

6.4 SUNSPOTS

Basic Data

Sunspots are dark markings on the Sun composed of a dark center called the umbra and a border region called the penumbra (Fig. 6.4-1). The umbra is rather structureless, but granulation has been found in it. With good seeing conditions, the penumbra is found to consist of a group of small filaments radially oriented with respect to the center of the umbra. The ratio of the diameter of the penumbra d_p to the diameter of the umbra d_u is somewhat independent of spot size (as long as the spots are not too small or too large) and has the value $d_p/d_u \approx 2.4$. This value is lower for large spots. Some well-developed spots show a bright ring around the penumbra some 2 to 3 per cent brighter than the photosphere. The diameter of a sunspot ranges from several thousand to several tens of thousand kilometers. A large spot group (Fig. 6.4-2) can attain lengths of over 100,000 km. The shape of the upper boundary of sunspots can be inferred from direct observations, and it is concluded that the upper surface is actually a shallow, depressed area.

The formation of a spot group begins with the appearance of a small spot or pore between the granules. Ordinarily, the appearance of one pore is associated with the appearance of other, nearby pores, and a young spot group develops. This young spot group may disappear after a few hours, or it may develop into a large group similar to the one shown in Fig. 6.4-2.

The number of spots on the Sun is not the same at all times. As a measure of the number of spots visible on the solar surface, we have the Wolf "relative sunspot number,"

$$R = k(10g + f) \tag{1}$$

where f is the number of individual sunspots and g is the number of groups. The factor k is assigned to an individual observer and/or his equipment to reduce the individual sunspot numbers to a consistent scale. The Wolf system has been in use for over a hundred years and has shown itself to be of great value. Since the sunspots partake of the solar rotation, there is an obvious variation of the sunspot number over a 27-day period, and hence it is more meaningful to take 27-day means. Mean sunspot numbers beginning with the year 1700 are shown in Fig. 6.4-3. It is clear that the number of sunspots varies in a periodic manner. When the spots are very rare for some months, the situation is called sunspot minimum. At sunspot maximum, there are 10 or more groups on the disk. The average period between successive maxima is about 11.2 yr; but the cycle is not sym-

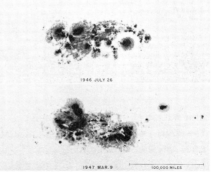

Fig. 6.4-2 Two large spot groups. (*Courtesy of the Mount Wilson Observatory.*)

1946 JULY 26

1947 MAR. 9   100,000 MILES

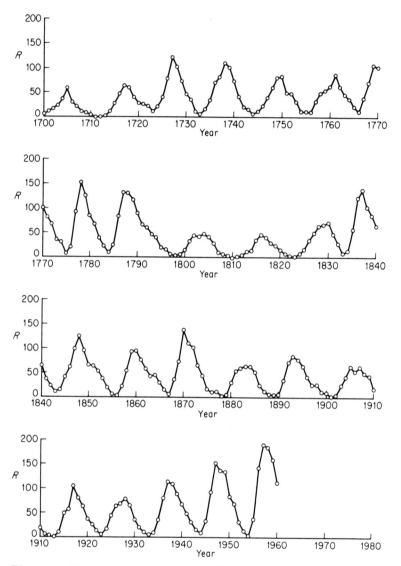

Fig. 6.4-3   The sunspot number since 1700, based on data in R 6.4-3.

metric, because it is, on the average, 6.7 yr from maximum to minimum but only 4.6 yr from minimum to maximum.

The location of sunspots on the solar disk is variable. Most all sunspots are found in two zones some 15 to 20° wide, parallel to the equator, and within ±45° latitude. The position of the sunspot zone varies through the solar cycle. It should be emphasized that only the locality of appearance varies throughout the cycle; the spots themselves have no appreciable motion in latitude during their lifetime of about 1 month. The first spots of a cycle appear at $\pm 30°$ latitude and reach $\pm 15°$ by sunspot maximum. The last spots of a cycle reach about $\pm 8°$. The phenomenon is clearly shown in a plot of the latitude of sunspots vs. time, called a butterfly diagram (Fig. 6.4-4). The migration of the sunspot zone is referred to as Spörer's law, which is clearly shown in the Maunder butterfly diagram.

Physical data for individual spots

Probably the single most important discovery (Hale, 1908) concerning sunspots is the fact that they contain magnetic fields ranging in strength from several hundred to several thousand gauss. The measurement of such fields involves the use of the Zeeman effect; classically, an observer looking along the magnetic field sees two opposite, circularly polarized components each displaced a distance $\delta\lambda$ from the normal position of the line. The displacement is given by

$$\delta\lambda = 4.7 \times 10^{-5} g\lambda^2 B \tag{2}$$

where g is the Landé factor, B is in gauss, and the wavelengths are measured in centimeters. For normal conditions encountered in sunspots, the separation $2\delta\lambda$ can amount to 0.1 A for the lines normally used (neutral iron lines in the red). The Zeeman splitting of a line in a sunspot is shown

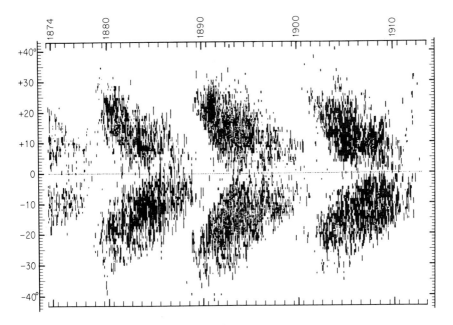

Fig. 6.4-4   The Maunder butterfly diagram showing the distribution of spot centers in heliographic latitude. (*Courtesy of the Monthly Notices of the Royal Astronomical Society, from R 6.4-4.*)

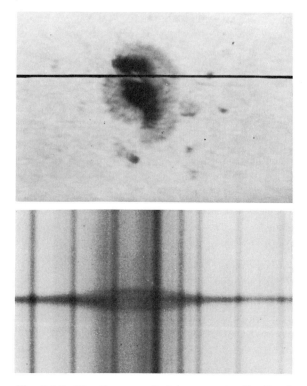

Fig. 6.4-5 The Zeeman effect in sunspots; the line is split in the sunspot and unaffected outside. (*Courtesy of the Mount Wilson and Palomar Observatories.*)

in Fig. 6.4-5. The orientation of the magnetic field in a sunspot along a diameter is shown in Fig. 6.4-6. The distribution of angles from the normal is roughly $\theta = (\rho/b) \times 90°$, where ρ is the distance from the center of the spot and b is the distance to the outer edge of the penumbra. At the boundary between umbra and penumbra, $\theta \approx 25°$.

Thus it is clear that the longitudinal Zeeman effect is appropriate for observations of sunspots near the center of the disk and the transverse Zeeman effect is appropriate for observations near the limb. In addition,

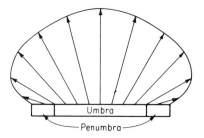

Fig. 6.4-6 A schematic diagram of the magnetic field along a sunspot diameter; the vectors represent the magnitude and direction of the field.

the effects of magnetic foreshortening and the possibility that the line is formed at different heights must be remembered when analyzing observations of sunspots taken at different positions on the disk. The distribution of field strength in a spot may be approximated as

$$B(\rho) = B_m \left(1 - \frac{\rho^2}{b^2}\right) \tag{3}$$

where B_m is the strength at the center (maximum) and ρ and b are as given above. The magnetic flux in a spot is $\approx \frac{1}{4} B_m \pi b^2$. The maximum field strength is related to the area by

$$B_m = 3700 \, \frac{A}{A + 66} \qquad \text{gauss} \tag{4}$$

where the area A is measured in millionths of the visible hemisphere.

The life history of a sunspot as shown by the variation of maximum field strength B_m and area A with time is shown in Fig. 6.4-7. Notice how

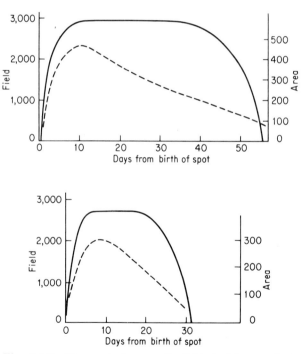

Fig. 6.4-7   The central magnetic field (solid curves), in gauss, and areas (dashed curves) in millionths of the Sun's visible hemisphere, plotted against days from birth of the sunspot. Upper curves give field for 55-day spots and area for 60-day spots; both lower curves are for 30-day spots. (*Courtesy of T. G. Cowling and The Monthly Notices of the Royal Astronomical Society, from R 6.4-6.*)

the maximum field strength remains relatively constant until the spot is on the verge of disappearing. Thus it appears that the field seems to decay by the progressive sinking or rising of the outer lines of force into the photosphere or the corona, and not by diffusion.

This viewpoint can be reinforced by a calculation of the lifetime for the magnetic field in a sunspot to decay by diffusion using Eq. (6.3-3b). In a sunspot the appropriate values are $\ell \approx 3 \times 10^8$ cm and $\sigma \approx 3 \times 10^{-8}$ emu; these values give $t_0 \approx 10^3$ years. This is a time much longer than the observed age of sunspots, and it constitutes a strong argument against diffusion. Thus, at this point, one has the impression that a sunspot appears because a subsurface field is occasionally brought up to the surface and that it disappears either by sinking back into the subsurface layers or by expanding outward into the corona.

Photometric observations of sunspots give $I_{spot}/I_{phot} \approx 0.7$ for the penumbra and $I_{spot}/I_{phot} \approx 0.3$ for the umbra. Thermocouple observations referring to the spectrum integrated over frequency give $I_{spot}/I_{phot} \approx 0.4$ for the center of an umbra. Since the emission goes as T^4, the effective temperature of a spot umbra is $\approx (0.4)^{1\!\!/\!\!4} \approx 0.795$ times the effective temperature of the photosphere. If the effective temperature for the Sun's photosphere is taken as 5750°K, the effective temperature of sunspot umbras is then 4600°K with an uncertainty of several hundred degrees. This temperature is consistent with studies of lines and bands and with the observed spot spectrum, which is classified as approximately K0. Since the surface gravity of a sunspot is the same as for the Sun, the classification must read K0 V (i.e., a main-sequence star, not a giant). This gives a temperature of about 4900°K. However, the radiation from the center of the disk is from the region of greatest temperature, and the spectral classification refers to the integrated intensity from a stellar disk. When this correction is applied, the temperature found by this method is in agreement with the value of 4600°K quoted above.

It is now known that the wavelength-energy curve and the limb-darkening profile are in reasonable agreement with an atmosphere in radiative equilibrium; hence, it is convenient to think of a sunspot as a cool portion of the photosphere, but essentially in radiative equilibrium. Models that reproduce the essential features of the observations can be constructed, but there is considerable difference between models.

Since sunspots are relatively long-lived, we may suppose that equilibrium is set up between the spot and the surrounding photosphere. Considering gas and magnetic pressure in the spot and only gas pressure in the photosphere, equilibrium requires

$$P_{spot} + \frac{B^2}{8\pi} = P_{phot} \tag{5}$$

Some of the available models satisfy this condition with $B \approx 10^3$ gauss.

Motions in sunspots have been known since 1909, when it was found that there is a general, horizontal, radial outflow from sunspots (Evershed effect) with velocities of ≈ 2 km/sec. The velocity in the faint metal lines is nearly zero in the umbra, grows in the penumbra, reaches a maximum (2 to 3 km/sec) at the border of the penumbra, decays as the material flows into the photosphere, and is nearly zero at $1.5b$ (where again b is the penumbral radius). The flow is not entirely radial because of the Coriolis force.

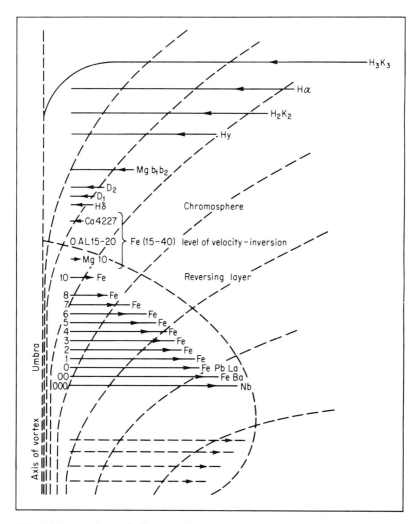

Fig. 6.4-8 A schematic diagram showing the observed velocities (proportional to the lengths of the solid lines) from each element; the magnetic field is represented by the curved, dashed lines. (*Copyright* 1913 *by the University of Chicago, Published by the University of Chicago Press, from R* 6.4-7.)

A different picture from the one described above is found when lines of different strength are used. In the stronger lines, no motion is found, and in the strongest lines (for example, H_α and the K line of Ca II), an inflow is found. The region of line formation can be thought of as increasing in height with increasing line strength, and a complete picture of the motions can be built up (Fig. 6.4-8). These motions in sunspots are not well understood.

Spot groups

Sunspots normally occur in spot groups such as the one shown in Fig. 6.4-2. Groups are usually classified as follows:

1. Unipolar groups, α. These are single spots or groups of spots with the same magnetic polarity.
2. Bipolar groups, β. The preceding (p) and following (f) spots, in the sense of the solar rotation, are of opposite polarity. The simplest form of a β spot group consists of one p and one f spot of opposite polarity.
3. Complex groups, γ. These groups have many spots of both polarities and cannot be legitimately classified as β groups.

Often, additional letters are added to the classification scheme outlined above to denote structure within the group or the relation of the spot group to faculae. There are other classification schemes in which the size or area of the group is a parameter. Roughly 90 per cent of spot groups are β, 10 per cent are α, and less than 1 per cent are γ. The distribution of magnetic fields in a γ group is shown in Fig. 6.4-9. The unipolar groups are usually the remaining p spot of an old bipolar group; often the distribution of faculae (Sec. 6.5) around a unipolar spot or group resembles the distribution of faculae around a bipolar group. In this latter case, a magnetic region is found in the expected position of the "missing" spot.

In essence, the magnetic field is often present, but for some reason, no sunspot develops. This discovery serves to emphasize that sunspots themselves are only one aspect of solar activity and that they may be only a by-product of processes which are more important. For example, faculae may well be much more important in the discussions of a bipolar magnetic region (BMR), since faculae appear before the sunspots and outlast them by several solar rotations (see Sec. 6.8).

The p and f spots of a β spot group are of opposite polarity, and the statement of the law of polarity is completed by noting that (1) the p spots are of different polarity in the northern and southern hemisphere and (2) the polarity of the p spots in each hemisphere reverses sign with each new solar cycle. The details of the polarity law and the relationship of the polarity law to the migration law are shown in Fig. 6.4-10. Since the general field also reverses polarity, it is clear that the length of the full solar cycle is actually some 22 years.

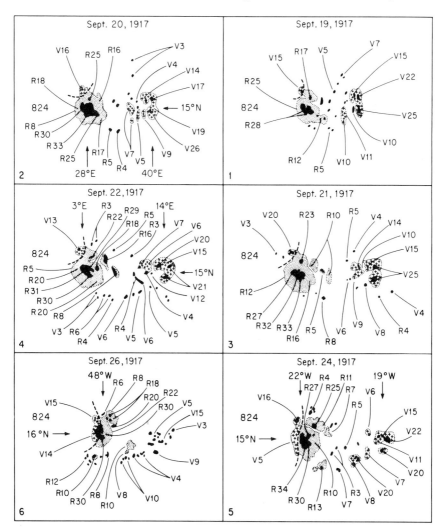

Fig. 6.4-9   Characteristics of a complex spot group. The designations R and V arise from instrumental considerations. The positive (or north-seeking) and negative fields are denoted by R and V, respectively, and the field is given in kilogauss. Thus, V9 denotes a field of 9,000 gauss which is negative or south-seeking. (*Courtesy of Mount Wilson and Palomar Observatories, from R 6.4-5.*)

On the average, the magnetic flux in the p spots is about three times that in the f spots. Also, p spots are usually somewhat larger and longer-lived than f spots. However, the BMR should be considered as the basis for the development of spot groups. The BMR's follow the law of polarity better than spots, and equal amounts of magnetic flux of opposite polarity are present in the p and f portions of the BMR. This is what one expects if the basic phenomenon involved is the emergence of flux loops from the sub-

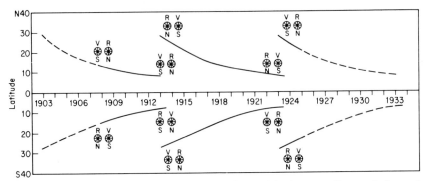

Fig. 6.4-10   The polarity law and migration law, with the preceding spot shown to the left. (*Courtesy of Mount Wilson and Palomar Observatories, from R 6.4-5.*)

photospheric field, as will be discussed in the next subsection. Thus, the development of a BMR as reflected in the spot group is undoubtedly more important than the behavior of individual spots. It is observed on magnetograms that BMR's appear to disappear by expansion. The properties of a BMR are clearly related to the properties of a "center of activity" (CA), as discussed in Sec. 6.8.

We note that important internal motions exist between various spots in a group and that these motions may be significant in the theory of solar flares.

Theory of sunspots

We now inquire into possible mechanisms for the emergence of BMR's from the subphotospheric layers as a basis for a theory of sunspots. Several sunspot theories have been proposed through the years, but here we restrict ourselves to a brief description of the theory developed by H. W. Babcock.

The theory begins (stage 1) with the type of general field shown in Fig. 6.3-4; here the field is a dipole field near the polar caps, but away from the polar caps it lies in a thin surface layer of thickness $\approx 0.1 R_\odot$. This field is considered as frozen-in to the solar material, and hence the field lines are carried along by the solar rotation and drawn out by the differential solar rotation. The result is an amplification (stage 2) of the field as shown in Fig. 6.4-11; the amplification of the field is a function of latitude.

A field of some 250 gauss (referred to as the critical value) is thought sufficient to produce "magnetic buoyancy" when amplified further to $\sim 10^3$ gauss by the twisting into flux ropes by distortions in the surfaces of constant angular velocity (isotachs) caused by convection. The critical value of the field is reached at a time n (measured in years from the beginning of a solar cycle) and at a solar latitude ϕ given by

$$\sin \phi = \pm \frac{1.5}{n+3} \tag{6}$$

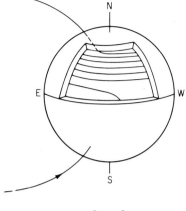

Fig. 6.4-11 Babcock's view of the sub-merged lines of force after they have been amplified by the differential solar rotation. (*Copyright* 1961 *by the University of Chicago, published by the University of Chicago Press, from R* 6.3-2.)

Stage 2

Since $n = 0$ at the beginning of a cycle, $\phi = \pm 30°$ as it should; the prediction of Eq. (6.4-6) gives a good fit to the observed laws of the migration of the sunspot zones. The flux ropes described above appear to be unstable, and the instability could result in the formation of a loop.

The formation of flux loops which protrude through the surface (stage 3) is thought to be the mechanism for the production of the observed BMR's. The loops in the flux ropes can arise from the instability mentioned in the preceding paragraph, or they can arise from magnetic buoyancy in regions where the field is large. From Eq. (6.4-5) and from the assumption of a constant temperature, we note that the density is less in a magnetic region, and hence the region will experience an upward buoyant force.

Detailed calculations show that a region with $B \approx 10^3$ gauss experiences appreciable buoyant force when brought close to the surface. Hence,

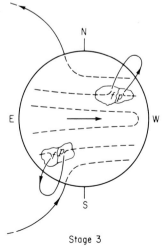

Fig. 6.4-12 Babcock's diagram illustrating stage 3; see the text for discussion. (*Copyright* 1961 *by the University of Chicago, published by the University of Chicago Press, from R* 6.3-2.)

Stage 3

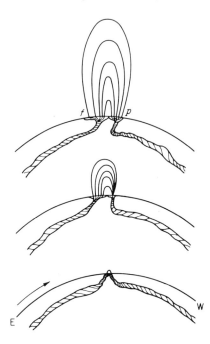

Fig. 6.4-13 The evolution of a BMR according to Babcock, with time moving from bottom to top. At first the BMR is compact, but it soon expands into the corona. The middle sketch shows how the BMR is advanced with respect to the submerged flux rope because of the differential solar rotation; this results in higher field strengths in the p part of the BMR. In the upper sketch, the expansion continues, the field strength decreases, and the signs of solar activity gradually disappear. (*Copyright* 1961, *by the Univeristy of Chicago, published by the University of Chicago Press, from R 6.3-2.*)

the instability and the buoyant force may both be important. The result is the formation of observable BMR's as shown in Fig. 6.4-12. The BMR continually expands; its subsequent evolution is shown in Fig. 6.4-13, which explains schematically why p spots tend to predominate. The production mechanism for BMR's naturally satisfies the polarity laws for p and f spots and the two hemispheres.

It remains to reverse the field, and the basic idea of stage 4 is shown in Fig. 6.4-14. Expanding lines of force from BMR's move outward toward the general dipole field. Severing and reconnection occur as shown in the diagram; and with each such process, a portion of the general field is neutralized. Continuation of this process results in the formation of a new general field of reversed sign. This process would have to be an irregular or "piecemeal" one; hence, it is not surprising that the reversal takes place at somewhat different times for the two hemispheres. Stage 5 is the same as stage 1, except for polarity. The model then runs through stages 2 to 4 to complete the 22-year cycle.

To sum up, the model accounts for the butterfly diagram, the polarity laws, the general field reversal, and the disappearance of BMR's by expansion. There are some difficulties with the model. A basic question concerns the energy supply for the maintenance of the differential rotation. The turbulent energy in the hydrogen convection zone could lead to meridianal circulation patterns which would produce differential rotation. Since this energy source is ultimately related to the nuclear energy generated in the interior, there appears to be no problem with the time scale.

Finally, we consider the question of the low temperature of sunspots, which seems to follow naturally from their magnetic origin. Consider the problem of convection in a plane-parallel layer of large conductivity with a uniform, horizontal magnetic field. Referring to Eq. (5.1-18), we see that a small blob of material which has a small, adiabatic displacement upward z experiences a buoyancy force,

$$F_b = \frac{V \rho g z}{T} \left[\left| \frac{dT}{dz} \right|_{str} - \left| \frac{dT}{dz} \right|_{ad} \right] \tag{7}$$

Since the conductivity is large, the lines of force are effectively frozen-in, and the displacement bends the lines of force. Considering the analogy to an elastic string (Sec. 6.2), the magnetic force per unit volume is just $B^2/4\pi$ times the curvature of the lines of force. If the distorted line of force is taken to be half a sine wave of wavelength λ, then the curvature is $d^2z/dx^2 = z(2\pi/\lambda)^2$, and the magnetic force becomes

$$F_m = \frac{z B^2 V}{4\pi} \left(\frac{2\pi}{\lambda} \right)^2 \tag{8}$$

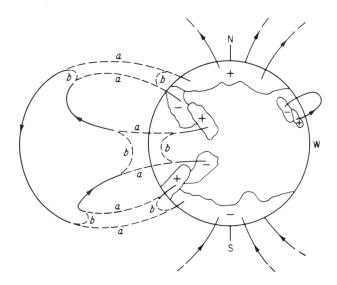

Fig. 6.4-14   Babcock's picture of the reversal of the main dipole field by the interaction with the expanding lines of force from old BMR's. In this process, severing and reconnection occur so that parts a are replaced by parts b and a partial neutralization occurs. Continuation of this process produces the reversal. (*Copyright* 1961 *by the University of Chicago, published by the University of Chicago Press, from R* 6.3-2.)

The ratio of the two forces is

$$\frac{F_b}{F_m} = \frac{\lambda^2 \rho g \left[\left| \dfrac{dT}{dz} \right|_{str} - \left| \dfrac{dT}{dz} \right|_{ad} \right]}{\pi B^2 T} \tag{9}$$

Thus, the size bubble which produces a balance between these two forces is

$$\lambda^2 = \frac{\pi B^2 T}{\rho g \left[\left| \dfrac{dT}{dz} \right|_{str} - \left| \dfrac{dT}{dz} \right|_{ad} \right]} \tag{10}$$

With the aid of Eq. (5.1-24), we may rewrite Eq. (6.4-10) as

$$\lambda^2 = \frac{\pi B^2 H}{\rho g \left[\left(\dfrac{d \log T}{d \log P} \right)_{str} - \left(\dfrac{d \log T}{d \log P} \right)_{ad} \right]} \tag{11}$$

where we recall that H is the scale height defined by Eq. (5.1-23). For the region substantially into the hydrogen convection zone, the quantity in brackets is ~ 0.1, $g \approx 2.5 \times 10^4$, $\rho \approx 10^{-5}$, and $B \approx 10^3$ gauss; this gives $\lambda \approx 10^3$ km.

Elements with characteristic sizes smaller than 10^3 km have their motions damped by the magnetic field. The fact that the magnetic field is not predominantly horizontal in a sunspot is not really of fundamental importance, since convection requires some sort of cellular pattern. Thus, some bending of the lines of force will occur and convection will, at least, be inhibited. Hence, we still have a qualitative explanation of sunspot coolness in terms of Eq. (6.4-11), which also shows why some BMR's do not produce sunspots. If the field is not strong enough, convection is not inhibited and no sunspot forms. It is clear that the magnetic field may also influence the mechanical equilibrium if it seriously hinders convection.

Since the scale height must be smaller in a sunspot than in the photosphere, the pressure at the surface is less in the spot than in the photosphere. This may be the explanation of the shallow depression of the solar surface over sunspots. Horizontal motions are presumably limited by the magnetic field, although the Evershed effect could be related to this pressure imbalance. The sunspot is also a relatively shallow phenomenon, as can be inferred from the sharp boundary of the umbra. This conclusion is reinforced by the fact that the energy density of turbulent motions and the magnetic energy density are approximately equal in the upper part of the hydrogen convection zone (but significantly below the photosphere). The magnetic field can hardly inhibit convection much below this point. The bright ring around sunspots is naturally explained as a consequence of the energy that is diverted by the presence of the sunspot.

Some attempt should be made to interpret the difference between the umbra and penumbra. From the Evershed effect and the distribution of the magnetic field in a sunspot (Fig. 6.4-6), the principal difference between umbra and penumbra appears to be the field strength (less in penumbra) and the field direction (essentially vertical in the umbra, nearly horizontal in the penumbra). The smaller magnetic field implies less hindrance of convection, in agreement with observations.

It has been suggested that the form of the convective element changes with the orientation of the magnetic field and that, in the presence of a horizontal magnetic field, this form is one of long convection cells (called convection rolls) with the long axis along the magnetic field. By analogy with the ordinary granulation, it seems appropriate to identify the bright penumbral filaments with rising elements and the dark filaments with descending elements. This view receives additional support from the fact that other possible models for the penumbra are found to be inadequate.

6.5 FACULAE

Terminology

The study of faculae is hindered somewhat by the confusing definitions and nomenclature pertaining to the phenomenon. Formerly, faculae referred to bright regions seen in white light near the limb as shown in Fig. 6.5-1. These regions are currently called photospheric faculae. Bright areas observed in K line or Hα spectroheliograms are labeled chromospheric faculae (Figs. 5.2-4 and 5.2-5) or *plages faculaires* (French). The latter term is often shortened to *plages*. In addition, "chromospheric faculae" is equivalent to "bright flocculi." *Flocculus* is currently used to denote a small, bright (but sometimes dark) area associated with chromospheric faculae.

Since it appears certain that we can identify a physical entity as being responsible for the various manifestations as described above, we call this entity a facula. It can be subdivided into photospheric and chromospheric faculae if a distinction is needed. A small bright or dark area in a facula is called a flocculus.

Structure and relation to other phenomena

Sunspots are invariably accompanied by faculae, but faculae can occur without sunspots. Faculae appear before the sunspots and usually last for several solar rotations after the spots disappear. The latitude distribution of faculae is roughly the same as the latitude distribution of sunspots, but with a somewhat broader belt. We mention, in passing, the existence of polar faculae; these are short-lived, ($\sim\frac{1}{2}$ hr) round faculae ($d \approx 2,000$ km) found at latitudes of $\pm 70°$. Since, as we find below, faculae are intimately

Fig. 6.5-1 The Sun in integrated white light showing the photospheric faculae (near the limb), limb darkening, and two large spot groups. (*Courtesy of Mount Wilson and Palomar Observatories.*)

related to magnetic fields, the polar faculae may exist because of the general solar field or the polar field suggested by the polar, coronal rays.

That faculae are observable only near the limb in white light and that they are indistinguishable from the photospheric background at the center of the disk means that (1) they are brighter than their surroundings in their upper portions, (2) they are cooler than their surroundings in the lower portions, and (3) they are not in radiative equilibrium. Hence, we immediately have the question of an energy supply. The faculae are approximately 100°K brighter than their surroundings at the photospheric surface.

Chromospheric faculae are generally somewhat larger in extent than photospheric faculae. Spectroheliograms in the strong hydrogen and metal lines show the chromospheric faculae quite well. Some height

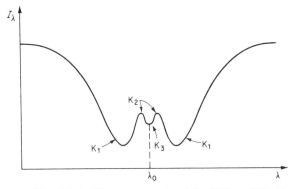

Fig. 6.5-2   The components of the K line of Ca II.

resolution can be achieved by using either lines of different strength or different parts of the same line. For example, the various components of the K line (λ3,934, Ca II) are shown in Fig. 6.5-2. The components originate in successively higher regions of the solar atmosphere with K_3 originating from the higher layers. The brightest faculae are those

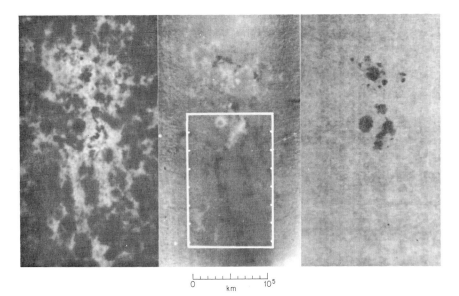

Fig. 6.5-3   A composite figure showing the close relationship between chromospheric faculae (plages) and the magnetic field. From left to right: a Ca II (K_2) spectrohelio-gram; a map (based on the Zeeman effect and the idea of comparison through photo-graphic subtraction) which shows the magnetic field as light (positive) or dark (nega-tive) depending on the polarity; a photograph showing the associated spot group. Notice the fine structure in the marked area and compare with the Ca II spectro-heliogram; the close correspondence is apparent. (*Courtesy of R. B. Leighton, California Institute of Technology. See also R 6.5-2.*)

observed in K_3; these faculae and others observed in the centers of strong lines occur over sunspots (covering them). Faculae are related to the magnetic fields associated with BMR's (Fig. 6.5-3) with B greater than 20 gauss.

Basically, faculae seem to be composed of a network of coarse mottles which, in turn, are composed of facular granules. These structures (the network, the coarse mottles, and the granules) are also found in spectroheliograms of the quiet chromosphere. The chief difference between the quiet chromosphere and the facular regions appears to be that the facular region has a higher density of the bright elements (granules or mottles) found in the normal chromosphere. This view is supported by the evolution of a facular area with time. At first, the bright, fine mottles are in a compact structure, but this structure gradually disperses with time. The facular areas become patchy and eventually merge into the normal chromospheric network. This last process seems to be quite smooth and continuous; a facular region has never been observed to disappear suddenly.

Theory of faculae

Much of the evidence summarized above points to a theory of faculae which takes the view that faculae occur because of an intensification or amplification of the process which normally heats the chromosphere. The magnetic fields were seen to be important, and this view is clearly illustrated in Fig. 6.5-3; the structure of the magnetic field shows a close correspondence with the structure of the facular area.

In Sec. 5.1 we described a mechanism for the deposition of mechanical energy and subsequent heating of the chromosphere. A qualitative theory of the energy supply for faculae is obtained by noting that there is extra noise generation in the hydrogen convection zone because of the magnetic field and, further, that the field enhances the energy deposition in the chromosphere. The magnetic field clearly arises from the emergence of a BMR.

6.6   FLARES

Basic data

A flare is a short-lived sudden burst of light in the vicinity of sunspots. Flares usually occur near γ or multipolar groups (often when a change in the structure is occurring). Flares are best observed in Hα, but some rare cases have been observed in white light. Flares are of interest for several reasons:

1. They are correlated (probably through the emission of corpuscular radiation) with disturbances in the ionosphere and the magnetic field of

the Earth. Such activity can then produce auroras and/or the interruption of radio communication.

2. Flares are associated with the emission of radio waves, ultraviolet radiation, X rays, and cosmic rays.

3. A phenomenon thought to be similar to flares has been observed on other stars. While the term "flare" refers to the visible burst of light, it could be that the process producing the high-energy particles and/or radiation is really the basic one.

Flares are not rare events. The number of flares (Imp $\geq$ 1, see below) per day is roughly $R/25$ where R is the sunspot number. If $R \approx 100$, we could have a flare every 6 hr. Flares of Imp. 1 are about one order of magnitude more frequent than flares of Imp. 3. Several flares often occur in virtually the same location. A more detailed study shows that the rate of flare production depends on the area A of a spot group and on dA/dt. Since virtually all flares occur within 100,000 km of a spot group, the distribution of flares over the solar disk closely follows the sunspot distribution. We note the existence of subflares (class 1$^-$) and the still smaller, but rather frequent, microflares.

Flares are classified according to area and brightness as 1$^-$, 1, 2, 3, and 3$^+$, in order of increasing importance. Flares of class 3 and especially 3$^+$ are generally responsible for terrestrial effects. Observational data concerning flares are difficult to obtain because of their short lifetimes. An Imp. 3$^+$ flare has an average lifetime of 3 hr, whereas an Imp. 1 flare lasts some 20 min. The development of flares seems to be nearly the same for all sizes. There is a rapid rise to peak intensity which is followed by a brief period of maximum brightness; then there is a slow return to the preflare brightness. These observations are usually made in Hα, but since the width and shape of Hα varies during the flare, the interpretation of such observations is not entirely straightforward.

Figure 6.6-1 shows the development of a solar flare. The flare pattern is usually complex, showing considerable filamentary structure. Flares often brighten up the existing chromospheric structure (or facular network), and often the appearance is that successive parts of the network are "activated." Flares leave the chromospheric structure essentially unchanged. A typical flare has an area of $\sim$10^{19} cm^2.

The visual spectrum of a flare contains many lines, and it is not strikingly different from the flash spectrum; one finds mostly emission lines of hydrogen, helium, and ionized calcium. An enhancement of the solar ultraviolet emission is expected; none has been observed for H Lyα (λ 1,216). Flares are known to produce X rays of sufficient intensity to, cause ionospheric effects. A model for flare radiation has been developed and it is discussed in Sec. 7.1. Several cosmic-ray flares have been observed, and it is now known that He^3 is produced in flares. From rocket measurements one sees that a flare is an event involving particles of rather

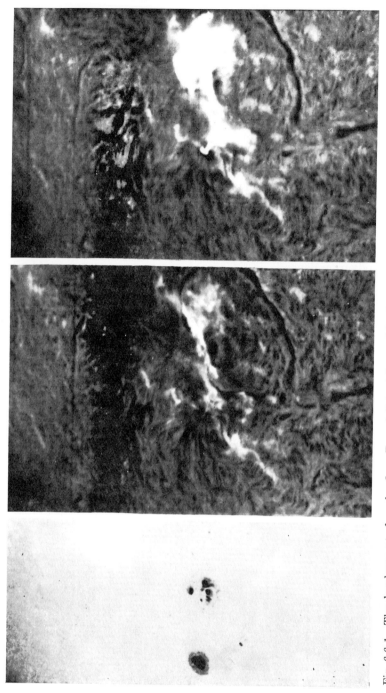

Fig. 6.6-1 The development of a solar flare. From left to right: a white-light photograph of the spot group; the flare in Hα 11 min later; the flare in Hα 22 min later. Notice the fine structure. (*Courtesy of Mount Wilson and Palomar Observatories*).

high energy. The observed (essentially visual) energy output of a flare can amount to $\sim 10^{27}$ ergs/sec for $\sim 10^3$ sec, or a total energy output of 10^{30} ergs. Energy emitted in corpuscular radiation could amount to 10^{29} to 10^{32} ergs, depending on the source of the estimate.

The energy in radio emission and cosmic rays is negligible, although a satisfactory theory of flares should provide a mechanism for production of radio waves and cosmic rays (Sec. 7.6). The height of flares is also important to the theory of flares. Such data can be derived from a statistical discussion of flare areas and from observations of limb flares. Flares are found to be flat structures located in the upper chromosphere or lower corona. Additional spectroscopic features associated with flares are moustaches—observed as broad emission primarily in the line wings—and Ellerman bombs. The bombs have larger size and longer lifetime than moustaches, but their principal effect is the brightening of the continuum around Hα.

Mass motions and related effects

Material is often thrown up from the region of the Sun near a flare. The most common occurrence is the flare surge. The surges appear to be shot up and decelerated at approximately the rate given by solar gravity; then they fall back into the Sun. On a spectrogram, the surge first appears as a blob displaced to the violet; then it becomes invisible (at zero velocity it is coincident with the line under observation, usually Hα), and finally it is seen as a red displaced blob. Speeds of up to 500 km/sec are found. Also, flare surges usually occur within 100,000 km of a flare. When flare surges occur on the limb, they are called surge prominences, which shoot up to heights of 100,000 km above the Sun (Fig. 6.6-2).

Repeated appearance of flare surges at the same location is quite common. These surge prominences shoot up at all angles and return to the Sun along the same path (sometimes curved). These paths are often influenced by nearby filaments, and the paths mirror the form of the filaments (i.e., prominences seen in projection against the disk, discussed in Sec. 6.7). The probability of flare surges increases with the importance of the flare.

It seems that both filaments and surge prominences are influenced by the same force field (presumably magnetic). However, the existence of a flare has a varied effect on nearby filaments ranging from no effect at all on a filament close to a large flare to the strong disturbance of a distant filament by a relatively weak flare. This point will not be discussed further, except to note that this behavior is possibly consistent with excitation by particles or waves channeled by the magnetic field, but not by radiative excitation.

Finally, there are the flare puffs which seem to be a very rapid expansion of the flare nearly at onset. This behavior should be contrasted with

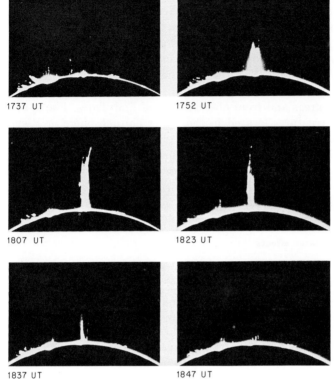

Fig. 6.6-2   A sequence of pictures showing a surge prominence. (*Courtesy of the High Altitude Observatory.*)

flare surges which can occur at any time during the life of the flare. The velocities found in flare puffs are often $\approx 10^3$ km/sec, which is in excess of the velocity of escape.

Theory of flares

It is possible that nuclear processes are important near the surfaces of some stars, and it might be supposed that solar flares could originate with nuclear reactions. However, the densities in the upper chromosphere or lower corona (site of flare origin) are so low that it is difficult to imagine that nuclear processes could originate there.

Considerable evidence points to a magnetic origin. If nuclear energy is ruled out, mass motions are found to be inadequate, whereas magnetic fields (using $B^2/8\pi$) can supply the estimated 10^3 ergs/cm^3 output of a solar flare with B of the order of a few hundred gauss. The figure 10^3 ergs/cm^3 was obtained by assuming a flare to be 10^8 cm thick, 10^{19} cm^2 in surface area, and of 10^{30} ergs total energy. If a total energy of 10^{32} ergs is assumed, we need a B of thousands of gauss. As we have mentioned previously, flares are observed near complex spot groups, usually when the groups are in a state of change. Also, magnetic fields are capable of accelerating particles to high energies, and these particles can, through free-free transitions, produce the high-energy photons observed.

A detailed theory of solar flares is not available, but the neutral-point theory of flares appears to be a step in the right direction. We seek a method of obtaining a discharge with a time scale of $\sim$minutes. One basic difficulty with the discharge theory arises from the fact that currents generated by a change in the magnetic field tend to oppose the change; this does not seem to be the case near the X-type neutral point shown in Fig. 6.6-3. Here the problem is idealized as one in two dimensions. Suppose the field distribution near a neutral point with a current flowing out of the paper is given. The limiting lines of force intersect at the neutral point X. For no current, the limiting field lines are normal; when a current flows, a magnetic force $\mathbf{F} = \mathbf{j} \times \mathbf{B}$ is generated as shown in Fig. 6.6-3. Since the conductivity is assumed to be large, the field lines are frozen-in; the lines of force move with the material, and the effect is to squeeze the material and the field in the x direction and stretch them in the y direction. This change in the material and the magnetic field reduces the acute angle between the limiting field lines. Thus, $\mathbf{j} \approx \mathbf{curl}\ \mathbf{B}/4\pi$ is increased at the neutral point. Starting with $\mathbf{j} = 0$, we see that a small perturbation leads to an increase in $\mathbf{j}$, and thus eventually to a discharge. On this simple picture, the rate of growth of the discharge is proportional to $|\nabla B|$.

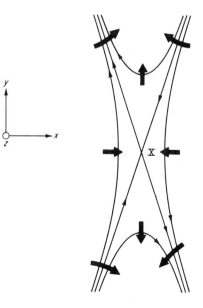

Fig. 6.6-3 The effect of the magnetic force at an X-type neutral point as described in the text. The light lines represent the field lines **B**, and the short, heavy arrows correspond to the magnetic force **j** ✗ **B**. (*After J. W. Dungey, from R 6.2-3 and R 6.6-2.*)

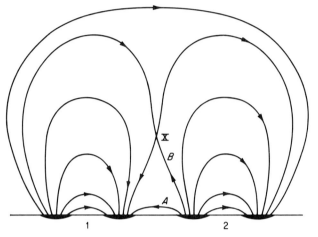

Fig. 6.6-4   A sketch showing a possible way for an X-type neutral point (X) to arise in the solar atmosphere owing to the interaction of the fields of the bimagnetic spot groups labeled (1) and (2). (*After P. A. Sweet in R* 6.6-3.)

In practice, the situation is much more complicated than indicated (e.g., pressure gradients), but the basic idea is attractive. Note that $|\nabla B|$ is large near neutral points. Also, for the discharge mechanism to be effective, collisions must be relatively unimportant. This places the discharge region high in the chromosphere (in agreement with the observations), especially to avoid collisions of electrons and neutral hydrogen, which has a large cross section.

An idealized picture of the mode of formation of an X-type neutral point is shown in Fig. 6.6-4. This type of configuration is expected to be encountered near complex (γ) spot groups, and we note that the usual bipolar (β) exhibit considerable internal structure. The small perturbation needed to trigger the discharge is probably associated with internal motions of spot groups (in accord with the observations). Thus it appears that we can provisionally identify the primary event associated with flares as a magnetic discharge near an X-type neutral point.

Estimates of the time scales involved have been made, and they all appear to be much too large. The discharge can build up a potential difference of $\sim 10^{10}$ volts. Cosmic rays with energies of $\sim 10^9$ to $\sim 10^{10}$ ev are known to originate from flares, since they are observed at the Earth. (Sec. 8.6). High-energy particles must also be emitted toward the Sun, and these would appear to interact with the denser material of the lower chromosphere to produce the observed visible and X-ray emission.

The neutral-point discharge theory may also give some insight into the mass motions associated with flares such as flare surges. The effect of the discharge is to reconnect the lines of force passing through the point, e.g., in Fig. 6.6-4 the line of force marked B would complete its loop, not as before, but now like line A. If the lines of force are thought of as elastic strings, it is easy to see how considerable mass motion could arise from the reconnection.

Two comparable theories of flares are available. The first is similar to the one sketched; it involves a discharge in a neutral plane. The second pictures twisted loops of magnetic flux. If these loops are sufficiently close, they attract and the flare can result from the subsequent annihilation of the magnetic field. These two theories also suffer from the difficulty with the time scale noted above.

Finally, we turn to the radio emission associated with flares. Several different types of transient radio emission are associated with flares. These emissions can probably be explained by plasma oscillations and/or synchrotron radiation (because electrons with energies of $\sim 10^6$ ev or greater are relativistic). We return to this point in Sec. 7.6, where a model for the production of the radio radiation is given.

6.7 PROMINENCES

General description

Prominences are easily observed on the limb as bright, arch-like structures resting on the chromosphere but extending into the corona. The part of the corona immediately surrounding the prominence is usually darker than would be expected. Prominences are also observed projected against the disk, where they appear as dark filaments. Changes in the appearance of a prominence as it moves off the disk are shown in Fig. 6.7-1. Chromospheric fine structure around a filament is usually arranged in a symmetrical manner with respect to the filament.

The prominence spectrum consists primarily of emission lines of hydrogen, helium, and ionized calcium; the spectrum indicates a temperature of $\approx 20,000°$K. Densities found in prominences are approximately two orders of magnitude higher than those in the surrounding corona, but the temperature is two orders of magnitude lower; hence, approximate pressure equilibrium exists between the prominence and the corona. Prominences are invariably associated with some kind of magnetic field, and this point is considered below.

Prominences have a large variety of forms, and several classification schemes have been devised; we do not discuss them in detail. The large-scale forms of prominences, by and large, remain constant. However, there appears to be considerable (mostly downward) motion associated with the fine structure of the prominence. The latitude distribution and the variation with solar cycle of prominences are somewhat similar to those of sunspots. Structural features found in prominences often seem to continue outward in the structure of the coronal rays.

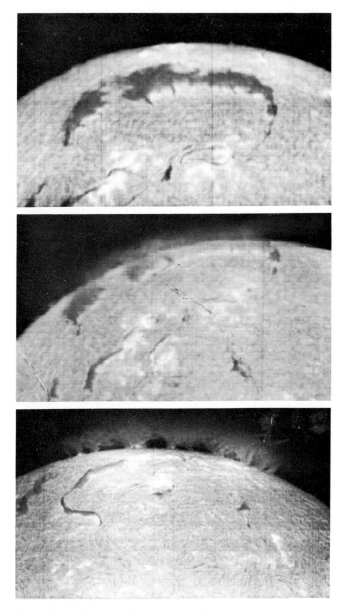

Fig. 6.7-1 Photographic sequence illustrating the correspondence between filaments and prominences. From top to bottom,
the photographs were taken on February 2, 3, and 5, 1959,
respectively. (*Observatoire de Paris–Meudon photographs, Courtesy
the Annals of the Observatory Paris–Meudon.*)

Quiescent and related prominences

Some ($\approx\frac{1}{3}$) of the quiescent prominences are associated with spot groups. They generally form on the polar side of the spot group, usually with the filament pointing toward the preceding spot. These quiescent prominences do not form in the early (apparently unstable or changing) part of the history of the spot group: instead, they appear approximately one solar rotation after the first spots form; by this time the spots are far past their maximum development. Initially, the filament makes an angle of some 38° with the meridian, but the differential solar rotation increases this angle and tends to make the filament lie east-west. The subsequent development of the filament is described in Sec. 6.8 concerning the development of the center of activity (CA).

The remainder ($\approx\frac{2}{3}$) of the quiescent prominences are found in the sunspot zone, away from spot groups but in facular regions. Thus, these quiescent prominences appear to avoid direct association with sunspots.

SOLAR EVENTS – 8 SEPT. 1948

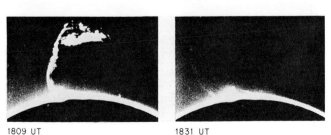

1632 UT   1659 UT

1724 UT   1751 UT

1809 UT   1831 UT

Fig. 6.7-2 A photographic sequence showing a rising prominence. (*Courtesy of the High Altitude Observatory.*)

There appears to be little difference between the quiescent prominences formed away from sunspots and those formed near spots. A typical developed filament has a thickness of 8,000 km, a height of 50,000 km. and a length of some 200,000 km. On the average, the length of a filament increases by about 100,000 km/solar rotation. The prominences show a bladelike structure which is remarkably maintained even though the prominence is not straight or exactly vertical.

Often during the life of a prominence, large-scale motions are present. This explosive stage can occur in a variety of ways. The prominence may rise and be thrown out into space (Fig. 6.7-2). The prominence may also shrink and disappear, or it may flow into the chromosphere along well-defined paths (Fig. 6.7-3). The point of entrance often coincides with a sunspot. These paths may be used repeatedly. Many of the phenomena associated with moving prominences are shown quite clearly on kinematograph films. These sudden disappearances usually take only a few hours.

SOLAR EVENTS — 13 AUG. 1951

1516 UT

1525 UT

1535 UT

1545 UT

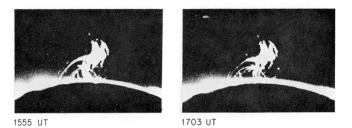

1555 UT

1703 UT

Fig. 6.7-3   A photographic sequence showing the flow of prominence material into the chromosphere. (*Courtesy of the High Altitude Observatory.*)

A new prominence of similar shape usually appears in the same location after a few days.

A theory of quiescent prominences must explain the creation and maintenance of a structure at a temperature of $\sim 10^4$ °K surrounded by the corona at $\sim 10^6$ °K for several rotations of the Sun. There are two basic problems:

1. The prominences require support. Even though they are in horizontal-pressure equilibrium with the corona, they cannot be in vertical hydrostatic equilibrium because they are 100 times more dense than the corona.

2. Some mechanism must operate to keep the prominence from being heated and ultimately dissipated by the corona. Here the magnetic field is of great importance.

We consider the second problem first, i.e., given a prominence, is there a mechanism for its maintenance? This involves a consideration of an energy balance. The mean free path for an electron of coronal energy in a prominence is about two orders of magnitude smaller than the thickness of a prominence. Hence each coronal electron deposits an energy of $\sim \frac{1}{2}kT$ (coronal) in the prominence. The gas current through a prominence can be calculated from standard formulas by assuming no shielding effects due to the magnetic field. The gas current times the energy of the coronal electron gives a rough estimate of the energy input into a prominence of $\sim 4 \times 10^5$ erg/(cm²)(sec).

At prominence temperatures, the major loss mechanism is free-bound emission in the Lyman continuum, which has a rate of $5 \times 10^{-22} T^{-\frac{1}{2}} N_e^2$ ergs/(cm³)(sec). As long as the prominence is optically thin, the emission per square centimeter is just the emission rate per cubic centimeter times the thickness of a prominence. Taking $N_e \approx 10^{10}/$ cm³ and $T_e \approx 10^{4°}$ K, equilibrium is found for a thickness of 10,000 km. This is the order of magnitude of the observed prominence thicknesses; if the prominence is less than this thickness, absorption exceeds emission and the prominence cannot exist. The prominence probably cannot greatly exceed this thickness, because it would then be optically thick in the Lyman continuum and absorption effects could become important.

The initial cooling could be caused by the expansion of a magnetic region; thus, we can qualitatively understand the existence of prominences from a thermal viewpoint by utilizing the magnetic field to produce the initial cooling and possibly to impede the inflow of mechanical energy from the corona. Since the prominences appear to be condensation from the corona, the coronal dark regions surrounding prominences receive a natural explanation.

We turn now to the problem of mechanical support, but first we review the results of magnetograph observations concerning the locations of filaments. Stable filaments are usually located between the regions of

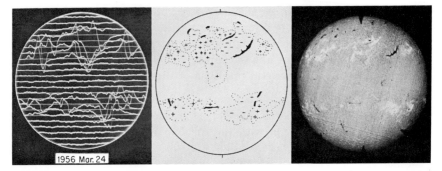

1956 Mar. 24

Fig. 6.7-4   A composite diagram showing, from left to right, a magnetogram, a sketch showing magnetic field polarities and the positions of stable filaments, and a hydrogen line spectroheliogram. This diagram clearly illustrates the positions of the filaments with respect to the magnetic areas; see the text for additional discussion. (*Courtesy of H. W. Babcock, Mount Wilson* and *Palomar Observatories, see R* 6.7-1.)

opposite polarity of a BMR or on the poleward side of a BMR or UMR (unipolar magnetic region). In the latter case, the magnetic region seemingly pushes the filament toward the polar regions. The relation of filaments to the magnetic regions is clearly shown in Fig. 6.7-4.

Invariably, the region where filaments occur is one where the magnetic field is parallel to the surface of the Sun. This situation is easy to visualize for the case of a filament straddling a BMR. It can also occur on the high-latitude side of a magnetic region owing to the interaction of the magnetic region with the general polar field. The property of the magnetic field being parallel to the Sun's surface is precisely the property required for support of the prominence by the magnetic field, because the field inhibits only motion that is perpendicular to the field lines.

The rapid changes occasionally observed in sunspots can be understood in terms of sudden changes in the magnetic field. A variety of phenomena (disappearances, inflows, rising prominences) could result, depending on the nature of the magnetic field variation.

Sunspot prominences

These prominences are made up of two general types, (1) the arch or loop type (Fig. 6.7-5) and (2) the condensation or knot type (Fig. 6.7-6). In the sunspot prominences downward motions predominate, and the sunspot prominences are in constant motion. The spot prominences correspond to the unstable filaments found in spot groups or CA's in the first week of their development.

The loop prominences and the trajectories of material in them give information concerning the magnetic field above the spot group. The trajectories can usually be explained as motion along the lines of force of a dipole situated just below the surface. The energy of the magnetic field in sunspot prominences greatly exceeds the energy in thermal or random motions. This should be contrasted with the quiescent prominences, where the two energy densities are of the same order of magnitude. The size of loop prominences is indicated by a mean projected length of $\approx 60,000$ km.

Condensation or knot prominences consist of a series of bright structures which form at approximately the same height (ranging from 50,000 to 100,000 km) above the surface. The bright structures are connected to the chromosphere (Fig. 6.7-6). Material apparently condenses into the knots and then flows downward and into the chromosphere. Condensation or knot prominences are associated with flare activity and with coronal condensations. This latter point is discussed in Sec. 6.8.

The general mechanism for the condensation of the sunspot prominences is probably the same as for the quiescent prominences. They are not mechanically supported, however. The sunspot prominence is maintained, for its short lifetime, by a balance between the rate of the condensation of material from the corona and the rate of flow along the field lines into the chromosphere.

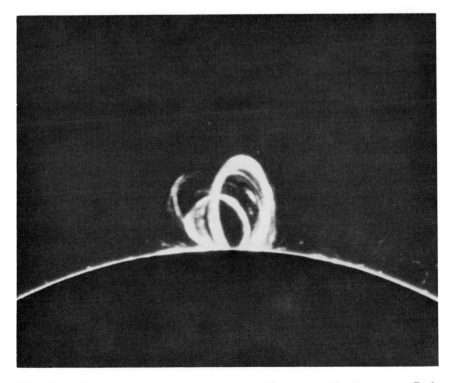

Fig. 6.7-5 Photograph of a loop prominence. (*Courtesy of the Sacramento Peak Observatory, Air Force Cambridge Research Laboratories.*)

Fig. 6.7-6   A photograph of a condensation prominence, "bird" type. (*Courtesy of the Sacramento Peak Observatory, Air Force Cambridge Research Laboratories.*)

6.8 CENTER OF ACTIVITY

An attempt has been made to somehow unify conceptually the many aspects of solar activity; this has led to the concept of the center of activity or CA. It summarizes the many phenomena associated with solar activity. The history of a CA is not always the same, but an average description can be given.

Figure 6.8-1 shows the development of a CA as seen in Hα. The following description of the development of a CA through 10 solar rotations (270 days) was given by Kiepenheuer (Copyright 1953 by the University of Chicago, from R 6.4-1):

> 1 day—In a seemingly undisturbed photospheric region within one of the spot belts, a change occurs in the fine structure of the chromosphere, visible in good Hα spectroheliograms as a transformation of round elements into stretched structures similar to filaments, which show a certain systematic alignment. Simultaneously or shortly afterward a small, bright facular speck is formed, visible in Hα and K, and on the limb also in white light. This speck rapidly becomes elongated in the east-west direction. The west end is somewhat closer to the equator.

2 days—Within the facular region the first spot is formed at the west end. The facula becomes very bright, close to the spot. A rapid extension of the chromospheric fine structure occurs, with the individual elements grouping themselves around the facular region. On the limb such small chromospheric filaments show as a weak prominence activity.

5 days—A second spot has formed in the east part of the facular region. Between the eastern (*f*) and the western (*p*) spot, numerous small spots have appeared. The total brightness of the facula still

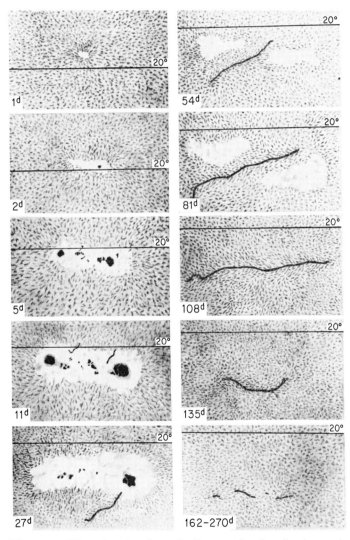

Fig. 6.8-1 Kiepenheur's schematic diagram showing development of a center of activity as seen in Hα through 10 solar rotations. (*Copyright 1953 by the University of Chicago, from R 6.4-1.*)

increases. The first flares appear mostly in the region between the main spots. Within the facular region short-lived filaments appear, and chromospheric ejections are observed in connection with flares (flare surges). On the solar limb fountain-like spot prominences become visible.

11 days—The spot group approaches the climax of its evolution and has formed large penumbrae. The brightness and extent of the facular region are still growing. The extent of the associated chromospheric structures exceeds 150,000 km and almost reaches the spot belt of the other hemisphere. The flare activity has increased.

27 days—Nearly all spots, except the p spot, have disappeared. The size of the facular region has further increased, and flares have become rare. On the poleward side of the facular region, an initially variable filament has become stable. It points almost exactly to the p spot and forms an angle of some 40° with the meridian. The alignment of the chromospheric fine structure is adapted to the filament.

54 days—All spots have disappeared. The facular region is decreasing in brightness and is cut in half by the filament. Within the last rotation the length of the filament has grown by some 100,000 km. The filament turns increasingly toward east-west.

81 days—The facular region dissolves into a transparent network. The chromospheric structures are unchanged. The filament is still increasing its length and turning east-west.

108 days—The facula has dissolved completely, the chromospheric structures still show the old arrangement. The filament has reached its maximum length and is almost east-west.

135 days—The CA region differs no longer from the undisturbed surroundings, either in the photosphere or in the chromosphere. The filament has decreased in length and has become independent. It is now east-west and seems to migrate poleward with irregular speed. It is still surrounded by a feather-like chromospheric fine structure.

162–270 days—The filament approaches the polar crown of filaments with decreasing velocity and is incorporated in it. It may exist there for 5 more rotations. It changes its form continuously and is difficult to follow as an individual.

Coronal development

We also find that a CA has effects visible in the corona. The regions over a CA are bright in λ5,303, Fe XIV (the coronal green line). The brightness of the green line has essentially the same behavior as the brightness of the facular regions, namely, the green patch appears immediately (≈ 1 day) after the beginning of the CA and reaches maximum brightness after one rotation. The green patch decreases in brightness faster than the facular area. The most active coronal areas are called permanent coronal condensations. They have higher densities and temperatures than the undisturbed corona has.

A radiation model of a coronal condensation is available; it is discussed in Sec. 7.1. The permanent coronal condensations exhibit considerable structure (short rays) and show the coronal yellow line ($\lambda 5,694$, Ca XV). This yellow line becomes enhanced, and a continuous spectrum is visible during periods of flare activity. The structure of the coronal emission usually parallels the structure of sunspot prominences.

We now mention briefly the other types of active regions in the corona, the so-called sporadic coronal condensations. They show the coronal green line, red line ($\lambda 6,379$, Fe X), and Hα. They appear to be objects with lower temperatures than the permanent condenstaions. Finally, there are the regions associated with UM regions. These were first called M regions to account for geophysical disturbances with a 27-day period. They were later discovered as C regions with a very bright green line, but *no* yellow line. These regions fall in the sunspot zones but are not associated with CA's or any other photospheric phenomena. The UMR's, C regions, and M regions are undoubtedly identical. They appear to occur at the location of old CA's. These regions are associated with the long coronal streamers. Since the long coronal streamers and the quiescent prominences have the same distribution over the solar disk, it could be that a coronal streamer is the last stage of development of a quiescent prominence.

The magnetic regions

While the CA develops as outlined above, there is also development of the magnetic region as revealed on the magnetograms. The magnetic field is first observed a day or two before the first spots or faculae. The field shortly assumes a bipolar character and increases in strength, reaching maximum magnetic flux at 27 days (one rotation). Just before maximum flux the field distribution is rather irregular and variable; this period corresponds (as one would expect) with the maximum in the flare activity. After three rotations, the field strength decreases; by five rotations, the field is somewhat scattered, and the total area has increased to one-twentieth of the disk. From seven to ten rotations, the area continuously increases; this observation gives rise to the impression that BMR's disappear by expansion. The area can grow quite large up to 0.2 of the disk. Finally, the BMR changes into a UM region.

It seems clear that the idea of the development of a magnetic region is a unifying concept which enables understanding of the myriad of phenomena comprising solar activity. Thus a most useful hypothesis is that all manifestations of solar activity are due to the emergence and subsequent evolution of a magnetic region.

BIBLIOGRAPHICAL NOTES

Section 6.1. Historical points relating to Chap. 6 are covered in:

R 6.1-1. Goldberg, L.: In "The Sun," ed. G. P. Kuiper, pp. 1–35, The University of Chicago Press, Chicago, 1953.

Section 6.2. Most of the material in this section is covered in standard texts such as:

R 6.2-1. Spitzer, L.: "Physics of Fully Ionized Gases," Interscience Publishers, Inc., New York, 1956.

R 6.2-2. Cowling, T. G.: "Magnetohydrodynamics," Interscience Publishers, Inc., New York, 1957.

R 6.2-3. Dungey, J. W.: "Cosmic Electrodynamics," Cambridge University Press, London, 1958.

R 6.2-4. Delcroix, J. L.: "Introduction to the Theory of Ionized Gases," Interscience Publishers, Inc., New York, 1960.

The following references deal with the theory and the application to solar and solar system problems.

R 6.2-5. Clauser, F. H. (ed.): "Symposium of Plasma Dynamics," Addison-Wesley Publishing Company, Inc., Reading, Mass., 1960.

R 6.2-6. Cowling, T. G.: In "The Sun," ed. G. P. Kuiper, pp. 532–591, The University of Chicago Press, Chicago, 1953.

R 6.2-7. Alfvén, H.: "Cosmical Electrodynamics," Clarendon Press, Oxford, 1950.

A comprehensive bibliography is given in R 6.2-5. Problems relating to radiative energy loss are discussed in many of the references for this section. See also:

R 6.2-8. Westfold, K. C.: *Astrophys. J.*, **130**: 241 (1959).

R 6.2-9. Jelley, J. V.: "Čerenkov Radiation and Its Applications," Pergamon Press, New York, 1958.

Section 6.3. The general magnetic field is discussed in R 6.1-1, R 6.2-2, R 6.2-3, R 6.2-6, and R 6.2-7. Also, see:

R 6.3-1. Cowling, T. G.: *Monthly Notices. Roy. Astron. Soc.*, **105**: 166 (1945).

R 6.3-2. Babcock, H. W.: *Astrophys. J.*, **133**: 572 (1961).

Section 6.4. Sunspots are discussed in R 6.2-2, R 6.2-3, R 6.2-6, R 6.2-7, and:

R 6.4-1. Kiepenheuer, K. O.: In "The Sun," ed. G. P. Kuiper, pp. 322–465, The University of Chicago Press, Chicago, 1953.

R 6.4-2. de Jager, C.: In "Handbuch der Physik," vol. 52, ed. S. Flügge, pp. 80–362, Springer-Verlag OHG, Berlin, 1959.

Sunspot numbers are contained in:

R 6.4-3. Waldmeier, M.: "The Sunspot: Activity in the Years 1610–1960," Schulthess and Co. A. G., Zürich, 1961.

Papers on the properties of sunspots are:

R 6.4-4. Maunder, E. W.: *Monthly Notices Roy. Astron Soc.*, **82**: 534 (1922).

R 6.4-5. Hale, G. E., and S. B. Nicholson: "Magnetic Observations of Sunspots, 1917–1924," part I, Carnegie Institution, Washington, D.C., 1938.

R 6.4-6. Cowling, T. G.: *Monthly Notices Roy. Astron. Soc.*, **106**: 218 (1946).

R 6.4-7. St. John, C. E.: *Astrophys. J.*, **37**: 322 (1913).

The theory of sunspots is developed in R 6.3-2, which also contains a summation of the observational facts. See also R 6.5-1, and R 6.7-1.
A reversal of the high-latitude magnetic field is investigated in:

R 6.4-8. Babcock, H. D.: *Astrophys. J.*, **130**: 364 (1959). Convective envelopes and differential rotation are discussed in:

R 6.4-9. Kippenhahn, R.: *Astrophys. J.*, **137**: 664 (1963).

The theory of sunspot penumbrae follows:

R 6.4-10. Danielson, R. E.: *Astrophys. J.*, **134**: 289 (1961).

Section 6.5. The basic data are given in R 6.4-1 and R 6.4-2. The relation between faculae and magnetic fields is covered in:

R 6.5-1. Babcock, H. W., and H. D. Babcock: *Astrophys. J.*, **121**: 349 (1955).

R 6.5-2. Leighton, R. B.: *Astrophys. J.*, **130**: 366 (1959).

R 6.5-3. Osterbrock, D. E.: *Astrophys. J.*, **134**: 347 (1961).

Section 6.6. The observational material is presented in R 6.4-1 and R 6.4-2. See also:

R 6.6-1. Goldberg, L., and E. R. Dyer: In "Science in Space," eds. L. V. Berkner and H. Odishaw, pp. 307–340, McGraw-Hill Book Company, New York, 1961.

The theory of flares is discussed in R 6.4-1, R 6.4-2, R 6.2-3, R 6.2-6, and:

R 6.6-2. Dungey, J. W.: In "I.A.U. Symposium No. 6: Electromagnetic Phenomena in Cosmical Physics," ed. B. Lehnert, pp. 135–139, Cambridge University Press, London, 1958.

R 6.6-3. Sweet, P. A.: In "I.A.U. Symposium No. 6: Electromagnetic Phenomena in Cosmical Physics," ed. B. Lehnert, pp. 123–134, Cambridge University Press, London, 1958.

R 6.6-4. Gold, T., and F. Hoyle: *Monthly Notices Roy. Astron. Soc.*, **120** : 89 (1960).

See also:

R 6.6-5. Smith, H. J., and E. v. P. Smith: "Solar Flares," The Macmillan Company, New York, 1963.

Section 6.7. See R 6.4-1 and R 6.4-2. The relation of filaments to the magnetic regions is discussed in:

R 6.7-1. Babcock, H. W., and H. D. Babcock: In "I.A.U. Symposium No. 6: Electromagnetic Phenomena in Cosmical Physics," ed. B. Lehnert, pp. 239–244, Cambridge University Press, London, 1958.

Section 6.8. The properties of a CA are summarized in R 6.4-1 and R 6.4-2.

The solar spectrum

7

Observations of the solar spectrum are greatly hampered by the presence of the terrestrial atmosphere, which in general is opaque to a great deal of electromagnetic radiation. A schematic representation of the properties of the atmosphere is given in Fig. 7-1, where it is shown that ground-based observations are possible only in the so-called optical and radio windows. Thus in this chapter, we must touch on the properties of the terrestrial atmosphere and, in particular, on the depth to which each type of radiation penetrates.

7.1 GAMMA RAYS AND X RAYS

Electromagnetic radiation of γ-ray energies is not expected from the quiet Sun. High-energy events on the Sun associated with flares could, however, provide a source of high-energy particles capable of producing γ rays by

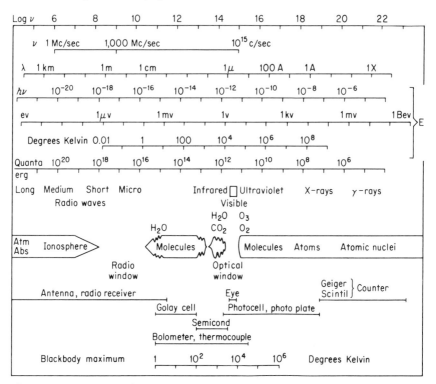

Fig. 7-1   A representation of the transparency of the terrestrial atmosphere. (*Courtesy of A. D. Code and the Editors of The Astronomical Journal, from R 7-1.*)

free-free transitions. At least one flare (of Imp. 2) has produced γ rays of measurable intensity; that was the flare of March 20, 1958, which produced an 18-sec burst of 0.5 Mev radiation. The burst was observed at balloon altitudes; it had a flux of 2×10^{-5} ergs/(cm²)(sec).

Hard X rays are also not expected from the quiet Sun, but, similarly, they are expected from regions associated with CA's. Figure 7.1-1 shows the height in the atmosphere required to observe X rays and extreme ultraviolet radiation. For X rays of wavelength 2 to 20 A a height of at least 100 km is needed. Table 7.1-1 shows the observations of X rays over a solar cycle, where the correlation with solar activity is quite clear. Also, a photograph of the Sun in X radiation (20 to 60 A) shows a close correspondence between the regions of X radiation and Ca II chromospheric faculae.

A radiation model of a flare is available; it corresponds to an energy given by a temperature of some 10^8 °K. Similarly, a radiation model is available for a hot region, or coronal condensation, which has an energy given by a temperature of some 6×10^6 °K. These models are shown in Fig. 7.1-2. Note that the emission consists of two parts; there is both continuous (free-free) and line emission. The line emission is excited by elec-

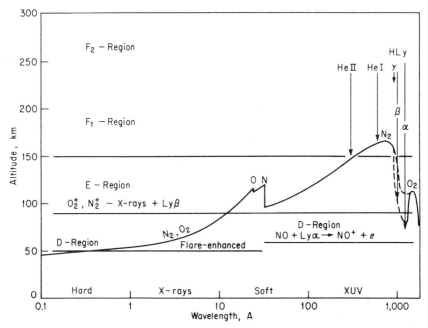

Fig. 7.1-1 The depth to which $1/e$ of the incident solar intensity penetrates for X-ray and extreme ultraviolet wavelengths. (*From R. Tousey, in R 7.1-3*).

tron collisions; the lines of Fe XXVI could be important (near 2 A); this is iron with but one electron remaining. The wavelengths of the resonance lines of a one-electron system are proportional to Z^{-2} (from the Rydberg formula). Hence, we conclude that there are probably no important lines shortward of about 2 A, because iron is the last abundant heavy element.

Table 7.1-1 X-ray counting rates observed over a solar cycle*

Time (UT)	Date	Counting rate, counts/(cm²)(sec) 2 to 8 A	8 to 20 A	Solar activity
1730	9/29/49	1.0×10^4		$2\frac{1}{2}$ hr after class 1 flare
1459	6/1/52	495		Quiet
1344	5/5/52	<125		Quiet
2240	11/15/53	<40		Quiet
1546	11/25/53	332		Quiet
1529	12/1/53		4.5×10^4	Quiet
2250	10/18/55		1.4×10^5	Quiet
1915	7/20/56	1.2×10^5		Late in class 1
1634	7/24/59	2.4×10^4	1.0×10^7	Quiet
1600	8/14/59	1.3×10^4	2.0×10^6	Quiet
2253	8/31/59	$>7 \times 10^5$	$>1 \times 10^7$	Class 2+

* As given by H. Friedman in R 7.1-4.

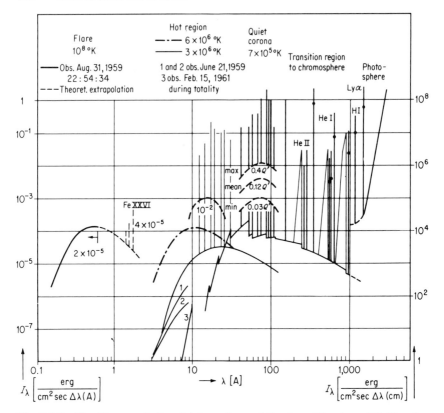

Fig. 7.1-2   The X-ray and ultraviolet spectrum of the Sun. (*Courtesy of G. Elwert, Tübingen.*)

The soft X-ray spectrum (40 to 100 A) of the Sun is thought to be composed primarily of permitted lines of highly ionized elements excited by electron collisions. This also is shown in Fig. 7.1-2. The observed values of the flux in the 40- to 100-A range are approximately 0.1 erg/(cm²)(sec) at solar minimum and 1 erg/(cm²)(sec) at solar maximum; these values are roughly consistent with theoretical work.

7.2   EXTREME AND FAR–ULTRAVIOLET RADIATION

We discuss here the radiation between 100 and 3,000 A. The high-energy radiation comes from the corona and the transition region; when we reach 3,000 A, the radiation comes from the lower chromosphere and the photosphere. Much of this radiation is thought to originate from the quiet Sun, but a variation through the solar cycle is possible. Figures 7.1-1 and 7.2-1 show the rocket heights required for observation. For a description of ultraviolet absorption processes, see R 7.3-4. Section 7.3 is devoted to Lyman-α.

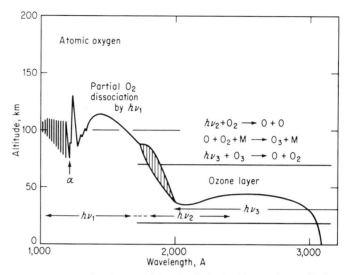

Fig. 7.2-1 The depth to which $1/e$ of the incident solar radiation penetrates for 1,000 to 3,000 A. (*From R. Tousey, in R 7.1-3.*)

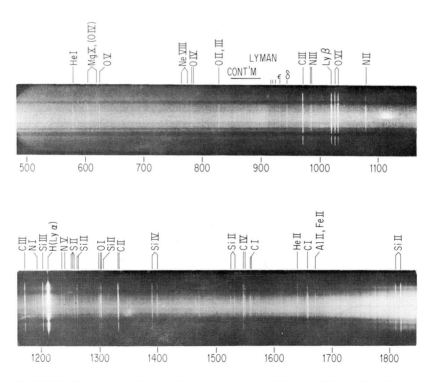

Fig. 7.2-2 Photograph of the solar spectrum from 500 to 1,800 A. (*Courtesy of J. D. Purcell, D. M. Packer, and R. Tousey, U.S. Naval Research Laboratory, Official United States Navy Photograph.*)

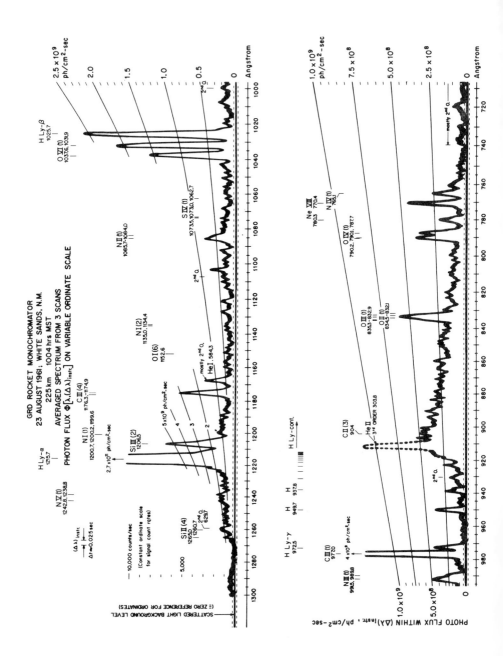

GRD ROCKET MONOCHROMATOR
23 AUGUST 1961: WHITE SANDS, N.M.
225 km 1004 hrs MST
AVERAGED SPECTRUM FROM 3 SCANS
PHOTON FLUX $\Phi[\lambda,(\Delta\lambda)_{instr}]$ ON VARIABLE ORDINATE SCALE

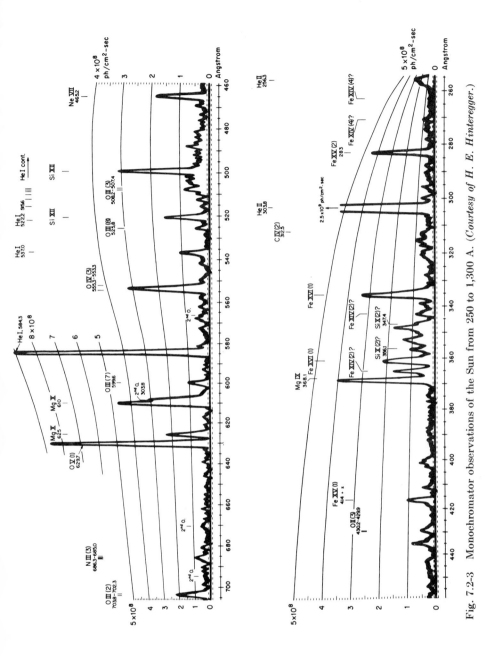

Fig. 7.2-3   Monochromator observations of the Sun from 250 to 1,300 A. (Courtesy of H. E. Hinteregger.)

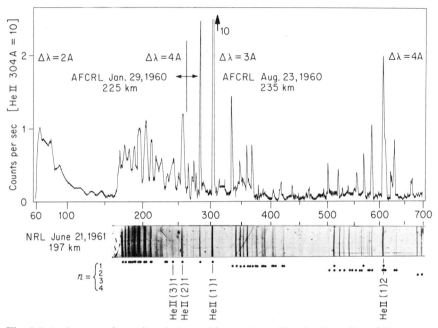

Fig. 7.2-4 A comparison of a photographic spectrum (Austin, Purcell, and Tousey) with the monochromator results (Hinteregger). (*Courtesy of R. Tousey, U.S. Naval Research Laboratory, Official United States Navy Photograph.*)

The two basic methods of obtaining information in this wavelength region are through spectra obtained from recoverable rockets and through data telemetered back to the ground by monochrometers in satellites or space vehicles. A representative spectrum for the region 500 to 1,850 A is shown in Fig. 7.2-2. Notice the beginning of the continuous spectrum at 1,800 A and longward. At 2,000 A, the blackbody temperature of the Sun is approximately 5000°K; the temperature increases as we go longward. By the time we reach 3,500 A, the temperature approaches 6000°K, which approximates the solar spectrum in the visual region. A sample monochrometer record is shown in Fig. 7.2-3. Figure 7.2-4 shows both a spectrum and a monochrometer record for the very short wavelengths.

The ultraviolet spectrum near 1,200 A is completely dominated by Lyman-α (see next section). The blackbody temperature in the Lyman continuum ($\lambda < 912$) is some 6500 to 7000°K; this emission is visible in Fig. 7.2-2.

7.3 LYMAN-α

The Lyman-α line is the dominant feature of the solar extreme ultraviolet spectrum. The measured ·flux is about 6 ergs/(cm²)(sec). This radiation is not enhanced in flares, and, in fact, the flux of Lyman-α is usually considered to be constant. Nevertheless, there is probably some variation over the solar cycle, because a direct photograph of the Sun in Lyman-α light (Fig. 7.3-1) shows that the Lyman-α radiation comes from regions associated with solar activity.

The profile of Lyman-α is shown in Fig. 7.3-2. The width is about 1 A, and the shallow depression at the top of the profile is caused by self-absorption in the solar atmosphere. This line is apparently formed in the transition zone of enhanced regions in the solar atmosphere. The large line width comes from opacity broadening rather than from characteristic velocities in the region of formation. The narrow, deep absorption core is caused by cool, terrestrial hydrogen.

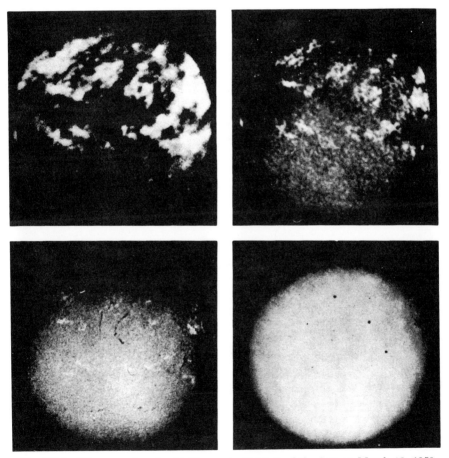

Fig. 7.3-1   Diagram, given by R. Tousey in R 5.1-3, of the Sun on March 13, 1959, showing: (upper left) U.S. Naval Research Laboratory Photograph of the Sun in Lyman-α taken from an Aerobee-Hi rocket, (upper right) McMath-Hulbert Observatory spectroheliogram in $K_{2,3,2}$, (lower left) U.S. Naval Research Laboratory photograph in Hα with a 0.7-A monochromatic filter, (lower right) U.S. Naval Observatory photograph in white light. (*Courtesy of the U.S. Naval Research Laboratory.*)

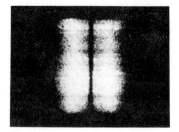

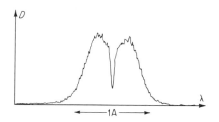

Fig. 7.3-2 The profile of the Lyman-α line obtained at a mean height of approximately 150 km, given by R. Tousey in R 7.1-3 (*Courtesy of the U.S. Naval Research Laboratory.*)

Lyman-α radiation can be observed as low as 80 km altitude in the terrestrial atmosphere, the result of a coincidence of the Lyman-α wavelength (1,215.67 A) with a minimum in the O_2 absorption coefficient, which dominates the absorption of solar radiation near 1,200 A. The extreme variation (with wavelength) possible in the various absorption coefficients

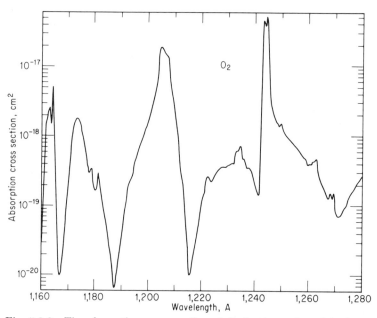

Fig. 7.3-3 The absorption cross section of O_2 in the region of hydrogen Lyman-α (λ1,216) showing the extreme variations possible. (*Courtesy of Academic Press, Inc., from R 7.3-4.*)

of atmospheric constituents is not always realized, and we illustrate this fact with Fig. 7.3-3.

Because it is the resonance line of hydrogen, the most abundant element, the Lyman-α line is important as a probe of the solar corona, the interplanetary medium, and planetary atmospheres.

7.4 OPTICAL RADIATION

In this text, optical radiation refers to radiation that reaches the Earth through the optical window, which is determined by ozone absorption at 0.3 μ and by H_2O absorption at 1.38 μ.

It is possible to specify the essential features of the frequency distribution through the judicious assignment of a blackbody temperature. This requires the observation of the frequency distribution of solar radiation at the Earth's surface and the extrapolation to outside the atmosphere. The procedure is shown schematically in Fig. 7.4-1, which also shows that the Sun can be reasonably represented by a blackbody at 6000°K. A temperature determined from Wien's law ($\lambda_{max} \times T = $ const; $\lambda_{max} = $ wavelength of maximum intensity) would not be reliable, because the wavelength of the maximum emission is influenced by the absorption lines in the Sun. The 6000°K quoted above refers to the center of the disk; the effective temperature of integrated sunlight (including limb darkening) is somewhat less, namely, 5750°K (see Sec. 3.1).

The optical radiation carries the bulk of the solar energy flux. We have already utilized this radiation many times in our discussions of the solar limb darkening, continuous opacity, and many other problems in the physics of the photosphere. Hence, we do not repeat this discussion but refer the reader to Sec. 4.2.

The optical region also contains the absorption line spectrum, often called the Fraunhofer spectrum. Many of the strongest absorption lines have been given letter designations (e.g., the sodium D lines, λ5,890, and the K line, λ3,934, of singly ionized calcium). These are also of great value in the study of the photosphere and for abundance studies (see Secs. 4.3 and 4.4). Emission lines are quite useful for the study of the chromosphere and corona (see Chap. 5); for example, helium was discovered on the Sun in the chromospheric flash spectrum before it was found on Earth.

7.5 INFRARED REGION

This is the spectral region (1.4 to 24 μ) characterized by absorption in the Earth's atmosphere by molecular constituents such as H_2O and CO_2. It contains a few "windows" in the spectrum where some solar observations are possible and is terminated at 24 μ by strong water vapor absorption. Studies in this spectral region yield valuable information concerning the existence and abundance of various constituents in the terrestrial

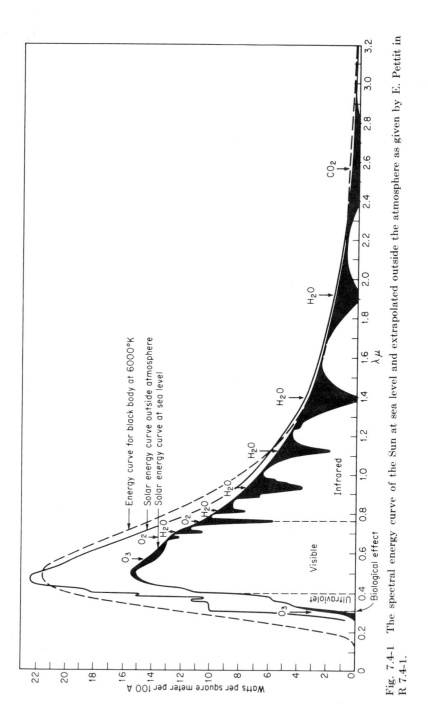

Fig. 7.4-1 The spectral energy curve of the Sun at sea level and extrapolated outside the atmosphere as given by E. Pettit in R 7.4-1.

atmosphere, including H_2O, the two isotopic forms of CO_2 ($C^{13}O_2^{16}$ and $C^{12}O^{16}O^{18}$), CH_4, HDO, N_2O, O_3, and CO.

While the information obtained from the infrared region refers primarily to the atmosphere of the Earth, solar applications do exist. The solar opacity goes through a minimum near 17,000 A, and at this wavelength the Earth's atmosphere is semitransparent. Observations at this wavelength have maximum penetration into the Sun and have proved to be quite valuable.

7.6 RADIO WAVES

The radio window shown in Fig. 7-1 extends from approximately 8 mm to 15 m. The short-wavelength limit is determined by molecular absorption of H_2O and O_2; the long-wavelength limit is determined by critical reflection in the ionosphere.

Since radio measures and techniques have not been emphasized in Chaps. 5 and 6 (except Sec. 5.3), we give here a survey of the observations and the mechanisms thought to explain them.

General features

The salient features of the solar radio emission are summarized in Fig. 7.6-1. The base line (denoted by B in the figure) corresponds to a radiation temperature of 10^4 °K at 1-cm wavelength, and this temperature increases to 10^6 °K at 1 m. Limb brightening on the quiet Sun has been detected at $\lambda \approx 20$ cm. The cause of the limb brightening is basically the same as the cause of the limb darkening for optical radiation except that the temperature increases with height in the part of the solar atmosphere probed by radio waves. These results are expected on the basis of the optical data and the type of analysis discussed in Sec. 5.3.

The basic component must be untangled from the gradual rise and fall observed at decimetric wavelengths, called the "slowly varying component." This component, connected with the solar activity cycle, can be eliminated by plotting the apparent temperature vs. projected sunspot area and extrapolating to zero sunspot area to obtain the basic component. The basic component is thermal in origin and shows random polarization.

The slowly varying component arises from regions at a height of $\approx 100,000$ km above the photosphere and associated with chromospheric faculae. The temperatures measured for these regions at some 300,000 km above the photosphere are approximately 1×10^6 °K, that is, the normal coronal values. However, the densities inferred are ≈ 3 times the normal coronal values. Hence, the slowly varying component appears to be thermal radiation originating in overdense coronal regions of normal temperature. These regions could be the so-called coronal condensations. In agreement with this picture is the fact that the slowly varying component is

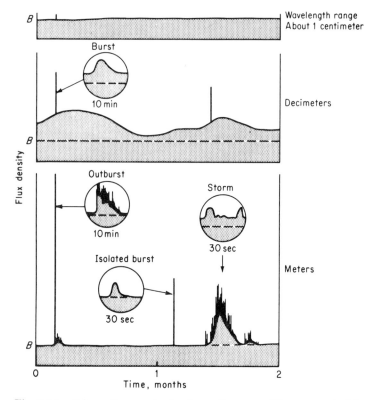

Fig. 7.6-1   Schematic records of solar radio waves. The apparent disk temperature of the base level B increases approximately linearly from $10^{4.°}$K at 1 cm to 10^{6} °K at 1 m. (*From J. L. Pawsey and R. N. Bracewell in R 7.6-1, Courtesy of Oxford University Press.*)

unpolarized except at wavelengths shorter than 10 cm. Here is observed weak circular polarization that may result from the origination of this radiation in the lower layers, which could be influenced by the magnetic fields associated with chromospheric faculae. In addition, the solar radio spectrum is characterized by intense, transient emission.

Transient radiations

Examples of the various types of solar radio bursts are illustrated in Fig. 7.6-2. These transient emissions are characterized by orders of magnitude changes within times of a few seconds. The fluxes and intensities of the sporadic emission are relatively high compared to the quiet Sun emission in decimeter and meter wavelengths. Temperatures for these emissions are probably not too meaningful, but the observed equivalent blackbody temperatures are in the range of 10^{10} to 10^{15} °K.

The type I burst or noise storm consists of narrow peaks superimposed on a continuum. The storms occur above spots which are larger than a certain minimum value (area > 4 to 5×10^{-4} solar disk). Thus, noise storms occur during the "active" phase of a CA. The radiation is strongly circularly polarized and is clearly nonthermal in origin, although the exact mechanism is not known. The storms appear to have *some* relationship to flares, but this also is poorly understood. The region of noise storms must occur high in the solar atmosphere ($0.3R_\odot$ to $1.0R_\odot$ above the photosphere), because the storm region moves across the solar disk faster than the associated spot group. In addition, the storm center rises later and sets earlier (on the Sun) than the spot group because of the limitations on the directions in which radio waves can escape from the solar atmosphere.

We note (Sec. 5.3) that the problem of escape of radio-frequency radiation from an ionized atmosphere depends on the magnetoionic parameters x, y, and z and is different for the ordinary and extraordinary modes. This problem is not considered here.

We now consider the flare-associated radio emission, or the "outburst." A complete idealized outburst is shown in the inset in Fig. 7.6-2; burst types II to V are involved. As is shown in the figure, types II and IV seem to be associated with each other, as are types III and V. Some insight into the problem is gained by postulating that types II and III are plasma oscillations at the plasma frequency (Sec. 6.2). If so, for a given coronal model, the plasma frequency can be computed as a function of height in the corona. With this information, the frequency drift with time

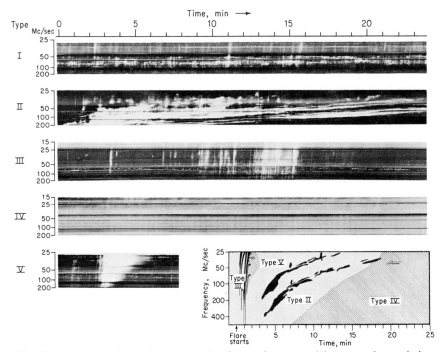

Fig. 7.6-2 Sample dynamic spectra showing main types of intense solar emission. (*Courtesy of J. P. Wild; see R 7.6-5.*)

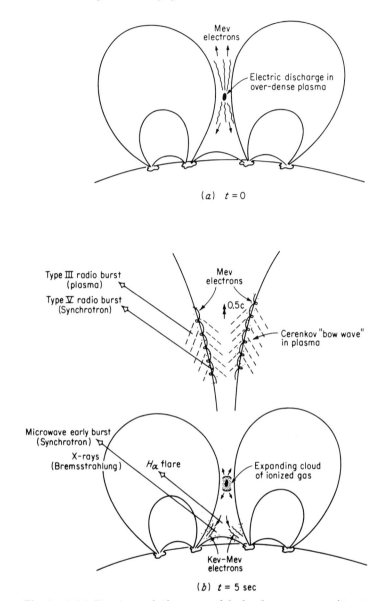

Fig. 7.6-3 (a),(b)   An evolutionary model of a flare event consistent with the general characteristics observed in radio, optical, X-ray, and corpuscular radiation. The model, as illustrated, presumes a neutral-point origin of the flare; with trivial modification it may be applied to other configurations. The first phase of the flare event shows the ejection of fast electrons and the accompanying electromagnetic emissions.

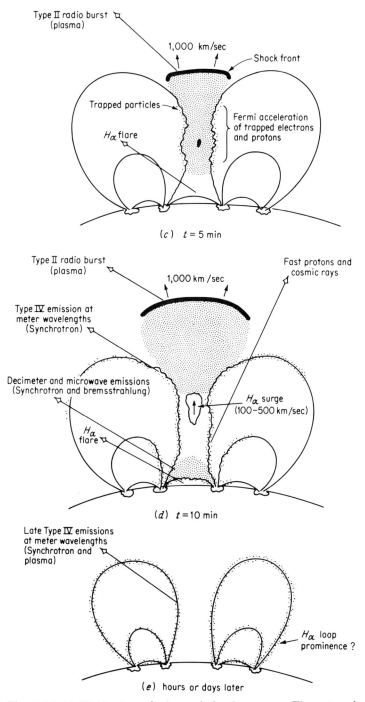

Fig. 7.6-3 (c),(d),(e)   Second phase of the flare event: The outward moving shock front with particle acceleration and trapping in its wake and the accompanying particle and electromagnetic emissions. (*Courtesy of J. P. Wild; see R 7.6-5.*)

gives the velocity of the disturbance causing the plasma oscillations. Thus we find that the type III burst arises from a disturbance traveling at $\frac{1}{3}c$ to $\frac{1}{2}c$; on the other hand, the type II burst gives velocities of some 500 to 1,000 km/sec.

The results indicate that a flare gives rise to two groups of particles. The fast group, presumably a cloud of electrons, passes through the atmosphere at a velocity of order $c/2$ and excites plasma oscillations which we observe as a type III burst. The identification of type III bursts with plasma oscillations seems certain, because harmonics are occasionally observed. The type V burst then results from synchrotron radiation from the electrons themselves. Similarly, the slow group of protons and electrons (perhaps associated with flare puffs) propagates at a velocity of $\sim 10^3$ km/sec in a shock front which excites the plasma oscillations observed as type II bursts. The type IV burst is due to synchrotron radiation and plasma oscillations caused by accelerated electrons and protons created in the complicated region behind the shock.

The polarizations of type IV and V emission support their identification as synchrotron radiation. A possible model which accounts for the major features of flare radiation is shown in Fig. 7.6-3.

The velocities associated with the type II bursts strikingly resemble those for the particle streams that are thought to be responsible for geomagnetic effects. However, geomagnetic effects are generally observed only when the type II burst is followed by a type IV burst. Physically, this means that there must be sufficient material behind the shock to produce type IV emission before geomagnetic effects are possible. The structure of type IV bursts is quite complicated, and several subclasses have been designated.

The isolated bursts appear to be type III bursts which occur outside outbursts. Also, there is considerable similarity between the type III burst and the U-type burst which first drifts toward low frequencies and then back to high frequencies. The mechanism appears to be the same as for type III bursts, but with the disturbance channeled first up and then down in the solar atmosphere by magnetic fields.

BIOGRAPHICAL NOTES

The transparency of the atmosphere is discussed in:

R 7-1. Goldberg, L., and E. R. Dyer: In "Science in Space," ed. L. V. Berkner and H. Odishaw, pp. 341–399, McGraw-Hill Book Company, New York, 1961.

Section 7.1. The γ-ray burst described was reported in:

R 7.1-1. Peterson, L. E., and J. R. Winckler: *J. Geophys. Res.*, **64**: 697 (1959).

See also:

R 7.1-2. Greenstein, J. L.: "Space Age Astronomy," eds. A. J. Deutsch and W. B. Klemperer, pp. 214–218, Academic Press Inc., New York, 1962.

R 7.1-3. Tousey, R.: In "Space Astrophysics," ed. W. Liller, pp. 1–16, McGraw-Hill Book Company, New York, 1961.

R 7.1-4. Friedman, H: In "Space Astrophysics," ed. W. Liller, pp. 107–120, McGraw-Hill Book Company, New York, 1961.

The observations of X rays are reviewed in:

R 7.1-5. Friedman, H: In "The Solar Corona," ed. J. W. Evans, pp. 45–58, Academic Press Inc., New York, 1963.

The theory is discussed in:

R 7.1-6. Elwert, G.: *J. Geophys. Res.*, **66**: 391 (1961).

Section 7.2. The following references are primarily to review articles which summarize the data and give the detailed references. See:

R 7.2-1. Purcell, J. D., D. M. Packer, and R. Tousey: In "Space Research," ed. H. Kallmann-Bijl, pp. 581–589, North Holland Publishing Company, Amsterdam, 1960.

R 7.2-2. Rense, W. A.: In "Space Research," ed. H. Kallmann-Bijl, pp. 608–614, North Holland Publishing Company, Amsterdam, 1960.

R 7.2-3. Friedman, H.: In "Space Research II," eds. H. C. van de Hulst, C. de Jager, and A. F. Moore, pp. 1021–1035, North Holland Publishing Company, Amsterdam, 1961.

R 7.2-4. Hinteregger, H. E.: *J. Geophys. Res*, **66**: 2367 (1961).

R 7.2-5. Tousey, R.: In "Space Age Astronomy," eds. A. J. Deutsch and W. B. Klemperer, pp. 104–114, Academic Press Inc., New York, 1962.

R 7.2-6. Rense, W. A.: In "Space Astrophysics," ed. W. Liller, pp. 17–33, McGraw-Hill Book Company, New York, 1961.

See also R 7.1-3 and R 7.1-4.

Section 7.3. The early work on the flux in Lyman-α is summarized in:

R 7.3-1. Byram, E. T., T. A. Chubb, H. Friedman, J. E. Kupperian, Jr., and R. W. Kreplin, *Astrophys. J.*, **128**: 738 (1958).

Recent flux observations are reported in most of the references for Sec. 7.2. The photography of the Sun in Lyman-α is described by:

R 7.3-2. Purcell, J. D., D. M. Packer, and R. Tousey: In "Space Research," ed. H. Kallmann-Bijl, pp. 594–598, North Holland Publishing Company, Amsterdam, 1960.

High-resolution spectra of Lyman-α are discussed in:

R 7.3-3. Purcell, J. D., and R. Tousey: In "Space Research," ed. H. Kallmann-Bijl, pp. 590–593, North Holland Publishing Company, Amsterdam, 1960.

Also, see R 7.2-6 concerning the width of Lyman-α. A valuable reference for ultraviolet absorption processes in the upper atmosphere is:

R 7.3-4. Watanabe, K.: *Advan. Geophys.*, **5** : 153 (1958).

A discussion of the theory of the formation of Lyman-α is contained in:

R 7.3-5. Morton, D. C., and K. G. Widing: *Astrophys. J.*, **133** : 596 (1961).

Section 7.4. The optical spectrum is discussed by:

R 7.4-1. Pettit, E.: In "Astrophysics," ed. J. A. Hynek, pp. 259–301, McGraw-Hill Book Company, New York, 1951.

See also:

R 7.4-2. Goldberg, L., and A. K. Pierce: In "Handbuch der Physik," vol. 52, ed. S. Flügge, pp. 1–79, Springer-Verlag OHG, Berlin, 1959.

Several atlases of the solar spectrum are referenced in R 7.4-2. The absorption spectrum of the atmosphere is covered in:

R 7.4-3. Goldberg, L.: In "The Earth as a Planet," ed. G. P. Kuiper, pp. 434–490, The University of Chicago Press, Chicago, 1954.

Section 7.5. The spectrum in this region is discussed in R 7.4-3 and R 7.4-2; see also the references in these articles.

Section 7.6. The absorption properties of the atmosphere are discussed in the textbooks on radio astronomy and in R 7.4-3. Reviews of solar radio astronomy are contained in:

R 7.6-1. Pawsey, J. L., and R. N. Bracewell: "Radio Astronomy," Clarendon Press, Oxford, 1955.

R 7.6-2. Pawsey, J. L., and S. F. Smerd: In "The Sun," ed. G. P. Kuiper, pp. 466–531, The University of Chicago Press, Chicago, 1953.

R 7.6-3. van de Hulst, H. C. (ed.): "Radio Astronomy," Cambridge University Press, London, 1957.

R 7.6-4. Bracewell, R. N. (ed.): "Paris Symposium on Radio Astronomy," Stanford University Press, Stanford, Calif., 1959.

Also of interest are the references for Sec. 5.3, Chap. 6, and pp. 283–322 of R 5.2-2. Recent developments are summarized in:

R 7.6-5. Wild, J. P.: In "The Solar Corona," ed. J. W. Evans, pp. 115–127, Academic Press Inc., New York, 1963.

R 7.6-6. Wild, J. P.: *J. Phys. Soc. Japan*, **17**(suppl. A-II): 249 (1962).

See also additional papers and discussion in the supplement which accompanies R 7.6-6.

The
interplanetary gas

8.1 INTRODUCTION

The interplanetary gas is a topic of great current interest. The "ancient history" of this subject goes back only a few years, and when new developments are occurring rapidly in a field, it is often quite difficult or impossible to present the subject as systematically as would be desirable. Since the field of the physics of the interplanetary gas is in a state of rapid change, our approach will be somewhat historical.

Existence of an interplanetary gas or a medium between the planets was first suspected from the zodiacal light (discussed in Chap. 13). This bright band of light along the ecliptic arises from sunlight scattered by particles in the interplanetary medium. The zodiacal light can be seen easily with the unaided eye in favorable locations and times of year. The question that then arises is the nature of the particles producing the scattered radiation. For some years an adequate explanation seemed to be

197

that the zodiacal light was simply sunlight reflected or scattered by dust. Then, Behr and Siedentopf observed the polarization of the zodiacal light. The degree of polarization obtained was considered too high to be explained by dust, and hence it was assumed that a sizable portion of the zodiacal light was due to scattering of sunlight by free electrons. An electron density near the orbit of Earth of about 600 per cm^3 was obtained from an analysis of the polarized component of the zodiacal light, under the assumption that all of the polarized radiation came from scattering by electrons. We shall find that this density is actually much too high and that the polarization must arise from dust. Nonetheless, these observations, together with Biermann's work on comet tails, stimulated considerable interest in the interplanetary medium.

Biermann's observations (Chap. 9) of comet tails also indicated the existence of an interplanetary plasma. One can distinguish knots in the tails of comets, and their motions can be followed. These motions, and particularly the accelerations, can be interpreted in terms of a constant flow of material from the Sun, i.e., the "solar corpuscular radiation" or "solar wind." The idea of a flow of gas from the Sun goes back many years; for example, Chapman and Ferraro advocated neutral plasma streams from the Sun in connection with auroral and geomagnetic theories. Biermann extended this concept to include emission in all directions at essentially all times. A simple interpretation of the phenomena indicated that an electron density of about 600 per cm^3 and expansion velocities w of some 500 to 1,000 km/sec were needed. The agreement with these numbers and the results of Behr and Siedentopf was considered favorable. We shall consider later how they must be revised. At the time they agreed also with the densities obtained from studies of whistlers (Chap. 18).

We should now consider how the interplanetary gas may arise. An approach (due to Chapman and Parker) which has been found to be rather profitable is simply to consider the interplanetary medium as a tenuous extension of the solar corona. This leads us to the study of models of the interplanetary medium. Notice that simply regarding the interplanetary plasma as a tenuous extension of the solar corona does not specify the physical process involved in maintaining it. Several specific mechanisms are discussed below. At present, three components of the interplanetary gas are distinguished:

1. Flare-associated events; see Secs. 6.6 and 7.6.

2. Apparently discrete streams with a 27-day period; these are thought to be associated with unipolar magnetic regions on the Sun (Sec. 6.8). The streams may be the distant extension of large coronal streamers.

3. The general, steady, windlike expansion which is the component under discussion in the major portion of this chapter.

8.2   THEORETICAL MODELS

The interplanetary gas is assumed to be spherically symmetric and in a steady state; no account is taken of magnetic fields. The basic equations are the equation of motion,

$$\frac{NM}{2} \nabla w^2 = -\nabla(NkT) - NM\nabla\phi \tag{1}$$

the equation of continuity,

$$\nabla \cdot (N\mathbf{w}) = 0 \tag{2}$$

and the first law of thermodynamics with heat conduction and energy deposition,

$$\nabla \cdot (K\nabla T) + F(r,N,T) = -kT\mathbf{w} \cdot \nabla N + \tfrac{3}{2}Nk\mathbf{w} \cdot \nabla T \tag{3}$$

In these equations, N ($= 2N_e$) is the total particle density, M ($=M_H/2$) is the mean particle mass, w is the expansion velocity, T is the temperature, $\phi = -M_\odot G/r$, r is the heliocentric distance, K is the coefficient of heat conduction, and k is Boltzmann's constant. Equation (8.2-1) neglects viscosity. In Eq. (8.2-3), the heat conduction is referred to the mass motion of the gas using the relation $d/dt = \partial/\partial t + \mathbf{w} \cdot \nabla$ on the right-hand side. This equation states that the net flow of energy into a volume [from the divergence of the conductive energy flux or from energy deposition represented by $F(r,N,T)$] must go into the work involved in expanding the gas or into the internal energy of the gas by raising the temperature.

Two integrals of these equations are immediately obtainable. Equation (8.2-2) gives

$$Nwr^2 = C \tag{4}$$

where $4\pi C$ is the total number of particles escaping from the Sun per second. In Eq. (8.2-3), the energy deposition can be written as $-\nabla \cdot \mathbf{b}(r)$, where $\mathbf{b}(r)$ is a flux of energy (say, mechanical). Then, Eqs. (8.2-1) and (8.2-3) can be written out, combined and integrated to yield

$$\frac{1}{wN}\left(K\frac{dT}{dr} - b\right) + E_\infty = \frac{Mw^2}{2} + \frac{5}{2}kT + M\phi \tag{5}$$

The right-hand side of this equation gives the total energy per particle; the term $\tfrac{5}{2}kT$ includes the internal energy $\tfrac{3}{2}kT$ and the potential due to adiabatic expansion, kT. The left-hand side expresses the particle energy in terms of the energy at infinity E_∞ less the energy still to be gained by conduction and energy deposition as the particle moves to infinity.

Consider now how various authors handle this problem. Chapman considers the case of a static corona; this corresponds to the postulate of a barrier at large distances so that the equilibrium configuration is static. Also, no energy deposition (or loss) was considered. Hence, Eq. (8.2-3) for $w = 0$ becomes

$$\nabla \cdot (K \nabla T) = 0 \tag{6}$$

In all cases, it is considered that the interplanetary medium is a plasma (i.e., a proton-electron gas). Hence, the coefficient of thermal conductivity is given by

$$K = K_0 T^{5/2} \qquad \text{erg}/(\text{cm})(\text{sec})(°\text{K}) \tag{7}$$

where $K_0 = 5 \times 10^{-7}$ (cgs). When Eq. (8.2-7) is substituted into Eq. (8.2-6), the resulting equation is easily integrated. With the condition $T \to 0$ as $r \to \infty$, we have

$$\frac{T}{T_0} = \left(\frac{r_0}{r}\right)^{2/7} \tag{8}$$

This solution implies a very slow decrease in the temperature as we move away from the Sun. If we assume a temperature of 1×10^6 °K at the base of the corona, we then have a temperature of 220,000°K at the orbit of Earth. The density can be computed from the temperature and the solar gravity through the equation of hydrostatic equilibrium. For a coronal temperature of 1×10^6 °K, the density near the orbit of Earth is in the range 300 to 400 electrons/cm³. This is in essential agreement with the measures of Behr and Siedentopf, etc. However, the density [determined from Eq. (8.2-1) with $w = 0$] actually goes through a minimum and then increases at large distances. This leads to the result that the pressure remains finite at large distances and hence cannot be balanced.

Thus, it seems that expansion is a characteristic feature of models of the interplanetary medium, because the barrier effectively postulated to guarantee $w = 0$ does not exist. Other evidence (e.g., acceleration of knots in comet tails) supports this conclusion. However, Eq. (8.2-8) may still give a reasonable estimate of the temperature if conduction remains important despite the expansion.

Consider now the expanding models. The procedure adopted by Parker is to assume that the corona is held at some constant temperature out to a certain point (say, 5 to $20R_\odot$) and that the corona expands adiabatically beyond (no net flow of heat into a volume element). This corresponds to adjusting $F(r,N,T)$ in Eq. (8.2-3) so that T is constant in the inner region. This type of model implies that the corona is heated to fairly large distances. The region outside corresponds to $F(r,N,T) = K = 0$ in Eq. (8.2-3). With this type of model, Parker was able to obtain velocities (taken as known from comet data) and also densities which could be identified with the solar wind.

Parker's latest values for the region near the orbit of Earth are $N_e \approx 30/\text{cm}^3$ and $w \approx 400$ km/sec for solar minimum and $N_e \approx 150/\text{cm}^3$ and $w \approx 550$ km/sec for solar maximum. On Parker's original model these high velocities extended to very large distances from the Sun. The temperature at the Earth is found to be about $100,000°$K. The density is somewhat lower than on the basis of the zodiacal light observations and Chapman's model, but other evidence indicates that this is in the right direction.

Chamberlain's approach to the problem is to set b and E_∞ equal to zero in Eq. (8.2-5). Hence, energy is supplied to the corona only at the base. The results near the orbit of Earth are $T \approx 20,000°$K, $N_e \approx 30$ per cm³, and $w \approx 20$ km/sec. The basic difference between the treatments of Chamberlain (solar breeze or subsonic solution) and Parker (solar wind or supersonic solution) would seem to be the manner of the supplying of heat to the corona. Chamberlain supplies it only at the base, while Parker's assumption of a constant temperature out to an appreciable number of solar radii implies a substantial deposition of energy. The real situation may well be an intermediate one, because we saw in Sec. 5.1 that some heating of the corona occurred through slow-mode disturbances created in the chromosphere by the collisions of shocks.

Noble and Scarf have given solutions corresponding to $b = 0$, but $E_\infty \neq 0$, in Eq. (8.2-5). These authors have assumed the conditions near the Earth and integrated back into the corona; the agreement (in the corona) is reasonable but not definitive. A useful review of the hydrodynamic models is contained in R 8.2-7.

The difference in the forms of the expansion velocity curves obtained on the basis of the two treatments outlined above can be seen in Fig. 8.2-1. The heavy line denotes the probable state of affairs in the interplanetary gas. Note that the high-velocity or supersonic solution undergoes a shock transition to the slow-velocity or subsonic solution, as has been noted by F. H. Clauser. The transition is analogous to a phenomenon observable in a bathtub. When the tap is turned on, one notes two regimes. The first

Fig. 8.2-1   A schematic diagram showing the velocity in the interplanetary gas on the solar wind and solar breeze model. Also shown is the shock front and the probable state of affairs, denoted by the heavy line. (*After E. Schatzman, in R 8.2-10.*)

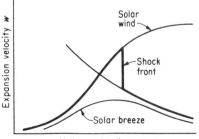

is a shallow, roughly circular area characterized by high velocities; this area is surrounded by a deeper, essentially stationary medium. The choppy rim between these two areas is the "transition zone." The transition zones in both bathtub and interplanetary gas occur for the same reason: the back pressure of the surrounding, stationary medium.

We expect that the transition occurs when the dynamic pressure in the solar wind ($\sim N_e m_H w^2$) becomes comparable to the pressure in the stationary medium. For a constant velocity of expansion (believed appropriate for the region exterior to 1 AU), the density and hence the pressure vary as r^{-2}; thus, it eventually becomes comparable to the interstellar pressure and the transition occurs. On the outside of the transition zone, the mean thermal velocities are of the order of w inside; for the solar case, this implies a temperature of $\sim 10^7$ °K.

The two approaches considered above take the interplanetary gas to be hydrodynamic in origin. Two other approaches are available. The gas can be considered to result from evaporation of ions and electrons from the corona (Secs. 18.7 and 18.8). Also, there is the "melon seed" mechanism of Schlüter. In a medium with **B** decreasing outward, a diamagnetic blob experiences a greater magnetic pressure ($B^2/8\pi$) on the inward side than on the outward. Thus, the blob is squeezed outward like a melon seed. The diamagnetic blobs are thought to be ejected into the coronal magnetic field from the hydrogen convection zone.

8.3 EMPIRICAL RESULTS AND MODELS

The assumption that the zodiacal light is caused essentially by scattering due to electrons can be tested in a way which is independent of the polarization measures. The electron scattering of radiation introduces, through the thermal motion of the electrons and the Doppler effect, a broadening of the lines in the Fraunhofer spectrum. This effect also changes the central intensities of these lines. Hence, the electron density can be inferred, in principle, from a comparison of the direct Fraunhofer spectrum with the scattered Fraunhofer spectrum from the zodiacal light (see also Sec. 5.3).

In practice, such observations require a very good observing site; Blackwell and Ingham have used a location in the Bolivian Andes at an altitude of 17,100 ft. The site is at geomagnetic latitude 3°S and hence should be as free as possible from the influences of faint auroras. By taking spectra of the zodiacal light, they were able to compare these spectra with spectra of the Sun and look for the presence of interplanetary electrons. The problem of obtaining the spectra involves the elimination of scattered light in the spectrograph, and the interpretation involves the subtraction of the night sky or auroral background. For these reasons, it was imperative to have the high-altitude site.

Blackwell and Ingham were able to find no evidence of line broadening by interplanetary electrons, and hence the upper limit to the electron density is given by the limits of the errors of the observations. Their original upper limit of about 100 electrons/cm^3 has been lowered by more recent work to 30. Blackwell and Ingham also observed fluctuations in the zodiacal light which can be attributed to electrons in a corpuscular stream with an electron density of about 300 per cm^3. This higher value is associated with discrete streams and is not a typical figure. The results of Blackwell and Ingham taken together with the observations of Behr and Siedentopf mean that the polarization must come from dust particles. This problem is discussed further in Sec. 13.1. The densities obtained on the models due to Parker and Chamberlain are consistent with Blackwell and Ingham's observations, but it should be noted that the 600 electrons/cm^3 originally supposed necessary to explain the acceleration of knots in comet tails by particle collisions is not consistent with those observations.

Models of the interplanetary medium have also been derived from empirical evidence. These models have so far not relied heavily on the rocket and satellite evidence, but natural probes such as the planets and comets were utilized as much as possible.

The velocity w of the solar wind can be estimated from the orientations of type I comet tails; in this case, the orientation is determined by dynamical aberration (Sec. 9.5), and thus we can determine w for the region of space probed by type I comets. For spherical symmetry, the equation of continuity, $N_e w r^2 = $ const, gives the run of the density, provided the density is known at one point. In Chap. 18, we describe the results of rocket surveys of the distant geomagnetic field. These observations show a termination or cutoff of the geomagnetic field at approximately $14R_\oplus$. When one considers that there is an approximate pressure balance between the solar wind $N_e m_H w^2$ and the geomagnetic field $B_c^2/8\pi$, where B_c is the value of the geomagnetic field at the cutoff, one obtains $N_e \approx 1$ per cm^3 for $w = 300$ km/sec. The model can be extended into the corona with the aid of observed coronal electron densities and velocities determined from the equation of continuity.

These empirical values near the orbit of Earth can be checked for consistency with a theoretical formula based on the distribution function, $f(r,v,t)$ (Sec. 6.2). By taking moments of this distribution function, we may find a relationship connecting parameters in the corona ($r = 4R_\odot$, say) with parameters near the orbit of Earth. For plausible parameters in the corona and a temperature near the orbit of Earth in the range 50,000 to 100,000°K, we find that reasonable parameters near Earth are $w = 200$ to 400 km/sec and $N_e = 1$ to 5 per cm^3. The principal change from the empirical model to this one (called the semiempirical model) is an increase in the density. A version of the semiempirical model is shown in Fig. 8.3-1.

We explicitly call attention to the fact that the electron density obtained is a mean in space and time. Our knowledge of coronal structure leads us to expect considerable fine structure in the interplanetary gas.

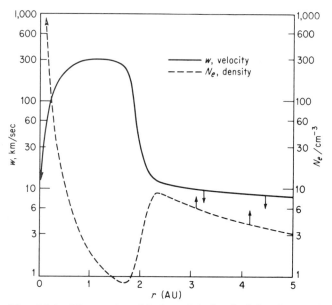

Fig. 8.3-1 The semiempirical model sketched in the text.
(*by J. C. Brandt and R. W. Michie in R 8.3-3.*)

This fine structure has been studied directly by occultations of radio sources, such as the Crab nebula, as they pass through the solar corona. As the position of the Crab nebula approaches the point of closest approach to the Sun, the total flux from the Crab nebula decreases while its angular size increases. This behavior has been attributed to scattering of radio radiation by irregularities in the electron density, not only in the corona, but well into interplanetary space.

The observations now extend to $100R_\odot$ and are consistent with scattering from elongated, radially aligned density fluctuations. The alignment presumably arises because of the influence of the magnetic field. Note that our discussion of the transfer of radio wavelength radiation in Sec. 5.3, thought to be appropriate to the corona, assumes a homogeneous medium without density fluctuations. The results here indicate that some correction to the results described in Sec. 5.3 may be required.

The temperature ($\sim 10^5$ °K) and densities (~ 2 per cm^3) thought to be probable near the orbit of Earth lead to another problem. The mean free path for protons in a plasma can be written as

$$\lambda \approx \frac{1}{2} \times 10^{-9} \frac{T^2}{N_e} \qquad \text{AU} \tag{1}$$

Equation (8.3-1) follows from the collision frequency for protons and the mean velocity of a particle in a gas at temperature T. This formula gives $\lambda \approx 1$ AU near the orbit of Earth; it means that there are not enough collisions to maintain an isotropic velocity distribution of particles in the coordinate system moving at the mean expansion velocity. Since the velocity distribution may well be anisotropic, the use of Eq. (8.2-8), which requires isotropy, may not be valid. Thus, conclusions drawn from the available hydrodynamic models should be used with caution. The velocity distribution must lie between an isotropic and radial one, and it may well be influenced by the presence of the interplanetary magnetic field. The assumption of fluid behavior must rest on the existence of the interplanetary magnetic field.

The interplanetary gas exterior to 1 AU is much more uncertain than the interior part. Presumably, the regime is one of a constant w and $N_e \propto r^{-2}$ until the transition region (discussed in Sec. 8.2) is reached. The orientations of the type II tails at $r \gtrsim 2$ AU suggest to some workers a stopping of the solar wind near 2 AU, a feature that has been included in the empirical and semiempirical models.

Certain other properties of comets (besides the orientation of the tail) seem to be consistent with these models. For example, the form of the relation between the diameter of comet comas vs. heliocentric distance changes somewhere between $1\frac{1}{2}$ and 2 AU. This apparent transition suggests a change in the properties of the interplanetary medium. Also, the type I comets have been found so far only interior to $1\frac{1}{2}$ to 2 AU. They are characterized by their ionized tails composed mainly of CO^+. Type I may appear only in regions near the Sun because the solar wind is responsible (directly or indirectly) for the ionization observed in comet tails, but this speculation is still controversial.

Finally, a transition zone near 2 AU is consistent with our knowledge of galactic structure and the local interstellar medium. The interaction between the solar wind and the interstellar medium is undoubtedly magnetic in nature—much as is the interaction with the terrestrial atmosphere via the geomagnetic field. Hence, we may compare the fields which are able to persist under the action of the solar wind and thus obtain an estimate of the location of the transition region. The geomagnetic field with strengths of 10 to 20 γ (1 $\gamma = 10^{-5}$ gauss) maintains itself against the solar wind; we adopt the 10 γ figure as the higher one, for the region in question appears to result from a compression of the geomagnetic field by the solar wind. When the pressures are compared for the wind and the local interstellar magnetic field B_I, we find that the heliocentric distance of the transition is proportional to B_I^{-1}.

If we assume that the interaction mechanism is the same for the geomagnetic and interstellar cases, we have a transition at $10/B_I$ AU (B_I in γ). Current estimates for interstellar fields are 1 to 3 γ, and, if correct, the transition would come at 3 to 10 AU. The actual average distance from the Sun may even be less than these quoted values—since the magnetic observations were made at solar maximum—and the interstellar cosmic-ray pressure may also be important.

In addition, the concave nature of the interplanetary-interstellar boundary means that the so-called "interchange instability" may be operative. This allows puffs of plasma to pass through the boundary, and it means that the solar wind is relatively less effective in pushing back the magnetic field compared to the geomagnetic (convex) case. The nature of the interplanetary-interstellar interface is quite uncertain. An alternate model has been discussed by Parker (see R 8.3-9). The role of the interplanetary magnetic field in the physics of the interface also needs study and clarification.

The general picture outlined here appears to be consistent with the requirements of cosmic-ray storage. However, we note that there is no general agreement on the location of the transition zone and that the interpretation of the distant type II comet tails sketched above is controversial.

8.4 SPACE PROBE RESULTS

The Mariner II plasma probe, sent a large distance from the Earth, has removed much of the uncertainty in the results described above. Some plasma flux was observed essentially all the time (Fig. 8.4-1); quiet conditions appear to be an electron density of 2 per cm^3 and $w = 500$ km/sec. These values are roughly those of the semiempirical model. For disturbed conditions, the density is doubled, and $w = 800$ km/sec. (Fig. 8.4-2). Some difficulty in the interpretation arises from the fact that there appears to be an appreciable helium component in the solar wind, in addition to the expected component of protons.

The observations also allowed an estimate of the temperature to be made via the velocity dispersion; Neugebauer and Snyder found 2×10^5 °K. The results from Explorer X are somewhat different from those of Mariner II, but the two experiments can be reconciled (Sec. 18.9). The Mariner II results are also compatible with the results obtained from ion traps on Soviet interplanetary probes.

The interplanetary magnetic field was also studied with instruments carried on Mariner II. The field varies between 2 and 10 γ; it is predominantly radial, but a definite transverse component exists. We return to the interplanetary magnetic field in Sec. 8.6.

8.5 NEUTRALS IN THE INTERPLANETARY GAS

For some time it was believed that the night-sky Lyman-α radiation (Chap. 18) was caused by neutral hydrogen in the interplanetary medium scattering Lyman-α photons back toward the Earth. Hence, there was some interest in computing the distribution of neutral hydrogen in the interplanetary medium.

This problem is approached by assuming a steady state. Hence, the various ways of creating and destroying neutral hydrogen in a fixed vol-

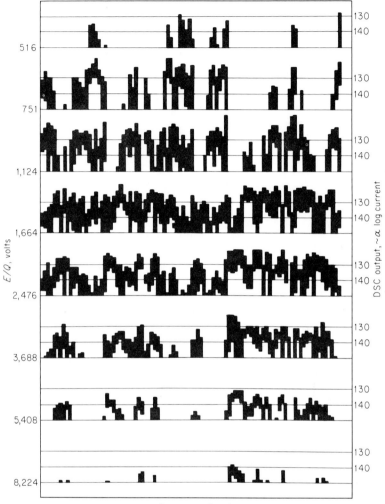

Fig. 8.4-1 A summary of data obtained by the Mariner II solar plasma experiment from August 20 through October 31, 1962, as a function of time and energy. The lines marked 130 and 140 correspond approximately to 10^{-11} and 10^{-12} amp, respectively; the length of the bar represents the total spread in the measured current over a period of approximately 16 hr. Notice that there are large variations and also that a current is measurable essentially all of the time. (*Courtesy of M. Neugebauer and C. W. Snyder, The Jet Propulsion Laboratory, see R 8.4-1.*)

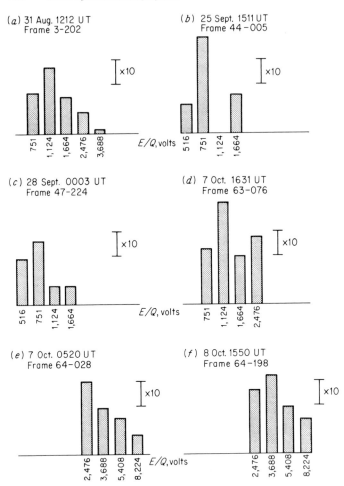

Fig. 8.4-2   Some selected plasma spectra obtained on the Mariner II probe. (*Courtesy of M. Neugebauer and C. W. Snyder, The Jet Propulsion Laboratory, see R 8.4-1.*)

ume must yield no change in the neutral hydrogen concentration with time. Thus, we need to solve an equation of the general form

$$\frac{\partial N_H}{\partial t}\bigg]_{\text{local processes}} + \frac{\partial N_H}{\partial t}\bigg]_{\text{mass motions}} = 0 \tag{1}$$

The term due to mass motions is given by the equation of continuity, where we consider motions due to the expanding plasma and diffusion. For the case of spherical symmetry,

$$\frac{\partial N_H}{\partial t}\bigg]_{\text{mass motions}} = \boldsymbol{\nabla} \cdot N_H(\boldsymbol{C}_H + \boldsymbol{w}) \tag{2a}$$

$$= \frac{1}{r^2} \cdot \frac{d}{dr}\left[r^2 N_H(\boldsymbol{C}_H + \boldsymbol{w})\right] \tag{2b}$$

where C_H is the diffusion velocity relative to the plasma. The term due to local processes describes the rate of recombination and ionization. The recombination rate is given approximately by

$$\frac{N_e^2 K_0}{T^{1/2}} \tag{3}$$

where K_0 is a constant. The photo-ionization rate is $N_H \chi$, where

$$\chi = \int_{\nu_1}^{\infty} (\pi F_\nu) \alpha_\nu \, d\nu \tag{4}$$

Here πF_ν is the solar flux and α_ν is the absorption coefficient for photo-ionization. The integral is over all wavelengths shortward of the ionization limit ν_1. The collisional ionization rate is given by $N_e N_H \alpha_c$, where α_c is the appropriate coefficient for collisional ionization.

We may collect the various terms to write

$$\frac{N_e^2 K_0}{T^{1/2}} - N_H(\chi + N_e \alpha_c) = \frac{1}{r^2} \cdot \frac{d}{dr} [r^2 N_H(C_H + w)] \tag{5}$$

The solution to this problem is obtained subject to the appropriate boundary conditions. For the solar wind region, it is not necessary to solve the full equation to obtain a clear picture of the physical situation. We simply compute a characteristic lifetime for recombination and compare it with the flight time. Since hydrogen is ionized in the corona, the ratio τ_F/τ_{rec} is roughly the fraction of hydrogen which could recombine. This gives an upper limit to the neutral component, because photo-ionization is neglected. Now

$$\tau_F \approx \frac{r}{\langle w \rangle} \tag{6}$$

and

$$\tau_{rec} \approx \langle N_e \alpha_{rec} \rangle^{-1} \tag{7}$$

where

$$\alpha_{rec} = \frac{K_0}{T^{1/2}} \tag{8}$$

The τ_{rec} is estimated from a "mean density and temperature" assigned to the region between the point r and the corona. With any reasonable model, we always find

$$\frac{\tau_F}{\tau_{rec}} \ll 1 \tag{9}$$

Hence, we find

$$\frac{N_H}{N_e} \ll 1 \tag{10}$$

in the solar wind. The same is true of helium and essentially all other elements and ions. In essence, the stage of ionization of elements in the interplanetary medium just outside the Earth is the same as in the corona, and hence the interplanetary medium is a plasma.

It is possible for recombination to occur beyond 2 AU. As one goes away from the Sun, the degree of ionization should approach the interstellar value. This may involve consideration of nearby early-type stars. The neutral hydrogen density outside the transition zone is of interest in connection with the night-sky Lyman-α problem; it has been suggested that the thermalized protons on the outside of the transition zone undergo charge exchange with interstellar neutral hydrogen, thereby creating neutral hydrogen atoms with velocities of several hundreds of kilometers per second. The velocities are isotropic, and this "hot" hydrogen could penetrate into the inner part of the solar system to form an important component of the night-sky Lyman-α radiation. This hypothesis appears unlikely, since the radiation from the Sun and nearby hot stars is thought to keep the interstellar gas ionized in the neighborhood of the Sun.

8.6 COSMIC RAYS AND THE INTERPLANETARY MAGNETIC FIELD

Cosmic rays were first discovered as a mysterious source of ionization in the atmosphere. Samples of air which were thought to be well shielded from outside influences always seemed to have some residual ionization. This source was at first thought to be associated with the radioactivity in the Earth's crust, since cosmic rays could be detected in deep mines. However, early balloon flight experiments showed that the cosmic-ray intensity increased with height above the Earth's surface and clearly established the extraterrestrial nature of these rays.

The early experiments dealt not with the primary cosmic-ray particles, but only with the secondary particles produced in the atmosphere. The primary cosmic-ray particles are particles with energies between 10^8 and 10^{19} ev (Fig. 8.6-1). These particles are thought to be produced largely in the galaxy, but there is also a solar component. The primaries (galactic component) contain about 85 per cent protons, 14 per cent α particles, and 1 per cent nuclei of elements from lithium to iron. Near the surface of the Earth, we find only the secondaries composed mainly of neutrons and μ mesons; there are also some electrons and γ rays (Fig. 8.6-2).

The solar system can influence the cosmic-ray spectrum by producing some cosmic-ray particles locally or by modulating the galactic component. Let us consider the first influence. It is known that solar cosmic-ray particles in the energy range 10^9 to 10^{10} ev are produced in solar events associated with flares (Sec. 6.6). In the appropriate energy range, the intensity can jump by orders of magnitude over the background intensity.

At the beginning of a solar cosmic-ray event (flare associated, ~ 5

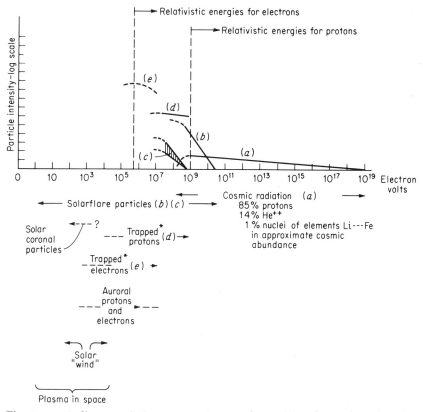

Fig. 8.6-1 A diagram of the spectra of energetic particles observed in the solar system. The dashed lines indicate extrapolations, and the asterisks denote particles trapped in the geomagnetic field. All particles except cosmic radiation (a) arise from processes within the solar system, and even (a) is modulated by solar system mechanisms. (*From J. A. Simpson in R 8.6-4.*)

events known), the particles are incident on the Earth from one general direction which includes the Sun. After some time, the angular distribution of the cosmic-ray particles incident on the Earth is isotropic. The later stages of a solar cosmic-ray event include an exponential decay of the intensity and subsequent return to the preflare level. It seems that this behavior can be given a simple interpretation in terms of the interplanetary magnetic field. The fact that the first particles arrive from one direction means that they are not appreciably deviated by the interplanetary magnetic field. This implies that the field interior to the Earth is either essentially radial or $\lesssim 10^{-6}$ gauss.

The isotropy implies that a storage mechanism exists. This can be accounted for by postulating that there are disordered magnetic fields outside the Earth's orbit which can scatter the cosmic rays. Thus we may

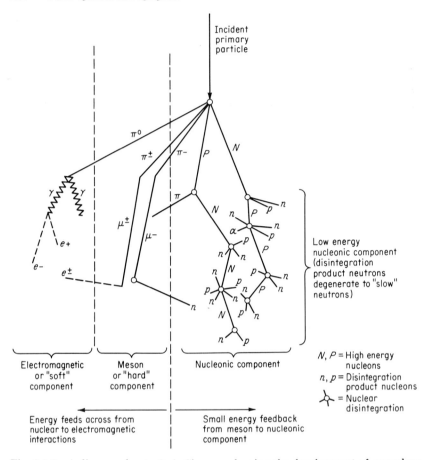

Fig. 8.6-2   A diagram due to J. A. Simpson showing the development of secondary components of the cosmic radiation in the atmosphere from incident primary cosmic-ray particles. (*From J. A. Simpson in R 8.6-4.*)

think of the cosmic-ray particles as "diffusing" through the interplanetary magnetic field by scattering from local irregularities in the magnetic field. If the diffusion coefficient is taken as $K(E)$, where E is the energy, and if $J(E)$ is the density of cosmic-ray particles with energies between E and $E + dE$, then the appropriate diffusion equation is

$$\frac{\partial J(E)}{\partial t} = K(E)\nabla^2 J(E) \qquad (1)$$

If the medium is taken as infinite and a burst of particles is released at $t = 0$, then a special solution of Eq. (8.6-1) is

$$J(E) = \frac{C}{(\pi K t)^{3/2}} \exp\left(-\frac{r^2}{\pi K t}\right) \qquad (2)$$

For the region near the Earth, r is sufficiently small to allow the neglect of the exponential term, and a simple $t^{-3/2}$ law is obtained.

A disordered field with a root-mean-square strength of about 10^{-5} gauss will suffice for this mechanism. The thickness of the shell of disordered fields can be estimated from the decay rate, because the cosmic-ray particles eventually escape into the galaxy. It is found that a shell between the orbits of Mars and Jupiter (approximately 2 to 5 AU) can explain the observations. The detailed model gives a good fit to the data (Fig. 8.6-3). It seems that we would expect this type of behavior on the basis of the empirical model of the interplanetary medium. Interior to 2 AU, the energy density in the wind exceeds the magnetic energy density. Hence, we expect that the expansion dominates and draws the magnetic lines of force out radially. However, the pertinent energy densities become comparable near 2 AU. This fact and the eventual merging of the interplanetary magnetic field with the interstellar field lead one to expect a disordered field in the proper region. The disordered fields can also be explained by instabilities in the magnetic field exterior to the Earth. A general picture of the interplanetary magnetic field is given in Fig. 8.6-4.

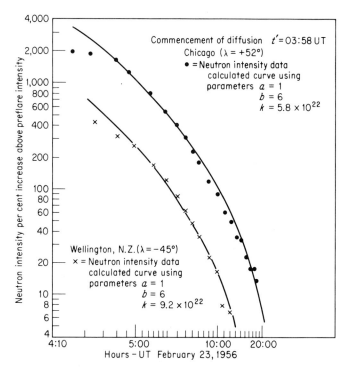

Fig. 8.6-3　A comparison of the theory sketched in the text for cosmic-ray diffusion in the solar system with the observations (solid curve denotes theory). (*By J. A. Simpson in R* 8.6-4.)

This simple picture is complicated by the solar rotation; possibly, the magnetic field picks up an azimuthal component. This is also reflected in the cosmic-ray data; flares on the western limb of the Sun produce more observable cosmic-ray events on the Earth than flares on the eastern limb. This is exactly what one would expect if these particles are guided along magnetic lines of force joining the Earth and the Sun, the field lines being curved because of solar rotation. One picture of the interplanetary magnetic field emphasizes the role of the solar rotation, which gives the field lines a spiral shape like water from a rotating garden hose. At the Earth, this model has an angle between the radial direction and the field lines of some 30 to 40°. The Mariner II magnetic field observations are consistent with but do not require spiral structure; these observations do seem to rule out a "tongue-like" magnetic field starting and ending in a localized region on the Sun. Hence, the storage of cosmic rays by such a tongue-like magnetic field (which envelops the Earth) appears to be ruled out. Note that the asymmetry in the cosmic rays may be due to fields near the Sun.

The variations of the galactic cosmic-ray intensity have been observed for some years. A comparatively recent advance established that these changes are caused by changes in the intensity of the primary beam impinging on the top of the atmosphere. This is the evidence for modulation. The first type of change is with the solar cycle. When the sunspot number is greatest, the intensity of cosmic rays is the least, and vice versa (Fig. 8.6-5). This relationship is clearly associated with changes in the

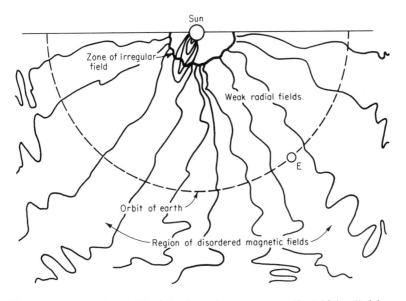

Fig. 8.6-4   A simple model of the interplanetary magnetic field implied by the studies of cosmic rays. Note however, that some large-scale spiral structure may exist. (*From R 8.6-4 by J. A. Simpson.*)

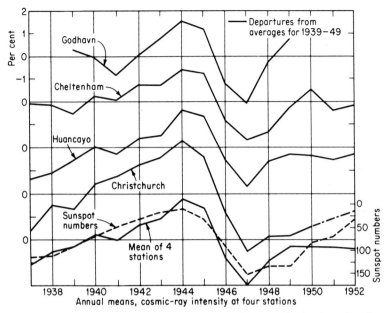

Fig. 8.6-5 A plot of the inverse correlation between ionization chamber intensity and solar activity. (*From S. E. Forbush in R 8.6-4.*)

interplanetary magnetic field caused by variations of the model of the interplanetary medium with solar cycle.

We imagine that the region of disordered fields would be thicker and the fields more disordered during sunspot maximum. Thus, a galactic cosmic-ray particle will have a harder time "diffusing" into the inner solar system during sunspot maximum than during sunspot minimum. We may think of the cosmic-ray particle as encountering an "escalator," i.e., the outward motion of a region of tangled magnetic fields. The escalator is longer and runs faster at sunspot maximum.

The second type of change is the so-called Forbush decrease in the secondary-neutron or μ-meson intensity due to a sudden 30 to 40 per cent decrease in the intensity of the primary beam. This means that the Earth is sometimes enveloped by clouds of magnetized plasma ejected from the Sun: these clouds would tend to shield the Earth from the galactic cosmic rays. These events occur about one day after some large solar flares.

BIBLIOGRAPHICAL NOTES

Section 8.1. The early results concerning the polarization of the zodiacal light and the electron content of the interplanetary gas is given in:

R 8.1-1. Behr, A., and H. Siedentopf: *Z. Astrophys.*, **32**: 19 (1953).

The early work on the acceleration of knots in comet tails is summarized in:

R 8.1-2. Biermann, L.: "La Physique des Comètes," p. 291–302, Ceuterick, Louvain, 1953. (Liège Symposium, September, 1952).

Section 8.2. The work on stationary models is reviewed in:

R 8.2-1. Chapman, S.: In "Space Astrophysics," ed. W. Liller, pp. 133–149, McGraw-Hill Book Company, New York, 1961.

For details of work on expanding models and summaries, see:

R 8.2-2. Biermann, L.: In "Space Astrophysics," ed. W. Liller, pp. 150–156, McGraw-Hill Book Company, New York, 1961.

R 8.2-3. Parker, E. N.: In "Space Astrophysics," ed. W. Liller, pp. 157–170, McGraw-Hill Book Company, New York, 1961.

R 8.2-4. Parker, E. N.: *Astrophys. J.*, **132**: 821 (1960).

R 8.2-5. Chamberlain, J. W.: *Astrophys. J.*, **131**: 47 (1960).

R 8.2-6. Chamberlain, J. W.: *Astrophys. J.*, **133**: 675 (1961).

R 8.2-7. Noble, L. M., and F. L. Scarf: *J. Geophys. Res.*, **67**: 4577 (1962).

R 8.2-8. Clauser, F. H. (ed.): "Symposium of Plasma Dynamics," chap. 8, Addison-Wesley Publishing Company, Inc., Reading, Mass., 1960.

R 8.2-9. Thomas, R. N. (ed.): "Proceedings of the Fourth Symposium on Cosmical Gas Dynamics: Aerodynamic Phenomena in Stellar Atmospheres," *Suppl. Nuovo Cimento*, **XXII** (1961). (I.A.U. Symposium No. 12.)

R 8.2-10. Schatzman, E.: In "Space Age Astronomy," eds. A. J. Deutsch and W. B. Klemperer, pp. 171–188, Academic Press Inc., New York, 1962.

R 8.2-11. Parker, E. N.: In "Science in Space," eds. L. V. Berkner and H. Odishaw, pp. 229–238, McGraw-Hill Book Company, New York, 1961.

R 8.2-12. de Jager, C.: *Space Sci. Rev.*, **1**: 487 (1963).

R 8.2-13. Lüst, R.: *Space Sci. Rev.*, **1**: 522 (1963).

The melon seed mechanism is treated in:

R 8.2-14. Schlüter, A.: *Z. Naturforsch.*, **5a**: 72 (1950).

R 8.2-15. Parker, E. N.: *Astrophys. J. Suppl.*, **III**: 51 (1957).

Section 8.3. The Bolivian observations of the zodiacal light appear in a series of four consecutive papers beginning with:

R 8.3-1. Blackwell, D. E., and M. F. Ingham: *Monthly Notices Roy. Astron. Soc.*, **122**: 129 (1961).

The ideas used in the construction of an empirical model and a discussion of the model are contained in:

R 8.3-2. Brandt, J. C.: *Icarus*, **1**: 1 (1962).

See also references given there and:

R 8.3-3. Brandt, J. C., and R. W. Michie: *Phys. Rev. Letters*, **8**: 195 (1962).

The details of the approach using the distribution function and a discussion of the anisotropy are contained in:

R 8.3-4. Brandt, J. C., and R. W. Michie: *Astrophys. J.*, **136**: 1023 (1962).

The radio observations of density irregularities in the corona and interplanetary gas are contained in:

R 8.3-5. Hewish, A.: In "Paris Symposium on Radio Astronomy," ed. R. N. Bracewell, pp. 268–273, Stanford University Press, Stanford, Calif., 1959.

R 8.3-6. Vitkevich, V. V.: In "Paris Symposium on Radio Astronomy," ed. R. N. Bracewell, pp. 275–281, Stanford University Press, Palo Alto, Calif., 1959.

R 8.3-7. Slee, O. B.: *Monthly Notices Roy. Astron. Soc.*, **123**: 223 (1961).

The location of the transition region is discussed in:

R 8.3-8. Davis, L.: *J. Phys. Soc. Japan*, **17**(suppl. A-II): 543 (1962).

R 8.3-9. Parker, E. N.: *Astrophys. J.*, **134**: 20 (1961).

R 8.3-10. Parker, E. N.: *Planet. Space Sci.*, **9**: 461 (1962).

R 8.3-11. Brandt, J. C.: *Proc. Fourth Intern. Space Sci. Symp.*, Warsaw, June, 1963.

Section 8.4. The Mariner II results are reported in:

R 8.4-1. Neugebauer, M., and C. W. Snyder: *Science*, **138**: 1095 (1962).

R 8.4-2. Coleman, P. J., L. Davis, E. J. Smith, and C. P. Sonett: *Science*, **138**: 1099 (1962).

Section 8.5. The early work is summarized by:

R 8.5-1. Elsässer, H.: *Mitt. Astron. Ges.*, **1957 II**: 61 (1957).

Later work is contained in:

R 8.5-2. Brandt, J. C.: *Astrophys. J.*, **133**: 688 (1961).

R 8.5-3. Brandt, J. C.: *Astrophys. J.*, **134**: 975 (1961).

Section 8.6. See the texts:

R 8.6-1. Wolfendale, A. W.: "Cosmic Rays," Philosophical Library, Inc., New York, 1963.

R 8.6-2. Leighton, R. B.: "Principles of Modern Physics," pp. 680–707, McGraw-Hill Book Company, New York, 1959.

Various topics on cosmic-ray physics are summarized in:

R 8.6-3. Savedoff, M. P. (ed.): *Astrophys. J. Suppl.*, **IV** : 369 (1960).

R 8.6-4. Simpson, J. A.: In "Science in Space," eds. L. V. Berkner and H. Odishaw, pp. 221–227, 239–259, and 261–274, McGraw-Hill Book Company, New York, 1961.

See also R 8.2-8, R 8.2-11, R 8.3-7, R 8.4-2, and:

R 8.6-5. Davis, L.: In "Space Age Astronomy," eds. A. J. Deutsch and W. B. Klemperer, pp. 189–193, Academic Press Inc., New York, 1962.

Comets

chapter

Some comets (e.g., Halley's Comet) have been known to mankind for centuries. Occasionally, naked-eye comets are seen in the sky, and these appearances engender considerable popular interest. Centuries ago the form of the interest was not casual or detached, since comets were greatly feared. Indeed, old prayers asked for deliverance from such things as the plague and the comet.

We now feel that comets are usually harmless, but our knowledge of them remains meager, qualitative, and largely descriptive.

9.1 GENERAL DATA

Orbits

Most comets have orbits which are highly elliptical or parabolic. The few hyperbolic orbits can usually be ascribed to planetary perturbations. The majority of cometary orbits can be taken to be highly elongated ellipses with perihelia of $\sim$1 AU and aphelia of many AU. A few comets have

219

nearly circular orbits. The inclinations to the ecliptic plane are random, and comets may be both direct and retrograde (e.g., Halley's Comet). The problems associated with cometary orbits have been studied in considerable detail. These efforts lead to a picture of the storage of comets in a large cloud about the Sun. Occasionally, a perturbation sends a comet toward the Sun, and we then observe it in a highly eccentric orbit.

It is also known that comet families exist. These are comets which were originally in highly eccentric orbits but which have been captured through a planetary encounter. Jupiter is the most important influence in this respect. If a comet approaches within 300,000 km of Jupiter, it is likely to be thrown into an orbit with aphelion of ≈ 5 AU. Because of the details of the encounter, Jupiter's comet family is composed mainly of direct comets. Those comets which move in virtually the same orbit are called a *comet group*. A group is often thought of as originating from one great comet which was disrupted.

Comets probe virtually the entire interplanetary space from the corona to many AU. This feature has stimulated considerable interest in them, since an understanding of the properties of comets becomes essential to the study of certain properties of the interplanetary gas.

Nomenclature and dimensions

Comets are very individualistic, and a normal or typical comet does not exist. Many comets, however, do exhibit the three basic parts: the nucleus, the coma, and the tail. Quite often the nucleus and the coma together are called the head. The appearance of a comet normally varies with heliocentric distance; a sequence of photographs showing Halley's Comet from 0.6 to 5.0 AU is given in R 9.1-2.

The nucleus is observed as a very bright, starlike part of the comet. Estimates of the size of such an object are very difficult to make; current values are 1 to 100 km. Often a nucleus is not visible, and sometimes the nucleus is multiple. Some upper limits to sizes of comet nuclei have been reported as the result of attempted observations of comets as they transit the solar disk. In these upper-limit determinations contrast and diffraction effects may be quite important.

The coma is the essentially spherical, permanent, and bright (compared to the tail) part of the comet (Fig. 9.1-1). An average size for the coma is 10^5 km. The coma size varies with heliocentric distance, but it has a maximum between 1.5 to 2.0 AU. The location of the maximum is probably not well established, but a definite "contraction of the coma" occurs for some comets as they approach the Sun from distances of ~ 1 AU. The comas of comets are apparently quite small at large distances $(r \geq 4$ AU); and hence we find ourselves with a maximum at an intermediate distance. Strictly, the coma does not include tail particles which are passing through it; see Sec. 9.5 and discussion on mass loss below.

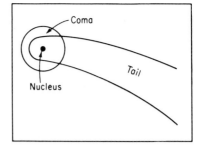

Fig. 9.1-1   A schematic diagram showing the parts of a comet.

The tail is the most impressive feature of a comet. Lengths of tails range from almost zero to a common value of 10^7 km; exceptional comets have tails of $\sim$1 AU.

Approximately 1,000 comets are known; 400 of them were discovered before the telescope. Comets are discovered at the rate of approximately 10 per year. Unofficially, comets are named after their discoverer (e.g., Comet Humason) or after an orbit computer (e.g., Halley's Comet). Officially, comets are designated 1962a, 1962b, etc., as they are discovered. Later, permanent designations such as 1962 I and 1962 II are given in order of perihelion passage. There are inconsistencies that are due to errors in early ephemerides.

Masses

Cometary masses have not been determined directly. An upper limit can be inferred from the fact that no definite effect in a planetary orbit due to a comet-planet encounter has ever been observed; this leads to an upper limit of some 10^{-6} times the mass of the Earth, or 10^{22} g. A lower limit can be obtained from the amount of material required to produce the observed brightness. Additional data on masses comes from the fact that two comets have passed within the satellite system of Jupiter with no discernible effect. A value of $4 \times 10^{-7} M_{\oplus}(10^{21}$ g) has been derived from the relative motion of the two parts of Biela's Comet after it split in 1846. Masses of $\sim 10^{18}$ to 10^{19} g are found in the literature.

Association with meteors

An important point is that meteor swarms are associated with comets. For example, the reliable Perseids (seen on about August 10) are associated with Comet Tuttle 1862 III. This subject is covered in Chap. 10.

Brightness

The law of cometary brightness (strictly the flux) is usually written as

$$J = J_0 f(\Delta) F(r) \psi(\cos \Theta) \qquad \text{ergs/(cm}^2\text{)(sec)(frequency interval)} \qquad (1)$$

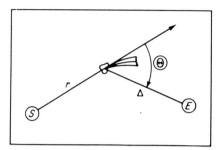

Fig. 9.1-2 A schematic drawing showing the geometry and quantities used
in the discussion of cometary brightness.

where Δ is the distance from the Earth to the comet and r is the heliocentric distance of the comet. The geometry is shown in Fig. 9.1-2. The function $f(\Delta)$ can be put equal to Δ^{-2}, but $F(r)$ is much more difficult. The function $\psi(\cos \Theta)$ is to account for variations of the brightness with phase. The brightness of comets has been observed over a large range of heliocentric distances, and no effect that could be ascribed to phase has been found. Hence, we set $\psi(\cos \Theta) = 1$ and write the brightness equation as

$$J = \frac{J_0}{\Delta^2} F(r) \tag{2}$$

We now postulate that $F(r) = r^{-n}$, and hence

$$J = \frac{J_0}{\Delta^2 r^n} \tag{3}$$

Expressing these quantities in magnitudes,

$$H = H_0 + 5 \log \Delta + 2.5n \log r \tag{4}$$

where H_0 is the absolute brightness of the comet, i.e., at $\Delta = r = 1$, and the distances are in AU. If we denote $(H - 5 \log \Delta) = H_\Delta$ as the magnitude reduced to the Earth, we then have

$$H_\Delta = H_0 + 2.5n \log r \tag{5}$$

Thus a plot of cometary magnitude versus $\log r$ is a straight line with slope $2.5r$. The observations show that this formula can provide a meaningful representation of the data, provided that n is allowed to vary from comet to comet. If the physical process involved in cometary brightnesses were simply reflection from a constant amount of gas or dust in the coma, we would expect $n = 2$. However, the average value of n is about 4 (with individual values between 2 and 6), which indicates that we also have a process of gas generation from the nucleus which varies with heliocentric distance. It should be noted that there exist sudden brightness variations in comets. Sometimes these variations are a minor feature of the light curve, but for a few comets the fluctuations prohibit a meaningful construction of a light curve. A satisfactory model of the cometary nucleus and coma is required to give some insight into the value of n and to provide a mechanism for brightness variations. Beyer has shown that brightness variations are correlated with solar activity through the sunspot number; hence, the ultimate explanation is probably in terms of corpuscular streams in the interplanetary plasma.

Mass loss

Finally, we should mention that there is no reason to believe that comets ever recover the mass that is driven into the tail and deposited or dispersed along the orbit. Hence, comets have a finite lifetime. This continual depletion of material may account for the fact that some comets are not found when they should return, even when it is believed that an accurate orbit is available. It may be that the last stages of depletion have actually been observed. Several comets have faded and vanished as they have moved toward perihelion; examples are Comet Perrine 1897 III and Comet Ensor 1926 III. This behavior is consistent with our ideas concerning the structure of comets (Sec. 9.3).

9.2 SPECTROSCOPIC DATA

Cometary spectra are quite complex; they are composed of a continuum, emission lines, and molecular bands. The continuum is thought to result from reflection from the nucleus or from dust in the immediate vicinity. Comets which show nuclei invariably show a continuous spectrum. Atomic lines rarely are found in the coma. Gases identified in the coma from their spectrum are CN, C_2, C_3, CH, NH, NH_2, and OH. Gases found in the tail are CO^+, N_2^+, OH^+, CO_2^+, and CH^+. Most of these gases are chemically unstable, which gives some indication of the very low densities found in comets.

The spectrum of a comet varies with heliocentric distance. The very distant comets show only a continuous spectrum with CN appearing at ≈ 3 AU. Near 2 AU, C_3 and NH_2 appear. As the comet approaches 1.5 AU, C_2 (Swan bands), CH, OH, and NH appear and increase. Inside 1.5 AU, CO^+, OH^+, N_2^+, and CH^+ appear in the tail. Near 0.8 AU, Na appears, and if the perihelion distance is very close (≈ 0.1 AU), Fe, Cr, and Ni appear. The forbidden lines of oxygen $\lambda 6{,}300$ and $\lambda 6{,}364$ have also been observed in at least one comet. This discussion refers, of course, to an idealized sequence.

Observations of radio emission from comets have been reported; but some of them appear to be spurious, and only radio emission from CH appears established.

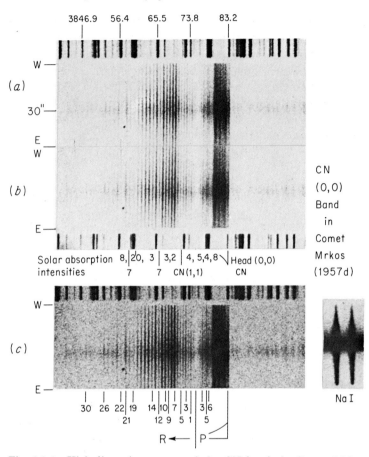

Fig. 9.2-1 High-dispersion spectra of the CN bands in Comet Mrkös clearly showing irregularities in the CN intensities caused by the (marked) solar absorption lines. (*Courtesy of J. L. Greenstein, Mount Wilson and Palomar Observatories.*)

One interesting subject in cometary physics does seem to be fairly well understood; that is the question of the mechanism which provides the radiation observed from comets. It is one of resonance fluorescence, as has been suggested by Swings. Consider the λ4,315 band of CH. The emission of this band is caused by an electronic transition from one energy state to a lower one. However, the electronic energy states are split into many levels by the rotational energy of the molecule. Thus the emission appears as a "band" which is composed of several individual lines. The intensities are determined by the populations of the upper levels. On the Swings mechanism, the populations of the upper levels are determined by transitions from the lower levels due to resonance absorption of solar continuous radiation.

Roughly, we may think of the situation as resonance scattering, though the actual situation is more complicated. This means that each absorbed photon is reemitted at almost the same frequency but in a random direction. Thus, the relative distribution of intensity in a band depends on the normal distribution among the lower states, the atomic parameters governing the transition (f values), and the variation of the intensity in the continuous solar radiation.

McKeller finds that the structure of the λ4,315 CH band in Comet Cunningham (1940c) reflects the variations with wavelength in the solar continuous spectrum. Greenstein has examined this problem with the aid of high-dispersion spectrograms of Comet Mrkös (1957d) taken with the 200-in coudé spectrograph. The variation of the intensities in the λ3,883 band of CN clearly shows the influence of solar absorption lines in the same wavelength region (Fig. 9.2-1). Thus the excitation mechanism of cometary molecular bands is considered known.

9.3 THE NUCLEUS

The *nucleus* as observed is a bright point of light within the coma. As mentioned above, a nucleus may be unobservable or it may be multiple. However, these last two circumstances are rather rare. It is probable that a reasonable understanding of the nucleus is the breakthrough which will lead to the understanding of comets as a whole.

The sand bank model

Here the nucleus is taken to be a swarm of independent solid particles that weigh a few milligrams each and are about one meter apart. This nucleus may alternatively be thought of as a swarm of meteoritic particles. This concentration of particles is the source of the reflected or scattered sunlight observed in the spectra of cometary nuclei. It is also consistent with the observation of no phase effect.

The sand bank model is not generally accepted at present. It appears difficult to produce the amount of observed gases in the coma from solid bodies; also, there is some question concerning the survival of the dust particles. We note that 1 g of meteoritic material can supply $\sim 10^{19}$ gas molecules. Another objection appears to be that such a model would be unable to withstand a close encounter with a planet or the Sun without being tidally disrupted.

The icy conglomerate model

Here the nucleus is taken to be a spongy mass of ices such as H_2O, NH_3, CH_4, CO_2, and C_2N_2 with some small ($\sim 1 \mu$) particles embedded throughout. The structure is envisioned as having some tensile strength. The ices are generally poor conductors of heat; incident radiation then heats only a surface layer, resulting in the sublimation of molecules and atoms. The more volatile molecules evaporate at larger heliocentric distances; this effect coupled with subsequent dissociation of the parent molecules listed above appears to satisfactorily account for the order of appearance of the molecular bands of the various constituents. However, it may be necessary to consider more complicated molecules to obtain complete accord with the observations. The ices postulated here are better sources of gas than are meteoritic grains, since each gram of ices can supply 10^{22} to 10^{23} gas molecules.

On this picture, the continuous spectrum of the nucleus originates from a cloud of particles in the immediate vicinity of the solid body. The model usually has 70 to 80 per cent of the mass in ices and the remainder in meteoritic dust. The ices appear to be essential as the source of gas. However, it is not permissible simply to add, say, "ice grains" to the sand bank model, since the ice grains would have a relatively short lifetime. Hence, it is necessary to shield some of the ices by placing them in a single structure.

The low thermal conductivity confines the heating largely to a relatively thin surface layer. After the surface layer of ices has been sublimated, a surface dust structure remains. Heat transfer to the interior apparently occurs by radiation and is inefficient. Because of the complicated manner in which the ices are heated, sublimated, and allowed to escape, the simple adsorption-desorption picture (often used to compute the gas production) may not be adequate. *Adsorption* is the attachment of a dense layer or film (usually monomolecular) of gas to a solid body such as a dust grain. The inverse process is called *desorption*. If the gas molecules penetrate deep into the solid, the process is termed *occlusion*.

These processes may well be important, but there is some question concerning the application of the simple theory to the complex situation envisioned on the icy conglomerate model of the nucleus. Such a model has some structural strength and thus is able to stand perturbing forces as we require. Eventually, all the ices are sublimated and we are left with dust spread out (by perturbations) along the orbit of the comet, and the meteor stream is formed.

The structure is thought to be rather inhomogeneous. Thus, pockets of gas may be able to develop. The release of such pockets of gas may be responsible for "jet-like" phenomena observed on comets.

The solar radiation heats the comet nucleus on the side facing the Sun. If the comet is rotating, the molecules evaporate in a preferential direction, owing to the time lag involved in transferring heat to the interior. This constitutes a net force on the comet nucleus and may explain the secular acceleration observed, for example, on Comet Enke.

9.4 THE COMA

The essentially spherical coma is composed of molecules which presumably have first sublimated and then evaporated from the dust layer of the nucleus. The physical picture is one in which the parent molecules evaporate from the nucleus and then are dissociated by the solar ultraviolet radiation into the simpler constituents, which we observe by the fluorescence mechanism described above. This picture can be checked by using observations with filters which isolate the molecular bands of one constituent, such as CN or C_2.

Consider the problem of the isotropic evaporation of molecules from a spherical source (a comet nucleus) and the subsequent photodissociation under the action of solar radiation with a time scale τ_0. Because of the low masses associated with cometary nuclei, the mass of the comet has no appreciable effect on particles ejected from the nucleus at the typical velocity of ~ 1 km/sec. This can be ascertained by computing the escape velocity, using Eq. (2.2-4), from a comet of mass 10^{18} g and radius 1 km. Since the result is two orders of magnitude below 1 km/sec, we conclude that the molecules that leave the nucleus of a comet do so at constant velocity v_0.

Hence, we find that on the average, a particle is photodissociated in a distance $R_0 = \tau_0 v_0$. The definition of the time scale τ_0 is such that $dN/dt = -N/\tau_0$, and hence τ_0 is the time for the number density to fall to e^{-1} of its original value under the assumption of a constant flux of dissociating radiation, which is the case of interest in comet comas. Thus the dissociation alone causes the density to vary as e^{-r/R_0}.

Also, the equation of continuity for a spherical system, Eq. (8.2-4), gives a variation as r^{-2}. Hence, the dependence of the density on the distance from the comet is approximately

$$D(r) = \left(\frac{R}{r}\right)^2 D(R)e^{-r/R_0} \tag{1}$$

where R is the radius of the comet.

The situation thought to prevail in comet comas is more complicated. The molecules which evaporate from the nucleus are postulated to be the relatively complex parent molecules which do not contribute to the observed light from the coma. These molecules then decay into simpler, daughter molecules from which we receive scattered solar radiation. These molecules are, in turn, ionized or photodissociated. If we let $\beta_0 = (R_0)^{-1}$, then Eq. (9.4-1) can be generalized in an obvious manner to include two decay processes, giving

$$D(r) = \left(\frac{R}{r}\right)^2 D(R)(e^{-\beta_0 r} - e^{-\beta_1 r}) \tag{2}$$

where β_0 refers to the daughter molecules and β_1 to the parent molecules. Note that Eq. (9.4-2) reduces to Eq. (9.4-1) when $\beta_1/\beta_0 = \infty$.

To compare this scheme with the observations of the surface brightness of comets, Eq. (9.4-2) must be integrated along the line of sight. This procedure is lengthy and leads to expressions involving Bessel functions; it is not reproduced here. A comparison of the theory with observations is given in Fig. 9.4-1; a satisfactory fit is obtained with $\beta_1/\beta_0 = 9$, but the fit is poor for $\beta_1/\beta_0 = \infty$. Typical densities for molecular constituents (for example, C_2) in comet comas range up to 10^4 to 10^6 molecules/cm^3.

Additional evidence for this scheme comes from the discussion of the variation of the brightness of comets (Sec. 9.1). There we found that an n of about 4 implied a generation process for the material under observation. A limiting process for the outer boundary of the comas may be implied by the heliocentric variation of coma diameters.

The approximately parabolic form of the coma boundary is easily understood on the basis of the Bessel-Bredichin theory of comet tails discussed in Chap. 2. Halos are expanding and drifting shells of gas which appear to be made up of material ejected at one instant from the nucleus. The mechanism responsible for halos is unclear, but it may be related to plasma streams and the observed brightness variations. Fine structure in comas is observed as structures which resemble fans.

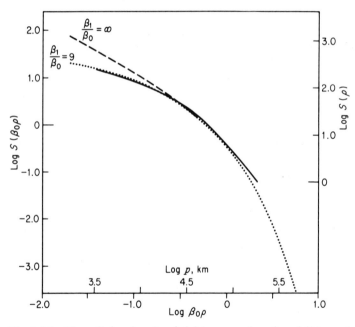

Fig. 9.4-1   Mean C_2-band surface brightness as a function of distance from the nucleus compared with the theory discussed in the text. (*Given by C. R. O'Dell and D. E. Osterbrock in R 9.4-1, Copyright 1962 by The University of Chicago, published by the University of Chicago Press.*)

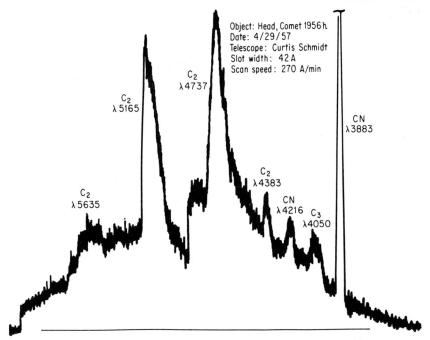

Fig. 9.4-2   Photoelectric scan of Comet Arend-Roland. Note that a yellow filter was inserted in the light path at wavelengths greater than λ5,000 to eliminate effects of overlapping orders. (*From R 9.4-5 by W. Liller, Courtesy of The Astronomical Journal.*)

In our above discussion, we imply that comas are a gaseous phenomenon. This is normally correct, but dust comas (showing a continuous spectrum) are sometimes found. These dust comas should probably be considered as somewhat distinct from the gas comas. Sometimes they are considered characteristic of "new comets," i.e., comets which only recently have penetrated into the observable portion of the solar system.

The observational distinction between dust comas and gas comas is easily made with the aid of photoelectric spectral scans; examples of the scans of the heads of two comets are shown in Figs. 9.4-2 and 9.4-3. These examples well illustrate the variations to be expected in the spectra of comet comas.

9.5   THE TAIL

Types

There are two basic types of comet tails. Type I tails are observed to consist entirely of ionized molecules, principally CO^+ but also C_2^+, CH^+, and CN^+ These tails are straight, show fine structure, and make an angle of

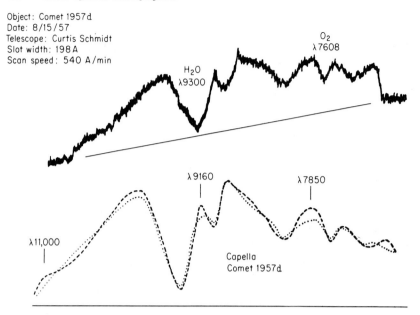

Object: Comet 1957d
Date: 8/15/57
Telescope: Curtis Schmidt
Slot width: 198 A
Scan speed: 540 A/min

H_2O
$\lambda 9300$

O_2
$\lambda 7608$

$\lambda 9160$

$\lambda 7850$

$\lambda 11,000$

Capella
Comet 1957d

Fig. 9.4-3   Photoelectric scan of the head of Comet Mrkös. The cometary scans (dashed line) are compared with Capella (dotted line), which is a yellow star of approximately the same color as the Sun. (*From R 9.4-5 by W. Liller, Courtesy of The Astronomical Journal.*)

a few degrees with the prolonged radius vector in the direction opposite to the comet's motion. Type I comets are found out to heliocentric distances of 1.5 to 2.0 AU. The fraction of comets which show the type I tail is larger near the solar equator than at the pole.

Type II tails are curved, but they are rather homogeneous and lacking in fine structure. The spectra of these tails appear to be reflected solar spectra; thus, type II comet tails are probably composed of dust. Type III tails are strongly curved dust tails. The size of the dust particles can be inferred from photometric and polarimetric measures; sizes of $\approx \frac{1}{2}\,\mu$ are found (see R 9.5-6 and references given there).

Comet Mrkös (1957 V) showed both a type I and a type II tail; these are shown in Fig. 9.5-1.

Structure and structural development

The structure of type II tails (homogeneous) appears to be compatible with the Bessel-Bredichin mechanical picture of comet tails. It is generally assumed (Chap. 2 and elsewhere) that the tails are in the plane of the comet's orbit and that the type II tails are essentially flat structures. This view is supported by observations of Comet Arend-Roland (1957 III). The Earth passed through the plane of this comet's orbit; a plate taken at that time is shown in Fig. 9.5-2. The tail is clearly confined rather closely to the plane of the orbit. Figure 9.5-2 also shows an "anomolous tail" or "sunward spike." It is sunward only in perspective, and possibly it is not a tail at all. Probably this is an observation of dust which experiences a negligible radiation pressure and is being dispersed along the orbit of the comet, such as found in meteor streams.

The type I tails are very complex and poorly understood. They exhibit considerable fine structure, the most characteristic feature being the tail ray. The matter in type I comet tails is apparently concentrated into thin bundles or streamers (CO^+ density $\approx 10^3$ per cm^3) which constitute the tail rays. These rays appear to be ejected from (or immediately in front of) the nucleus in the sunward direction. The tip of the ray is then bent back away from the Sun while the ray lengthens. As the ray lengthens still further, it turns into the tail axis and merges with the tail rays already there. The tail rays are created in groups called outbreaks or outbursts ($\sim$10 rays) lasting a few days.

Thus, the tail ions (predominantly CO^+) exist in tubes that run up to the immediate vicinity of the nucleus, which poses the question of the mechanism of the ionization of CO. This molecule has the same ionization potential as several of the coma molecules which remain unionized for

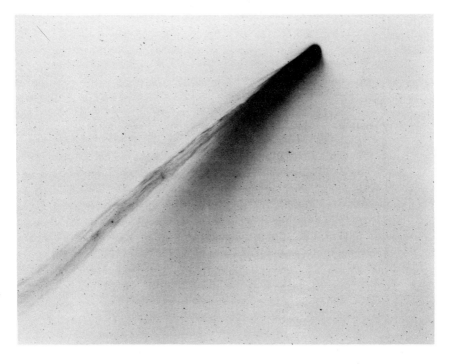

Fig. 9.5-1 A 48-in Schmidt photograph of Comet Mrkös showing both a type I and a type II tail. (*Courtesy of the Mount Wilson and Palomar Observatories.*)

Fig. 9.5-2   Comet Arend-Roland as the Earth was approximately in the plane of the Comet's orbit. (*Taken by C.A. Wirtanen, Courtesy of the Lick Observatory.*)

large distances from the nucleus. Thus, ionization is probably not due to solar radiation. From the spatial distribution of type I comets and the model of the interplanetary gas discussed in Chap. 8, it appears that a solar wind is necessary to produce CO^+. This immediately suggests the possibility of charge exchange, that is,

$$H^+ + CO \rightarrow CO^+ + H \tag{1}$$

Charge exchange appears to be inadequate, particularly with respect to the fine structure and the tail rays. A possible solution could be the transfer of energy from the solar wind to localized regions of the nucleus by means of a magnetic field embedded in the nucleus. A localized deposition of energy could account for the tail rays and CO ionization at the same time. Magnetic fields are possibly indicated from the very existence of the tail rays, and $B \sim 10^{-5}$ gauss is indicated for magnetic confinement of the ions into the thin streamers.

Besides the tail rays, type I tails also show cloudlike structures or condensations of CO^+ (Fig. 9.5-3). The knots are quite interesting, because historically they led to the concept of the solar wind. Accelerations of the knots were observed by following individual knots from day to day. If one assumes that it is constant, the acceleration can be derived readily, and accelerations of $1 - \mu \approx 10^2$ are quite common. The quantity $1 - \mu$ gives the extra force (such as radiation pressure or plasma drag) in units of the solar gravitation. The formula for the force of the solar radiation pressure is

$$F_r = \frac{2\pi^2 h e^2}{m_e c \lambda^3} \left(\frac{R_\odot}{r}\right)^2 \frac{f}{[e^{hc/\lambda kT} - 1]} \tag{2}$$

where h is the Planck constant, e is the electron charge, m_e is the mass of the electron, c is the velocity of light, r is the heliocentric distance, $R_\odot$ is the solar radius, T is the appropriate solar temperature, k is the Boltzmann constant, λ is the wavelength of the transition in question, and f is the oscillator strength (f value) for the transition. This formula follows from the expression

$$F_r = \frac{[\pi F_\nu]}{c} \times \frac{\pi e^2}{mc} f \tag{3}$$

which gives the force as the incident momentum per second per square centimeter, $[\pi F_\nu]/c$, times the effective area of the molecule [Eq. (4.3-26)].

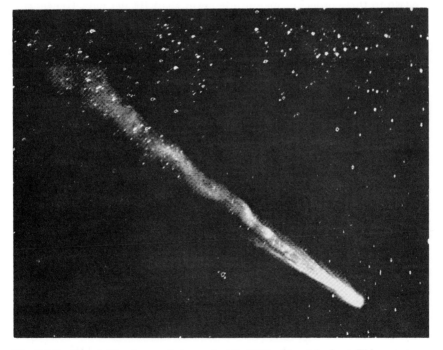

Fig. 9.5-3   Comet Morehouse photographed in 1908 with a 6-in. lens. This comet was very active and shows several tail knots. (*Courtesy of the Lick Observatory.*)

One assumes that the photons are scattered isotropically; hence, the effect is for each photon to impart (on the average) its entire momentum to the molecule. The flux at the comet follows from the flux at the surface of the Sun $[\pi B_\nu]$ (which comes from a source of constant intensity over a hemisphere; B_ν is the Planck function) and the appropriate dilution $(R_\odot/r)^2$. These various factors produce Eq. (9.5-4). The appropriate f value for CO^+ is quite small and cannot explain the observed accelerations. This failure led to the idea of these accelerations being caused by the drag of an ionized plasma streaming past the comet in the radial direction.

A discussion of the momentum equations shows that little momentum is transferred directly from the solar protons to the tail ions. The momentum transfer is effectively accomplished through the electrons, which have a large amount of friction with both the solar protons and the tail ions. The acceleration on the tail ions is found to be

$$\frac{dv_i}{dt} \approx \frac{e^2 N_e v_e m_e}{\sigma m_i} \approx 10^{-4.3} \left(\frac{m_e}{m_i}\right) N_e v_e \tag{4}$$

The conductivity σ (proportional to the inverse of the electron-ion collision frequency) was evaluated by using $T = 10^4\ °K$. For $N_e = 10^3/cm^3$ and $v_e \approx 10^8\ cm/sec$, Eq. (9.5-4) gives an acceleration of $\sim 10^2\ cm/sec^2$ as required. The densities in the solar wind on the basis of current models are two to three orders of magnitude lower than 10^3 per cm^3. Hence, this picture is not sufficient. However, it was realized from the beginning that magnetic fields would greatly enhance the coupling. These fields could be in the solar wind (Sec. 8.6) and/or in the tail knot. A magnetic field in the comet is consistent with our discussion of the tail rays and may also help in preserving the identity of the knot.

High accelerations and tail activity appear to be correlated with solar and geomagnetic activity, the latter when the geometry is favorable.

Orientations

The orientations of comet tails with respect to the prolonged radius vector are important not only for the study of comets but also for the study of the interplanetary gas. Within our present state of knowledge, the orientation of type I comet tails appears to be determined by the direction of the solar wind as seen by an observer on the comet (dynamical aberration). This view is supported by the fact that $\tan \alpha$ is proportional to the tangential velocity of the comet for many cases. Here the problem is purely geometrical and

$$\cot \alpha = \frac{\mathbf{r} \cdot (\mathbf{w} + \mathbf{V})}{-\boldsymbol{\phi} \cdot (\mathbf{w} + \mathbf{V})} \tag{5}$$

where α is the angle between the prolonged radius vector and the tail. The plasma velocity is $\mathbf{w}$, and $\mathbf{V}$ is the velocity of the comet. We also use unit vectors $\mathbf{r}$ in the radial direction and $-\boldsymbol{\phi}$ for the azimuthal direction in the sense opposed to the comet's motion (but $-\boldsymbol{\phi} \cdot \mathbf{r} = 0$). Under the assumption that $\mathbf{w}$ is radial,

$$\cot \alpha = \frac{w + V \cos \theta}{V \sin \theta} \tag{6}$$

where θ is the angle between $\mathbf{r}$ and $\mathbf{V}$. At perihelion, $\theta = 90°$, and we have $\cot \alpha = w/v$.

Type II tails are much more difficult. The type II tails at $r \lesssim 1$ AU seem to be explicable on the basis of the Bessel-Bredichin theory (Sec. 2.4) with radiation pressure acting on dust particles with sizes of ~ 1 μ. The forces on the various types of tails can be inferred from the shape (curvature) of the tails. One finds $1 - \mu \approx 10$ to 100 for type I tails, $1 - \mu \approx 1$ for type II, and $1 - \mu \approx 10^{-1}$ for type III. The force due to radiation pressure on a dust grain is

$$F_r = \frac{[\pi F]}{c} \pi s^2 Q(s) \tag{7}$$

The derivation of this formula is entirely analogous to Eq. (9.5-2); here, $[\pi F]$ is the solar radiation flux integrated over frequency and $Q(s)$ is the efficiency factor, which is the ratio of the effective area to the geometrical area πs^2. The force of solar gravity is GMm/r^2, and hence

$$1 - \mu = \frac{r^2 [\pi F] \pi s^2 Q(s)}{cGMm} = \frac{5.6 \times 10^{-5} \, Q(s)}{s\rho} \tag{8}$$

where ρ is the density of the material. For almost all substances, the efficiency factor $Q(s)$ is approximately 1 for sizes of the order of or greater than the mean wavelength involved (see R 9.5-7). Then, sizes of ~ 1 μ and densities of 1 g/cm³ or less give a $1 - \mu > 10^{-1}$, as we would require for an explanation of type II comet tails. The force on an atom or molecule is given by Eq. (9.5-2). Radiation pressure is not thought to be important for the gas tails (especially CO^+), but it can be important in producing an asymmetry in the distribution of atomic constituents such as sodium.

There is some evidence that the type II tails do not always emerge from the nuclear region in the radial direction. This appears to result from the dust near the nucleus being carried along by the fairly dense concentration of gas there. The observed orientations are consistent with this hypothesis and with the observed expansion velocities of the interplanetary gas [see Eq. (9.5-6)], which determine the orientation of the gas tail. Thus, we should think of the ordinary ($r \lesssim 1$ AU) type II comet tails as being governed by radiation pressure, but with the possibility of a significant interaction with the gas tail near the nucleus.

The distant type II tails ($r \geq 2$ AU, usually 2 to 5 AU) are somewhat of a mystery. They lie at an angle of some $45°$ from the radius vector in the direction opposite to the comet's motion. This angle appears to hold right up to the nucleus. Nevertheless, a formal fit for $1 - \mu$ on the Bessel-Bredichin theory can be made, and one finds $1 - \mu \approx 10^{-3}$. Immediately we see that the dust in these tails cannot be the same as in the ordinary type II tails, if we desire an explanation on the basis of radiation pressure, since $1 - \mu$ is independent of r. A simple explanation on the basis of radiation pressure would require dust particles several orders of magnitude larger than sizes of ~ 1 μ; however, there is no evidence for particles of this size in comet tails.

If radiation pressure is discarded, then the only explanation appears to be in terms of a strong interaction with the solar wind, which, then, must have had its velocity greatly reduced compared to its velocity near the orbit of Earth. The observations of the distant type II tails constitute one of the arguments for stopping the solar wind at a few AU, but the entire situation is still somewhat uncertain. For example, the mechanism for the interaction between the dust and the solar wind is not well understood, though the possibility of a buildup of charge on the grains appears promising.

9.6 COMETARY SPACE EXPERIMENTS

Two types of space experiments have been suggested in connection with comet physics. The first is simply to rendezvous a suitably instrumented probe with a comet to measure densities, fine structure, etc. Such experiments will undoubtedly be carried out, though the required rendezvous may be difficult to achieve.

The second type of experiment involves the launching of an "artificial comet." The general idea is to place some 100 kg of ices of H_2O, CO_2, etc. into orbit. The properties of such a "comet" could be studied, but with the tremendous advantage that the physical properties of the nucleus would be known.

BIBLIOGRAPHICAL NOTES

Section 9.1. The basic facts are presented in:

R 9.1-1. Richter, N. B.: "The Nature of Comets," Methuen & Co., Ltd., London, 1963.

R 9.1-2. Wurm, K.: In "Handbuch der Physik," vol. 52, ed. S. Flügge, pp. 465–518, Springer-Verlag OHG, Berlin, 1959.

R 9.1-3. Bobrovnikoff N. T.: In "Astrophysics," ed. J. A. Hynek, pp. 302–356, McGraw-Hill Book Company, New York, 1951.

R 9.1-4. Watson, F. G.: "Between the Planets," Harvard University Press, Cambridge, Mass., 1956.

R 9.1-5. Wurm, K.: In "The Moon, Meteorites, and Comets," eds. B. M. Middlehurst and G. P. Kuiper, pp. 573–617, The University of Chicago Press, Chicago, 1963.

R 9.1-6. Beyer, M.: In "La Physique des Comètes," pp. 276–286, Ceuterick, Louvain, 1953 (Liége Symposium, September, 1952).

For a catalogue of comet orbits see:

R 9.1-7. Porter, J. G.: *Mem. B.A.A.*, **39**(3): (1961).

Section 9.2. A compendium of cometary spectra is contained in:

R 9.2-1. Swings, P., and L. Haser: "Atlas of Representative Cometary Spectra," Institut d'Astrophysique, Liége, 1956.

See also R 9.1-1 to R 9.1-3 and:

R 9.2-2. Herzberg, G.: "Molecular Spectra and Molecular Structure I. Spectra of Diatomic Molecules," pp. 482–497, D. Van Nostrand Company, Inc., Princeton, N.J., 1950.

R 9.2-3. Swings, P., In "Astrophysics," ed. J. A. Hynek, pp. 145–171, McGraw-Hill Book Company, New York, 1951.

High-dispersion cometary spectra are presented in:

R 9.2-4. Greenstein, J. L.: *Astrophys. J.*, **128**: 106 (1958).

R 9.2-5. Greenstein, J. L., and C. Arpigny: *Astrophys. J.*, **135**: 892 (1962).

Section 9.3. See R 9.1-1. The icy conglomerate model is presented and discussed in:

R 9.3-1. Whipple, F. L.: *Astrophys. J.*, **111**: 375 (1950).

R 9.3-2. Whipple, F. L.: *Astrophys. J.*, **113**: 464 (1951).

R 9.3-3. Whipple, F. L.: *Astrophys. J.*, **121**: 750 (1955).

R 9.3-4. Whipple, F. L.: In "La Physique des Comètes," pp. 321–328, Ceuterick, Louvain, 1953 (Liége Symposium, September, 1952).

R 9.3-5. Whipple, F. L.: *Astron. J.*, **66**: 375 (1961).

The possible role of magnetic fields embedded in the nucleus is sketched in:

R 9.3-6. Brandt, J. C.: *Astron. J.*, **67**: 180 (1962).

The stability of ices in the solar system is the subject of:

R 9.3-7. Watson, K., B. C. Murray, and H. Brown: *Icarus*, **1**: 317 (1963).

See also:

R 9.3-8. Whipple, F. L.: In "The Moon, Meteorites, and Comets," eds. B. M. Middlehurst and G. P. Kuiper, pp. 639–664, The University of Chicago Press, Chicago, 1963.

Section 9.4. See R 9.1-1 to R 9.1-3. The density distribution in comet comas is the subject of:

R 9.4-1. O'Dell, C. R., and D. E. Osterbrock: *Astrophys. J.*, **136**: 559 (1962).

R 9.4-2. Haser, L.: *Bull. Acad. Roy. Belg. (Classe Sci.)*, *5th Series*, **43**: 740 (1957).

R 9.4-3. Miller, F. D.: *Astrophys. J.*, **134**: 1007 (1961).

R 9.4-4. Wurm, K.: *Astron. J.*, **66**: 362 (1961).

The photoelectric scans of comets heads are discussed in:

R 9.4-5. Liller, W.: *Astron. J.*, **66**: 372 (1961).

Comet comas are considered as plasmas in:

R 9.4-6. Marochnik, L. S.: *Soviet Astron.*, **6**: 532 (1963).

Section 9.5. See R 9.1-1 to R 9.1-3, R 9.4-4, and:

R 9.5-1. Wurm, K.: In "La Physique des Comètes," pp. 260–275, Ceuterick, Louvain, 1953 (Liége Symposium, September, 1952).

The ionization of CO is discussed in R 9.4-4, R 9.3-5, and R 9.5-2. The acceleration of the tail knots is described in:

R 9.5-2. Biermann, L.: In "La Physique des Comètes," pp. 291–302, Ceuterick, Louvain, 1953 (Liége Symposium, September, 1952).

R 9.5-3. Harwit, M., and F. Hoyle: *Astrophys. J.*, **135**: 875 (1962).

Tail orientations are discussed in:

R 9.5-4. Brandt, J. C.: *Icarus*, **1**: 1 (1962).

For the observations of orientations see the references in R 9.5-4. The distant tails are discussed in:

R 9.5-5. Osterbrock, D. E.: *Astrophys. J.*, **128**: 95 (1958).

R 9.5-6. Belton, M. J. S., J. C. Brandt, and P. W. Hodge: *Ann. Astrophys.*, **26**: 250 (1963).

See also:

R 9.5-7. Hulst, H. C. van de, "Light Scattering by Small Particles," John Wiley & Sons, Inc., New York 1957.

R 9.5-8. Biermann, L., and Rh. Lüst: "The Moon, Meteorites, and Comets," eds. B. M. Middlehurst and G. P. Kuiper, pp. 618–638, The University of Chicago Press, Chicago, 1963.

Section 9.6. Rendezvous with comets are discussed in:

R 9.6-1. Corben, H. C.: In "Space Age Astronomy," eds. A. J. Deutsch and W. B. Klemperer, pp. 380–382, Academic Press Inc., New York, 1962.

Artificial comets and related subjects are considered in:

R 9.6-2. Biermann, L., R. Lüst, Rh. Lüst, and H. U. Schmidt: *Z. Astrophys.*, **53** : 226 (1961).

R 9.6-3. Shklovskii, I. S.: *ARS J.*, **31** : 699 (1961).

R 9.6-4. Swings, P.: In "Space Age Astronomy," eds. A. J. Deutsch and W. B. Klemperer, pp. 370–379, Academic Press Inc., New York, 1962.

Meteors

chapter 10

Although meteors have been observed and studied for centuries, an understanding of their nature, their physical and orbital properties, and their origin has been realized only in the last two or three decades. In this interval a concentrated attempt has been made to deduce all the important astronomical properties of meteors which we can hope to learn with current techniques, and it can be said that in general this attempt has succeeded. The astronomical problems—orbits, distribution in space, and origins—are now fairly well solved, but the physical processes, especially those taking place when the meteor encounters the atmosphere, are still only partially understood and in need of considerably more work.

At the meeting of the International Astronomical Union in 1961, an attempt was made to standardize the then-confused terminology of meteor and meteorite astronomy. We shall use these standardized terms, and so they are summarized here.

1. *Meteor*. The light phenomenon resulting from the entry into the atmosphere of a particle from space.

2. *Meteoroid.* Any object that moves in space and is larger than a molecule and smaller than an asteroid.

3. *Meteorite.* A meteoroid which passes through the atmosphere (producing a meteor) and reaches the surface of the Earth without being completely vaporized.

4. *Fireball.* A meteor which is brighter than the brightest planets.

5. *Micrometeorite.* A meteorite with diameter that is less than one millimeter but is at least a few microns.

6. *Meteoritic dust.* Very small particles, finer than micrometeorites.

7. *Absolute magnitude.* The stellar magnitude a meteor would have if placed at the zenith and at a height of 100 km.

8. *Trajectory.* The line of motion, in three dimensions, of the meteor in the atmosphere.

9. *Path.* The projection of the trajectory on the celestial sphere, as seen by an observer.

10. *Train.* Anything left behind, such as ionization, along the trajectory.

11. *Wake.* Very short duration trains, lasting less than a second.

12. *Radiant.* The point where the backward projection of the trajectory intersects the celestial sphere.

13. *Shower.* A large number of meteors with nearly parallel trajectories.

14. *Stream.* A group of meteoroids with nearly identical orbits.

10.1 VISUAL OBSERVATIONS

Meteor astronomy is one of the few fields of the science in which visual observations have played an important role in recent years. The duration of a meteor's flight through the atmosphere is so short that very little light reaches any one point on a photographic plate exposed in a camera, unless

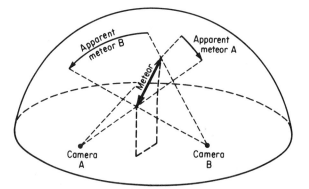

Fig. 10.1-1   The true path of a meteor and the apparent path as seen by two stations.

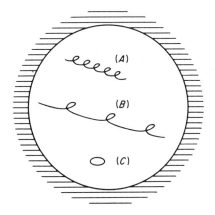

Fig. 10.1-2 Paths of (A) a slow meteor, (B) a fast meteor, and (C) a star, as seen in Öpik's rocking-mirror system.

the meteor is exceedingly bright. The human eye is capable of detecting meteors as faint as the fifth magnitude, whereas ordinary wide-field cameras can photograph only those brighter than zero or -1 apparent magnitude.

Systematic visual observations of meteors have been carried out in a large number of countries including Antarctica, with results usually in good agreement. Commonly, observations are made at two stations, separated by some 50 km, so that simultaneous observations of the same meteor may be used to determine the path in the atmosphere by triangulation (Fig. 10.1-1). Groups of trained observers at each of the two stations maintain a constant watch, usually with each individual responsible for a particular section of the sky. When a meteor is seen, the time is recorded, and the observer estimates its magnitude, its duration, the duration of its train if any, and its location with respect to the background of stars. Often this information is called out to a centrally located recorder, who writes down all information so that the observers may keep continuous watch of their sections of the sky.

Experienced observers are found to be able to estimate the position of the beginning and end of the meteor path to within about 3° and the direction to within 2°. The apparent brightness of the meteor is more difficult to estimate visually. This is especially true of the luminous meteors, for which two observers' estimates commonly differ by more than a magnitude.

A very ingenious method of visually estimating the velocities of meteors has been used by E. J. Öpik, first in Arizona and later in Tartu, Estonia. He devised a large flat mirror mounted on a rocking apparatus so that it oscillated with a small amplitude and a period of a fraction of a second. Any meteor seen in this mirror would appear to travel in a looped path (Fig. 10.1-2), the separations of the loops being a function of the angular velocity of the meteor.

Although visual meteor observations still are important sources of information on the problems of the hourly rates of meteors and the dis-

Fig. 10.2-1   One of the Baker Super-Schmidt meteor cameras. (*Courtesy of F. L. Whipple.*)

tribution of meteor magnitudes, the powerful photographic and radio techniques which have been devised provide other information much more accurately and efficiently.

10.2   PHOTOGRAPHIC OBSERVATIONS

The early days of meteor photography were in modern terms remarkably unproductive. The most successful of these early ventures, the program carried out by Whipple at Harvard from 1936 to 1946, photographed meteors at the slow rate of about one for every 100 hr of exposure time.

Previous programs had required even greater patience. The first successful double-station meteor photographs were obtained by Elkin at Yale between the years 1894 and 1909. He set up two batteries of four cameras each at stations two miles distant. At one station a bicycle wheel supported a rapidly rotating shutter which broke the meteor's trail into segments of equal time. When a meteor was photographed at both stations, Elkin was able to compute its height, its path, its duration, its brightness, and its velocity as a function of time.

The Harvard photographic meteor program originally made use of a base line of 38 km, the distance between Cambridge and Oak Ridge, and this increase over Elkin's 3-km base line provided for much greater accuracy. The cameras were equipped with $1\frac{1}{2}$-in-diameter $f4$ wide-angle lenses with a field of about 60°. These cameras photographed nearly 50 meteors at both stations, and the trails of these objects yielded very accurate information on the characteristics of the very brightest meteors, to which these cameras were limited.

A most important step in meteor astronomy occurred when James G. Baker designed a remarkable new camera based on the Schmidt principle (Fig. 10.2-1). The Super-Schmidt was designed with an effective aperture of 12 in, an optical focal ratio of 0.65, and a field of 55°. The first such camera was installed in New Mexico in 1951. It photographs approximately 250 times as many meteors per hour of exposure as the previously

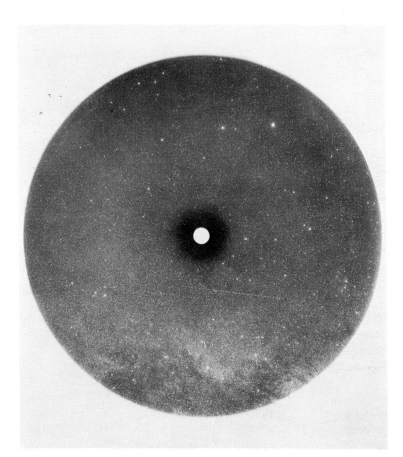

Fig. 10.2-2   Photograph of three meteors of the Perseid shower taken by a Baker Super-Schmidt camera. The center of the field is blocked optically by the plateholder. A rapid shutter produces breaks in the meteor trails. (*Courtesy of F. L. Whipple.*)

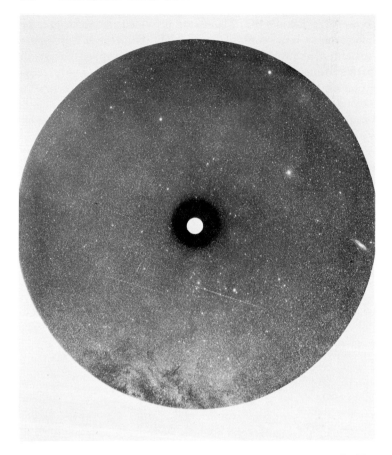

Fig. 10.2-3 Super-Schmidt photograph of the meteors shown in Fig.
10.2-2, but with a camera at the other New Mexico station 50 km distant. (*Courtesy of F. L. Whipple.*)

used cameras, and its use in pairs in New Mexico during the subsequent
years has provided us with a great wealth of photographic meteor data
(Figs. 10.2-2 and 10.2-3).

10.3 RADIO OBSERVATIONS

Meteor paths through the Earth's atmosphere were first detected by radio
techniques in 1928, although it was three years before it was realized that
such was the case. In the process of studying the ionized layers of the
atmosphere, radio waves were beamed upward and their reflections from
the ionized regions were received and studied. It was found that the electron density in the E region, as the strongly ionized layer at a height of
120 km is called, was very much higher in the daytime than at night,

varying by more than an order of magnitude diurnally. This was obviously an effect of solar radiations. However, it was noticed that very sudden increases in the electron density often occurred during the night, and it became necessary to postulate the existence of some ionizing agent other than the Sun which might have a brief and sudden effect of this sort.

In 1931 it was suggested that meteors might be the ionizing agent, and in the same year it was found that a distinct increase in the nighttime ionization of the E region corresponded in time with the Leonid shower (Sec. 10.7). In the following year conclusive proof was provided when sudden increases in electron density were observed simultaneously with visual bright meteors overhead (Fig. 10.3-1). The effects of meteors on the E regions are known to be quite impressive, especially during major meteor showers. During the maximum of the Leonids the electron density has reached a value of 10^6 electrons/cm³, about ten times that for a summer day at noon.

Distances to meteor paths in the atmosphere can be measured with radio techniques in a way quite different from that used photographically. A commonly used method is to send out a short pulse of radio waves and then observe the time it takes for the echo of the pulse, reflected from the ionized trail of the meteor, to return. The distance to the trail is then simply

$$D = \frac{ct}{2} \tag{1}$$

where t is the elapsed time between transmission of the pulse and reception of the echo and c is the velocity of the radio waves (Fig. 10.3-2). For such distance measurements the length of the pulse is generally about 10 μsec; the pulses recur at the rate of a few hundred per second.

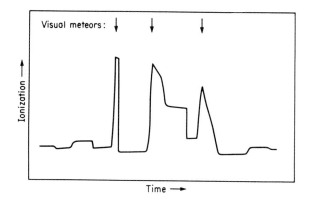

Fig. 10.3-1 An example of the coincidence of visual meteors with peaks in the ionization of the upper atmosphere.

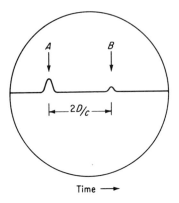

Time ⟶

Fig. 10.3-2   A cathode-ray-tube pattern showing (A) the ground pulse sent and (B), the echo received from the meteor. The distance is measured from the separation of the signals in time.

The actual path of a meteor is more difficult to determine by radio methods than by visual or photographic means. A number of different, rather indirect, methods are possible, however. Most of them take advantage of the fact that radio echoes are reflected only from that part of the trail of a meteor which is perpendicular to the radio beam, especially with the shorter wavelengths generally used (about 4 m). By using either directional signals or three stations, a statistical sampling of large numbers of meteors will allow an approximate radiant to be determined. Because these methods require observations of many meteor paths to establish the geometry of the situation, they are useful only for meteor showers and can give no information on individual objects.

A very different method has been used at longer wavelength (10 m), in which case very large meteors can be detected over a considerable portion of their path, not just at the point which is perpendicular to the beam. The use of three stations permits the path and velocity of the meteor to be determined unambiguously, and the orbit can be computed. However, the method is very inefficient because, to be observed sufficiently well at all three stations, the meteor's path must be very long, over 100 km, and it must be so situated that all three beams receive a usable signal. McKinley and Millman in Canada found in their original program using this method that an average of about 200 hr of observation was required to obtain a single usable meteor path.

Velocities of meteors can be obtained either by the above method or, more readily, by measuring the Doppler effects in the returned pulse used for range measures. Various ingenious methods of measuring the Doppler shift have been devised; they use the properties of the diffraction pattern of the signal.

10.4   THE RATE OF METEOR ENCOUNTERS

One of the first observed and most thoroughly studied features of meteor astronomy is the rate of occurrence of meteors in the atmosphere. The

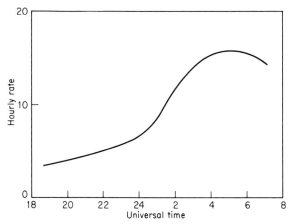

Fig. 10.5-1 The mean variation of the hourly rate of visual meteors as a function of time.

visual and radio techniques outlined above have been used extensively to measure this rate and to determine how it varies during the day and during the year. In addition to general diurnal and seasonal variations, it was long ago found that great increases in the number of meteors occur on certain dates; these increases are the "meteor showers."

10.5 DIURNAL DISTRIBUTION

The hourly rate of visual meteors is found to vary during the night. On the average, more than twice as many meteors occur after midnight as in the evening hours (Fig. 10.5-1). In 1866 the Italian astronomer Schiaparelli explained this fact in a qualitative way by pointing out that if

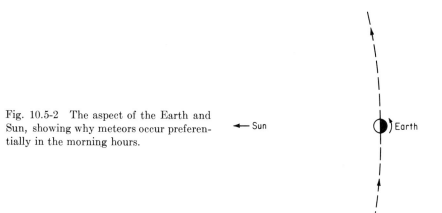

Fig. 10.5-2 The aspect of the Earth and Sun, showing why meteors occur preferentially in the morning hours.

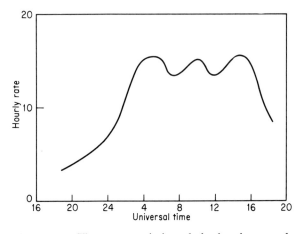

Fig. 10.5-3 The mean variation of the hourly rate of radio meteors as a function of time.

meteors are arranged randomly and uniformly in the solar system, there will be an apparent increase of encounters in the direction in which the Earth moves in its orbit. The morning side of the Earth is the side which faces the direction of the Earth's motion, and therefore it receives a larger number of encounters with meteors than does the evening side (Fig. 10.5-2). Schiaparelli's theory, however, is not able to explain the more recent observations in an *exact* way.

Rather than mere observations of meteors in general, if observations of their radiants are plotted as a function of the time of day, a more detailed and physically meaningful curve is derived, and it is possible to

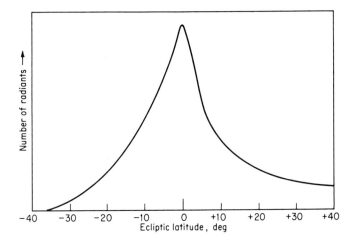

Fig. 10.5-4 The distribution of meteor radiants with ecliptic latitude. (*After Lovell.*)

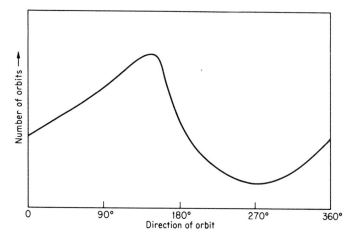

Fig. 10.5-5   The distribution of the directions of meteor orbits as deduced from radio studies. The Sun's direction is taken as 0°.

explain this curve adequately. The most useful tool for this experiment is the radio meteor telescope, which can operate in daylight and is not influenced by twilight or other sky brightness variations. Radio surveys of the mean hourly rate of meteor echoes as a function of the time of day show three maxima and a long, deep minimum (Fig. 10.5-3). The three high points correspond to the direction of the Sun, the direction opposite the Sun, and the direction of the Earth's motion in its orbit. This fact, in conjunction with the observed concentration of sporadic meteor radiants along the ecliptic (Fig. 10.5-4), permits the true distribution of meteor orbital directions to be determined (Fig. 10.5-5).

The general picture one constructs from the data in Figs. 10.5-4 and 10.5-5 is one in which in the vicinity of Earth's orbit the great majority of the meteor motions are in a direction close to the ecliptic and either toward the Sun, away from it, or in the direction of the Earth's motion. Such would be the case if the orbits of sporadic meteors have high eccentricities and have something of a tendency to be direct and close to the plane of the ecliptic. Detailed orbits, described below, indicate this to be the case.

10.6   SEASONAL DISTRIBUTION

The hourly rate of meteor encounters is also dependent on the season (Fig. 10.6-1). This is found not to be in any agreement whatsoever with Schiaparelli's theory, and also not in agreement with a prediction based on the distribution of directions determined from the diurnal variations. It can only be explained by rejecting the assumption that meteor orbits are uniformly distributed around the Sun. Instead, there is a maximum

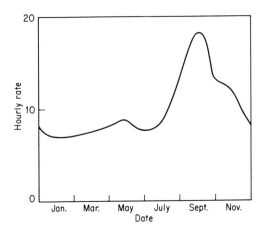

Fig. 10.6-1   The seasonal distribution of the hourly rate of visual meteors. (*After Denning.*)

number of orbits at solar longitude approximately 100° (which the Earth passes in June). The fact that there are more cometary orbits which make close approaches to the Earth's orbit at this solar longitude is an interesting and independent bit of evidence in favor of a cometary origin for sporadic meteors.

10.7   METEOR SHOWERS

By far the largest variations in the rate of meteor encounters occur during the times of meteor showers. Whereas the diurnal variations in the hourly rate may cause a range of from 6 to 16 visual meteors per hour, a major shower can increase this rate to 50 or 100. Occasional showers have reached (for brief periods of time) the phenomenal rate of 12,000 per hour, such as was the case for the Leonids in 1833.

Meteor showers consist of meteors with a common radiant, indicating that the meteoroids have parallel paths in space. The showers are usually named after the constellation in which their radiant lies; occasionally they are named after the comet with which they seem to be associated. In the case of the Quadrantids, the shower has outlived the constellation for which it was named, a nineteenth-century constellation near Hercules called Quadrans Muralis. Table 10.7-1 lists the major showers, those with an hourly rate for visual meteors of at least 20. Some of the showers listed are called permanent, indicating that they occur every year on the dates indicated, obviously because the orbit intersects that of the Earth at this point and the meteoroids are nearly uniformly distributed along their orbit. The remainder are called periodic, indicating that they occur every so many years. These meteoroids move in an orbit which intersects that of the Earth, but they must be heavily concentrated in one clump, moving

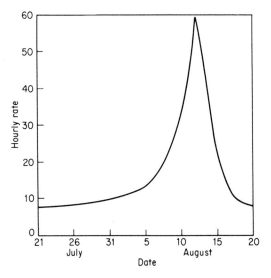

Fig. 10.7-1 The mean visual hourly rate curve for the Perseid meteor shower. (*After Denning.*)

along together in their orbit. The shower occurs whenever this clump and the Earth arrive simultaneously in the vicinity of the intersection of the orbits (the node).

An example of the permanent streams is the Perseid shower, which occurs in July and August with great regularity. Figure 10.7-1 shows the results of a 19-yr study by Denning made at the end of the last century. The hourly rate on the date of maximum for visual meteors is usually about 50, but in some years it has been 5 times this value and in others it has been barely detectable. A period, however, has not been established with any certainty. Figure 10.7-2 shows how the hourly rate of the Perseids on August 10 has varied during the first half of the twentieth century.

Table 10.7-1 Major meteor showers

Name	Date of maximum	Type
Quadrantids	Jan. 3	Permanent
Lyrids	Apr. 21	Permanent
η Aquarids	May 5	Permanent
δ Aquarids	July 28	Permanent
Summer daytime showers	May–July	Permanent and periodic
Perseids	Aug. 12	Permanent
Draconids	Oct. 10	Periodic
Orionids	Oct. 21	Permanent
Taurids	Nov. 7	Permanent
Leonids	Nov. 16	Periodic
Geminids	Dec. 12	Permanent
Ursids	Dec. 22	Permanent

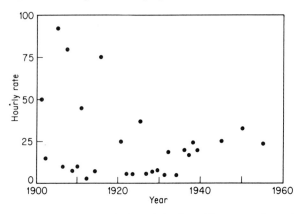

Fig. 10.7-2   The variation of the Perseid meteor shower's intensity for the last 60 yr. Points are visual hourly rates for August 10. (*After Lovell.*)

An example of a periodic stream is the Draconid, or Giacobinid shower. It is apparently related to the comet 1900 III, discovered by Giacobini and found to have a period of 6.5 yr. The orbit of this comet nearly intersects that of the Earth on about October 10, and whenever the comet has been near this portion of its orbit at the same time as the Earth, a brief spectacular shower of meteors is observed (Fig. 10.7-3). The most recent occurrence of a visually observed shower was in October, 1946, when the Earth passed the orbit 15 days after the comet. The shower lasted only 5 or 6 hr, during which time the visual hourly rate rose to over 4,000.

Table 10.7-2 summarizes the activity of the Draconid shower since the first definite observations of it. Apparently the meteoroids are heavily

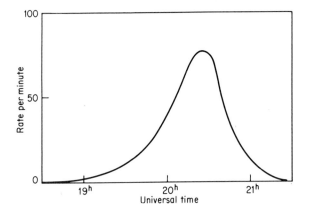

Fig. 10.7-3   The Giacobinid meteor shower as observed visually on October 9, 1933. (*After Olivier.*)

Table 10.7-2   The Draconid shower

Year	Earth at node	Hourly rate at maximum
1926	70 days before comet	17
1933	80 days after comet	5,000
1939	136 days before comet	. . .
1946	15 days after comet	5,000
1952	195 days before comet	200

concentrated in the immediate neighborhood of the comet. The 1952 occurrence was observed only by radio means in the daytime, the duration of the shower being so short that only one or two Draconids were found that evening.

An example of a spectacular lost meteor stream is the Bielid shower. A faint comet discovered by Biela in 1826 was found to have a period of 6.6 yr and an orbit which passes close to that of the Earth. On its return in 1845 the comet was seen to have broken in two, a small companion being visible near the main comet. This companion grew in brightness and formed a tail. By the return of 1852 the components were well separated in the orbit and both were abnormally faint. Neither was ever seen again. However, when the Earth crossed the orbit in 1872, 1885, 1892, and 1899, brilliant displays of meteors were observed, with hourly rates for visual meteors as high as 50,000 having been estimated (for 1885). After a feeble exhibition in 1904, the shower remained unobserved until 1940, when a very mild display occurred. Since then it has remained completely unobserved. The remarkable history of the Bielid comet and stream have not been thoroughly explained, but the evidence suggests that the orbit has been continually altered by close approaches to Jupiter.

10.8 VELOCITIES

The observed velocities of meteors range between about 11 and about 75 km/sec. These two limits are both readily explained in terms of escape velocities. The velocity of escape from the Earth is 11.2 km/sec, and no meteoroids will encounter the atmosphere with a lower relative velocity with respect to the Earth. The velocity of escape from the solar system at the Earth's distance is 42 km/sec. The Earth's orbital motion is approximately 30 km/sec. Therefore, the maximum velocity of a solar system meteoroid with respect to the Earth is approximately 72 km/sec. The fact that few, if any, meteors are observed to have a greater velocity indicates that by far the great majority of meteoroids are "permanent" members of the solar system, traveling in closed orbits. It is estimated that the interstellar component is probably less than 1 per cent of the observed meteors.

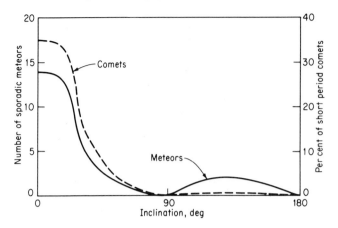

Fig. 10.9-1 A comparison of orbit inclinations of sporadic meteors and of comets with periods of less than 200 years. (*After Whipple.*)

The orbital velocities of the meteoroids are, of course, altered in the Earth's vicinity by gravitational attraction. The relative velocity between the Earth and the meteoroid is increased according to the equation:

$$v^2 = v_R{}^2 + \frac{2GM_E}{R} \cong v_R{}^2 + 125 \tag{1}$$

where v is the geocentric velocity, in kilometers per second, just outside the Earth's atmosphere, v_R is the original relative velocity, M_E and R are mass and radius of the Earth, and G is the constant of gravitation.

10.9 ORBITS OF SPORADIC METEORS

In order to compute an orbit of an individual meteor, the trajectory and velocity must be quite accurately determined. Visual and the early radar observations proved insufficiently accurate for these purposes. The Super-Schmidt photographic meteor program provided the first good meteor orbital data. Whipple has discussed the results of orbit computations for 51 sporadic meteors photographed with the Super-Schmidts. He found that 17 of these were retrograde and none were certainly hyperbolic. All but one had periods greater than 22 years and aphelion distances greater than 8 AU. Their inclinations were mildly concentrated to the ecliptic, and the distribution of inclinations resembles that for comets very strongly (Fig. 10.9-1); probably less than 15 per cent are not of cometary origin.

10.10 ORBITS OF SHOWER METEORS

The Super-Schmidt photographic survey, during the 10 years in which it operated, provided a wealth of accurate data on orbits of shower meteors. Figure 10.10-1 illustrates these results for meteors of various showers. In all cases the orbits agree well for their inner portions, near the Earth. Some show poor agreement at aphelion, a result of the combined effects of uncertainties in the measures, the dispersive action of the major planets, and other perturbations. For those showers known to be associated with an observed comet, the orbits of the meteors agree well with the orbit of the comet (as for the Lyrids, the Taurids, and the α Capricornids).

10.11 THE ORBITS OF FIREBALLS

Precise velocities have not generally been measured for those exceedingly bright and rare meteors called fireballs and bolides. They are definitely more massive than the ordinary meteors and become comparable in size to the meteorites which actually reach the ground. From studies of what information is available on the velocities of these objects, Whipple suggests that, as we look at brighter and brighter meteors, the orbits become less inclined, smaller, and more circular. Meteors large enough to give rise to meteorite falls move primarily in small, low-eccentricity orbits of small inclination that strongly resemble the asteroid's orbits. Apparently, the smallest meteors are almost entirely cometary in origin and the asteroidal component gradually increases with mass until the meteorites are reached. At the level of meteorite mass the cometary contribution is insignificant.

10.12 METEOR PHYSICS

The physical processes involved in the interactions of meteors with the atmosphere are still being actively investigated. The basic theory was

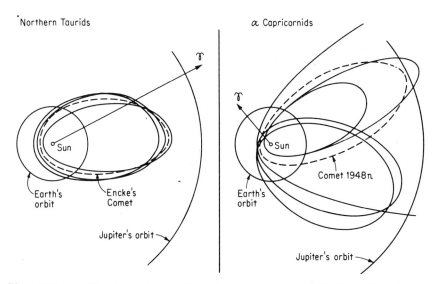

Fig. 10.10-1 Orbits for meteors of two showers, compared with the orbits of the associated comets. (*After F. W. Wright.*)

worked out in 1938 by Whipple, and it has been gradually refined through the results of the detailed photographic meteor surveys. Öpik also has treated the various aspects of the problem in considerable detail.

When a meteoroid enters the atmosphere with some velocity v, which lies between 11 and 72 km/sec, a momentum exchange occurs on the front surface of the incoming object between this body, which decelerates, and the air molecules, which are given a forward velocity. If ρ is the atmospheric density, Γ is the drag coefficient, and s is the effective cross-sectional area of the meteoroid, then for the momentum exchange, we have

$$m\,\frac{dv}{dt} = -\Gamma s\rho v^2 \tag{1}$$

Usually the cross section s is approximated by $\rho_m^{-\frac{2}{3}} m^{\frac{2}{3}}$, where ρ_m is the density of the meteoroid. The approximation holds fairly well for bodies of ordinary shapes. Thus we may write the *drag equation:*

$$\frac{dv}{dt} = -\Gamma \rho_m^{-\frac{2}{3}} m^{-\frac{1}{3}} \rho v^2 \tag{2}$$

The meteoroid loses mass as well as velocity as it penetrates the atmosphere. This mass loss, called *ablation,* can occur either by vaporization, melting, or fragmentation. From conservation of energy, we can derive an equation for the mass loss by equating the energy given to the meteor by the colliding molecules to the energy required for ablation. The kinetic energy lost by deceleration is negligible. We have

$$\zeta\,\frac{dm}{dt} = -\frac{1}{2}\,\Lambda \rho_m^{-\frac{2}{3}} m^{\frac{2}{3}} \rho v^3 \tag{3}$$

where ζ is the energy required to ablate 1 g of the meteor and Λ is the efficiency of energy exchange. Dividing (10.12-3) by (10.12-2), we have the *mass equation:*

$$\frac{1}{m}\,\frac{dm}{dt} = \frac{\Lambda}{2\Gamma\zeta}\,v\,\frac{dv}{dt} \tag{4}$$

When ablation occurs, atoms of the meteoroid are lost from the body and collide with atmospheric molecules in the forward direction with a velocity v. Each has sufficient energy to ionize and excite the air particles so that light is emitted. If τ is the percentage of the kinetic energy which is converted into light, then we have a *luminosity equation:*

$$I = -\frac{1}{2}\,\tau v^2\,\frac{dm}{dt} \tag{5}$$

where I is the total luminous energy, in ergs per second, emitted by the meteor.

Equations (10.12-2), (10.12-4), and (10.12-5) are basic to the theory of meteor physics. We have three variables: v, m, and I, and we have five constants: Γ, Λ, ρ_m, ζ, and τ. From double stations we can measure four quantities: v, dv/dt, $I(t)$, and $h(t)$, where h is height in the atmosphere. Meteor physics concerns itself with determining the measurable quantities and deducing the values of the constants and variables. Because of the large number of unknowns and the small number of equations relating them, the problem cannot be solved, even for this simplified theory, without more information from other sources.

Detailed theoretical investigations have been carried out in order to get a reliable idea of some of the constants involved, in particular, the drag coefficient Γ and the constants of the heat-transfer processes. Experiments carried out in the laboratory provide information on many of the ballistics problems. These experiments use artificial meteors, particles given high velocities by means of directive explosions. Artificial meteors can be set off on the ground, as well as from rockets, and they give information for widely different ρ. Such experimental studies are capable of giving us reliable information on the luminous efficiency; the actual processes of excitation, ionization, dissociation, and recombination which are involved; the heat-transfer efficiency; shock-front phenomena; the physical processes of vaporizing, spraying, and fragmentation; and the drag coefficient.

From our present knowledge of the details of the physical processes involved in meteor ablation, it has been possible to conclude that most meteors photographed by the Super-Schmidts are of very low density, certainly less than 1 g/cm³. Meteors of different showers apparently are of different density. It is also true that practically all meteors are remarkably fragile, and for that reason a theory which does not take into account the detailed processes of the fragmentation of the meteoroid is inadequate. Total masses for meteoroids are only roughly known. There is still a great deal of work, theoretical, observational, and experimentational, to be done on meteor physics.

10.13 METEOR SPECTROSCOPY

Meteor spectra, of which there are now nearly 200, are not at all well understood. Many of the elements involved in the emission spectra have been identified, but no adequate theories of the physical details of their production have been attempted. So far detected are neutral atoms of H, N, O, Na, Mg, Al, Si, Ca, Cr, Mn, Fe, and Ne. Ionized atoms of Mg, Si, Ca, and Fe have been identified. In general, those seen are just the elements expected from the known general cosmic abundances. The most common transitions are those from upper levels with energies only about 1 per cent of the kinetic energy of the evaporated meteor atoms. The energy levels involved appear to be higher and higher as the meteor progresses into the atmosphere; near the end of its path the lines are often from ionized atoms. This is probably an effect of the increasing density of air as the meteor penetrates lower and of the resultant increase in the efficiency of energy transfer.

Research is being carried out on the available meteor spectra, and it is expected that through this vital study a great deal of the uncertainty which characterizes detailed meteor physics theory will be resolved.

BIBLIOGRAPHICAL NOTES

A very thorough book dealing with most meteor problems is:

R 10-1. Lovell, A. C. B.: "Meteor Astronomy," Clarendon Press, Oxford, 1954.

An older but interesting account primarily of visual meteor observations is:

R 10-2. Olivier, C. P.: "Meteors," Williams & Wilkins Company, Baltimore, 1925.

A series of chapters on particular fields in meteor astronomy is collected in:

R 10-3. Kaiser, T. R.: "Meteors," Pergamon Press, New York, 1955.

A review of meteor astronomy and an excellent source of references is found in:

R 10-4. Whipple, F. L., and G. S. Hawkins: In "Handbuch der Physik," vol. 52, ed. S. Flügge, pp. 518–564, Springer-Verlag OHG, Berlin, 1959.

A more recent book with an excellent bibliography and good coverage of radio meteor astronomy is:

R 10-5. McKinley, D. W. R.: "Meteor Science and Engineering," McGraw-Hill Book Company, New York, 1961.

Section 10.1. A brief review of visual meteor observations is given by:

R 10.1-1. Millman, P. M.: *Sky and Telescope,* **16**: 222 (1957).

See also R 10-1 and R 10-2.

Section 10.2. Photographic meteor studies are reported in:

R 10.2-1. Jacchia, L. G., and F. L. Whipple: In "Vistas in Astronomy," ed. A. Beer, vol. 2, pp. 982–994, Pergamon Press, New York, 1956.

Sections 10.3 to 10.6. See R 10-1.

Section 10.7. A good summary of our knowledge of meteor showers is given in R 10-1, and there is also a great deal of information in:

R 10.7-1. Hoffmeister, C.: "Meteorströme" (in German), Verlag Werden und Wirken, Weimar, 1948.

Sections 10.8 to 10.11. A compilation of orbital data, diagrams, and useful references can be found in:

R 10.10-1. Wright, F. W.: *Astron. J.*, **65**: 33 (1960).

Sections 10.12 and 10.13. See R 10-3 and R 10-4, as well as the lucid monograph:

R 10.12-1. Öpik, E. J.: "Physics of Meteor Flight in the Atmosphere," Interscience Publishers, Inc., New York, 1958.

Meteorites

The Earth is continuously being bombarded by extraterrestrial bodies, called meteorites, which have given man a revealing preview of outer space. Meteorites fall indiscriminately into oceans and onto land, often landing in the wilderness but sometimes on surprised examples of man himself.

There are an estimated 500 tons of meteoritic material in museums, and the literature describing them far outweighs that explaining them. Aside from the important problem of the chemical composition of meteorites, only the last few years have seen much success in determining the physical and astronomical histories of these interlopers from interplanetary space.

11.1 FALLS AND FINDS

If a meteorite is seen or heard to fall, and for this reason is found, then it is called a *fall*. A very rough estimate of the number of meteorites falling

Table 11.2-1   Types of meteorites

Type	Characteristics
Irons:	Mostly Fe and Ni in metallic form
Octahedrites	Widmanstätten pattern; Ni content 6–15 per cent
Hexahedrites	Neumann bands; Ni content 5.5–6 per cent
Ataxites	No macrostructure; Ni content widely variable
Stones:	Mostly various stonelike combinations of minerals
Ordinary chondrites	Chondrules very common; olivine, feldspar, other common minerals
Carbonaceous chondrites	Usually black and fragile; carbon common; chondrules rare
Enstatite chondrites	Usually homogeneous; enstatite common
Achondrites	Similar to terrestrial igneous rocks; there are many subdivisions, including, for instance, urelites, which contain carbon, sometimes in the form of diamonds
Stony-irons:	Iron-nickel matrix with inclusions of stony material
Pallasites	Silicate crystal inclusions, Fe-Ni content 25–60 per cent
Mesosiderites	Texture and crystals finer than for pallasites, Fe-Ni content 40–70 per cent
Lodranites	Like pallasites, Fe-Ni content 30 per cent
Siderophyres	Like pallasites, Fe-Ni content 50 per cent

over the world is 2,000 per year, a figure based on the results of a program of public education carried out by Nininger in the central part of the United States, where he alerted the populace to watch for possible meteorite falls and to report them promptly. His remarkable success in this program has led the way for the present photographic recovery programs which are in progress in the United States and Czechoslovakia.

A *find* is a meteorite which is picked up and identified because of its appearance and not because of any witness of its fall. Meteorites are usually recognized by their surfaces (commonly glassy with flow marks), their density, and their chemical composition. A good chemical test is the Fe/Ni ratio, which usually ranges between 8 and 20 for meteorites of different types and which is normally very much smaller than that for the Earth minerals.   (Throughout this chapter we have been giving percentage compositions in terms of *mass*.)

11.2 TYPES OF METEORITES

There are three groups of meteorites, divided according to their composition. They are the *irons*, the *stony-irons*, and the *stones*. The numerous subdivisions are given in Table 11.2-1. The irons are nearly purely metallic, with iron as the principal constituent. They are of special interest because of the remarkable crystalline structures which show up when they are sliced and polished (Fig. 11.2-1). These patterns, called Widmanstätten figures, have not been duplicated artificially in the laboratory, and it is thought that they can arise only under conditions of very slow cooling and perhaps very high pressure. It is often suggested that they prove that the iron meteorites come from the centers of larger bodies which historically broke up into many fragments. Meteorite finds are predominately irons, but falls are only 10 per cent irons at most.

Some 90 per cent of the falls are stones, which are so easily mistaken for terrestrial rocks and which weather so easily that they are rarely found if not witnessed. The stones have a wide and complex variety of physical characteristics and chemical properties. The most common type of stone

Fig. 11.2-1   The etched surface of an iron meteorite, showing Widmanstätten figures. (*Courtesy of Chicago Natural History Museum.*)

is that called *chondritic* because of the presence of chondrules, inclusions of material similar to basic rocks of the Earth. The average chemical compositions of chondrites are quite uniform, in spite of an immense variety in structural, physical, and mineralogical characteristics. Stones without such inclusions are the rarer *achondrites,* which have characteristics very similar to those of the chondrules of the chondrites.

The stony-irons make up only about 2 per cent of the known meteorites. They are normally in the form of an iron-nickel matrix with stony inclusions.

11.3 CHEMICAL COMPOSITION

The composition of meteorites is of interest for two primary reasons: (1) such information can provide a clue to the mystery of the origin of meteorites and (2) it provides information on the abundances of the elements in the solar system—especially important for those elements undetectable in the solar spectrum.

Table 11.3-1 lists the average compositions of meteorites of various types. These averages are poor for the achondrites, which vary immensely in composition from one example to the next, but they are quite representative of the rest. Such information is the source of a great deal of interesting evidence and speculation on the origin of meteoritic material. Combined with mineralogical and isotopic data, the chemical analyses can be used to attempt to establish the existence (or nonexistence) of a large parent body and to explore the possibilities for its prebreakup structure. Unfortunately, the data are not yet sufficiently abundant or clear to lead to agreement between scientists on any of the major questions. The lack of accord between the investigators is remarkable, and it is probably equaled in solar system problems only by that for tektites (Sec. 11.9), puzzling objects of an even more obscure origin.

For meteorites, the major question that has been attacked, but not unequivocally answered, is the problem of the existence of a parent body or bodies. Many scientists believe that the meteorites originated in a fairly large parent planet or planets which broke up into many fragments long ago, or perhaps broke up gradually through numerous collisions in the asteroid belt (Chap. 12). The size of the body or bodies has been proposed to have been of the order of the Moon (3,000 km) by some scientists, of asteroid size (300 km) by others, and of their present size ($\sim$1 m) by others. There is evidence both for and against all three possibilities, and the only safe conclusion that can be made is that the meteorites have had a complicated history.

It is often claimed that the meteorites are our best source of information on the abundances of many of the chemical elements in the solar system. Spectra of the Sun and stars provide us with information on abundances of some, but not all, elements. For the rest, we must rely on

Table 11.3-1 Average chemical compositions of meteorites in per cent by weight*

Compound, element	Octahedrites	Hexahedrites	Ataxites	Ordinary chondrites	Carbonaceous chondrites	Enstatite chondrites	Achondrites	Pallasites	Mesosiderites	Lodranites	Siderophyres
Fe	88	93	84±	12	0.8	20	1±	49	46	28	46
Ni	8	6	14±	1.3	0.4	1.7	0.1±	5	4	4	5
Co	0.5		0.8	0.3	0.01	0.1	……	0.3	0.3	……	0.15
Cu	0.1	0.4	0.1	……	……	……	……	……	……	……	……
P	0.2	0.3	0.1	0.05	……	……	……	0.1	0.1	……	……
C	0.4	0.2	0.2	……	2.4	0.3	……	0.08	……	……	……
SiO$_2$	……	……	……	38	27±	39	47	17	20	29	35
MgO	……	……	……	24	19±	21	12±	20	6	23	10
FeO	……	……	……	12	20±	2	15±	7	6	8	4
Al$_2$O$_3$	……	……	……	2.7	2.3	2	8±	0.4	4	0.2	……
CaO	……	……	……	1.9	2.0	1	9±	0.3	3	0.2	……
FeS	……	……	……	5.9	9±	11	1±	0.5	3	7	……
Other	2.8	0.1	0.8	1.8	17.1	1.9	6.9	0.3	7.6	0.6	……

* A ± sign indicates a wide spread in the abundance of that element for that meteorite type.

Table 11.3-2 Abundances of some minor elements in
chondrites (relative to silicon)

Element	Abundance	Element	Abundance
Helium	1.1×10^{-7}	Copper	1.9×10^{-4}
Lithium	5×10^{-5}	Zinc	1.2×10^{-4}
Beryllium	6.4×10^{-7}	Silver	1.3×10^{-7}
Boron	4×10^{-5}	Xenon	7×10^{-12}
Carbon	2×10^{-2}	Gold	1.3×10^{-7}
Nitrogen	9×10^{-5}	Mercury	7.6×10^{-8}
Neon	1.5×10^{-9}	Lead	1.5×10^{-7}
Chlorine	1×10^{-3}	Thorium	2.6×10^{-8}
Argon	4×10^{-7}	Uranium	7.5×10^{-9}
Cobalt	1.2×10^{-3}		

the meteorites and the Earth's crust. We suspect the Earth's crust to be
not representative of the Earth as a whole; for the interior has a much
greater density than the crust. Therefore, the meteorites are the most
promising source of such fundamental data, but until more is known about
their mode of formation and about their history, we cannot rely completely on them for such information. Table 11.3-2 summarizes the abundances of a few of the minor elements found in meteorites.

11.4 SHAPE AND ABLATION

Aerodynamical studies of the surfaces of meteorites have disclosed information on the flight through the atmosphere. A cap of compressed air is
formed on the forward surface of the supersonic meteoritic body, and the
heat of the air cap melts the surface of the meteorite. Molten streams of
material apparently are swept away by the air stream, and these solidify
later into vast numbers of droplets. The surfaces of meteorites often show
the flow marks frozen on the surface (Fig. 11.4-1), and these droplets are
known to pervade the atmosphere. Almost every meteorite fall displays
a persistent train of smokelike appearance (Fig. 11.4-2) that is partly
vapor but is mostly made up of the ablated material from the meteorite's
surface. Some of it is made up of the molten droplets, but other ablation
products also probably exist. It is not known just how ablation takes place,
that is, just how important, relatively, are vaporization, melting, flaking,
and mechanical destruction.

Many meteorites have one face beautifully formed into a streamlined
shape with a smooth conical surface marked with shallow holes and flow
marks. These meteorites apparently entered the atmosphere without rotation. The back sides of such meteorites are often very rough and sharp,
with only slight evidence of any melting of any of the surface. Other

meteorites seem to have rotated during the ablation process, because they display no such symmetry.

Ablation is estimated to remove a great deal of meteoritic material before the meteorite is stopped. Recent mineralogical and thermomagnetic analyses of the surface layers of iron meteorites have led to estimates of the rate of ablation in the atmosphere. A typical value lies between 1.5 and 2.0 mm/sec, and the total amount of material lost ranges from a few per cent up to 60 per cent or so, for irons. Stones probably ablate faster and lose a larger percentage of their mass.

A different and independent method of determining the amount of meteoritic ablation has been used recently. While in space, the meteorite is constantly subjected to bombardment by the high-energy particles of cosmic radiation. As a result, spallation isotopes (formed by the breakup

Fig. 11.4-1 The Carbo iron meteorite, with a foot ruler for scale. (*Courtesy of F. L. Whipple.*)

Fig. 11.4-2   A painting of the train of dust and gas which persisted after the fall of the Siberian Sikhote-Alin iron meteorites. (*Courtesy of E. L. Krinov.*)

of larger nuclei) are formed, and the concentration of these spallation products shows a depth variation in the meteorite. A common cosmic-ray-produced isotope is He^3, which is found to be unusually abundant in the outer portions of meteorites.

As an example of how one can calculate the amount of ablation from the observed distribution of He^3, Fig. 11.4-3 shows the distribution of He^3 in the Grant meteorite, an iron which fell in New Mexico and which was analyzed in this way in 1959. The distribution of He^3 was determined by subjecting several samples of the meteorite, taken from different locations in the body, to a flux of slow neutrons in an atomic reactor. The He^3 was thus converted to H^3, tritium, which was extracted and easily counted, since it is radioactive. From the variation of He^3 content with depth, it is possible to estimate the average cosmic-ray energy involved (calibrations are made in the laboratory); from the contours of equal He^3, one can determine the original shape of the meteoroid; and from the absolute amounts of He^3, one can estimate the original size of the pre-encounter body. For the Grant meteorite, for example, the cosmic-ray energy was found to have averaged 6 Bev, the shape of the meteoroid was found to be irregular, and the encounter with the atmosphere was found to have caused approximately half its mass to be ablated away.

11.5 COSMIC-RAY INTENSITIES AND EXPOSURE AGES

The powerful methods of isotope analysis have greatly increased our knowledge of meteorite physics in recent years. Potentially, we are in a position to learn from isotope studies about the following: cosmic-ray intensities in various parts of the solar system and at different times in solar system history; collisions between asteroids and their frequency; the ages of meteorites; the shapes and masses of meteorites before encountering the Earth; and the difference in time between the formation of the elements and the formation of the meteorites.

Bombardment of meteorites by cosmic rays produces radioactive isotopes of various half-lives (Table 11.5-1). The abundances of the short-

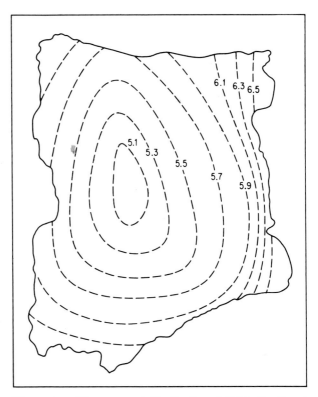

Fig. 11.4-3   The measured distribution of He³ in the Grant iron meteorite. The figures are in units of 10^{-6} cm³ of He³ per gram of meteorite. The meteorite in space can be seen to have been roughly egg-shaped, and calculations show that about half of its mass was lost in ablation. (*After Fireman.*)

Table 11.5-1   Cosmic-ray-produced unstable isotopes found in meteorites*

Isotope	Half-life	Isotope	Half-life
Be^{10}	2.5×10^6 years	V^{48}	16.0 days
Na^{22}	2.6 years	V^{49}	330 days
Al^{26}	7.4×10^5 years	Cr^{51}	27.8 days
Si^{32}	~700 years	Mn^{53}	$\geq 2 \times 10^6$ years
Cl^{36}	3.1×10^5 years	Mn^{54}	208 days
A^{39}	260 years	Co^{56}	~74 days
K^{40}	1.2×10^9 years	Co^{57}	270 days
Ca^{45}	164 days	Co^{60}	5.2 years
Sc^{46}	84 days	Ni^{59}	8×10^4 years
Ti^{44}	~200 years		

* After R 11.5-3.

lived isotopes, e.g., argon 37, tell us about cosmic-ray intensities near the Earth; and those of long-lived isotopes, e.g., tritium, argon 39, and chlorine 36, give an average of the cosmic-ray intensities for different ranges of time and location. The latter is especially important when the orbit of the meteorite is known as, for instance, for the Luhy meteorite (Fig. 11.5-1). Measures so far indicate that cosmic-ray intensities have been uniform over the last few million years, within a factor of 2 or 3.

Recently the cosmic-ray "exposure ages" of a number of meteorites have been measured. The exposure age is the time during which the mete-

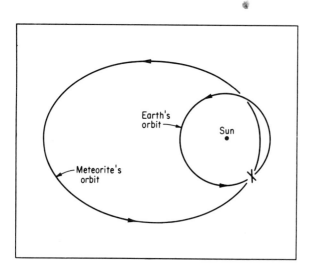

Fig. 11.5-1   Orbits of the Earth and the Luhy meteorite, first fall to have a photographically determined orbit. An X marks the point of collision.

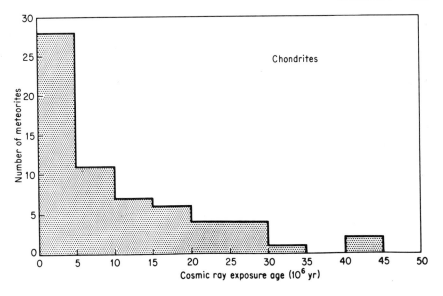

Fig. 11.5-2   The distribution of measured cosmic-ray ages for chondritic meteorites, as of 1962. The preponderance of short ages illustrates the effectiveness of meteoritic erosion in space.

oritic fragment was exposed to cosmic rays. For meteorites which were formed by the breakup of larger bodies, the determined age pinpoints the date of the breakup. The measured ages range from 10^6 to 2×10^9 years, and the distribution of these ages, once a sufficient number have been measured, is expected to tell us a considerable amount about collisions and their rate for asteroidal bodies.

As an example of how the cosmic-ray exposure age can be calculated, let us consider the radioactive isotope argon 39 (260-yr half-life), formed as a spallation product in iron meteorites while they are out in space. After a meteorite has fallen to the Earth, the rate of decay of A^{39} must equal its rate of production by cosmic rays previously out in space. Since the stable isotope A^{38} is produced at approximately the same rate as A^{39} by cosmic rays (laboratory experiments show this), and since probably all of the argon is cosmic-ray-produced, the measured amount of A^{38} gives a method for obtaining the length of exposure to bombardment. The cosmic-ray age is simply

$$T_{\text{CR}} = \frac{\text{number of } A^{38} \text{ atoms/g}}{\text{number of } A^{39} \text{ decays/(g)(sec)}} \qquad (1)$$

Similar arguments for other cosmic-ray-produced isotopes lead to similar ages. The results for numerous meteorites are shown in Fig. 11.5-2.

11.6 AGES OF METEORITES

Radiogenic ages, measures of the time since the meteoritic material last solidified, are also determined from isotopic abundances. An age measured in this way is especially interesting because it is expected to indicate the age of the solar system, or at least the age of the solid bodies of the system.

Most commonly, lead is used to determine ages of meteorites. The assumption is made that the isotopic composition of the lead at the time of formation was the same for all meteorites. Thus the differences now found in the ratios of lead isotopes in meteorites are due to the contribution of radiogenic lead arising from the decay of the uranium and thorium mixed with the lead at the time of formation. By intercomparisons, the original isotopic composition can be inferred and the present compositions can be explained by assigning radiogenic ages to individual specimens. For stony meteorites there are now available a large number of radiogenic ages, and all so far agree remarkably well on an age of 4.6×10^9 yr, which is therefore taken as the probable age for the solar system. Iron meteorites are more difficult to date, because there is much less of the proper element available for analysis. The ages of some iron meteorites, measured by the K to A ratios, are found to be approximately 10^{10} years.

A very fascinating possibility is the opportunity to measure a different type of age—the time difference between the formation of the elements and the solidification of the meteorite. Potentially, the abundance of the gas xenon 129 can indicate the length of this interval. Preliminary work based on straightforward interpretations of the data gave a time of 3×10^8 yr. However, more recently it has been found that the xenon in meteorites is very complicated in its interpretation and cannot be discussed in a simple way. When it is well understood, Xe^{129} should provide an exciting result for the history of the solar system.

11.7 DISTRIBUTION OF METEORITIC MASSES

It is well known that the number of meteorite falls is inversely related to the size of the meteoritic body, but just exactly what mathematical relation is involved is unknown, except to a crude approximation. Obviously, there must be a cutoff at the upper end of the scale (as well as the lower), but it may not be reached until bodies of asteroid size are reached, where the cutoff is effected by erosion and collision. The total influx of meteoritic material to the Earth is estimated to be some 2×10^8 g per year for meteoritic bodies.

The largest known meteorites are listed in Table 11.7-1. The Hoba West meteorite, largest of all at 60 tons, lies in Southwest Africa at its place of discovery. Admiral Peary discovered the second largest, Ahnighito, at Cape York, Greenland, and it now lies in the American Museum of Natural History. The nearly hypothetical mammoth Chinguetti meteorite,

Table 11.7-1   Largest known meteorites

Meteorite	Weight, 10^6 g	Place of discovery	Present location
Hoba West	60	South West Africa	Place of fall
Ahnighito	50	Greenland	New York
Bacubirits	24	Mexico	Place of fall
Morite	20	Mexico	Mexico City
Willamette	14	Oregon	New York
Chupaderos	14 and 6	Mexico	Mexico City
Chinguetti (?)	10^5 (?)	French West Africa	Unknown

reported by explorers to lie in the Adrar Desert of Africa, has never been seen by a scientist, although a sample of it brought back to Europe showed it to be unmistakably an iron meteorite. Its estimated size is probably greatly exaggerated.

11.8 METEORITE CRATERS

When a very large meteorite encounters the Earth, its deceleration by the atmosphere is practically negligible. Therefore, the tremendous amount of energy released by the collision is often enough to completely pulverize and vaporize most if not all of the meteorite as well as the Earth at the point of impact. A crater is formed by the event, which is akin to an explosion because meteorite and the rock are partly vaporized by the collision. Fragments and molten droplets of meteoritic and Earth material are scattered over a wide area surrounding the crater, and the geological strata are usually severely deformed.

The three best-known meteorite craters are the Barringer crater near Winslow, Arizona, and two Siberian crater areas, the Tunguska, which was formed in 1908, possibly formed by impact of a small comet with the atmosphere (there are no proper craters at the place of impact, just a devastated forest) and the Sikhote-Alin system of 106 craters, formed in 1947 (Fig. 11.8-1). Table 11.8-1 lists 14 craters and crater systems which are proved to be of meteorite origin. Many others are suspected to be meteorite craters and will probably be proved so in the future.

"Fossil craters" are also now recognized by geologists. Numerous instances of the discovery of certain minerals, e.g., coesite, can be shown to be the result of a meteorite crater now entirely eroded away. Often this once-pulverized rock material is the only clue to the past presence of such a crater. "Shatter cones," conical shock-formed structures, are also useful indicators of impact. Two possible craters of immense size whose identity is still somewhat in doubt are the Vredefort formation, a huge circular rock formation which has no other reasonable explanation,

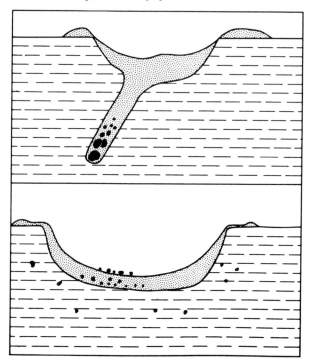

Fig. 11.8-1   Profiles of two meteorite craters of the Sikhote-Alin group. In the upper crater (6 m in diameter) the meteorite (black fragments) remained almost intact. In the lower crater (10 m in diameter) it was apparently disintegrated by explosive impact. (*After Krinov.*)

and the possible Wilkes Land "crater," a depression in Antarctica which, under hundreds of meters of ice, was discovered by magnetic anomaly measures.

Two features of Table 11.8-1 which are immediately evident are the facts that almost all crater-producing meteorites are irons and that usually a very tiny fraction of the meteoritic matter has been found in or near the crater. The first fact tells us that the largest meteoritic bodies in space must be irons, though stones far outnumber irons in the smaller size ranges. This is very likely a consequence of the greater resistance of iron bodies to erosion and collisions in space. The second fact illustrates how completely the meteoritic matter must be pulverized and vaporized by the explosive collision, because so little is left of the original body.

Let us look into the problem of the dispersion of the meteoritic mass on collision by examining the Arizona event in more detail. Many years ago it was suggested that the meteorite that formed the crater in Arizona must be somewhere beneath it. Estimates of the mass which would be expected to make such a crater ranged from 10^{10} to 10^{12} g. Only 10^6 g or

Table 11.8-1   Proven meteorite craters

Name	Location	Number	Diameter,* m	Type of meteorites	Total mass found	Date of fall
Wolf Creek	Australia	1	1,300	Stony-iron	<1 ton	
Barringer	Arizona	1	1,200	Iron	12,000 tons	~50,000 B.C.
Henbury	Australia	15	200	Iron	200 kg	
Boxhole	Australia	1	175	Iron	100 kg	
Odessa	Texas	2	170	Iron	?	>10,000 B.C.
Wabar	Arabia	2	100	Iron	A few kg	
Oesel	Estonia	6	100	Iron	110 g	
Campo del Cielo	Argentina	Many	75	Iron	~3 tons	
Dalgaranga	Australia	1	25	Iron	<1 ton	
Tunguska	Siberia	?	?	Comet?	A few g	1908
Sikhote-Alin	Siberia	106	28	Iron	5 tons	1947
Brenham	Kansas	1	17	Stony-iron	~1 ton	

* Where more than one crater exists, diameter quoted is for largest.

so of meteorite material has been picked up around the crater, so it was argued that most of the original meteorite must be underground. Holes were drilled near the center of the crater floor through a few hundred meters of shattered rock without any large meteoritic mass being found.

It was then conjectured that the meteorite may have come in at a large angle and that the main body might lie under the south rim. A drill hole was dug there and the drill stuck fast at 420 m below the crater rim in a layer rich in meteoritic nickel-iron. Presumably a sizable meteoritic mass lies at this position, but its size is still a matter of conjecture. More recently, a survey of the soil around the crater showed that tiny bits of meteoritic material pervade the soil down as far as a meter or more and as far from the crater as 8 km (Fig. 11.8-2). The total mass contained in this microscopic form is some 10^{10} g, enough to account for the entire crater. Possibly most or, at least, much of the meteorite was pulverized, melted, or vaporized by the explosion of impact and is now buried in the surroundings.

11.9   TEKTITES

Among the most puzzling objects known to man are the small pieces of natural glass called tektites. Although they have been analyzed and studied for nearly a hundred years, it is still not known whether they are extraterrestrial in origin. We discuss them here because this possibility has been seriously considered for many years. Their properties are so baffling when viewed altogether that if all scientists' conclusions about them are accepted, the tektites have no possible origin in the heavens or on the Earth and thus cannot exist. Thousands of them existing all over the world are mute evidence that our conclusions conflict with reality.

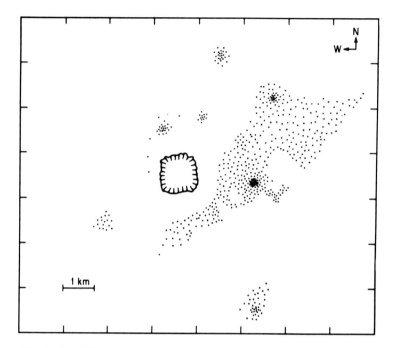

Fig. 11.8-2   Map of the Arizona meteorite crater and its surroundings, showing the location of fine meteoritic debris recovered from a soil survey. (*After Rinehart.*)

One of the most interesting problems of meteorite-aligned research is to resolve this conflict.

Appearance

Tektites are small, smooth, rounded objects of glassy material resembling molten droplets in a wide variety of spherical, teardrop, and dumbbell shapes (Fig. 11.9-1). They range in size from diameters of a few millimeters to diameters of some 10 to 20 cm. The mean weight of some 2,000 tektites from Australia has been found to be 0.93 g. In some other areas, such as Indochina, tektites average larger. Although most resemble some variant of a spheroidal shape, two unusual and remarkable shapes occasionally found are "buttons" and thin round plates, some very thin at the center.

Occurrence

One of the more remarkable things about tektites is the location in which they are found. Unlike meteorites, which are found uniformly over the

Fig. 11.9-1 Typical forms of tektites: teardrops, buttons, spheres, dumbbells, and grooves.

Earth's surface, tektites have been found in only a few special localities. They are often densely concentrated in these areas and completely absent in nearby ones. For example, the southern two-thirds of Australia is rather densely sprinkled with tektites in numerous areas, whereas in the northern one-third they are unknown. From an area of occurrence of some 2 million square miles, a total of 50,000 tektites have been collected in Australia, and undoubtedly many more remain undiscovered. The sources of tektites have given them their individual names (Table 11.9-1).

This rather odd distribution over the globe has led scientists to believe that tektites cannot be terrestrial in origin, but must have come, possibly in showers, from a cosmic source. One possible source is the Moon,

Table 11.9-1   Types of tektites

Name	Location
Australites	Australia and Tasmania
Bediasites	Grimes County, Texas
Billitonites	Billiton (Indonesia), Borneo, Java, Bunguran (Natuna Archipelago)
Georgia tektites	Empire, Georgia
Indochinites	Indochina, Thailand
Ivory Coast tektites	Ivory Coast, Africa
Moldavites	Bohemia and Moravia, Czechoslovakia
Philippinites	Philippine Islands

and detailed calculations show that ejected material from meteorite impacts on the Moon could reach the Earth in the form of a shower of melted material which would be distributed much like the australites, for instance. A more distant source is unlikely, however, because the tektites could not stay together in such a cosmically small cluster for any appreciable length of time.

Only one tektite-like object has been identified as a meteorite fall, and there is some doubt as to whether or not it is a fraud. A glassy object with the chemical composition of a tektite is reported to have fallen in Igast, Estonia, in 1855. Unfortunately, spurious specimens of the "Igast meteorite" were sold to many museums by a dealer of the period who actually, it turned out later, sold them blobs of melted brick. The real Igast meteorite may exist in some European museum, and it may be a tektite fall.

Recent investigations of a large crater near Adrar, Western Sahara, suggest that it may be of tektite origin. The material formed by the melting on impact of the rock at this location is a glassy substance called *Aouellel glass*. The lack of any meteoritic matter in it has led to the suggestion that the impact of a large tektite body caused the crater and that Aouellel glass is an impacted mixture of tektite and Earth material, a fascinating but still otherwise unsupported speculation.

Physical properties

Many of the physical properties of tektites have been investigated in the laboratory and compared with those of common glasses such as obsidian, quartz, and commercial glass.

1. *Viscosity*. The viscosity of tektites is intermediate between that of common glass and obsidian.

2. *Magnetism*. No total magnetization is present, so the tektites must have been heated well above 1,400°C. Magnetization intensity is much less than for obsidian.

3. *Flow structures*. Variations in the index of refraction cause the appearance of flow structures. These can only develop in small masses of glass that cool rapidly. Flow structures disappear after 30 min of subjection to temperatures above the melting temperature.

4. *Evidence of melting*. All tektites show surface features indicative of a formerly molten condition, but some, particularly the button-shaped australites, indicate two periods of melting with a period of solidification between.

5. *Quartz inclusions*. Tiny fused quartz particles, called lechatelierite, are found in many tektites. Their presence indicates a very brief melting period, with temperatures in excess of 1,710°C, of a previously nonglassy material.

6. *Vacuum bubbles.* Occasional bubbles found in tektites are very good vacuums. This has been taken to indicate an extraterrestrial origin, but it may merely be due to shrinkage of the glass on cooling.

7. *Surface erosion.* Some meteoriticists believe that many of the tektites have suffered surface erosion at their place of fall, but that none exhibit any features indicating erosion by ablation on entering the atmosphere.

8. *Meteoritic inclusions.* Tiny nickel-iron particles have been found in a few tektites.

Chemical properties

The gross chemical composition of tektites is very different from that of meteorites but rather similar to that of sedimentary rocks. A general consensus of opinion is that the composition could be simulated by fusing together at some temperature in excess of 1700°C a mixture of 75 per cent shale and 25 per cent quartz. A comparison of the abundances of the Fe family of elements with those of sedimentary rocks and of meteorites indicates good agreement only with the former.

The abundances of nickel, deuterium, the different leads, strontium, rubidium, potassium, and uranium isotopes are all much more similar to those of terrestrial rocks than those of meteorites. The main chemical anomaly is the water content, which is low compared to that of terrestrial glasses.

Ages

The ages of tektites measured since they were last molten can be estimated from the potassium-argon method, as for meteorites, as well as by the standard geological methods of dating the formation in which they are

Table 11.9-2 Ages of tektites (in million years)

Type	K-A age	Geological age	Cosmic-ray exposure age (Ne^{21})
Australites	0.7	Recent	<0.03
	0.7		<0.5
Bediasites	34	Eocene (~40)	
Empirites	34		
Indochinites	0.7	Middle Pleistocene (~0.5)	<0.3
			<0.5
Moldavites	15	Miocene (~20)	
Philippinites	0.7	Middle Pleistocene (~0.5)	<0.04

found. Ages so determined range from 700,000 years to 34 million years (Table 11.9-2). Cosmic-ray exposure ages, measured also as for meteorites, are always very small, normally less than the limit of the experiment.

Conclusions

There is a widespread disagreement on the conclusions to be drawn from our knowledge of the properties of tektites. Many formation mechanisms have been proposed, some complex, others fantastic, but no mechanism has won universal support. Hopefully, the next few years, with their concentrated interest on space problems, will straighten out the confusion caused by the tektites, these rare glass objects of unknown heritage.

BIBLIOGRAPHICAL NOTES

A good technical treatise covering many meteoritical problems is:

R 11-1. Krinov, E. L.: "Principles of Meteoritics," translated from the Russian by I. Vidziunas and H. Brown, Pergamon Press, New York, 1960.

Other good but more popular books dealing with meteorites are:

R 11-2. Nininger, H. H.: "Out of the Sky," Dover Publication, Inc., New York, 1959.

R 11-3. Watson, F. G.: "Between the Planets," chaps. 9 and 10, Harvard University Press, Cambridge, Mass., 1956.

A good source of references to the literature up to the early 1950s is:

R 11-4. Brown, H. S.: "A Bibliography on Meteorites," The University of Chicago Press, Chicago, 1953.

An excellent summary of meteorite problems with a good review of mineralogical findings by J. A. Wood is contained in:

R 11-5. Middlehurst, B. M. and G. P. Kuiper (eds.): "The Moon Meteorites and Comets," The University of Chicago Press, Chicago, 1963.

Sections 11.1 and 11.2. A complete listing of meteorite falls is contained in:

R 11.1-1. Leonard, F. C.: "A Classification Catalog of the Meteoritic Falls of the World," University of California Press, Berkeley, 1956.

A standard classification of meteorites is that found in:

R 11.1-2. Prior, G. T.: *Mineral. Mag.*, **19**: 51 (1920).

A good listing of most known meteorites is:

R 11.1-3. Prior, G. T., and M. H. Hey: "Catalog of Meteorites," British Museum of Natural History, London, 1953.

Section 11.3. Two compilations of chemical analyses of meteorites are:

R 11.3-1. Buddhue, J. D.: *Popular Astron.*, **54**: 149 (1946).

R 11.3-2. Urey, H. C., and H. Craig: *Geochim. Cosmochim. Acta,* **4**: 36 (1953).

Most of the more recent analyses for minor and rare elements in meteorites are published in *Geochimica et Cosmochimica Acta.*

Section 11.4. Three papers dealing with the shapes of meteorites and their relation to aerodynamics are:

R 11.4-1. Nininger, H. H.: *Am. J. Sci.*, **32**: 1 (1936).

R 11.4-2. Rinehart, J. S., "Meteorites and Ballistics," Smithsonian Astrophysical Observatory, Cambridge, Mass., 1958.

R 11.4-3. Henderson, E. P., and D. T. Williams: "Evidence on the Nature of Airflow around Stony Meteorites and Ballistics," Smithsonian Astrophysical Observatory, Cambridge, Mass., 1958.

A description of the principle behind isotopic studies of preencounter shapes and sizes is given by:

R 11.4-4. Fireman, E. L., and J. Zahringer: *Phys. Rev.*, **107**: 1695 (1957).

Section 11.5. Many recent papers in journals deal with cosmic-ray exposure ages. See, for example:

R 11.5-1. Honda, M., J. P. Shedlovsky, and J. R. Arnold: *Geochim. Cosmochim Acta,* **22**: 133 (1961).

R 11.5-2. Fireman, E. L., and J. de Felice: *J. Geophys. Res.*, **65**: 3035 (1960).

R 11.5-3. Honda, M., and J. R. Arnold: *Geochim. Cosmochim. Acta,* **23**:219 (1961).

See also R 11.1-3.

Section 11.6. Reference R 11.1-3 contains excellent discussions and sources of references on ages of meteorites.

Section 11.7. See R 11.1-4.

Section 11.8. A good discussion of meteorite craters is found in:

R 11.8-1. Watson, F.: *Popular Astron.*, **44**: 1 (1936).

A description of the soil survey of the Arizona Crater is found in:

R 11.8-2. Rinehart, J. S.: *Smithsonian Contrib. Astrophys.*, **2**: 145 (1958).

A description of the huge possible meteorite crater in Antarctica is given by:

R 11.8-3. Schmidt, R. A.: *Science,* **138**: 443 (1962).

See also R 11-1 which gives excellent accounts of meteorite craters in the U.S.S.R. and references to the Russian literature on the subject.

Section 11.9. A good summary of tektite research with plentiful references is:

R 11.9-1. O'Keefe, J. A. (ed.): "Tektites," The University of Chicago Press, Chicago, 1963.

Asteroids

12

On the first of January, 1801, while making observations of star positions for a routine program, the astronomer Piazzi found a peculiar object. On succeeding nights, Piazzi found that this apparently stellar object moved slowly among the stars as does a planet. He announced it as a new planet and named it Ceres Ferdinandea, later shortened to just Ceres. The new planet was faint and it moved rapidly, so that after a few weeks Piazzi lost it.

At that time the physicist Gauss developed a method of using Newtonian mechanics to determine an orbit from three observations of position. Gauss applied his method to Piazzi's position measurements for Ceres, found that its orbit lay between the orbits of Mars and Jupiter, and predicted its location accurately enough for it to be rediscovered. Its fame as a new planet was short-lived, however, because in the following year, 1802, another faint planet with a similar orbit was found by an astronomer who was looking for Ceres. This planet was called Pallas, and its discovery was shortly followed by the discoveries of Juno (1804) and Vesta (1807).

Table 12.1-1   Orbital parameters of several important asteroids

No.	Name	Period, years	Semi-major axis, AU	Eccen-tricity	Incli-nation, deg	Notes
1	Ceres	4.60	2.77	0.08	10.6	The four largest and brightest; their orbits are typical
2	Pallas	4.61	2.77	0.23	34.7	
3	Juno	4.36	2.67	0.25	13.0	
4	Vesta	3.63	2.36	0.09	7.1	
433	Eros	1.76	1.46	0.22	10.8	Approach to Earth: 23,000,000 km
588	Achilles	11.98	5.24	0.15	10.3	Trojan: 60° ahead of Jupiter
617	Patroclus	11.82	5.19	0.14	22.1	Trojan: 60° behind Jupiter
944	Hidalgo	14.0	5.80	0.65	42.5	Largest mean distance
...	Hermes	1.47	1.29	0.47	4.7	Approach to Earth: 800,000 km
...	Icarus	1.10	1.08	0.83	23.0	Small perihelion distance and largest eccentricity

All of these new planets were faint, normally too faint to be seen without a telescope, and all had nearly identical orbits lying between the orbits of Mars and Jupiter. By 1891, a total of 322 of these minor planets, usually called asteroids, had been found visually. Most of them were named by their discoverer; and when all of the mythological possibilities had been exhausted, the discoverers derived names from those of their wives, friends, cities, colleges, etc. Officially, asteroids are given numbers as well as names. By 1949, 1,565 had been assigned numbers, and orbits had been computed for all of them. Many more asteroids have been discovered and then lost.

The number of asteroids increases very greatly with fainter magnitudes, so that large telescopes are capable of discovering immense numbers of these minor planets. It is estimated that the 200-in. telescope at Palomar, if it photographed the entire sky, would register almost 100,000 asteroids. On one plate taken with the 48-in. Schmidt telescope at Palomar, nearly 90 asteroids were found. The number of these objects in the solar system must be truly immense.

12.1 ASTEROID ORBITS

All orbits so far determined for asteroids are direct and of low inclination. Most asteroids have orbital periods between 4 and 7 yr, with a few as large as 12 and some less than 3 yr. The eccentricity of their orbits is generally small, with a few values as large as 0.4, but most lying between 0.0

and 0.2. From the point of view of their orbits, the majority of asteroids behave very much like the larger planets (Table 12.1-1).

One of the most interesting findings about asteroids is the way in which their orbital parameters are influenced by the planet Jupiter. The most striking example of Jupiter's dominance of the asteroid belt is the way in which gaps (called Kirkwood's gaps) occur in the distribution of periods at certain fractions of the period of Jupiter.

Figure 12.1-1 illustrates the distribution of periods for the asteroids with known orbits and shows that there are very distinct gaps at periods of 5.95, 4.76, and 3.97 yr, which are exactly $\frac{1}{2}$, $\frac{2}{5}$, and $\frac{1}{3}$ the period of Jupiter. Gaps also can be found at other fractions of Jupiter's period, for instance at $\frac{1}{4}$, $\frac{1}{5}$, $\frac{3}{5}$, and $\frac{3}{7}$. This is obviously a result of a resonance between the periods, one of the more interesting problems of celestial mechanics to be attacked. It is found that perturbations on a small body with orbital parameters which are a simple fraction of those of a nearby large body are severe enough to cause instability and a change of orbit. The details of the solution to this problem are complicated and will not be discussed here.

Another example of Jupiter's dominance of the asteroids is the fact that several asteroids have been found to lie in Jupiter's orbit (Fig. 12.1-2). These objects, called Trojans, lie at the equilateral lagrangian points of the Jupiter-Sun system (Sec. 2.3). These lagrangian points of Jupiter are known to be stable, so that it is not surprising that any small body which might have at some time crossed these points should be captured in them, or oscillate about them. A total of 15 Trojans are now known.

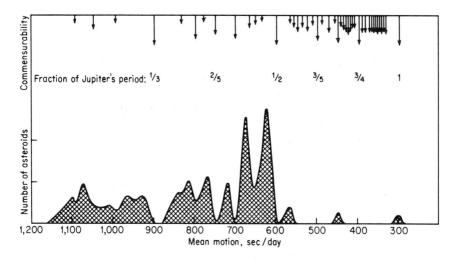

Fig. 12.1-1   The distribution of the mean daily motions of asteroids (lower), compared with the computed perturbations due to Jupiter (upper). Commensurabilities with Jupiter's period are indicated.   (*After Brouwer.*)

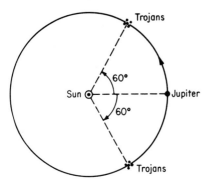

Fig. 12.1-2 Orbits of the Trojan asteroids.

Some asteroids have sufficiently small orbits or large enough eccentricities that they come quite near to the Earth and are therefore of great interest from the point of view of the distance scale of the solar system (Chap. 14). Examples are Eros, which came within 23,000,000 km of Earth, and Hermes, which came within 800,000 km (Table 12.1-1). It may well be that asteroids have come even closer; some of the largest meteorite craters (Sec. 11.8) may in fact be evidence of the collision of an asteroid with the Earth. Another unusual asteroid is Icarus, which has a perihelion distance of only 2.8×10^7 km, a distance from the Sun which causes its temperature to be raised to some 800°K.

12.2 DIAMETERS

The asteroids are all so small that only a very few can be distinguished as being nonstellar through the largest telescopes. Micrometer and interferometer measurements have yielded diameters for four asteroids (Table 12.2-1). The remaining asteroids are all probably smaller than 200 km in diameter, with perhaps 200 larger than 50 km and the vast majority only a few kilometers across. The only method of estimating the sizes of the smaller asteroids is measuring their magnitudes and estimating that their albedos roughly correspond to the mean albedos for the four asteroids for which this quantity has been measured. The faintest asteroids which can be photographed with the 48-in. Schmidt telescope at Palomar mountain are estimated on this basis to have diameters of only one or two kilometers.

If one integrates over the dimensions calculated in this way for all asteroids estimated to be in the solar system, one finds that the total volume is approximately 2×10^{24} cm^3. Thus, assuming a density of 3 g/cm^3, the total mass of asteroidal material is computed to be only one-thousandth that of the Earth, or $\sim 10^{25}$ g.

12.3 ALBEDOS AND SURFACES

The albedos for those four asteroids for which sizes have been obtained are also listed in Table 12.2-1. It is seen that two of these asteroids have

Table 12.2-1   Diameters and albedos of four asteroids

Name	Number	Diameter, km	Albedo
Ceres	1	770	0.06
Pallas	2	490	0.07
Juno	3	190	0.12
Vesta	4	390	0.26

albedos very similar to those of Mercury or the Moon (Chaps. 16 and 19). Juno and Vesta, however, have larger albedos and may possibly be covered with some lighter colored material, perhaps ices or dust of some sort. Those asteroids so far measured show very steep phase variation of luminosity, indicating that surfaces must be exceedingly rough (Sec. 16.2). The phase coefficient is 0.03 mag/deg for asteroids, in excellent agreement with that for Mercury and the Moon and twice the value for Venus and Mars. Thus, there must be no atmosphere on any of the asteroids, certainly not a surprising conclusion in view of the obvious inability of such a small mass to retain a gaseous atmosphere (Chap. 18).

The colors of asteroids have been measured photoelectrically and turn out to be very similar to colors of stony meteorites and most terrestrial rocks, i.e., somewhat yellower than the Sun. Polarization measurements of the asteroid Vesta show that it is no doubt covered with a layer of dusty material.

12.4   SHAPE AND ROTATION

For bodies as small as the asteroids, it can be shown that gravitational forces are not necessarily sufficient to induce a spherical form. Yield for ordinary materials occurs when the load reaches approximately

$$S = 10^9 \text{ g/(cm)(sec}^2) \tag{1}$$

We take, as the characteristic length l of yielding, the length of a column of unit cross section and of density ρ, the weight of which equals the critical load. Thus,

$$S = l\rho g \tag{2}$$

where g is the surface gravity. For an asteroid the surface gravity in terms of that of the Earth is

$$\frac{g}{g_e} = \frac{R}{R_e} \cdot \frac{\langle \rho \rangle}{\langle \rho_e \rangle} \tag{3}$$

For the asteroid, we take $\langle \rho \rangle = \rho$ and find the critical radius R_c which equals l:

$$R_c = \frac{1}{\rho}\left(\frac{SR_e\rho_e}{g_e}\right)^{\frac{1}{2}} \tag{4}$$

If the density of the asteroid is 4 g/cm³, then the critical radius is approximately 150 km. Thus it is not a surprise that many asteroids have been found to be very irregularly shaped. For one of these asteroids, Eros, this irregular shape has actually been seen at the telescope. When Eros was at one of its close approaches to the Earth in 1931 (it came within 23 million km), it was seen as an elongated image with an appearance similar to that of an unresolved double star of 0″.18 separation. The astronomers observing it detected the rotation of Eros, which turned counterclockwise in 5 hr 17 min. This period is exactly the same as that found by photometric observations of variation in brightness of Eros.

Many asteroids have been photometrically observed to be variable, with periods of between 2 or 3 to more than 10 hr. It has been assumed that this variation in luminosity is connected with the irregular shape of the asteroid or with irregular surface characteristics. Possibly very accurate photometry combined with polarimetry could allow the shape and surface to be uniquely determined for a given asteroid, but so far this has been attempted only in a rough way for a few of the asteroids so observed. Eros, for instance, has been computed from its light curve to be approximately cylindrical in shape with a length of approximately 25 km and a diameter of some 10 km. In actual fact, Eros is undoubtedly more irregu-

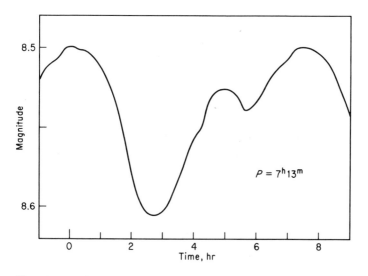

Fig. 12.4-1   Light curve of the asteroid Juno. (*After Groeneveld and Kuiper.*)

lar than indicated by these calculations. Figure 12.4-1 gives a representative light curve for the asteroid Juno. One finds, of course, that the light curve varies with the angle at which we see the asteroid in its orbit. For Eros, for instance, the variation from maximum to minimum is sometimes a factor of 3 in luminosity and at other times is unmeasurably small.

BIBLIOGRAPHICAL NOTES

A partly descriptive book dealing entirely with asteroids is:

R 12-1. Roth, G. D., "The System of Minor Planets," Faber & Faber, Ltd., London, 1962.

Section 12.1. An interesting historical account of the derivations of orbital parameters for 21 important asteroids is:

R 12.1-1. Leuschner, A. O.: *Bull. Natl. Res. Council,* **4**(part 7): (1922).

See also the frequent publications issued by the Minor Planet Center, University of Cincinnati, Ohio.

Sections 12.2 and 12.3. A good popular account of asteroids, with many details as to size and total mass, is:

R 12.2-1. Watson, F. G.: "Between the Planets," Harvard University Press, Cambridge, Mass., 1956.

Section 12.4. An account of a survey of asteroids, including reference to photometric work, is contained in:

R 12.4-1. Kuiper, G. P., et al.: *Astrophys. J., Suppl. Ser.* 32 (1958).

Interplanetary dust

Even without direct observations, it is possible to infer the presence of dust in the space between the planets. In preceding chapters it has been shown that the characteristics of comets, meteors, and meteorites all argue that such dust must be abundant. The ejection of cometary material as we see it in the dust tails is a process which continually supplies microscopic material to interplanetary space.

The fact that meteors increase in number rapidly with decreasing size suggests that there must be vast numbers of very small meteors, of such dimensions that we should call them meteoric dust. And the similar frequency-mass curve for meteorites argues for a great abundance of very small meteoritic material. We have inferred dust, therefore, from at least two sources; the comets (from which the meteors come) and the asteroidal material (from which the meteorites come).

Direct observations of interplanetary dust are available from many sources, and they all verify what we have inferred, namely, that micro-

Fig. 13.1-1   Photograph of the zodiacal light. (*Courtesy Blackwell and Ingham.*)

scopic particles are very abundant in interplanetary space. We can readily observe dust optically in the zodiacal light and also detect it physically
by using detectors on artificial satellites; and we can collect it from the
atmosphere, the ground, arctic ice, and the ocean.

13.1   THE ZODIACAL LIGHT

The zodiacal light, which may be observed on a dark night as a faint band
of light oriented along the ecliptic and increasing in intensity toward the
Sun, has been subjected to extensive observations in recent years because
of the potentially great amount of information it can give us regarding
the interplanetary medium, especially the dust component.

Early attempts to deduce the detailed characteristics of interplanetary dust from the zodiacal light measurements were those of van de
Hulst and Allen, working independently in 1946. Since then, accurate photometry and polarization measurements have been carried out by many
astronomers at various latitudes and widely ranging altitudes. Because of

the need for very dark skies, many measurements have been carried out at high altitudes, such as recently by Blackwell and Ingham from a 17,000 ft high station in the Bolivian Andes. We now have measures of the brightness, polarization, and variations in these features, as well as spectra of the zodiacal light (Fig. 13.1-1).

It was realized years ago that the zodiacal light must be made up of scattered sunlight, because the spectra show the normal solar spectrum without enhancement of the night-sky emission lines. The scattering material was at first assumed to be solid particles distributed liberally along the ecliptic between the Earth and the Sun.

An idea of the actual spatial density of these particles could be obtained, it was thought, by simple geometry. Let us take I as the solar radiation flux, in ergs per second per square centimeter, at the Earth's distance and consider the energy received by a cylinder, in the line of sight, with a length dx, a cross section a, a distance from the Sun y, and a distance from the Earth x (Fig. 13.1-2). The energy received per second by the particles, if their space density is ρ (cm^{-3}), within the cylinder is

$$\frac{I\rho a A \, dx}{y^2}$$

where A is the mean cross-sectional area of the particles. A certain percentage of this radiation is scattered through an angle θ so that it reaches the Earth. The intensity of this radiation will be proportional to $1/x^2$ and to the efficiency of the scattering process for this particular angle. The latter is called the phase function, $f(\theta)$. Thus the flux of radiation received from this cylinder at the Earth is

$$\frac{I\rho A \, (a/x^2) f(\theta) \, dx}{y^2} \tag{1}$$

Dividing by the solid angle in steradians of a seen at distance x, that is, a/x^2, we obtain the flux per steradian:

$$\frac{I\rho A f(\theta) \, dx}{y^2} \tag{2}$$

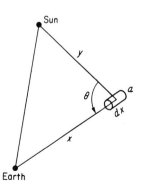

Fig. 13.1-2 Diagram for analysis of the zodiacal light.

Now, the total surface brightness as seen from the Earth at this particular angle ϵ from the Sun is

$$B(\epsilon) = I \int_0^\infty \frac{\rho A f(\theta)}{y^2} \, dx \tag{3}$$

To put this in terms of the scattering angle θ, we use

$$y = \frac{\sin \epsilon}{\sin \theta} \quad \text{and} \quad dx = \frac{\sin \epsilon \, d\theta}{\sin^2 \theta}$$

So that

$$B(\epsilon) = \frac{I}{\sin \epsilon} \int_\epsilon^\pi \rho A f(\theta) \, d\theta \tag{4}$$

Thus, if we measure $B(\epsilon)$ and know the behavior of the phase function $f(\theta)$, we need only to know A to obtain the exact distribution of particles in space.

Before attempting to deduce this distribution, let us first examine in detail the observations which have been made. Photometry of the zodiacal light is very difficult and not all observers have agreed on even its crude properties, such as shape and absolute brightness. Table 13.1-1 lists measures of the observed surface brightness of the zodiacal light at elongation ϵ of 40°, as deduced at eight different times. The differences between the various results are probably primarily due to experimental errors, although it is not impossible that variations as large as those observed might be real. Elvey and Roach detected annual variations which may amount to differences of as much as a factor of 2.

The symmetry of the zodiacal light now seems well established by the Bolivian observations (Fig. 13.1-3), although earlier measures did not agree among themselves at all on this point. Also, the degree and distri-

Table 13.1-1   Observations of the zodiacal light

Observer	Latitude, deg	Height, ft	Date	Brightness*
Behr and Siedentopf	+46	11,700	1952	3.17
Barbier	+44	1,900	1952/3	3.35
Roach et al.	+36	5,415	1952/3	5.38
Regener	+34	9,200	1953/4	5.52
Blackwell	−16	9,000	1955	2.90
Elsässer	−29	5,550	1956	2.85
Divari and Asaad	+24	660	1957	3.26
Blackwell and Ingham	−16	17,100	1958	4.42

* Brightness of the zodiacal light on the ecliptic at longitude $\epsilon = 40°$, in units of 10^{-13} times the mean solar disk brightness.

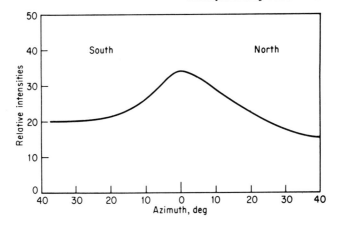

Fig. 13.1-3 A sample scan in azimuth of the zodiacal light intensity. (*After Blackwell and Ingham.*)

bution of polarization now seem fairly well established (Fig. 13.1-4). Similarly, the color has been determined by a number of observers who agree that the color is very close to that of the Sun. At elongation 40°, Behr and Siedentopf quote a color of CI = +0.46, whereas for the Sun it is CI = +0.53 (in mag.)

Since the outer corona is also the same color as the Sun, one might ask whether this portion of the corona is not just the inward extension of the zodiacal light. It can be seen and measured during eclipses, and Allen and later Blackwell have made careful measurements of it from aircraft during solar eclipses. As Fig. 13.1-5 shows, the eclipse observations fit very well to the nighttime zodiacal light measurements, and we take the two as being the same phenomenon.

Now let us return to the problem of analysis of the zodiacal light. We found that Eq. (13.1-4) will give us the distribution of scattering par-

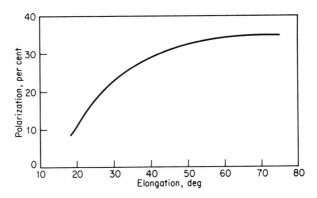

Fig. 13.1-4 Polarization curve for the zodiacal light. (*After Blackwell and Ingham.*)

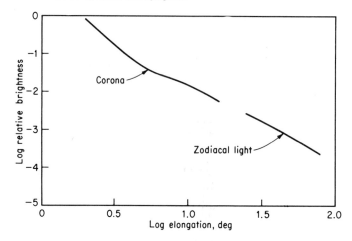

Fig. 13.1-5   A comparison of the outer coronal intensity with the intensity of the zodiacal light. (*After Blackwell and Ingham.*)

ticles if we know the phase function $f(\theta)$ and the optical cross section of the particles A. The existence of polarization, averaging about 20 per cent, in the zodiacal light suggests that part, at least, of the light is scattered by free electrons. From the formula for Thomson scattering, we find that for the polarized component of scattered light,

$$f(\theta)A = \left(\frac{e^2}{mc^2}\right)^2 \frac{\sin^2 \theta}{2} \tag{5}$$

where c is the velocity of light and e and m are charge and mass of the electron. If we substitute (13.1-5) into (13.1-4) we find that

$$B(\epsilon) = \frac{I(e^2/mc^2)^2}{2 \sin \epsilon} \int_\epsilon^\pi \rho \sin \theta \, d\theta \tag{6}$$

This provides us with values for ρ at various distances from the Sun. Assuming that all of the polarized light is scattered from free electrons leads to electron densities of 600 per cm³ at 1 AU from the Sun. As we have pointed out in Chap. 8, this value is impossible, because a large body of evidence (including results from space probes) indicates an electron density of 1 to 10 per cm³ at 1 AU. Therefore, we conclude that much of the polarization is produced by dust particles.

In order to derive the distribution of dust which might give rise to the observed zodiacal light, we must in some way arrive at a value for A, and we must state the appropriate phase function. We know that we are not just observing reflected light from solid particles, because this would mean that the particles must exist right up very close to the Sun in order to explain the corona. This is impossible, because it is unlikely that dust will remain in a solid state closer than about 4 solar radii. Instead, the brightening close to the Sun must be explained by diffraction of light by particles between us and the Sun. These particles, in order to produce the observed results, must be small, of the order of 10 μ. This size restriction follows from the observed color, because scattered light from particles smaller than a few microns is bluer than the incident light and that from particles larger than 100 μ or so is redder.

The detailed theory of diffraction by particles in a range of sizes of this order is very complicated, being based on the Mie diffraction formulas generalized to arbitrarily shaped particles in a range of sizes. A rigorous solution has not been attempted, and anyway it is certain that the present observations can be explained by a rather wide variety of size distributions, albedos, and distributions in space. Ingham has evaluated the probable mass density and particle space density that one computes from various assumed values of the above parameters combined with the Bolivian zodiacal light measures. Characteristic values are $\sim 10^{-24}$ g/cm³ for the mass density and ~ 200 per km³ for the number of particles of all sizes in the Earth's vicinity. Direct measures of these quantities by means of artificial satellites are providing us with even better values.

13.2 MICROMETEORITES

Both Öpik and Whipple have shown that it is possible for very small particles to pass through the atmosphere without suffering ablation. At a certain size the particle is capable of radiating energy away as fast as it is generated, so that the melting temperature is never reached. Such unablated particles are called *micrometeorites*. The actual evaluation of the critical size is complicated, but the principles are simple and straightforward. Let us examine them.

First, we find an expression for the increment of energy contained in the molecules which collide with the front of the incoming body. The mass of the air which is encountered is simply

$$dm = A\rho V\,dt \tag{1}$$

where A is the cross-sectional area of the meteorite, ρ is the density of the air, and V is the velocity of the meteorite. The energy gained by the molecules is thus

$$dE_g = \tfrac{1}{2}V^2\,dm = \tfrac{1}{2}A\rho V^3\,dt \tag{2}$$

Now let us consider how this energy is dissipated. Most of this energy will be transmitted to the micrometeorite. Part of the energy will heat up the body, part will be radiated, part will go into dissociation, excitation, and ionization of the material, and part will be used in mechanically removing material from the surface of the body. Let us say for the moment that the radiation accounts for most of the energy used up. Whipple has shown that this is not too far wrong. Also, let us assume that the particle radiates as a blackbody. Then, from Stefan's law, the energy radiated is

$$dE_r = a\sigma T^4 \, dt \tag{3}$$

where a is the radiating area of the object, σ is the Stefan-Boltzmann constant, and T is the temperature of the surface. The radiating area a is normally just 4 times the cross-sectional area A, so that (13.2-3) can be written

$$dE_r = 4A\sigma T^4 \, dt \tag{4}$$

Under our present assumptions and because of the conservation of energy we can equate (13.2-2) and (13.2-4). The result is

$$T^4 = \frac{\rho V^3}{8\sigma} \tag{5}$$

Now as the meteorite penetrates into the atmosphere, ρ increases, which causes V to decrease in an amount depending upon its size A. Let us now find an expression relating A, ρ, and V. In Sec. 10.12 we saw that

$$m \, dV = -A\Gamma\rho V^2 \, dt \tag{6}$$

where m is the mass of the meteorite and Γ is the drag coefficient, approximately equal to 1. For a spherical particle of density 3 g/cm^3, $m = 4A^{3/2}/\pi^{1/2}$, so that Eq. (13.2-6) becomes

$$dV = \frac{-\pi^{1/2}\rho V^2}{4A^{1/2}} \, dt \tag{7}$$

Now ρ varies with height h above sea level as

$$\rho = \rho_0 e^{-bh} \tag{8}$$

where ρ_0 is constant and b is a constant for an isothermal atmosphere. Furthermore, for a body entering the relatively flat atmosphere straight down (taking the zenith angle Z equal to zero) we have

$$dh = -V \, dt \tag{9}$$

Let us substitute Eq. (13.2-8) for ρ and Eq. (13.2-9) for dt in Eq. (13.2-7). We then have

$$\frac{dV}{V} = \frac{\pi^{1/2}\rho_0 e^{-bh}}{4A^{1/2}} \, dh \tag{10}$$

Now let us integrate this equation over the path of the meteorite from outside the atmosphere to height h, where the velocity has a value V smaller than its initial value V_i.

$$\int_{V_i}^{V} \frac{dV}{V} = \frac{\pi^{1/2}\rho_0}{4A^{1/2}} \int_{\infty}^{h} e^{-bh} \, dh \tag{11}$$

This is easily evaluated:

$$\log \frac{V}{V_i} = -\frac{\pi^{1/2}\rho_0}{4A^{1/2}b} e^{-bh} \tag{12}$$

By resubstituting in the expression for ρ from Eq. (13.2-8), we obtain

$$\log \frac{V}{V_i} = -\frac{\pi^{1/2}\rho}{4A^{1/2}b} \tag{13}$$

or

$$\rho = -\frac{4A^{1/2}b}{\pi^{1/2}} \log \frac{V}{V_i} \tag{14}$$

Substituting this expression for ρ into Eq. (13.2-5) gives us

$$T^4 = -\frac{A^{1/2}bV^3}{2\pi^{1/2}\sigma} \log \frac{V}{V_i} \tag{15}$$

Now in order that our particle will not be melted, its maximum temperature must be somewhat below the melting temperature of its material. From Eq. (13.2-15) we can express this in terms of a critical velocity V_c, the velocity corresponding to this maximum temperature. Thus if we impose a maximal condition on T, by differentiation of Eq. (13.2-15) we can find V_c. We get, by putting the differential of Eq. (13.2-15) equal to zero, the nontrivial relation

$$0 = \frac{d}{dV} \left(V^3 \log \frac{V}{V_i} \right) \tag{16}$$

and this gives

$$\log \frac{V_c}{V_i} = -\frac{1}{3} \tag{17}$$

or

$$V_c = \frac{V_i}{e^{1/3}} \tag{18}$$

Now we may calculate a critical size above which melting occurs. From Eq. (13.2-15), substituting in our values for V_c, we get

$$T^4_{\max} = \frac{A^{1/2}bV_i^3}{6\pi^{1/2}\sigma e} \tag{19}$$

For a spherical particle,

$$A \approx \pi r^2 \tag{20}$$

So that we find a maximum radius of

$$r_c = \frac{6e\sigma T_{max}^4}{bV_i^3} \tag{21}$$

Taking a melting temperature of 1500°K for T_{max}, a value for b of 1.1×10^{-6} cm^{-1}, and a value for σ of 5.7×10^{-5} erg/(cm²)(deg⁴)(sec), we calculate a critical radius of

$$r_c = \frac{4.2 \times 10^{15}}{V_i^3} \tag{22}$$

in cgs units. Thus for vertical incidence at 11.7 km/sec, the minimum velocity for a meteoroid, we calculate that a particle 26 μ in radius or smaller will not have suffered ablation by melting. Whipple has calculated this radius more vigorously, without most of our assumptions, and gets $r = 30$ μ for this particular critical radius. His complete formula for an isothermal atmosphere (later, he makes corrections for variation of temperature in the atmosphere) is

$$r_c = \frac{9e\beta\sigma\Gamma(T_m^4 - T_0^4)}{\alpha\rho_s b(\cos Z)V_i^3} \tag{23}$$

where β = gray emissivity coefficient
  σ = 5.7×10^{15} erg/(cm²)(deg⁴)(sec)
  Γ = drag coefficient, a function of V
  T_m = melting temperature
  T_0 = temperature of the body outside the atmosphere
  α = accommodation coefficient (fraction of molecular energy transferred to the micrometeorite)
  ρ_s = density of particle
  b = a parameter in the ρ_{air} formula which varies with air temperature
  Z = zenith angle of the micrometeorite's path
  V_i = velocity of the meteorite at the top of the atmosphere

Table 13.2-1   Numerical values for critical radii

V_i, km/sec	r_c, μ
11.3	30
20.0	7
40.0	1
70.0	0.3

Table 13.2-1 gives values calculated by Whipple for spheres with various velocities and for $\rho = 3$, $Z = 0°$. We see that for objects in orbits similar to the orbit of the Earth, so that V_i is low, particles of the size estimated to predominate in the zodiacal light will for the most part penetrate the atmosphere relatively unchanged. They are probably stopped at heights of some 150 km, from which elevation they experience free fall into the lower atmosphere, where they mingle, unrecognized, with the abundant dust of terrestrial origin.

13.3 METEORITIC DUST AND THE EARTH

On the evening of November 14, 1856, the clipper ship *Joshua Bates* lay approximately 200 miles southeast of the island of Bali. Out of a calm sky the crew was suddenly startled by a barrage of fine shot which fell profusely over the deck. Captain D. S. McCallum collected a sample of this puzzling material and found it to be made up of tiny spherical metallic particles. When back at home port, the Captain sent a sample to Washington, where scientists were stumped as to its origin. They in turn sent a sample to Germany, where chemical analysis showed the material to be metallic iron and iron oxide, and the suggestion was made that the material must be meteoritic and had probably resulted from the passage of a bolide through the atmosphere above the ship.

At least a hundred other instances of dust falls of this nature are recorded. In 1885, Dr. Batchelder of Pelham, New Hampshire, walked out his front door after a brief thunder shower and discovered a layer of peculiar fine dust covering his walk. He sent some to the *Scientific American*, who found it was made up of iron, nickel, and silica and was therefore most probably meteoritic in origin. Hailstones which fell in a great storm on Padua, Italy, on August 26, 1834, were found by Prof. D. L. Cosari to contain sandy nuclei, and later analysis of these grains suggested that they were meteoritic in origin.

When the extremely spectacular Bielid, or Andromedid, meteor shower (Chap. 10) occurred on November 27, 1885, the rain which fell that day and on the next few days in Ghent, Belgium, was found to contain large amounts of "meteoritic" dust, according to the scientist Yung. Numerous reports have been made of falls of "red snow," such as that in Iceland on May 27, 1903. The red color was due to oxidized iron, and the snow was full of shiny, black metallic spherules.

More than 50 falls of dust, supposedly meteoritic, were listed by Chladni in 1819 as having occurred between the years 472 and 1816. Such dust falls have not been reported in recent scientific literature, except for a brief account by H. E. Landsberg of an attempt to collect particles resulting from the great 1946 Draconid shower and an account by the French scientist L. Rudaux, who found high numbers of magnetic particles falling to the Earth two days after passage of a bright bolide in 1927.

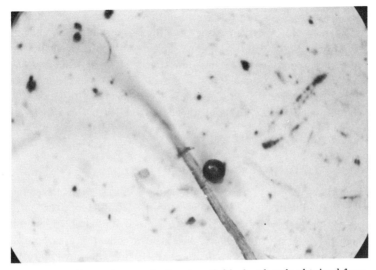

Fig. 13.3-1   Photomicrograph of a smooth black spherule obtained from 750-yr-old Greenland ice. The spherule is 40 μ in diameter. (*Courtesy of C. C. Langway, Jr., U.S.A. CRREL.*)

If it is true that large amounts of dust fall to the Earth after spectacular showers or bright bolides, then smaller amounts of meteoric dust must fall to the Earth at all times. A number of scientists have attempted to collect such particles simply by separating out the magnetic fraction of dust that settles to the Earth each day. It has been found that a principal regular magnetic constituent of this dust is made up of small, smooth, shiny spherules, with diameters ranging from a few to 100 μ or so (Fig. 13.3-1). Analyses of these particles show that they are usually iron or iron oxide, with nickel only rarely detected. In both appearance and chemical composition, they strongly resemble the spheres of molten material which are often found in the vicinity of a recently fallen meteorite.

It seems reasonable to suggest that they are the molten fraction of asteroidal (high-density) meteors, most of which do not reach the Earth's surface. Unfortunately, they also resemble, in both appearance and chemical composition, certain industrial by-products that are spewed into the atmosphere by the Earth's millions of smokestacks and which permeate the air near most centers of civilization. No physical or chemical means has yet been devised to tell whether a particular spherule is meteoritic or industrial, and investigators have been forced to abandon the attempt to collect such objects except in very remote areas, such as the Arctic, or by high-altitude aircraft.

For example, in the center of New Haven, Connecticut, approximately 100 of these spherules larger than 5 μ in diameter fall per square centimeter per day, while this rate falls to 25 at a distance of 10 miles from New Haven, and to approximately 0.15 in the Arctic. In spite of these difficulties—the fact that metallic, shiny spherules are so easy to recognize and are so rare compared to the bulk of atmospheric dust— much effort has gone into the study of them, primarily in the Arctic, in deep-sea cores, and in the upper atmosphere.

13.4 ARCTIC COLLECTIONS

In the process of studying the rate of deposit of snow through history, scientists in the Arctic regions have occasionally noted the presence of possible meteoritic dust deep in the Arctic ice. Studies in Greenland and in Antarctica have shown that black, shiny magnetic spherules exist throughout cores in the ice, taken at depths in the ice so great that the ice (and spherules) are as much as 750 years old. The mere occurrence of these particles so deep in the ice precludes any industrial origin, and their shape and surface characteristics are not compatible with a volcanic origin. Systematic studies of such Arctic ice cores are being used to provide us with information on historical fluctuations in the yearly influx rate of such particles.

Because of its isolation, the Arctic has been the site of searches for airborne meteoritic particles as well as "fossil" deposits. In one program, simultaneous daily deposits were collected for an entire year at two Arctic stations, one in central Alaska, and one on Cornwallis Island, just west of Greenland. It was found that at both stations the rate of fall of tiny magnetic spherules, made up primarily of iron, was 1 per cm^2 per day, larger than the diameter of 3 μ. The agreement of these two data and their further agreement with similar collections made on a mountain top above the Mojave Desert in California and in New Mexico lend considerable support to the hypothesis that these particles are indeed of meteoritic origin. Chemical analyses of the Arctic particles show that they are primarily magnetite and that they strongly resemble meteorites in composition.

13.5 DEEP-SEA CORES

In 1884 it was found that microscopic spherules were fairly common in deposits collected from the ocean bottom, and the origin of these particles was tentatively suggested to be meteoritic. They have since been found to be quite common in the globigerina ooze, where they occur to a depth of at least 3 m, which indicates a deposit age of at least 1 to 3 million years. Nearly 1,000 of them are found per kilogram of sediment. Their chemical composition as established from the abundances of iron, cobalt, nickel, and copper is remarkably similar to meteoritic composition and is unlike Earth minerals. The cosmic origin of these deep-sea spherules seems firmly established.

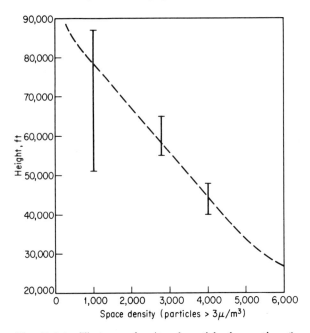

Fig. 13.6-1   The space density of particles larger than 3 μ in diameter as a function of height above sea level, determined by aircraft. (*After Hodge.*)

13.6   UPPER ATMOSPHERE COLLECTIONS

In order to avoid the difficulty of identifying extraterrestrial material after it has mixed with the exceedingly abundant Earth dust that permeates the lower atmosphere, a number of attempts have been made to collect dust from higher in the atmosphere, above the tropopause. High-altitude jet aircraft have been used, and collections have ranged in height from 30,000 to 90,000 feet (Fig. 13.6-1). The samples obtained show that the air at these altitudes is far cleaner than that at lower altitudes, although terrestrial dust is still present even in the highest samples. Tiny spherules, apparently identical to those collected in the Arctic, are found in the samples, and the abundance is the same as that deduced from the Arctic ground collections.

The spherules, however, are only a very minor component of the microscopic material which is collected from the stratosphere (approximately one one-thousandth the total number of particles larger than 3 μ in mean dimensions). Of the remaining material, a small amount is of obvious terrestrial origin, while the majority is a mixture of high- and low-density particles which may contain cometary meteor debris and micrometeorites. Chemical analysis cannot prove or disprove an extraterrestrial origin, because we have no good criteria for such particles. However, when it becomes possible to obtain vast numbers of these particles, we can hope to accumulate enough mass to analyze them collectively for cosmic-ray-induced radioactivity, the presence of which would prove a cosmic origin.

13.7   ROCKET AND SATELLITE RESULTS

With the advent of artificial satellites and high-flying rockets, it became possible to physically detect interplanetary dust outside the atmosphere. Because of the high velocity of such cosmic material—probably at least 15 km/sec—actual collection is exceedingly difficult; the dust is immediately destroyed on impact with most surfaces. For that reason satellite and rocket data consist mostly of records of impacts. Two common methods are detection of impacts by acoustical means and by means of breakage of very fine wires in a grid. Both methods require that a number of assumptions be made; in particular, the density, velocity, and structure of the particles must be assumed in order to draw conclusions about size distributions and spatial densities.

There is a tendency for different methods and different satellites to give very different results. For instance, the spatial density for particles of mass 10^{-8} g as calculated from sounding rocket data is nearly 50,000 times the value inferred from satellite Explorer VI (1959δ). And the data from Explorer I (1958α) are approximately 300 times larger than this value. Whipple has developed a partial explanation of these discrepancies by pointing out a possible relation between spatial density of particles and height (Fig. 13.7-1). On this picture, the Earth is surrounded by a localized cloud of dust, produced most probably by meteorite impacts on the Moon. Whipple has shown that if the high-velocity component of

Fig. 13.7-1 The space density of particles of mass 10^{-9} g as a function of distance from the surface of the Earth, determined by space craft. (*After Whipple.*)

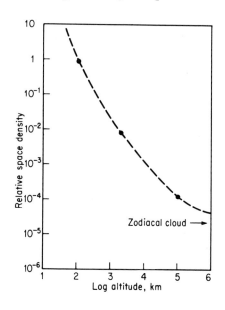

Table 13.7-1   Rate of deposit of cosmic material over the Earth

Type of object	Method of discovery	Diameter	Rate of deposit, tons/year
Meteorites	Observed falls	$> \sim 5$ cm	10^2
Meteors	Visual counts	$> \sim 5$ mm	10^3
Dust spherules	Deep-sea deposits	$> 25\ \mu$	10^2
Dust spherules	Antarctic ice	$> 15\ \mu$	2×10^5
Dust spherules	Arctic ice	$> 5\ \mu$	2×10^5
Dust spherules	Arctic air	$> 3\ \mu$	5×10^5
Dust spherules	California mountains	$> 3\ \mu$	5×10^5
Dust spherules	New Mexico mountains	$> 5\ \mu$	2×10^5
Dust spherules	Stratosphere	$> 3\ \mu$	2×10^5
All dust	Nickel in deep sea	All	10^6
All dust	Zodiacal cloud	All	10^6
All dust	Satellite data	All	10^6

lunar material ejected in the formation of impact craters is reasonably large, then the Earth's dust cloud should be dense enough to explain the satellite data. Material would be ejected from the Moon if its velocity is greater than 2.38 km/sec, the lunar velocity of escape. This material would go into a temporary circumterrestrial orbit if the velocity is less than from 2.42 km/sec to 3.43 km/sec, depending on the direction of ejection.

In a general way, the satellite results agree, at least for the most distant measures, with the spatial densities of interplanetary dust that are computed from the zodiacal cloud observations and the surface collections (Table 13.7-1).

13.8   THE DYNAMICS OF INTERPLANETARY PARTICLES

The dust particles which give rise to the zodiacal light revolve about the Sun, as do the planets, but they are subject to three influences (in addition to solar gravity) which are relatively unimportant for larger bodies. First, their orbits are influenced by close approaches to the planets, with the result of greatly perturbed orbits or, often, capture. It is estimated that the Earth captures of the order of 10^{16} of these particles per day, most of which fall immediately into the atmosphere. The other influences on particle dynamics are those of the Poynting-Robertson effect and of light pressure, both of which we shall now examine.

13.9   THE POYNTING-ROBERTSON EFFECT

In 1903 Poynting discussed the effects of the absorption and reemission of light on the motions of particles near the Sun, and how the particles must thus lose orbital angular momentum and spiral inward. Robertson later discussed the problem in terms of relativistic effects as applied to small bodies of the solar system. He showed that the equations of motion for a particle in orbit about the Sun are

$$\ddot{r} - r\dot{\theta}^2 = -\frac{GM}{r^2} + \frac{\alpha c}{r^2} - \frac{2\alpha \dot{r}}{r^2} \tag{1}$$

and

$$\frac{1}{r}\frac{d}{dt}(r^2\dot{\theta}) = -\frac{\alpha \dot{\theta}}{r^2} \tag{2}$$

where r, θ, G, and M are the usual parameters and constants (Chap. 2) and the parameter α introduces the radiation pressure explicitly. Robertson shows that α has a value of $(3.55 \times 10^{-8}/s\rho)$ $(AU)^2/yr$, where s is the radius of the particle and ρ is its density, both in cgs units. This simple treatment assumes $Q(s) = 1$ (Sec. 13.10). For a circular orbit, the solution for the secular perturbation in a, the semimajor axis, gives

$$\frac{da}{dt} = -\frac{2\alpha}{a} \tag{3}$$

Integrating this gives us

$$-t = \frac{a^2}{4\alpha} = 7.0 \times 10^6 s\rho a^2 \qquad \text{yr} \tag{4}$$

where s is radius and ρ is density of the particle, a is the initial distance, in AU, and t is the time of fall into the Sun, in years. Table 13.9-1 lists the times of fall for particles of various sizes and orbits calculated with more complete formulas, including the eccentricity. The Poynting-Robertson effect is quite efficient in clearing the solar system of small particles. It is possible that corpuscular radiation makes it even more efficient than Table 13.9-1 shows.

Table 13.9-1   Times of fall for particles with various orbits

a, AU		e	$t/10^7$ yr $\times$ $s\rho$	Type of orbit
3		0.0	6	Asteroidal
3		0.7	0.7	Asteroidal
1.4	(Geminids)	0.9	0.14	Meteor showers
3.5	(Bielids)	0.7	3	Meteor showers
10	(Leonids)	0.9	7	Meteor showers
55	(Lyrids)	0.98	20	Meteor showers

13.10   RADIATION PRESSURE

For very small particles, in the submicron range, the pressure exerted by the Sun's radiation is large enough to give them an appreciable outward motion. The radial force due to radiation pressure is

$$F_r = \frac{[\pi F]}{c} \pi s^2 Q(s) \tag{1}$$

where πF is the flux of radiation, in ergs/(cm²)(sec), c is the velocity of light, s is the radius of the particle, and $Q(s)$ is the efficiency factor for the particle for radiation pressure, all in cgs units. $Q(s)$, which is the ratio of the effective cross section to the geometrical cross section, can be quite small; but for values of s comparable to the wavelength of the radiation, it is of the order of 1. Particles of such dimensions (about 0.5 μ for those in the solar system) are rapidly blown away by the radiation pressure.

13.11   THE GEGENSCHEIN

On exceedingly dark, clear nights it is usually possible to detect (visually) a faint, diffuse patch of light almost exactly opposite the Sun in the night sky (Fig. 13.11-1). Called the *gegenschein*, this phenomenon is the subject of a continuing controversy. Because most suggested explanations propose that the observed illumination is sunlight reflected from dust particles, a discussion of the gegenschein is given here.

Although hard to detect and even harder to measure, the gegenschein has been investigated in a number of ways. The following properties seem now to be fairly well established:

1. It lies approximately 3° west of the antisolar point.
2. Its color is slightly redder than that of the Sun.

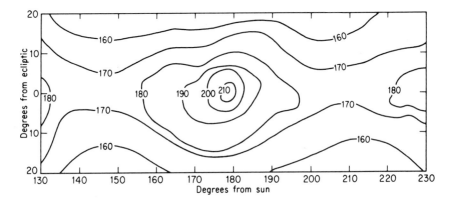

Fig. 13.11-1   An idealized isophotal diagram of the gegenschein. (*Compiled from typical scans measured by Roach and Rees.*)

3. The maximum surface brightness of the zodiacal light reaches a value of the equivalent of 200 tenth-magnitude stars per square degree.

4. It can be detected out to about 20° from its center.

Explanations of this feeble phenomenon have had first to find some reason for its mere existence, without reference to its detailed properties. An early hypothesis, due to the celestial mechanics experts Glyden and Moulton, explained the gegenschein as a quasi-stable concentration of interplanetary particles caught at the antisolar libration point of the Earth-Sun system (Sec. 2.3). This idea, however, fails to explain the observed 3° difference between the location of the gegenschein and the true antisolar point. It also fails to account for the amount of total luminosity observed in the gegenschein, which would be much too faint to see according to the Glyden-Moulton hypothesis.

It has been pointed out by Hoffmeister that there may be a phase function for the zodiacal light such that a brightening exists at phase 180° from the Sun, but this hypothesis is inconsistent with the observed 3° position difference. The gaseous tail hypothesis, due to Evershed and supported by Fesenkov, suggests that the light is the result of the excitation of Earth-escaped gases by the interplanetary plasma (Chap. 8), but this predicts a spectrum of discrete lines which is not observed. Scattering from molecules would give a color bluer than sunlight, rather than redder as observed.

A recent suggestion, not yet thoroughly explored theoretically, seems able to predict the observed features of the gegenschein consistently. It is hypothesized that the lunar dust cloud about the Earth (Sec. 13.7) could be the source of a dust tail of the Earth, blown away by radiation pressure, as are type II comet tails (Chap. 9). On this picture, material is constantly produced by impacts at the lunar surface and captured in temporary orbits around the Earth. The larger particles gradually fall into the Earth, but the smaller ones are blown away by solar radiation pressure to form a tail of dust seen visually as the gegenschein.

BIBLIOGRAPHICAL NOTES

Two fairly complete annotated bibliographies on the subject of extraterrestrial dust are:

R 13-1. Schmidt, R. A.: *Res. Rept. Series 63-2, University of Wisconsin, Geophys. Polar Res. Center*, January, 1963.

R 13-2. Hodge, P. W., F. W. Wright, and D. Hoffleit: *Smithsonian Contrib. Astrophys.*, **5**: 85 (1961).

Section 13.1. This section is treated in detail in many papers in journals, for instance:

R 13.1-1. Blackwell, D. E., and M. F. Ingham: *Monthly Notices Roy. Astron. Soc.*, **122**: 113 (1961).

Section 13.2. Material on micrometeorites is covered by:

R 13.2-1. Whipple, F. L.: *Proc. Natl. Acad. Sci. U.S.*, **36**: 687 (1950).

Sections 13.3 to 13.10. These subjects are treated in many research papers which can be located through R 13-1 or R 13-2.
A general paper is:

R 13.3-1. Öpik, E. J.: *Irish Astron. J.*, **4**: 84 (1956).

Section 13.11. A historical discussion of the gegenschein can be found in:

R 13.11-1. Brandt, J. C.: *Leaflets Publ. Astron. Soc. Pacific, No.* 391, 1962.

The planets: introduction

The principal planets are among the most interesting objects studied in astronomy. Although insignificant compared to the larger aggregates of the universe, their proximity and their intriguing properties present a challenge to the imagination and ingenuity of modern scientists. They are nine in number, and their names in order of distance from the Sun are Mercury, Venus, Earth, Mars, Jupiter, Saturn, Uranus, Neptune, and Pluto.

14.1 DISTANCES, THE ASTRONOMICAL UNIT

The distance scale of the solar system is established by direct physical or geometrical measurement. Since the periods of revolution of the planets can be measured readily, the relative distances of the planets from the Sun can be determined from Kepler's third law (Sec. 2.1). Thus the entire distance scale of the solar system is known once these relative distances are transformed into absolute distances by means of some independent measurement. The fundamental constant of the solar system distance scale is the "solar parallax," defined as the angle subtended by the equatorial diameter of the Earth at the Sun's mean distance from the Earth.

There are two methods of obtaining absolute measurements of the solar parallax. The first has been triangulation. The most accurate such determination results from measuring the parallax of the asteroid Eros during its close approach to the Earth (Sec. 12.1). Simultaneous measurements made of the position of Eros by observatories at different locations on the Earth provide a very accurate instantaneous linear distance to Eros. Combining this distance with the known orbital parameters for Eros and the Earth makes it possible to compute an accurate value for the solar parallax. The most reliable value derived in this way was that found in 1950; it is $8\overset{''}{.}7984 \pm 0\overset{''}{.}0004$.

A second method can also be employed. Radar observations of the nearest planets, in particular Venus, can be used to determine the absolute linear distance scale of the solar system. The method consists of accurately timing the interval between the transmission and the reception of a radar signal reflected from the surface of Venus. By knowing the orbital elements of Venus and the Earth and by knowing the velocity of light, a solar parallax can be computed. The result is $8\overset{''}{.}794098 \pm 0\overset{''}{.}000015$. This value disagrees somewhat with the value obtained from Eros, and it is hoped that additional radar measurements will eliminate this discrepancy.

It is important to note that both computations of the solar parallax depend heavily upon other constants of the solar system. For instance, in the case of the triangulation on an asteroid the following constants must be known accurately:

1. The orbital elements of the asteroid
2. The orbital elements of the Earth
3. The masses of the inner planets
4. The equatorial radius of the Earth
5. The ratio of the masses of the Earth and the Moon
6. The constants of the shape and mass distribution of the Earth
7. The constant of gravitation
8. The exact positions of the comparison stars used in measuring the position of the asteroid

The radar method requires the following constants to be known accurately:

1. The velocity of light
2. The orbital elements of the planet
3. The orbital elements of the Earth

4. The exact rates of change of these elements computed from per-turbation theory

5. The equatorial radius of the Earth

In order for high accuracy to be obtained for the value of the solar parallax, *all* of these constants must also be known with appropriate accuracy.

14.2 ORBITAL PARAMETERS

The nine principal planets revolve around the Sun in orbits which obey to a high degree of accuracy the general law of gravitation of Newton. Only for certain small changes observed for rapidly revolving planets (e.g., Mercury) is it necessary to include the general relativistic corrections to Newton's theory. The orbits of the planets are all elliptical and are normally described by a set of numerical constants called orbital parameters (Fig. 14.2-1). Seven of these parameters are needed to describe the orbit completely and to allow the position of the planet at any time to be calculated (neglecting perturbations caused by other planets). The orbital parameters are defined in the following way:

1. a, the semimajor axis of the orbit, usually given in astronomical units (AU); 1 AU is the mean distance from Sun to Earth.

2. e, the eccentricity of the orbit.

3. i, the inclination of the orbit to the plane of the ecliptic.

4. Ω, longitude of the ascending node of the orbit.

5. ω, the angle between the ascending node and perihelion point.

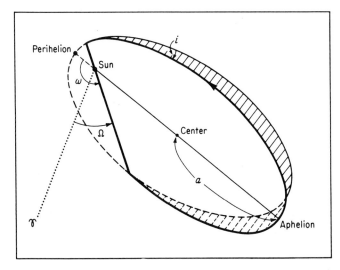

Fig. 14.2-1 A planetary orbit showing the definitions of several orbital parameters. The plane of the paper is the ecliptic plane.

Table 14.2-1 Orbital elements of the planets

Planet	a, AU	e	i	Ω	ω	P, yr
Mercury	0.3871	0.206	7°00′	47°9′	75°54′	0.241
Venus	0.7233	0.007	3°24′	75°47′	130°9′	0.615
Earth	1.0000	0.017	0°00′	00°00′	101°13′	1.000
Mars	1.5237	0.093	1°51′	48°47′	334°13′	1.881
Jupiter	5.2027	0.048	1°19′	99°27′	12°43′	11.86
Saturn	9.546	0.056	2°30′	112°47′	91°6′	29.46
Uranus	19.20	0.047	0°46′	73°29′	169°3′	84.02
Neptune	30.09	0.009	1°47′	130°41′	43°50′	164.8
Pluto	39.5	0.247	17°9′	108°57′	222°48′	248.4

6. P, the period, sometimes expressed as the mean daily motion n (Sec. 2.1).

7. T, the time of passage of perihelion, sometimes expressed as E, the epoch.

Orbital elements for the nine planets are given in Table 14.2-1.

14.3 CLASSIFICATION OF THE PLANETS

From many points of view, the planets naturally divide themselves into two classes, terrestrial planets and Jovian planets. The terrestrial planets are five in number: Mercury, Venus, Earth, Mars, and (probably) Pluto. The remainder, Jupiter, Saturn, Uranus, and Neptune, are the Jovian planets. Table 14.3-1 lists and contrasts the characteristics of these two classes of planets. The key difference seems to be the mass of the body. It is believed that the planets formed out of interstellar material rotating about the primitive Sun. When they condensed into planetary bodies, those with high mass retained essentially their original chemical composition and became the Jovian planets, with extensive atmospheres made up primarily of hydrogen and helium. The planets nearer the Sun and of lower mass were unable to retain light gases, so that their atmospheres escaped, except perhaps for heavier gases such as nitrogen and oxygen.

Table 14.3-1 Characteristics of the planets

Feature	Terrestrial planets	Jovian planets
Mass	Small ($\sim 10^{27}$ g)	Large ($\sim 10^{29}$ g)
Density	Large (~ 5 g/cm^3)	Small (~ 1 g/cm^3)
Distance from Sun	Small ($\sim 10^{13}$ cm)	Large ($\sim 10^{14}$ cm)
Atmosphere	None or thin	Extensive
Satellites	Few or none	Many
Composition	Mostly silicates, rocks	Mostly H, He

It may be that even these gases were lost back in the high-temperature history of the terrestrial planets and that the present atmospheres are secondary, derived more recently from volcanic escape from the interiors.

In any case, the differences between the terrestrial and the Jovian planets are very striking and must have some explanation tied intimately to the history of the solar system. Until this history is better understood, we can do little more than note these contrasts and explore them critically. In the next chapters, we discuss the various planets from the inside out, from their interiors to their atmospheres.

BIBLIOGRAPHICAL NOTES

Section 14.1. An excellent review of the situation with respect to the solar system distance scale is contained in:

R 14.1-1. Brouwer, D., and G. M. Clemence: In "Planets and Satellites," eds. G. P. Kuiper and B. M. Middlehurst, pp. 31–94, The University of Chicago Press, Chicago, 1961.

An account of the measurement of the solar parallax by means of observations of the asteroid Eros can be found in:

R 14.1-2. Rabe E.: *Astron. J.*, **55**: 112 (1950).

The determination of the solar parallax measured by radar observations of Venus is discussed in:

R 14.1-3. Muhleman, D. O., D. B. Holdridge, and N. Block.: *Tech. Rept. 32-221, Jet Propulsion Lab.*, Pasadena, California, 1962.

Section 14.2. The orbital parameters of the planets are discussed in detail in the general references given at the end of Chap. 2. See also R 14.1-1 for information on the subject.

Planetary interiors

chapter

15

The internal structure of the planets is of considerable interest, especially for what it can tell about the origin and formation of the solar system. Unfortunately, the problem is an extremely difficult one theoretically and a nearly impossible one observationally. We know less about the interior of the nearest planet, Venus, than we know about the interiors of stars millions of times more distant. Our experimental knowledge even of the Earth's structure is very limited and variously interpreted, and observations of the other planets are literally only skin deep. Nevertheless, there are certain data which can be combined with certain theoretical models to give us some information on this basic solar system problem.

15.1 RELEVANT DATA

There are seven sources of observational data which bear on the problem of the interiors of the planets. We examine them in this section from the point of view of their relevance and reliability.

Table 15.1-1   Masses of the planets

Planet	Date	Method	Mass ratio: Sun/planet
Mercury	1895	Motions of four inner planets	6,000,000
	1895	Perturbations on Venus	7,210,000
	1960	Perturbations on Venus	5,880,000
	1950	Perturbations on Earth	6,480,000
	1950	Perturbations on Eros	6,120,000
Venus	1895	Motions of four inner planets	408,000
	1939	Perturbations on Earth	407,000
	1943	Perturbations on Mercury	409,300
	1950	Perturbations on Eros	408,645
	1950	Perturbations on Earth	408,000
Mars	1878	Motions of the satellites	3,093,500
	1927	Motions of the satellites	3,088,000
	1960	Motions of the satellites	3,088,000
Jupiter	1895	Motions of satellites, comets, and planets	1,047.35
	1908	Motions of satellites	1,047.42
Saturn	1833	Motions of Titan	3,501.6
	1954	Motions of satellites	3,494.8
	1953	Perturbations on Jupiter	3,497.64
Uranus	1898	Perturbations on Saturn	23,239
	1927	Motions of satellites	22,887
	1950	Motions of satellites	22,934
Neptune	1874	Perturbations on Uranus	19,700
	1910	Perturbations on Uranus	19,094
	1926	Motions of Triton	19,416
	1957	Motions of Nereid	18,889
Pluto	1951	Perturbations on Neptune and Uranus	360,000
	1955	Perturbations on Neptune and Uranus	400,000
	1955	Perturbations on Neptune and Uranus	450,000

Masses

The total masses of the planets are of obvious importance to their structure and composition. Table 15.1-1 lists the various values for planetary masses which have been obtained in recent years. The comparisons show that the masses for most planets are accurately known and that these data are not likely to be a major source of uncertainty in a treatment of a planet's structure.

Densities

The mean density of a planet is also of obvious importance to the question at hand. It is computed from the calculated mass and the measured radius. Unfortunately, radii are difficult to measure for some of the planets (Table

15.1-2), either because (1) the location of the surface is in some doubt owing to a dense atmosphere (Venus), (2) the apparent radius is dependent on the wavelength used and this is affected by the atmosphere (Mars), or (3) severe observational difficulties are caused by chronic bad seeing (Mercury). The radii of the major planets are for the whole visible disk, so that the quoted mean densities include the extensive atmospheres. Finally, for Pluto the measures are uncertain simply because the size of the disk is never much greater than the resolving power of the largest telescopes.

Oblateness

The oblateness of a planet is of great importance in the problem of internal structure, because it reflects the distribution of mass in a fairly straightforward way. It can be seen intuitively that a rotating planet with all the mass concentrated at the center will be more oblate than a similar planet with a uniform density throughout. We discuss this in more detail in Sec. 15.3. Oblatenesses are known only for a few planets (Table 15.1-2).

The oblateness, or ellipticity of a planet's image, is normally defined by

$$\epsilon = 1 - \frac{b}{a} \tag{1}$$

where a and b are the major and minor axes (equatorial and polar radii) of the elliptical planetary image.

Dynamic ellipticity

For a planet with a close satellite, it is possible to compute, from perturbing effects on the motions of the satellite, the dynamically effective

Table 15.1-2   Radii, mean densities, and ellipticities of the planets*

Planet	Radius, km	Mean density, g/cm³	Ellipticity
Mercury	2,500 ±200	5.30 ±0.8	?
Venus	6,200 ±50	4.95 ±0.1	?
Mars	3,350 ±30	3.95 ±0.2	0.0052
Jupiter	71,200 ±200	1.33 ±0.05	0.062
Saturn	60,300 ±300	0.68 ±0.05	0.096
Uranus	23,800 ±500	1.56 ±0.08	0.06
Neptune	22,000 ±500	2.47 ±0.09	0.017
Pluto	~6,000	?	?

* Compiled and averaged from numerous sources. Quoted uncertainties indicate the spread in values found in the recent literature.

ellipticity of the planet's gravitational potential. This will often differ from the geometrical oblateness of the planet's surface, depending on the distribution of mass in the interior. Planets with sufficiently close satellites are Jupiter, Mars, Neptune, and the Earth (artificial satellites). The dynamic ellipticity is also formally defined by Eq. (15.1-1), and equals $C-A/C$ (see Sec. 2.5).

Rate of rotation

The rotation period enters into the quantitative interpretation of oblateness and mass distribution. Periods are known accurately for most planets (Sec. 15.7), though there is still some uncertainty for Venus.

Surface temperature

A comparison of the observed surface temperature with a predicted temperature based on the solar distance and the known properties of the atmosphere of the planet can give some indication of the amount of heat which might be generated by the radioactive elements in the core. So far this comparison has usually been taken as indicating an upper limit, because for most planets the observed and predicted temperatures agree fairly well within the combined uncertainty of each. For Venus, which has a somewhat higher surface temperature than predicted, this difference is probably explained by the atmosphere's characteristics.

Meteorite compositions

Scientists interested in the radioactive heating of planetary interiors are hard put to find empirical evidence of the amounts of various radioactive elements which might exist in the planets. The most relevant evidence seems to come from studies of the meteorites, which may be representative of interior conditions in planets (Chap. 11). Careful analyses in the laboratory allow determination of characteristic meteorite compositions, and these are often postulated to hold true for planets' rocky or metallic cores.

15.2 DESIRED INFORMATION

In order to solve the problem of the planetary interiors, the data discussed in the preceding section are used to establish, under various assumptions and with more or less sophisticated theoretical considerations, the run of *pressure, temperature, density,* and *chemical and minerological composition* with radius for the planet. The problem is somewhat similar to that of the solar interior, with the added complication of a nongaseous substance as the major constituent.

15.3   THEORETICAL CONSIDERATIONS

For very simple models of planetary interiors, it has been shown that the dynamic ellipticity is related to the rotational centrifugal acceleration $\omega^2 R$ and the gravity g in a simple way for different internal mass distributions. Here R is the planet's radius and ω is the angular rotation speed. For a planet with density everywhere the same, we have

$$\frac{\epsilon g}{\omega^2 R} = 1.25 \tag{1}$$

and for a planet with all of its mass at the center we have

$$\frac{\epsilon g}{\omega^2 R} = 0.5 \tag{2}$$

Between these two extremes, the value for this expression varies continuously between 1.25 and 0.5, provided the density never *increases* with distance from the center. Although not the basis for a unique determination of the structure of a planet, the ellipticity can put very definite restrictions on possible models. Planets for which fairly reliable ellipticities are known are listed in Table 15.3-1, where values are given for $\epsilon g/\omega^2 R$. When these values are compared with Eqs. (15.3-1) and (15.3-2), it is seen that Mars must have very little central concentration, while Jupiter and Saturn must have small, very dense cores.

A common and normally justifiable assumption made in treating planetary interiors is that the interior is in hydrostatic equilibrium. This no doubt holds true throughout most of the interior of a moderately large planet, where the great pressure and high temperature cause the material either to be liquid or to be in equilibrium in any case over a reasonable length of time. In the rocky mantle of the Earth, the mechanical strength of the material is similar in magnitude to the pressure, or greater, so that here hydrostatic equilibrium does not apply. However, for most of a planet we have [from Eq. (3.3-1) and by adding the term for the radial compo-

Table 15.3-1   Values of $\dfrac{\epsilon g}{\omega^2 R}$ for three planets

Planet	$\dfrac{\epsilon g}{\omega^2 R}$
Mars	1.14
Jupiter	0.77
Saturn	0.69

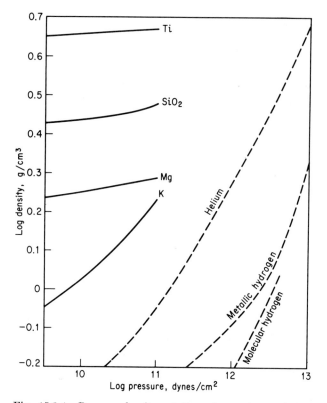

Fig. 15.3-1   Pressure-density relations for various substances. The four left-hand curves are from experimental results, and the three right-hand curves are computed from theory. (*After Elsasser.*)

nent of the centrifugal acceleration averaged over a sphere of radius r]

$$\frac{dP}{dr} = -[g(r) - \tfrac{2}{3}\omega^2 r]\rho(P) \tag{3}$$

where

$$g(r) = \frac{GM(r)}{r^2} = \frac{4\pi G}{r^2}\int_0^r \rho(x)x^2\,dx \tag{4}$$

Here P is pressure, r is distance from the center, g is the acceleration of gravitation, G is the constant of gravitation, $M(r)$ is the mass interior to r, ω is the angular velocity, and $\rho(P)$ is the density for pressure P. The relation $\rho(P)$ is obtained from the equation of state, and it can be determined if the chemical composition and temperature are known, as well as the pressure. In actual cases, it has been found that equations of state for very high pressures are rather difficult to determine. Figure 15.3-2 illustrates the behavior of ice under various pressures and temperatures. As seen in this figure, ice is found to exist in various phases (Ice I, Ice II, etc.), which are different crystal structures of the material.

It has been shown that for gaseous stars, the central pressure P_c must satisfy the inequality

$$\frac{3}{8\pi}\frac{GM^2}{R^4} \leq P_c \leq \frac{3}{8\pi}\frac{GM^2}{R^4}\left(\frac{\rho_c}{\bar{\rho}}\right)^{\frac{4}{3}} \tag{5}$$

and that the mean pressure $\bar{P}$ defined by

$$M\bar{P} = \int_0^R P\, dM(r) \tag{6}$$

must be bounded by

$$\frac{3}{20\pi}\frac{GM^2}{R^4} \leq \bar{P} \leq \frac{3}{20\pi}\frac{GM^2}{R^4}\left(\frac{\rho_c}{\bar{\rho}}\right)^{\frac{4}{3}} \tag{7}$$

This probably also holds true for the larger planets (but not for the asteroids), because their interiors do not have sufficient strength to act very differently from gaseous substances. On this basis we can compute the lower limits to the central and mean pressures for planets, because we know their masses M and radii R. These are listed in Table 15.3-2.

If the material behaves like an ideal gas and if we assume no internal heat source then we can use the perfect-gas law to show that the central

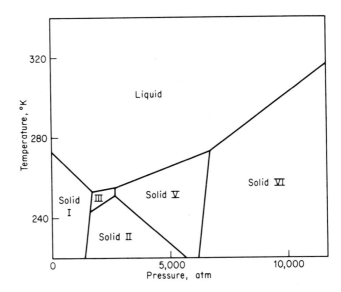

Fig. 15.3-2   Phase diagram for water under different pressures and temperatures. (*After Wildt.*)

Table 15.3-2   Limits to densities, pressures, and temperatures

Planet	Central density >, g/cm³	Mean pressure >, atm	Central pressure >, atm	Mean temp >, °K	Central temp >, °K
Mercury	. . .	1.2×10^5	3×10^5	400	650
Venus	. . .	4.8×10^5	1.2×10^6	1,200	1,900
Mars	4.4	7.0×10^4	1.6×10^5	300	1,600
Jupiter	2.7	4.1×10^6	1.0×10^7	42,000	68,000
Saturn	1.7	7.7×10^5	1.9×10^6	16,000	24,000
Uranus	2.8	7.5×10^5	1.8×10^6	7,000	11,000
Neptune	4.0	1.5×10^5	3.6×10^6	8,000	12,000

temperature must be greater than a certain minimum value:

$$T_c \geq \frac{1}{2} \frac{\mu m_{\mathrm{H}}}{k} \frac{GM}{R} Q \tag{8}$$

where μ, m_{H}, and k are given in Eq. (3.3-7) and where Q is of the order 0.640 for planets but is mass-dependent. If we define the mean temperature $\bar{T}$ by

$$M\bar{T} = \int_0^R T \, dM(r) \tag{9}$$

it has been shown that

$$\frac{1}{5} \frac{\mu m_{\mathrm{H}}}{k} \frac{GM}{R} \leq \bar{T} \leq \frac{1}{5} \frac{\mu m_{\mathrm{H}}}{k} \frac{GM}{R} \left(\frac{\rho_c}{\bar{\rho}}\right)^{\frac{1}{3}} \tag{10}$$

These values are tabulated in Table 15.3-2.

A lower limit to the central density ρ_c can be computed by considering that the moment of inertia I of the planet is larger than it would be if all mass were at the center and the rest of the planet's material had a negligible effect. Let us consider a dense core of radius r_0 and density ρ_0. From the equation for the moment of inertia of a rotating sphere,

$$I \geq \frac{8\pi}{3} \int_0^R \rho(r) r^4 \, dr \tag{11}$$

we find, for a constant-density core

$$I \geq \frac{8\pi \rho_0 r_0^5}{15} \tag{12}$$

Since

$$\rho_0 = \frac{M}{\frac{4}{3}\pi r_0^3} \qquad \text{and} \qquad \bar{\rho} = \frac{M}{\frac{4}{3}\pi R^3} \tag{13}$$

we find that

$$\rho_0 r_0{}^3 = \bar{\rho} R^3 \tag{14}$$

Thus

$$\rho_0 \geq \left(\frac{5}{2}\frac{I}{MR^2}\right)^{-3/2} \bar{\rho} \tag{15}$$

for our lower limit to the central density.

15.4 THE INTERIOR OF THE EARTH

Although more properly and traditionally a subject of geophysics, the interior of the Earth will be discussed briefly here because of its relevance to the problems of the interiors of all the terrestrial planets. The similarity of the mean densities and radii of the terrestrial planets has lead to the assumption that these planets are similarly constructed.

The simplest physical model of the Earth, first proposed more than 50 yr ago, is one in which there are two components, the core and the mantle, both uniform in density. A recent solution of this model by Jeffreys makes use of seismic data to determine the depth of the discontinuity. If $\alpha R_\oplus$ is the boundary of the core, then seismic data (see below) give $\alpha = 0.545$ ($R_\oplus$ is the Earth's radius). Then in order that the mass of the Earth be given correctly by the model, we have

$$\rho_m + (\rho_c - \rho_m)\alpha^3 = \bar{\rho} \tag{1}$$

where ρ_m, ρ_c, and $\bar{\rho}$ are densities of the mantle, the core, and the mean Earth. Also, we have

$$\rho_m + (\rho_c - \rho_m)\alpha^5 = \frac{5}{2}\frac{\bar{\rho}}{MR_\oplus{}^2} \tag{2}$$

Solving for ρ_m and ρ_c gives values of 4.22 and 12.33 g/cm³, respectively. Originally, mainly because of the compositions of meteorites, the material making up the core was assumed to be iron (or nickel-iron), and that of the mantle, silicate rocks.

A more recent suggestion has put forward a rather different model of the Earth in which the chemical composition is uniform throughout. The common mineral olivine has been shown to undergo a change in crystal structure at the pressures that probably exist at 500 km, where seismic evidence (the 20° discontinuity) indicates a rather sudden change in the material involved. This discontinuity is found by plotting the earthquake wave travel times as a function of the angular distance from the earthquake; a rapid change occurs at $\Delta = 20°$. This datum and seismic data of a similar nature suggest the possibility of the existence of a core

Table 15.4-1   Interior of the Earth computed by Bullen

Distance from center, km	Density, g/cm³	Pressure, 10^{12} dynes/cm²
6,000	3.61	0.13
5,000	4.90	0.56
4,000	5.42	1.06
3,473*	5.68	1.37
3,473*	9.43	1.37
3,000	10.09	1.80
2,000	11.07	2.68
1,000	16.92	3.40
0	17.20	3.64

* Boundary of core.

which may be due to another high-pressure-induced change in the phase of silicate rocks. So far, opinion is still divided on whether the Earth's core is made up of iron or of silicates in a metallic phase. The chances of determining which model is correct are increasing as methods are developed for determining experimentally the behavior of various substances under high pressure. Theoretical predictions of this behavior are presently too complicated and unreliable for them to be substituted for actual experiments.

By collecting together the abundant available data on the velocities of seismic waves, both longitudinal and transverse, and by interpreting them semitheoretically, it has been possible to construct a fairly reliable set of densities and pressures in the Earth, without stipulating anything about composition. Table 15.4-1 lists the run of densities and pressures so derived by Bullen.

The thermal constitution of the Earth can be derived if the amount and distribution of radioactive elements (as well as residual initial heat) are known. A common and probably reasonable assumption is that the radioactivity of the interiors of the terrestrial planets is like that of chondritic meteorites, that is, $K = 8.0 \times 10^{-4}$ g/g, Th $= 4.4 \times 10^{-8}$ g/g, and $U = 1.1 \times 10^{-8}$ g/g. A wide variety of models which use such a combination can be derived; a critical variable is the initial thermal condition inside the Earth. Geophysicists have measured the outward heat flow at the Earth's surface to be some 50 ergs/(cm²)(sec), but this value is not yet sufficiently accurate to permit the derivation of a unique thermal constitution.

15.5   INTERIORS OF THE OTHER TERRESTRIAL PLANETS

It has been customary to interpret the similarities of the terrestrial planets as evidence of similar constitution. Some very recent work has thrown some doubt on this assumption, but as yet the basic data which determine the details of the problem are still for the most part too uncertain for final models to be derived. When it is realized that for the Earth, with abundant seismic and gravitational data at our disposal, we are still very uncertain on details, it is obvious that for other planets only the general structure can be hoped for.

For Mercury the greatest problem has been due to uncertainty of its mass and radius. The latter is especially hard to measure, and since the density is dependent on the cube of the radius, the density of Mercury is only roughly known. Over the last 20 yr quoted values for the mean density of Mercury have ranged from 0.37 to 0.61 g/cm³. A recent measurement of Mercury's diameter, made during the 1960 transit of the planet across the Sun, leads to a mean density of 0.53 g/cm³. This value is somewhat too large to allow the interior of Mercury to be assumed homologous with that of the Earth. It has been suggested that, since Mercury may well have once had a more eccentric orbit, it lost some of its less dense mantle during close approaches to the Sun in the early history of the solar system.

For Venus, we again have uncertainty because of its extensive atmosphere and its unknown period of rotation. On the assumption of similarity with the Earth, a model can be derived in which 22 per cent of the material is in the core and 78 per cent is in the mantle. Table 15.5-1 lists the run of pressures and densities derived in this way. Possible thermal constitutions of Venus, calculated on the assumption of uniformly distributed radioactive elements of chondritic abundances, are shown in Fig. 15.5-1.

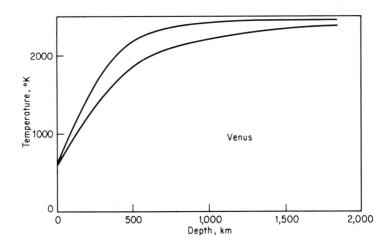

Fig. 15.5-1 Two possible thermal profiles of the interior of Venus, computed by McDonald. The difference of the curves is due to differences in the assumed opacity and density of the material. Chondritic abundances of radioactive elements were assumed.

Table 15.5-1   Interior of Venus computed by Jeffreys

Distance from center, km	Density, g/cm³	Pressure, 10^{12} dynes/cm²
6,000	3.41	0.04
5,617*	3.69	0.16
5,617*	4.23	0.16
5,000	4.58	0.39
4,000	5.01	0.78
2,911*	5.44	1.24
2,911*	9.64	1.24
2,000	10.41	1.89
1,000	10.97	2.39
0	11.15	2.56

* Boundaries.

For Mars, the difficulty of measuring the diameter works against an accurate model for the interior. However, the presence of two very close satellites helps restrict the problem of the Martian interior somewhat, because a value for the dynamical ellipticity can be obtained. The problem is nevertheless still indeterminate, because the data are just not yet complete and accurate enough.

Table 15.5-2 gives an early model of Mars that is based on the assumption of homology of the pressure-density relation with that of the Earth. More recent evidence has lead to the possible conclusion that Mars actually contains no core, or only a negligibly small one. A suggested thermal profile, based on chondritic radioactivity, is given in Fig. 15.5-2.

The mass and radius of Pluto are so poorly known that the interior of the planet cannot be discussed at this time.

Table 15.5-2   Interior of Mars Computed by Jeffreys

Distance from center, km	Density, g/cm³	Pressure, 10^{12} dynes/cm²
3,000	3.42	0.05
2,500	3.57	0.11
2,034*	3.69	0.16
2,034*	4.23	0.16
1,500	4.35	0.24
1,424*	4.37	0.25
1,424*	8.28	0.25
1,000	8.45	0.35
0	8.60	0.44

* Boundaries.

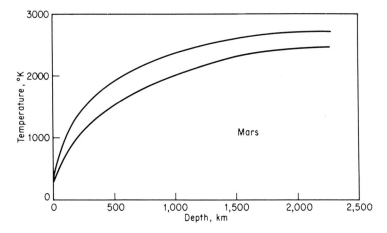

Fig. 15.5-2   Two possible thermal profiles of the interior of Mars, computed as for Fig. 15.5-1. (*After McDonald.*)

15.6   INTERIORS OF THE MAJOR PLANETS

As can be readily seen by their very low densities, the Jovian planets must have interiors very different from those discussed above. The densities alone strongly suggest the presence of light elements such as hydrogen and helium as common constituents. Combined with masses, radii, and ellipticity (geometrical and dynamical), the measured densities can be used to compare with physical models of the interiors. So far, there is no unique model of the Jovian planets which can be claimed unarguably correct, but a number of recent investigations have resulted in models of these four planets which agree sufficiently well with observations to be considered very likely close to the truth.

The most recently calculated model for the interior of the planet Jupiter assumes that almost all of that planet consists of hydrogen and helium, with only a small contamination of heavier elements in the core. This is a reasonable assumption, not only because it provides a model agreeing with the observations, but also because hydrogen and helium are the most cosmically abundant elements.

Table 15.6-1 lists the properties of the Jovian model calculated by DeMarcus in 1958. He based this model on the information, only recently obtained experimentally and theoretically, concerning the equations of state of cold solid hydrogen and helium. Although these equations of state are not yet absolutely certain, they are reliable enough to produce a fairly reasonable picture of the interior of a cold hydrogen-helium planet. The model given in Table 15.6-1 is consistent with Jupiter's mass, radius, density, and ellipticity. In order to make this fit, it was necessary to assume a density in the center of the planet Jupiter approximately double that for a pure helium-hydrogen planet. This is very probably a reason-

Table 15.6-1   Interior of Jupiter Computed by DeMarcus

Distance from center, km	Density, g/cm^3	Pressure, 10^{12} dynes/cm^2	Per cent He, by weight
71,200	0.00016	0	0
70,800	0.14	0.007	0
70,400*	0.18	0.02	0
70,400*	0.20	0.02	0
60,000	0.62	1.20	0.10
57,200*	0.78	1.93	0.13
57,200*	1.08	1.93	0.13
50,000	1.56	5.07	0.16
40,000	2.23	11.3	0.24
30,000	3.04	19.9	0.26
20,000	3.68	30.9	0.26
10,000	4.50	45.2	0.27
7,120	19.09	63.5	1.00
0	30.84	110	1.00

* Boundaries.

able assumption, because a core of heavier elements is certainly not unexpected.

Similar models have been constructed for the planets Saturn, Uranus, and Neptune. In each case the hydrogen-helium content of the planet is very high, although a core consisting partly of heavier elements had each time to be assumed. Tables 15.6-2 and 15.6-3 summarize the properties of the models for these planets.

One of the questions which is being actively investigated is the source and amount of heat in the interior of the Jovian planets. Assuming chon-

Table 15.6-2   Interior of Saturn computed by DeMarcus

Distance from center, km	Density, g/cm^3	Pressure, 10^{12} dynes/cm^2	Per cent He, by weight
60,300	0.00016	0	0
58,000*	0.18	0.02	0
58,000*	0.20	0.02	0
50,000	0.38	0.36	0
40,000	0.54	0.92	0
31,500*	0.72	1.93	0
31,500*	1.00	1.93	0
20,000	3.19	7.14	0
10,000	10.9	31.0	1.0
0	15.6	55.5	1.0

* Boundaries.

Table 15.6-3   Data on interiors of Uranus and Neptune*

Quantity	Uranus	Neptune
Possible hydrogen mass fractions	0.2–0.03	0.16–0.00
Maximum helium mass fraction	0.9	0.6
Minimum heavy element mass fraction	0	0.12

* DeMarcus and Reynolds. Based on models computed on the assumption of a cold planet.

dritic radioactivity for the heavy elements in the cores of the planets leads to temperatures which are too high, of the order of a million degrees. The observed temperatures of the planets, although higher than blackbody temperatures for objects at the appropriate solar distance, are consistent with an assumed central temperature of only a few thousand degrees (Sec. 16.7).

15.7 PLANETARY MAGNETIC FIELDS AND ROTATION

The magnetic fields of planets are still poorly understood and fragmentarily observed. Only the detailed properties of the Earth's field are well known, and even the Earth's field is not understood completely. It has a strength at the equator of 0.31 gauss, and its general shape is very much like that of a dipole. The magnetic axis of the Earth is oriented $11°4$ from the rotational axis; the north geomagnetic pole lies at a position of approximately 79°N latitude, 70° W longitude.

In detail, the Earth's magnetic field departs from a dipole field in two puzzling ways. There are anomalies in field strength, the more local due to the immediate presence of large masses of magnetite or other magnetic materials, and the more general due to an unknown cause. These large-scale anomalies amount to as much as 0.15 gauss and are distributed over the globe without obvious correlation with geological features. The second kind of departure from a perfect dipole field for the Earth is the variation with time observed for the field strength at many localities. The greatest changes observed so far amount to as much as 30 per cent in a hundred years.

The magnetic field of Venus was searched for when Mariner II approached the planet in 1962. No field was detected, and the upper limit for the surface field was therefore set at approximately 0.03 gauss. Jupiter is the only other planet for which there is some evidence of a magnetic field. From interpretations of the Jovian radio noise (Sec. 17.6), the surface magnetic field strength is inferred to be of the order of 2 to 5 gauss.

The most promising explanation of planetary magnetic fields connects them with the presence of a possible dynamo-type action in the molten interior. Convection currents, possibly generated by radioactive

Table 15.7-1   Planetary rotation periods and magnetic field strengths

Planet	Period of rotation (equatorial)	Surface magnetic field strength (equatorial)
Mercury	88^d	—
Venus	240^d?	<0.03 gauss
Earth	$23^h55^m4.1^s$	0.31 gauss
Mars	$24^h37^m22.6^s$	—
Jupiter	$9^h50^m30^s$	2–5 gauss
Saturn	10^h14^m	—
Uranus	10^h49^m	—
Neptune	15^h40^m	—
Pluto	16^h	—

heating in the core, may set up electric currents in the molten metallic material, which can explain the dipole field. The rapid changes of the Earth's field can be reasonably explained in general by ascribing them to rapid changes in the molten interior of the Earth.

If planetary magnetic fields are produced by a dynamo action, then the strength of the field can be expected to be correlated with the period of rotation of the planet. This is indeed found to be so for those three planets for which there is some evidence regarding the strength of magnetic field (Table 15.7-1).

BIBLIOGRAPHICAL NOTES

Two excellent review articles, with extensive bibliographies, are:

R 15-1. Wildt, R.: In "Planets and Satellites," eds. G. P. Kuiper and B. M. Middlehurst, pp. 159–212, The University of Chicago Press, Chicago, 1961.

R 15-2. DeMarcus, W. C.: In "Handbuch der Physik," vol. 52, ed. S. Flügge, pp. 419–448, Springer-Verlag OHG, Berlin, 1959.

Sections 15.1 and 15.2. See R 15-1, R 15-2, and R 2.5-1.

Section 15.3. See especially R 15-1 and the many papers quoted there.

Section 15.4. See R 15-1 and R 15-2 and also a technical discussion of a detailed model in:

R 15.4-1. Bullen, K. E.: *Monthly Notices Roy. Astron. Soc., Geophys. Suppl.*, **6**: 50 (1950).

R 15.4-2. Bullard, E.: In "The Earth as a Planet," ed. G. P. Kuiper, pp. 57–137, The University of Chicago Press, Chicago, 1954.

Section 15.5. Three discussions of models of the terrestrial planets are found in:

R 15.5-1. Jeffreys, H.: *Monthly Notices Roy. Astron. Soc., Geophys. Suppl.*, **4**: 62 (1937).

R 15.5-2. Ramsey, W. H.: *Monthly Notices Roy. Astron. Soc.*, **108**: 406 (1948) and **111**: 427 (1951).

R 15.5-3. Bullen, K. E.: *Monthly Notices Roy. Astron. Soc.*, **110**: 256 (1950).

A more up to date discussion, including details of thermal properties, is:

R 15.5-4. MacDonald, G. J. F.: *J. Geophys. Res.*, **67**: 2945 (1962).

Section 15.6. See especially R 15-1 and R 15-2, as well as a brief discussion of Uranus and Neptune in:

R 15.6-1. DeMarcus, W. C., and R. T. Reynolds: *Cong. Colloq. Univ Liége*, **24**: 51 (1962).

An interesting discussion of Jupiter's interior can be found in:

R 15.6-2. Öpik, E. J.: *Icarus*, **1**: 200 (1962).

Planetary
surfaces

The advent of space travel and exploration has brought about a renewed interest in the observations of planetary surfaces, a field in which relatively little was accomplished in preceding decades. In the early part of this century the emphasis in astronomy swung from the solar system to the stellar universe, partly because of the discovery of external galaxies, partly because of increased understanding of stellar atmospheres and structure, partly because of the discovery of the size and shape of the galaxy, and partly because planetary astronomy had come to something of a dead end. The latter resulted from the disappointments brought on by the giant telescopes which were built at Yerkes, Lick, and Mt. Wilson Observatories. In spite of their excellent optics, these mammoth instruments were found to be only occasionally and slightly better than smaller instruments when it came to resolving fine detail. Telescopes in 1830 had resolving powers as good as $0''.5$ of arc; by 1930, this was seldom better than $0''.4$ of arc. The reason for this limit was found to be that atmospheric

Fig. 16-1   The 36-in. refractor at Lick Observatory, typical of the type of telescope long used for planetary observations. (*Courtesy of Lick Observatory.*)

effects—called seeing—distorted the image enough on even the calmest days as to artificially limit the smallness of the image. Only very rarely is the seeing good enough, in ordinary locations, to take full advantage of the aperture of a large telescope.

Fortunately, there are some few extraordinary locations where seeing conditions are unusually good, and it has been at such places that recent advances in the study of the surface details of solar system objects have taken place (Fig. 16-1). But other features than planetary surface details are of interest and importance. Integrated properties of the disk, such as albedo, color, temperature, and polarization, are all observable and productive of information, and all are not seriously limited by bad seeing. But at mountain-top observatories or, even better, at extraterrestrial observatories lies the future of the study of planetary surfaces.

16.1   METHODS OF OBSERVATION

In general the methods of observing planets are somewhat different from standard stellar astronomical techniques. Serious visual observations, motion picture photography, and thermocouple measurements, for instance, are techniques which are almost completely limited to planetary astronomy.

Surface detail

Both historically and currently, *visual* observations have been important in the discovery and measurement of planetary surface detail. The eye, having both a quick response time and the ability to discriminate, is capable of more efficient work at high magnifications than the ordinary photographic plate. Visual observations of Mercury, for instance, show details that have rarely, if ever, been photographed. Similarly, the surface of Mars has disclosed more of its detail to the eye than to the camera. It should be mentioned, however, that the human being is not an entirely reliable instrument unless used with great care. When working at the very limit of visibility, the eye occasionally sees more than is really distinguishable; for instance, it occasionally connects into straight lines things which are really just diffuse patches. Especially for Mars, the history of visual observations is riddled with unconfirmed details and semi-imaginary features.

Photography: Photographic observations of planetary surfaces show less detail but do it more reliably than visual observations. The planetary image is often enlarged with a negative lens and exposures and image size are adjusted to bring out the greatest contrast for areas of delicate shadings, for the particular emulsion used. The exposures normally run from a fraction of a second for Venus to a few seconds for the major planets. Many exposures are often made before a good one is obtained, because to get a plate which shows much detail on any planet, the seeing must remain excellent throughout the exposure.

In some cases, the limit to the quality of the image is set by the graininess, rather than by the telescopic or atmospheric resolution. Then the image quality can be improved by composite printing, which is done by selecting the best images taken at that particular time and successively enlarging them on the same print, which becomes a composite of all the images. The resolution is not improved, but the graininess is greatly reduced. Occasionally, motion picture cameras are used in order to obtain a maximum number of exposures during long periods of good seeing.

Photoelectric Photometry: Integrated properties, such as apparent magnitude and color, have been measured for all the planets by *photoelectric techniques*. A photoelectric photometer (Fig. 16.1-1) consists of a

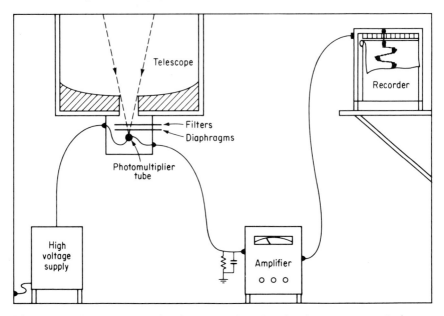

Fig. 16.1-1   Semischematic drawing of a photoelectric photometer attached to a Cassegrainian telescope.

surface extremely sensitive to light (in a photomultiplier tube) which, when a planet's image is projected on it by a telescope, generates a small electric signal. This in turn is greatly magnified by an electronic amplifier and recorded for later reduction to magnitude and color by comparison with standard stars. Potentially, such a device can be also effective in determining accurate color and intensity differences in different parts of the disk of a planet. So far, because of the seeing problem coupled with the very small size of planetary images, photoelectric observations of details on planets' surfaces have not been very extensive.

   Spectroscopy: Spectrographs are used extensively not only for the planetary atmospheres, but also to test for the nature of various surface features, such as the polar caps of Mars. Spectrophotometry, in the infrared especially, has been useful for these problems.

Temperatures

The temperatures of bodies in the solar system can be determined by measuring their radiation in various wavelengths and subtracting out the reflected sunlight. The spectral energy distribution of the reflected light is nearly identical to that of the Sun, and because of the Sun's high temperature, it is essentially restricted to wavelengths between 0.3 and 3 μ. Radiation from the much cooler planets is concentrated in longer wavelengths, roughly between 2 and 30 μ. Thus measurements in the far infrared detect almost exclusively the heat radiation from the warmed planet itself.

Three methods have been used to determine planetary temperatures: thermocouple and bolometer measures, infrared spectrophotometry, and centimeter-wavelength radio emission detection.

Thermocouple Measurements: Thermocouples were first used successfully for astronomical temperature measurements by the Earl of Rosse in 1869 with his 36-in. reflector. In the intervening hundred years, this technique has been exploited quite fully, especially at the Mt. Wilson and Lowell Observatories. The best couple was found to be bismuth against a combination of bismuth plus 5 per cent tin. In a vacuum such a thermocouple can be made to be very sensitive, able to detect temperatures as low as 120°K, for the dark side of the Moon. A common method is to separate the planetary heat from the reflected sunlight by using a sheet of glass to suppress the short wavelengths or a water cell to suppress the long wavelengths and then compare the energy generated with that obtained when no filter is used. Great care must be taken to calibrate the device properly and to correct accurately for atmospheric transparency effects, especially those connected with variable water vapor content.

Spectrophotometry: Infrared spectrophotometry can be carried out with thermocouples or other detectors and special narrow-band infrared filters or a prism spectrometer. Detailed temperature measurements of various surface features on Mars, for example, recently have been made by such means. The results of the studies using spectrophotometry have been in good agreement with the earlier thermocouple measurements.

Radio Measurements: Radio telescopes (Fig. 16.1-2) are capable of detecting thermal emission from the planets at centimeter wavelengths. For instance, for Venus the radio spectrum between wavelengths of 3 to 10 cm is like that of a blackbody at approximately 600°K. Techniques which extend the detected part of the thermal emission spectrum to such long wavelengths are severely limited by the size, distance, and temperature of the planet.

Polarization

Visual Polarimeters: Measurements of the polarization of planetary surfaces have been made visually, photographically, and photoelectrically. Lyot developed methods of measuring per cent polarizations for small areas of planetary surfaces with a visual polarimeter which uses a birefringent prism as an analyzer and shows fringes wherever the surface viewed is reflecting polarized light. Calibration is by a polarizing film in the beam, which is adjusted to compensate for the instrumental polarization. Accuracies are remarkable for the Lyot-type visual polarimeter; polarizations as slight as 0.001 (0.1 per cent) can be detected. The advantage of the visual device is its ability to detect polarizations in areas only as large as a few seconds of arc.

Fig. 16.1-2   The parabolic radio telescope of the Space Sciences Laboratory, University of California. It is used extensively for planetary research. (*Courtesy of S. Silver.*)

Photographic Polarimeters: The photographic polarimeters have been developed along the lines of the visual instruments, but they have not been used extensively for planetary work. They have an advantage of being able to detect polarization in images much fainter than can be measured visually.

Very accurate polarization measures can be made with the more recently developed photoelectric polarimeters.

Radio emission

Radio telescopes of sufficient size to have a reasonably small field and high sensitivity can be used to study the thermal and nonthermal radio emission from at least some of the planets, in particular, from Mercury, Venus, Mars, Jupiter, and Saturn. For Jupiter, the situation is rather unique. Most of the radiation is not like that of a blackbody at a unique temperature; rather, it must have a nonthermal origin, because the indicated temperature varies from 150°K at 3 cm to nearly 50,000°K at 68 cm. Because of this remarkable situation and. because both long-term and very short-term variations occur in the Jupiter radio radiation, special antennas and unique receivers and analytical equipment have been designed especially to study Jupiter.

16.2 MERCURY

Mercury, the innermost planet, is one of the most difficult to observe, owing to the fact that it is never more than 28° from the Sun. Observations of its surface are carried out almost exclusively in the daytime.

Magnitude

The apparent magnitudes of planets are indices of size and reflection properties. As fundamental data, measured magnitudes are important for computing planetary albedos and for looking for and detecting any short-term variations in brightness correlated with rotation period or any long-term variation of an evolutionary nature. D. L. Harris has introduced the notation $V(1,0)$ to represent the visual *absolute* magnitude of a planet computed for unit distance from the Sun and Earth and for zero phase angle. Thus the apparent magnitude is

$$V = V(1,0) + 5 \log rd + \Delta m(\alpha) \tag{1}$$

where r is the planet's distance from the Sun, d its distance from the Earth, and $\Delta m(\alpha)$ is the correction for variation with phase angle.

The magnitude of Mercury has been determined to be $V(1,0) = -0.36$ by Danjon. He found very little evidence for variation in this value for different faces of the planet, although because of the fact that Mercury keeps the same face to the Sun, only librations allow us to test for such variation. As far as we know, Mercury's surface on the side opposite the Sun may be quite different in reflecting properties from the sunward hemisphere.

Albedo

The albedo of a planet has been defined by Bond as the ratio of the amount of light reflected by the planet in all directions to the amount of sunlight incident on the planet. Values for planetary albedos vary between nearly 1.0 for the whitest to less than 0.1 for the blackest. The tentative value for Mercury is 0.056, the lowest of all the planets' albedos. It is somewhat uncertain because the diameter of Mercury is difficult to measure precisely. This very low value, nearly the same as that for the Moon (0.067), indicates that Mercury's surface is covered with very dark material, as black as dark basalt.

Color

The color of Mercury is difficult to measure accurately, because the planet is always close to either the daytime Sun or the horizon. Hardie has found the color index on the Yerkes-McDonald system to be $B - V = 0.93$. The corresponding value for the Sun is $B - V = 0.63$. Here B and V are blue and visual magnitudes, respectively, defined in a standard way. Thus Mercury's reflected light is somewhat redder than the sunlight incident on it. This is also true of the Moon, the colors of which are very similar to Mercury's. Kuiper has found that Mercury is relatively very bright in the far infrared (2μ), much more so than any other planet. This is due to the high temperature of Mercury's surface, which causes planetary radiation to be important at these wavelengths.

Phase effects

In its variation of brightness with phase, Mercury again mimics the Moon. A very small amount of work has been done on this problem. Nevertheless, the similarity to the Moon is well enough established that we can conclude that Mercury's surface, like that of the Moon, has considerable roughness on a small scale. That is, the roughness probably consists primarily of surface irregularities of the order of centimeters in size.

Surface detail

Under ideal conditions, when observed from favorable locations at favorable times, certain rather vague and diffuse markings can be detected on the sunlighted side of Mercury (Fig. 16.2-1). These can be seen consistently from day to day, and they have been mapped in essentially the same form for over 50 yr. The markings are large diffuse areas which make the planet appear through the telescope much the way the Moon, with its dark maria, appears to the unaided eye. The markings have been photographed at the Pic du Midi Observatory, and the photographs, especially composite prints, confirm the visually drawn charts of the surface. Dollfus estimates that Mercury cannot be much more mountainous than the Moon, or it would be possible to see the shadows of mountains at the terminator. It may be that Mercury is considerably less mountainous than the Moon, of course, as Mars is known to be. The Moon and the Earth are the only solar system bodies *known* to be extensively mountain-

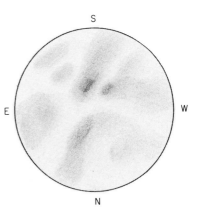

Fig. 16.2-1 Drawing of Mercury based on the sketches of Schiaparelli, Lyot, and Dollfus.

covered. There is some evidence (from the phase effect shown by Pettit and Nicholson's temperature measure) that the side of Mercury presented at western elongation is less rough than the other side. This may be due to the fact that that is the side which experiences the fewer meteoritic impacts.

The fact that the same markings are seen on the surface from day to day with position relatively unchanged with respect to the terminator indicates that Mercury's period of rotation on its axis is equal to its period of revolution about the Sun. Except for librations and the obliquity of the ecliptic, the same side of the planet always faces the Sun. Dollfus has shown that modern photography of the markings can be made to agree exactly with older visual drawings if an obliquity of about 6° is assumed for the plane of the orbit with respect to the equator, as defined by the pole of rotation. Thus Mercury has very slight seasons and the polar regions experience a rising and setting of the Sun once per Mercury year. However, the variation of temperature on any more temperate spot on the sunward side of the planet is probably brought about more by Mercury's varying distance from the Sun than by strictly seasonal changes.

Temperature

From thermocouple measurements made over a number of phase angles, Pettit and Nicholson derived a temperature for the subsolar point on Mercury of 613°K (340°C). They were not able to measure temperatures at other points on the disk because of the very small size of the image and the chronically bad seeing which one experiences with it. The temperature no doubt decreases with distance from the subsolar point until the twilight area is reached. The twilight zone on Mercury is a fairly wide band which experiences alternate sunlight and darkness and resultant rapidly varying temperatures. The dark side of the planet has as yet an unmeasured temperature; it is probably not much above absolute zero. That side would be heated only by internal radioactive sources, meteoritic impact, or conduction of heat from the sunny side.

Polarization

Measures of the polarization of sunlight reflected from Mercury have been made at the Pic du Midi by Lyot and by Dollfus. Lyot's observations of polarization from the whole disk agree extremely well with measures for the Moon. The polarization varies from 0 per cent at 20° phase to a maximum of nearly 7 per cent at 100° phase (the phase is the angle between the line of sight and the line joining the planet and the Sun). The great similarity with the lunar polarization curve indicates that the optical properties of the surface of Mercury are like those of the Moon (Chap. 19). Dollfus has detected a tendency for the polarization to be somewhat greater for the darker areas on Mercury, an effect also conspicuous for the Moon. Probably the surface of Mercury is covered by a layer of fine dust like that on the lunar surface. This is in no way unexpected, because Mercury is continuously being pelted by meteoritic particles large and small, the impacts of which would be expected to produce a rough and dusty surface.

16.3   VENUS

The atmosphere of Venus is so opaque that the planet surface is essentially unobservable from the Earth, except perhaps for occasional partings of clouds. Nevertheless, it is possible to deduce quite a bit about the planet's surface and atmosphere from studies of the integrated properties of the visible disk.

Magnitude

The visual magnitude of Venus, as defined for Mercury, is $V(1,0) = -4.29$. This is very much brighter than Mercury and demonstrates the larger size and the greater albedo of Venus. There has been no evidence of any variation of this value in the 90 yr that it has been measured. The *apparent* magnitude is sometimes as bright as $V = -4$, greater than for any other planet.

Albedo

Venus is an excellent reflector of sunlight; it has an albedo in visual light of 0.76, a very high value. Its extreme brilliance in the evening or morning sky is the result of this high albedo and of the planet's proximity to the Earth.

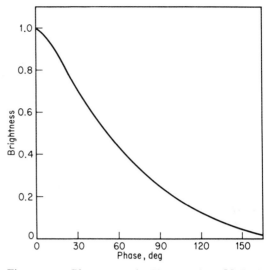

Fig. 16.3-1   Phase curve for Venus. (*After Muller.*)

Color

Venus is slightly redder than the Sun. It has a noticeably yellowish tinge when observed visually; and the photoelectrically measured color is $B - V = +0.82$, which makes Venus redder than the Sun but bluer than all the planets but Uranus, Neptune, and Pluto.

Phase effects

The variation of the brightness of Venus with phase angle is very different from that of Mercury. At half illumination (90° phase angle), Mercury is only 10 per cent of its full-phase brightness, and the corresponding figure for Venus is 25 per cent (Fig. 16.3-1). Obviously, the reflecting surface of Venus does not share the rough character which explains Mercury's (and the Moon's) phase curve. Instead, it behaves much more nearly like a white matte surface, as would be expected if, as all evidence suggests, the visible surface is the top of a white cloud layer which completely envelopes the planet.

Surface markings

Venus viewed through a telescope is normally devoid of any conspicuous markings (Fig. 16.3-2). However, under exceptional conditions faint diffuse patches slightly darker than the rest of the planet are sometimes seen and photographed. These are detectable only by exercising extreme care, skill, and patience, because the contrast is very low, much lower than between the limb and terminator region. There is some evidence that the

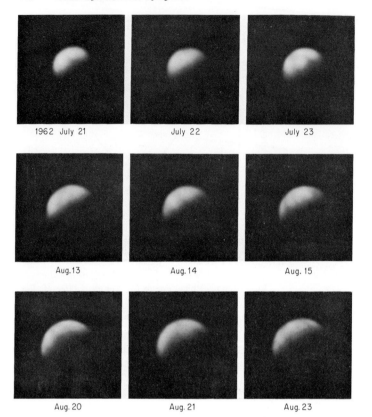

1962 July 21	July 22	July 23
Aug. 13	Aug. 14	Aug. 15
Aug. 20	Aug. 21	Aug. 23

Fig. 16.3-2   Photographs of Venus in ultraviolet light, taken by the 120-in. reflector. (*Courtesy of Lick Observatory.*)

faint markings are semipermanent in nature, indicating either a common atmospheric pattern of clouds or a portion of the surface of the planet seen through the clouds. In any case, the observations suggest that clouds above these dark markings commonly obscure portions of them from day to day, so these clouds are not entirely stable in location.

Ultraviolet photographs very conspicuously show highly variable *bright* areas; these too can be noticed visually, though less easily. The bright clouds seem to have little or nothing to do with the more permanent dark markings. Their relative brightness in ultraviolet light may indicate that they are higher than the general cloud cover and are therefore less obscured by the atmosphere at short wavelengths. They appear to be normally arranged in parallel wide bands roughly perpendicular to the terminator. Sometimes, very bright areas extend past the terminator, especially near the cusps. These circumstances have led to the hypothesis that these bands are parallel to Venus's equator, that the equator is nearly in the plane of the orbit, and that the bright areas near the cusps are polar haze due to cooler temperatures at the poles. A great deal of uncertainty is involved in these observations and their interpretation, however, and the true nature of the surface features of Venus is just not known. Perhaps certainty will only come with the successful completion of exploration of the planet by a manned or unmanned recoverable rocket.

Temperature

The temperature of Venus has been measured at optical and radio wavelengths and is found to be a function of the wavelength used. Thermocouple measurements, which take advantage of the terrestrial atmospheric window between 8 and 13 μ, give a temperature of the planet of 235°K. This is usually interpreted as the temperature of the top of the cloud layer, although it is more likely a composite temperature integrated over various depths in the atmosphere near this level.

Two temperatures have been derived from detailed analyses of the carbon dioxide bands in the 8,000-A area of the Venus spectrum. The bands show rotational fine structure, so that a temperature of 285°K has been derived by assuming a Boltzmann distribution of energy levels and a simple isotropically scattering, optically thick atmosphere. This is a composite value, as is the one given above. The lines also show pressure broadening, from which a temperature of 320°K has been derived for the bottom of the layer in which the bands originate.

Temperatures measured at longer wavelengths by using radio techniques differ considerably from the infrared values. Assuming blackbody radiation, a comparison with the Planck curve leads to a temperature of about 400° for the brightness of Venus at 8 mm. At longer wavelengths, between 3 and 21 cm, this value rises to 600°K. The picture, then, is one in which the measured temperature increases with the wavelength of the measurement until wavelengths of about 3 cm are reached. Above this the temperature remains a constant 600°K (Fig. 16.3-3).

The generally accepted explanation of the temperatures of Venus is based on the hypothesis that the surface of the planet has a temperature of about 600°K and that only wavelengths greater than a few centimeters penetrate the atmosphere down to the true surface. The 8-mm radio waves come, in this case, from the top of a cloud layer which, like terrestrial clouds, is opaque to those wavelengths but is transparent at 3 cm. The infrared measures refer to an even higher level in the atmosphere where the temperature ranges between 200 and 300°K, decreasing with altitude.

The reason for such a high temperature at Venus's surface is not merely nearness to the Sun. The theoretical temperature for a bright rotating body at that distance is only about 325°K, assuming no atmosphere. The observed high temperature must result from an exceedingly effective greenhouse effect. Sunlight passes through the atmosphere (rather ineffectively, to be sure, because of clouds) and heats up the surface, but the energy which is emitted by the heated surface at longer wavelengths

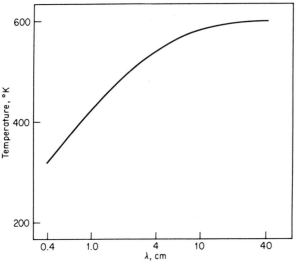

Fig. 16.3-3   The computed blackbody equivalent temperature of Venus as a function of wavelength.

does not escape from the planet, whose atmosphere is opaque at infrared wavelengths. The atmosphere of Venus must then have properties not unlike the glass of a greenhouse: more transparent to visual light than to infrared. The most likely molecule that can cause such an effect is water vapor, which is appropriately opaque in the 30-μ wavelength region. The amount of water required is of the order of 5 g/cm^2 column of atmosphere, roughly equal to that in the Earth's atmosphere.

16.4   MARS

The planet Mars has a fairly transparent atmosphere that permits scientists to see in considerable detail the characteristics of the planet's surface. These have been studied for centuries, and a great wealth of literature has resulted. Mars is never an easy object to observe, but the great pains which have been required to explore it astronomically have been well rewarded.

Magnitude

The absolute magnitude of Mars is variable; it depends primarily on which face of the planet is measured. The transparency of the Martian atmosphere also contributes to the variation; when there is an unusually large amount of haze, the absolute magnitude is greater than normal. The mean absolute magnitude is $V(1,0) = -1.52$, with an amplitude of variation of about 0.15 mag. There may also be a further variation over the Martian year owing to seasonal changes on the surface, but more observations are needed to establish this variation.

Albedo

Mars is a far better reflector of light than Mercury, but it is less efficient in this respect than Venus. This is probably a consequence of the nature of the Martian atmosphere, which is more transparent than Venus's and more extensive than Mercury's. The mean value of the albedo is 0.16 for visual light. The albedo is a function of color (Fig. 16.4-1) such that blue light is reflected much less efficiently than red light.

Color

Mars is well known for its red color, which is noticeable even with the naked eye. It is the reddest of the planets in the visual region, with a color of $B - V = +1.36$, 0.71 mag redder than the Sun. This color is traceable to the material making up most of the Martian surface, a substance as yet unidentified but probably similar to red desert rock or sand. The integrated color of Mars varies with the planet's longitude in a way such that it is reddest when brightest, at a longitude of about 120°. This portion of the Martian surface is conspicuous for its lack of dark markings (Fig. 16.4-2).

Phase effects

Although Mars is exterior to the Earth, its proximity is such that it still exhibits phases (gibbous), with a range of 47°. Photometric data suggest

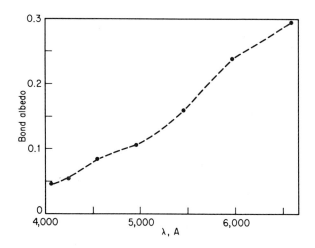

Fig. 16.4-1 The Bond albedo of Mars at various colors. (*After Woolley.*)

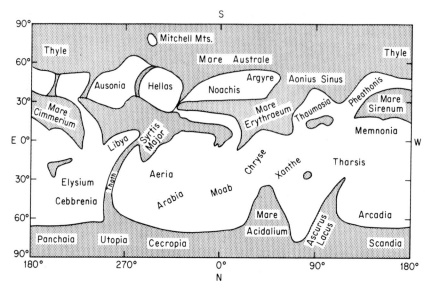

Fig. 16.4-2 Sketch map of Mars with some principal markings identified.

that the phase function is linear with a constant slope of 0.015 mag/deg. The significance of this value has not yet been thoroughly explored, though the value does indicate that the surface of Mars is not like that of the Moon.

Surface detail

The surface of Mars is covered with intricate details the nature of which has been a source of interest for many years. Most of these features are permanent in position on the Martian surface, and they have been given names, for clarity. Figure 16.4-2 shows a map of Mars with the chief surface features identified.

Permanent markings

The features of the Martian surface that are constant in location and in shape are divisible into two classes: bright areas of a reddish color and dark areas of a gray or greenish hue. There is a tendency in some areas for a smooth gradation between the two and in others for fairly sharp boundaries.

Bright areas

Most of the Martian surface is covered by bright areas of a light reddish-orange hue. There are five lines of evidence regarding the nature of these bright areas; all suggest a desert-like character, though they do not all agree on the material which makes up the desert surface.

1. The reddish color is suggestive of a desert rock cover, with the principal mineral being rich in iron oxide (such as Fe_2O_3).

2. Spectra of the near infrared have been likened by Kuiper to that of felsite, an igneous rock chiefly of feldspar (which contains aluminum silicates with potassium, sodium, calcium, or barium).

3. Polarization curves obtained by Dollfus are strong evidence that the bright surface is dust- or sand-covered. Dollfus believes that the polarization curve is sufficiently unique to indicate the exact material covering the surface. His experiments have singled out the mineral limonite ($Fe_2O_3 \cdot 3H_2O$) which, if finely pulverized, closely mimics the polarization properties of Mars' bright areas.

4. The temperature variations across the Martian disk can give further information on the surface material. Sinton and Strong have measured the temperature with the 100- and 200-in. telescopes. They were able to determine from their scans the variation of temperature with local time (Table 16.4-1). Not only was this of intrinsic interest, it also allowed them to compute the *thermal inertia* of the surface, usually expressed as $(K\rho c)^{1/2}$, where K is the thermal conductivity, ρ is the density, and c is the specific heat of the surface material. Their value is approximately 0.004, which is very low. Ordinary rocks have values of about 0.05, and sand and dust have values near 0.01. The lack of moisture tends to lower the thermal inertia, so that the Martian value of 0.004 is what might be expected for a dry, dusty, or sandy surface.

5. Finally, there are frequently observed dust or sand storms on Mars; some of them nearly completely cover the planet. These are visible as either a local or a general covering of the usual markings by a diffuse yellow haze. Such an immense dust storm as that which obscured the entire surface of Mars in 1956 can occur only in the presence of an exceedingly dusty, dry, desertlike surface. Thus, it is fairly certain that the Martian bright areas are covered with a fine material, but whether this material is chiefly felsite, limonite, or some other mineral is still not settled.

Table 16.4-1 Martian temperatures

July 1954 variation of equatorial temperature during Martian day*

Local time:	0700ʰ	0800ʰ	0900ʰ	1000ʰ	1100ʰ	1200ʰ	1300ʰ	1400ʰ
Temperature, °K:	213	235	259	276	289	294	294	285

Average variation of temperature between perihelion and aphelion†

	Subsolar point	Limb	South polar cap
Perihelion T, °K:	300	279	221
Aphelion T, °K:	273	254	201

* After Sinton and Strong.
† After Pettit.

Dark markings

The many intricate dark markings on the Martian surface have long been the source of dispute with regard to their color, shape, and nature. With high magnification and excellent seeing, they appear to be greenish or gray in the Martian autumn and winter, but they turn brown in the spring and remain so through the summer. Visual observers do not always agree on the color, probably because of the difficulty introduced by contrast with the adjoining red desert areas. It has been suggested that the dark markings have no real color difference from the rest of Mars, but merely have a lower albedo. This conjecture is contradicted by detailed color measures, by color photographs and photographs in different colors, and by the diurnal color variations.

Variations

The dark markings are remarkable for their variability in intensity as well as color. Seasonal changes have been followed for some 70 yr, and these changes invariably follow the following pattern:

Martian Spring: The polar cap on the hemisphere which is experiencing spring shrinks in size rather rapidly and becomes surrounded with a dark band, which gradually increases in extent. The dark markings near the pole turn brownish and darken, and this transformation gradually proceeds toward the equator.

Martian Summer: The equatorial dark markings are now richer in color, but the polar cap is nearly or entirely gone and the dark areas in the polar regions are fading.

Martian Autumn: The pole becomes covered with clouds or haze and the dark areas of the entire hemisphere lighten and become less distinct.

Martian Winter: The polar cap reaches its maximum extent and the dark regions are once again faded and grayish green in color.

In addition to these seasonal changes, the dark markings also occasionally undergo irregular variation in shape, color, and intensity. Particular regions, such as the Thoth system, have repeatedly undergone changes of this type at irregular intervals (Fig. 16.4-3).

Nature of the dark markings

1. Polarization measurements show that the dark areas tend to decrease the amount of polarization for a given phase. But this effect varies noticeably with the seasons, indicating that the texture of the dark material changes, especially in the Martian spring. One type of material which might behave in this way is vegetation. Dollfus has shown that the observed polarization differences cannot be explained by assuming the presence of normal terrestrial seed plants but that they are consistent with an assumed covering of tiny microorganisms such as monocellular algae.

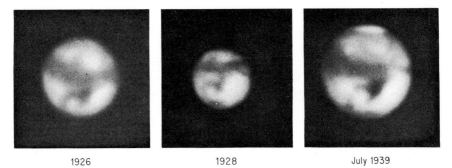

1926   1928   July 1939

Fig. 16.4-3   The area of Syrtis Major, showing changes in the Thoth canal system. Photographs taken, left to right, in 1926, 1928, and 1939 with the 36-in. Crossley reflector by W. H. Wright. (*Courtesy of Lick Observatory.*)

2. Temperature measures show that the dark areas are approximately 8°C warmer than their surroundings, which argues that they are covered with some material with a greater temperature inertia.

3. The spectral intensity in the near infrared is low, unlike that of most terrestrial plants. However, Kuiper has shown that the more simple and primitive plants (such as lichen) do not differ in this way from the Martian markings.

4. Sinton showed in 1957 and 1960 that possible evidence for the presence of vegetation on the Martian surface is the detection of three absorption bands in the infrared near 3.4 μ wavelength. Sinton's observations of Mars showed these bands clearly but there is some doubt of their identification and interpretation. A possible explanation is the presence of some sort of organic covering for the Martian surface, though one band may be due to acetaldehyde produced by the action of ultraviolet light on the Martian atmosphere.

5. It has been pointed out that the frequent violent yellow dust storms would certainly be expected to have covered over and obliterated the dark markings by now, and the fact that they are continuously visible indicates that they lie perhaps somewhat above the ground level and that they have some sort of regenerative power.

6. A final suggestion regarding the nature of the markings comes from the seasonal color and intensity variations. These can be explained most easily by the vegetation hypothesis; for the melting of the poles in spring increases the water vapor content of that hemisphere's atmosphere, and thus may cause changes in the color of a primitive plant cover; or perhaps such changes are more influenced by the increasing temperatures of the spring.

We have reviewed six lines of evidence regarding the nature of the Martian dark markings. All have been consistent with the suggestion that these markings indicate the presence of a cover of some primitive plant life, perhaps microscopic organisms. Alternative, mineralogical, and volcanological explanations can be made, and they agree about as well with all of the evidence. There may be life on Mars, but there is no completely convincing evidence yet. The lack of any appreciable oxygen (Chap. 18) in the Martian atmosphere, as well as the low nighttime temperatures, argues against the possibility of advanced life as we know it having developed there.

Canals

In the nineteenth century, observers of Mars occasionally saw faint bands or lines crisscrossing the surface. The Italian astronomer, Schiaparelli mapped these lines in 1877 and named them "canali"; subsequently they have become known as the Martian canals. The most extensive work on Martian canals was carried out by the astronomer Percival Lowell at his observatory in Arizona. Lowell mapped over 600 canals on the surface of Mars during the 25 years that he observed them. Some of the canals were apparently double, many joined at intersections, pictured by Lowell as circular "oases," and all were believed to be very thin, straight lines. Lowell estimated the width at only two or three kilometers and recorded that when the polar caps melted, the canals gradually darkened. He believed that these observations proved the presence of life of a reasonably intelligent nature, capable of engineering feats. According to his picture, Martians constructed artificial water irrigation canals to carry polar water to the arid Martian deserts.

It is now known that Lowell's interpretation of the canals cannot be correct because there is not enough water in the thin polar caps or elsewhere on Mars to support such a global irrigation system. In any case many astronomers believe that Lowell's observations are questionable in their details, for very few have been able to see the Martian canals as Lowell drew them. It is believed that instead of fine straight lines, the details are rather irregular smudges and borders between areas of slightly different intensity. There is no doubt that the most conspicuous canals seen visually can be photographed (Fig. 16.4-4), but their exact nature remains an unanswered question.

Polar caps

Normally the most conspicuous Martian surface features are the brilliant white polar caps. These were long ago associated with the similar polar caps of ice of the Earth. In winter the white caps completely cover the Martian polar area, commonly subtending an arc as great as 60°. At such times, the polar cap has an extent of some 10^6 km². With the coming of spring the polar cap gradually shrinks until by midsummer it almost

Fig. 16.4-4   The Mare Acidalium, Mare Erythraeum region of Mars, photographed by the 200-in. reflector. (*Courtesy of Mt. Wilson and Palomar Observatories.*)

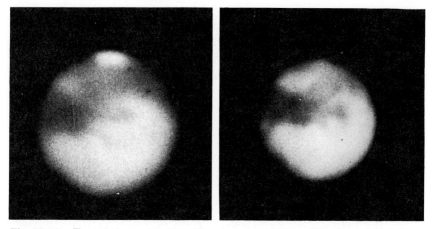

Fig. 16.4-5   Two photographs of the Tharsis region of Mars. The plate at the left was obtained in 1924 during spring at the Martian south pole and that at the right in 1926 during summer there. (*36-in. Crossley photographs courtesy of Lick Observatory.*)

entirely disappears (Fig. 16.4-5). Figure 16.4-6 shows the normal progress of the seasonal shrinkage of the south polar cap of Mars.

Often the border of the polar cap is seen, both visually and photographically, to be darkened, and this dark fringe shrinks with the polar cap. Also often seen are irregular patches of white that are separated from the main cap and lag behind the normal shrinkage of the cap. Such are the so-called Mountains of Mitchell, a place near the south pole of Mars which is interpreted to be an area of higher ground (Fig. 16.4-7).

Spectroscopic measurements in the infrared by Kuiper have shown that the Martian polar caps probably consist of ice. However, the ice cannot be glacierlike, because the lack of appreciable water vapor in the

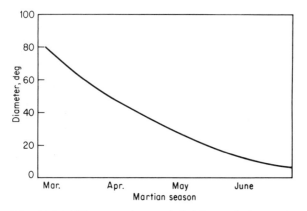

Fig. 16.4-6   The normal rate of shrinkage of the south pole cap during the Martian spring and summer. (*After Slipher.*)

Fig. 16.4-7   The normal appearance of the Mountains
of Mitchell.

Martian atmosphere (Chap. 18), and the fast rate with which the polar
caps melt suggest that they are no thicker than a centimeter or so, like
Arctic hoarfrost.

Clouds

Two types of Martian surface features have been identified, because of
their transitory motion, to be atmospheric clouds. These are distinguished
from each other by their color, some being white and some yellow. The
white clouds exist preferentially in specific regions and are often seen
covering the polar areas, especially in late autumn and winter. It is believed that these clouds are responsible for the deposition of the polar cap
in winter. White clouds are also seen at the Martian terminator and are
believed to be morning and evening fog at such times (Fig. 16.4-8). Also,
certain small areas on the Martian surface, such as the Tharsis region,
commonly are covered with clouds of this type. Polarization measurements indicate fairly reliably that these clouds are made up of ice crystals,
as are terrestrial cirrus clouds.

The yellow clouds often veil areas for days at a time, and sometimes,
as in 1956, they completely obscure the surface features of the entire
planet. The yellow clouds are probably dust storms stirred up by high
winds over large areas. It has also been suggested that they are a result
of intense volcanic activity on the Martian surface. The polarization
measures of the yellow clouds show a general decrease in polarization with
increase in the opacity of the cloud. A definite identification has not been
made from these polarization measurements, but they do not seem to be
inconsistent with the hypothesis that the yellow clouds are dust storms.

In general the atmospheric clouds of Mars are most conspicuous on
blue plates on which the dark markings usually are obscured. Occasionally
the general opaqueness of the Martian atmosphere to blue light diminishes
for short periods of time. This is called the *blue clearing* of the Martian
atmosphere.

Temperatures

At favorable oppositions of Mars it has been possible to measure the temperature of various portions of the Martian disk. These measurements
show that the temperature during the Martian day even on the equator

Fig. 16.4-8   Clouds at the polar regions and the terminators of Mars, photographed by the 200-in. reflector. (*Courtesy of Mt. Wilson and Palomar Observatories.*)

has a very large range, some 80 to 100°C. They also show that the Martian polar temperatures are very low, reaching some 200°K. Table 16.4-1 lists measurements of temperature on the equator at various times, and the table illustrates the variation in temperature between perihelion and aphelion. The Martian temperatures, except during midday on the equator, are uncomfortably low. They do not, however, make the presence of life of a primitive kind impossible.

16.5 JUPITER

The solid *surface* of the planet Jupiter cannot be discussed, because it has never been seen and may not even exist. Therefore, in this section we are limited to a discussion, as for Venus, of the visible disk. Markings on the face of Jupiter are very much more easily seen than those of Venus, and they have been studied in great detail since their discovery over 300 years ago. Jupiter, because of its large physical size, is an easy object to study in some detail in spite of its great distance.

Magnitude

The absolute magnitude of Jupiter is the greatest of all the planets, with an average value of $V(1,0) = -9.45$. It appears to vary slightly with both rotational phase and solar phase angle. This variation is not yet well established photoelectrically.

Albedo

The Bond albedo of Jupiter is believed to be approximately 0.73. Because of the lack of a large phase amplitude for Jupiter, this Bond albedo must be estimated theoretically from the observed geometric albedo, which in visual light is 0.44. It is not known exactly how the atmosphere and clouds scatter light in directions other than the incident direction.

Color

Jupiter is somewhat redder than the Sun but not as red as Mars. In fact, its color in $B - V$ is almost identical to the color of Venus. Detailed measures of Jupiter's color show that this quantity is slightly variable and depends on the colors of the cloud bands visible at the time of measurement. The cloud bands possess a wide range of color from deep blue and green to red and orange.

Surface detail

The visible surface of Jupiter's cloud layer is intricately covered with markings of various types (Fig. 16.5-1). Most conspicuous are the dark

Fig. 16.5-1   Jupiter photographed in blue light by the 200-in. reflector. The satellite Ganymede and its shadow are visible at the top of the photograph. (*Courtesy of Mt. Wilson and Palomar Observatories.*)

strips that run parallel to the equator at various latitudes. There are also spots and irregular markings, some permanent and many temporary. The nomenclature for the more or less permanent features is given in Fig. 16.5-2, where it is shown that the dark parallel strips are called belts and the light areas between belts are called zones.

Belts

Although their latitude tends to vary somewhat over long periods of time, the Jovian belts have been fairly consistently observed for many years. That they are parallel to the equator, are long, thin, and somewhat variable in shape, and have rotation periods dependent upon their latitude suggests that they are cloud formations drawn out by the rapidly rotating planet beneath. Rifts, spots, and eruptions of various appearances commonly are seen in the belts or bands from time to time. There is no known reason for these variations in the belts of Jupiter, but it has been suggested that perhaps outside influences, such as meteoritic infall or solar flares, may be the triggering mechanisms.

Great red spot

A remarkable feature of Jupiter's surface is a large, oval, usually reddish, spot observed consistently since at least 1830. This is called the "great red spot," and it is still a major puzzle because of the peculiarities of its behavior. Its maximum size is some 10,000 by 40,000 km; in shape it is a nearly perfect ellipse. It has a darkening at its border, and it is surrounded by a concentric whitish area. Its color and intensity vary from time to time, though it is normally dark red. Also, its length is variable, although its width has been fairly constant over the last 130 yr. Perhaps its most puzzling characteristic is its motion. Unlike most other spots observed on Jupiter's surface, the great red spot is variable in its rotation, with a range of some 12 secs (9 hr 55 min 32 sec to 9 hr 55 min 44 sec). This means that the great red spot drifts in longitude with respect to neighboring features on Jupiter's disk. Figure 16.5-3 shows the extent of this drift over the last 100 yr.

There have been many hypotheses regarding the nature of the great red spot and the reason for its permanence, but so far no explanation has been entirely satisfactory. Its permanence can be explained by suggesting that it is a result of a meteorological interaction with a permanent feature of some solid surface of Jupiter, but this cannot explain the variable rotation period. There does in fact appear to be evidence that the great red spot is floating in the atmosphere, because neighboring features have occasionally accelerated its motion. For instance, a feature conspicuous in the

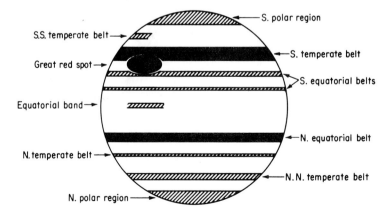

Fig. 16.5-2   Nomenclature of the bands of the Jovian cloud layer. Compare with Fig. 16.5-1.

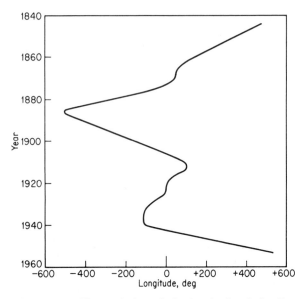

Fig. 16.5-3   The variation of the longitude of the Great
Red Spot over the last 120 yr. (*After Peek.*)

early part of the twentieth century, called the *south tropical disturbance*,
moved with a shorter period than that of the great red spot and appeared
to influence the spot's motion at the time of its greatest activity.

Polarization

The visible surface of Jupiter is believed to be a cloud layer overlain with
a transparent atmosphere (Chap. 17). If such is the case, then the polarization of the disk would be expected to increase greatly with phase angle
and should be very sensitive to wavelength:

$$P \text{ (per cent polarization)} \propto \lambda^{-4}$$

However, measures show that the wavelength dependence of the polarization of Jupiter is negligible. Also, it is found that the polarization is
greatest at the poles of Jupiter and decreases to almost 0 per cent near
the equator. Individual markings such as belts and the' great red spot,
show no difference in polarization from the surrounding area. The interpretation of these polarization observations is difficult to work out physically, but Dollfus believes that if the atmospheric clouds are overlain by
an extensive thin fog of particles approximately 1 μ in diameter, then the
observations can be completely explained. These particles are probably
droplets of ice or liquid which owe their existence to solar radiation; for
the observations suggest that they are not present at the poles of Jupiter,
hence the higher polarization there.

Table 16.6-1   Planetary surface data

Planet	$V(1,0)$	Bond albedo, visual light	$B - V$	Surface detail
Mercury	−0.36	0.056	0.93	Irregular markings
Venus	−4.29	0.76	0.82	Diffuse patches
Mars	−1.52	0.16	1.36	Intricate markings
Jupiter	−9.45	0.73	0.83	Parallel belts
Saturn	−8.88	0.76	1.04	Parallel belts
Uranus	−7.19	0.93	0.56	Belts?
Neptune	−6.87	0.84	0.41	?
Pluto	−1.01:	0.14:	0.80	?

16.6   THE OUTER PLANETS

The known characteristics of the visible surfaces of the outer planets, Saturn, Uranus, Neptune, and Pluto, are summarized in Table 16.6-1, and summaries for the other planets are given for comparison. Because of the great distance of the outer planets from the Earth, relatively little is known about the surfaces and surface markings. Only for Saturn —which has belts that are like Jupiter's (Fig. 16.6-1) but are more diffuse and difficult to see—do we have rotation periods determined from visible surface features. And even these periods are not precisely known because of the vagueness of the markings. The planet Uranus probably has faint belts like those of Jupiter and Saturn, but they are exceedingly difficult to detect. Little is seen on the surface of the planet Neptune, and

Fig. 16.6-1   Saturn and its rings photographed by the 100-in. reflector. (*Courtesy of Mt. Wilson and Palomar Observatories.*)

even to detect the disk of the planet Pluto is a difficult task. Among the four outer planets the most interesting feature probably is the ring system of Saturn. Since this is more appropriately a satellite phenomenon, we shall discuss it in Chap. 19.

16.7 BLACKBODY TEMPERATURES

It is possible to calculate the expected temperatures of the planets on the assumption that the Sun and the planets themselves radiate like black-bodies. From Eq. (3.1-2) we have a relation between temperature and radiation flux. Using this equation, the total rate of energy emitted by the Sun is $\sigma T_\odot{}^4$ times its surface area, or

$$\sigma T_\odot{}^4 \cdot 4\pi R_\odot{}^2 \tag{1}$$

where $R_\odot$ is the radius of the Sun. Thus, the rate of solar energy reaching any planet of radius R_p at distance r from the Sun is just

$$\sigma T_\odot{}^4 4\pi R_\odot{}^2 \cdot \frac{\pi R_p{}^2}{4\pi r^2} = \frac{\sigma T_\odot{}^4 \pi R_p{}^2 R_\odot{}^2}{r^2} \tag{2}$$

The planet reflects away some of this solar radiation and absorbs the rest; the amount depends upon its total albedo A. The rate of energy absorbed is

$$\frac{(1 - A)\sigma T_\odot{}^4 \pi R_p{}^2 R_\odot{}^2}{r^2} \tag{3}$$

For equilibrium, this must also be the rate of radiation of energy from the planet (at longer wavelengths, of course). For a rapidly rotating planet, which radiates equally from its bright and dark sides, applying Eq. (3.1-2) again leads to the equation

$$4\pi R_p{}^2 \sigma T_p{}^4 = \frac{(1 - A)\sigma T_\odot{}^4 \pi R_p{}^2 R_\odot{}^2}{r^2} \tag{4}$$

The planet's temperature, then, would be

$$T_p = \frac{T_\odot R_\odot{}^{1/2}(1 - A)^{1/4}}{(2r)^{1/2}} \tag{5}$$

For a slowly rotating planet, such as Mercury, most of the radiation is from the sunward side, so that the radiating area is one-half that used above and we have

$$T_p = \frac{T_\odot R_\odot{}^{1/2}(1 - A)^{1/4}}{2^{1/4} r^{1/2}} \tag{6}$$

Comparisons of temperatures calculated in this manner are given in Table 16.7-1, where agreement is shown to be surprisingly good. The disagree-

Table 16.7-1   Planetary temperatures

Planet	Temperature, °K Rapidly rotating	Temperature, °K Slowly rotating	Temperature, °K Measured
Mercury	441	525	610–1100
Venus	325	373	600
Mars	218	259	250
Jupiter	102	122	150
Saturn	76	90	88–106
Uranus	49	58	. . .
Neptune	40	47	. . .
Pluto	42	50	. . .

ments are primarily the effects of the atmospheres of the planets, which can (e.g., for Venus) cause anomolously high temperatures, and the effects due to nonblackbody radiation from the surfaces. The effect of an atmosphere is very sensitive to the composition of the atmosphere (Chaps. 17 and 18). It is possible that internally generated heat may explain part of the anomalous warmth of the major planets (Chap. 15).

The blackbody approximation is also useful in predicting the wavelengths of the radiation emitted by the planets. One of the blackbody approximations is Wien's law,

$$\lambda_{max} = \frac{A}{T} \tag{7}$$

where λ_{max} is the wavelength of greatest intensity of radiation, T is the temperature, and A is 0.2897 for cgs units. For planets, with temperatures between 100 and 600°K, the wavelengths of radiation of maximum intensity are in the range 50,000 to 300,000 A, deep in the infrared and radio regions. It should be mentioned that λ_{max} is the maximum of the intensity curve plotted as a function of wavelength only. When plotted as a function of frequency of the emitted radiation, the point of maximum emission is somewhat different from that given by Eq. (16.7-7).

BIBLIOGRAPHICAL NOTES

A good general reference to solar system problems and an excellent collection of references to the technical literature is:

R 16-1. Kuiper, G. P., and B. M. Middlehurst (eds.): "Planets and Satellites," chaps. 8 to 12 and 15 to 17. The University of Chicago Press, Chicago, 1961.

A more popular treatment of the planets is:

R 16-2. Whipple, F. L.: "Earth, Moon and Planets," Harvard University Press, Cambridge, Mass., 1963.

A treatment of the origin of planetary features is contained in:

R 16-3. Urey, H. C.: "The Planets," Yale University Press, New Haven, Conn., 1952.

Section 16.1. Methods of observation are described in:

R 16.1-1. Miczaika, G. R., and W. M. Sinton: "Tools of the Astronomer," Harvard University Press, Cambridge, Mass., 1961.

Section 16.2. See R 16-1.

Section 16.3. A rather popular account of the study of Venus is given in:

R 16.3-1. Moore, P.: "The Planet Venus," The Macmillan Company, New York, 1959.

Section 16.4. There are many popular books on Mars; of historical interest is:

R 16.4-1. Lowell, P.: "Mars as the Abode of Life," The Macmillan Company, New York, 1908.

An excellent set of photographs of Mars with a complete discussion of visible surface features is given in:

R 16.4-2. Slipher, E. C.: "Mars," Sky Publishing Corporation, Cambridge, Mass., 1962.

An account of many Martian problems is given by:

R 16.4-3. Vaucouleurs, G. de: "Physics of the Planet Mars," Faber & Faber, Ltd., London, 1954.

Two popular treatments of the subject are:

R 16.4-4. Moore, P.: "Guide to Mars," Muller, London, 1960.

R 16.4-5. Richardson, R. S.: "Exploring Mars," McGraw-Hill Book Company, New York, 1954.

The reader should also consult the numerous proceedings of astronomical and space symposia, which are being published with considerable frequency and which will be much more up to date than the above books.

Section 16.5. A rather complete account of the visible features of Jupiter's disk is:

R 16.5-1. Peek, B. M.: "The Planet Jupiter," Faber & Faber, Ltd., London, 1958.

Section 16.6. A book dealing, mostly historically, with the planet Saturn is:

R 16.6-1. Alexander, A. F. O'D.: "The Planet Saturn," The Macmillan Company, New York, 1962.

The other outer planets are discussed in some detail in R 16-1.

Atmospheres of the Jovian planets

The four Jovian planets have extensive atmospheres made up principally of the light gases found to make up their interiors. For Jupiter, the largest and nearest, the structure and composition of the atmosphere are best known. Most of this chapter, therefore, is devoted to Jupiter in particular; a discussion of the other Jovian planets' atmospheres is given in the last section.

17.1 SPECTRA

Spectra of the Jovian planets show the reflection spectrum of the Sun with superimposed absorption features consisting of molecular bands of hydrogen, methane, and ammonia (Fig. 17.1-1). The amount of methane in Jupiter's atmosphere above the opaque cloud layer can be determined from the strength of the bands; it is found to be approximately 11 g/cm². This is a small quantity, amounting to a total of only 6×10^{20} g, some 3×10^{-10} of Jupiter's total mass. The computed amount of gaseous am-

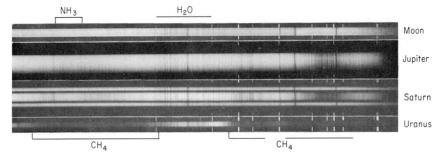

Fig. 17.1-1   Spectra of Jupiter, Saturn and rings, and Uranus in the wavelength region 7,500 to 8,800 A with the spectrum of the Moon for comparison. The H_2O bands are of terrestrial origin. The bands of NH_3 and CH_4 come from the atmosphere of the planet involved. Coudé spectra taken by the 120-in. reflector. (*Courtesy of Lick Observatory*.)

monia is even smaller, only 0.53 g/cm². The lines of hydrogen were discovered only in 1962; they indicate that the amount of molecular hydrogen is large, more than 100 times the amount of methane.

17.2   SCALE HEIGHT

A quantitative idea of the structure of the Jovian atmosphere is given by the measures of the dimming of the star σ Arietis when it was occulted by Jupiter in 1952. Most of the dimming, as shown by color measures, was due to refraction of the starlight by the planet's atmosphere, so that the slope of the intensity curve gives the distribution of gas in the atmosphere in a fairly straightforward way.

If an atmosphere obeys the equation of hydrostatic equilibrium

$$dP = -g\rho \, dr \tag{1}$$

and the perfect-gas law

$$P = \frac{k\rho T}{\mu m_H} \tag{2}$$

then we define the scale height H to be

$$H = \frac{kT}{\mu m_H g} \tag{3}$$

In these equations, P is the pressure, g is the local acceleration of gravity, ρ is the density, r is the planetocentric distance, k is the Boltzmann constant, and μ is the mean molecular weight in terms of the mass of the hydrogen atom m_H (Sec. 3.3). Dividing Eq. (17.2-1) by Eq. (17.2-2) and integrating gives us the variation of pressure with height,

$$P(r) = P(r_0) \exp\left[-\int_{r_0}^{r} \frac{dr}{H}\right] \tag{4}$$

and when g, T, and μ are nearly independent of r, we find

$$P(r) \approx P(r_0) \exp \left[- \frac{r - r_0}{H} \right] \tag{5}$$

Knowing the variation of pressure or density with height thus gives us the scale height. The value of H found by analysis of the occultation of σ Arietis is 8 km.

17.3 COMPOSITION

From spectroscopic evidence, it is known that Jupiter's atmosphere contains at least the molecules H_2, CH_4, and NH_3. Other inert gases may well also be present; helium, for instance, would not be detectable spectroscopically even if present. The presence of helium can be inferred, in fact, but from other, less direct evidence.

The mean molecular weight of the atmosphere can be determined from the measured scale height. From Eq. (17.2-3) we have

$$\mu = \frac{kT}{Hm_H g} \tag{1}$$

so that we can find μ, knowing the scale height and temperature. Values of T for the atmosphere have been estimated from the infrared and radio measures, combined with theoretical temperature profiles. Results range from values of 86 to 130°K, leading to mean molecular weights of $\bar{\mu} = 3.3$ to $\bar{\mu} = 5.0$, respectively. The difficulty in determining the temperature arises from the fact that only portions of Jupiter's infrared spectrum have been measured. The opacity of the Earth's atmosphere allows measurement only in atmospheric "windows." Elsewhere in the spectrum, Jupiter's radiation may be different from what is expected, because a planet with such an atmosphere is probably a poor approximation to a blackbody.

A mean molecular weight of the order 4 indicates the predominance of light constituents such as molecular hydrogen ($\mu = 2$) and helium ($\mu = 4$). The quantitative composition of the atmosphere remains uncertain, however. No doubt, either hydrogen or helium is the most abundant constituent, with possibly neon (not observed) next in abundance. Methane and ammonia are minor components, and other gases such as H_2O, CO_2, C_2H_6, and C_2H_4, which could be detected spectroscopically if present, are definitely not present to any important degree. Radiative transfer in planetary atmospheres (clearly related to the interpretation of spectra and the composition) is discussed in Sec. 18.10.

17.4 TEMPERATURES

The intensity of Jovian radiation in the infrared (measured in our atmosphere's window at wavelengths 8 to 14 μ) corresponds to that of a blackbody of temperature 130°K (with an uncertainty of some 10°K). The temperature measured by radio telescopes at a wavelength of 3 cm is 135°K. These values are somewhat higher than the expected temperature owing to solar radiation (Sec. 16.7), which is 102°K for Jupiter. This discrepancy may be due either to an internal heat source or a possible greenhouse effect that in turn is due to dissociated CH_4 or NH_3 and probably H_2O. At present it is not possible to choose between these possibilities with confidence.

The measures at 8 to 14 μ no doubt refer to the temperature of the top of the layer of ammonia, because ammonia absorbs strongly in this spectral region. The radio temperature refers to approximately the same level.

17.5 ATMOSPHERIC MODELS

It was pointed out in 1934 by Wildt that the density of the atmosphere of Jupiter must increase very rapidly with depth, so that the solid or liquid surface cannot be very far below the cloud layer. To estimate this depth, one must know the composition, the temperature and density profiles, and the pressures in the lower atmosphere. Estimates place the nongaseous mantle of Jupiter somewhere between 100 to 500 km below the visible cloud layer. This solid surface may be simply molecular hydrogen solidified under pressure.

Figure 17.5-1 shows a model of the atmosphere of Jupiter based on

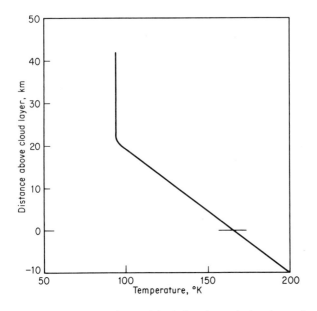

Fig. 17.5-1   An early model of the thermal structure of Jupiter's atmosphere. (*After Kuiper.*)

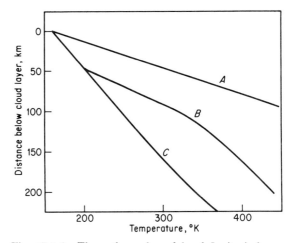

Fig. 17.5-2 Three thermal models of Jupiter's lower atmosphere. Curve A is for a dry adiabat, curve B for an atmosphere with 1 per cent NH_3, and curve C for 2 per cent NH_3. (*After Gallet.*)

Kuiper's calculations, assuming a predominantly hydrogen constitution. A later model, based on considerations of the effect of the energy released by the condensation of ammonia and water vapor on the structure, is shown in Fig. 17.5-2, demonstrating that such considerations imply an increased pressure gradient and decreased temperature gradient over previous models. On the basis of the latter model, it is predicted that there is a cloud of ammonia ice crystals (the visible surface) some 50 km thick, underlain by a region in which liquid ammonia may fall as rain. Below this the higher temperatures and pressures produce a layer of gaseous ammonia. Of course, hydrogen and helium are still the major constituents of these portions of the atmosphere. There may also be water ice clouds a few kilometers below the ammonia clouds, with water rain and water vapor below them.

The structure of the Jovian atmosphere above the visible cloud layer is still very hypothetical. There is evidence that the ammonia gas that produces the observed bands in the spectra sometimes has a slower (3–8 km/sec less) rotational velocity then the cloud surface, with supersonic shear velocities apparently resulting. The observed rotational tilt of the ammonia lines is variable; sometimes it equals that of the reflected solar spectral lines and sometimes it is much less. Figure 17.5-3 schematically represents the current picture of Jupiter's atmosphere.

17.6 NONTHERMAL RADIO EMISSION

The radio radiation from Jupiter at wavelengths shortward of about 4 cm is similar to that from a blackbody of temperature of 130°K. However,

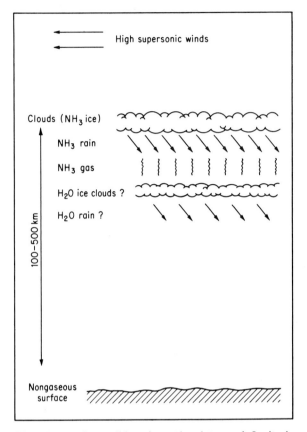

Fig. 17.5-3   A possible schematic picture of Jupiter's atmosphere.

the flux observed for radiation of wavelengths of 5 cm to a meter or so is very much larger than predicted for the thermal radiation. At 10 cm, one calculates a blackbody temperature of 600°K, and at 31 cm this has risen to nearly 10,000°K. Clearly, the decimeter radiation from Jupiter has a nonthermal source. Figure 17.6-1 shows the microwave spectrum of Jupiter and illustrates the obvious nonthermal component.

The most reasonable explanation put forward to explain the decimeter radiation is that it is synchrotron radiation (Sec. 6.2) coming from two radiation belts which surround Jupiter as the Van Allen belts surround the Earth (Sec. 18.9). Their location has been measured interferometrically to be at 3 Jovian radii from the planet's center, concentrated in the equatorial plane. The radiation coming from the outer belt is apparently linearly polarized in a plane that is nearly parallel to the equator. From the way in which the plane of polarization wobbles with the rotation of the planet, it is found that the belts are tilted approximately 10° with respect to the equatorial plane, and it is supposed that this is the angular separation of Jupiter's rotational and magnetic poles. The outer belt is correlated in intensity with solar activity; it is activated, apparently by solar particles, some 4 days following a solar outburst.

From the observed frequencies the magnetic field strength can be computed [see Eqs. (6.2-62) and (6.2-63)]. The field strength is found to be approximately 2 gauss, and the energies of the electrons are estimated to be of the order of 10 Mev.

In addition to the thermal and synchrotron radiation, radio telescopes have detected strong bursts of energy from Jupiter at much longer wavelengths. In fact, it was at a wavelength of 13.6 m that the first radio signals from Jupiter were detected in 1955. At decameter wavelengths, Jupiter is a strong, erratic, and complicated radio source. The exact mechanism involved is still obscure, but a great many observations and a surfeit of hypotheses are now available.

The decameter radiation is exceedingly sporadic and sudden, with a behavior somewhat reminiscent of solar noise storms. Major outbursts last from minutes to a few hours and are characterized by an intricate fine structure, with durations of individual bursts in the range of hundredths of seconds. Correlations with Jupiter's rotational period have shown that there is one strong discrete source on the planet and possibly two weak ones, with most longitudes of Jupiter silent. The rotational period of the source is $9^h55^m29.37^s$. That the source is in some way connected with the presence of the Jovian radiation belts seems indicated by the fact that the longitude of greatest decameter activity coincides with that of the magnetic pole inferred from the decimeter radiations.

17.7 ATMOSPHERES OF SATURN, URANUS, AND NEPTUNE

The outer three Jovian planets probably have atmospheres similar to the atmosphere of Jupiter except for lower temperatures. Most of the am-

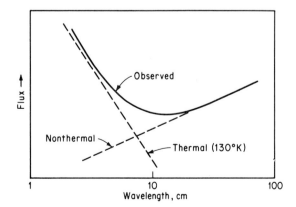

Fig. 17.6-1 The radio spectrum of Jupiter compared with a blackbody thermal curve for a temperature of 130°K.

Table 17.7-1   Atmospheres of the Jovian planets

Planet	Gas	Approximate amount, cm-atm (NTP)
Jupiter	H_2	3×10^6
	CH_4	1.5×10^4
	NH_3	7×10^2
	He	?
Saturn	CH_4	3.5×10^4
	NH_3	2×10^2
	H_2	4×10^6
	He	?
Uranus	CH_4	2.2×10^5
	H_2	9×10^6
	He	?
Neptune	CH_4	3.7×10^5
	H_2	10^7

monia is frozen out of the visible atmosphere of Saturn, and it does not show up at all in that of Uranus and Neptune. Table 17.7-1 lists the observed constituents of the atmospheres of all four Jovian planets.

Doppler measures of the spectrum of Saturn show that although the H_2 is apparently moving with the same rotational velocity as the visible surface of the planet, the CH_4 may have a faster speed. The spectra of Uranus and Neptune are interesting, because there are several spectral features still unidentified. These planets also show broad, weak absorption lines in the red and near infrared, probably due to H_2. These bands become noticeable in the laboratory when H_2 reacts under pressure with other molecules or with itself.

BIBLIOGRAPHICAL NOTES

Section 17.1. A review of spectroscopic analyses of planetary atmospheres is found in:

R 17.1-1. Kuiper, G. P. (ed.): "The Atmospheres of the Earth and Planets," 2d ed., The University of Chicago Press, Chicago, 1952.

The identification of the H_2 molecule is reported in two papers:

R 17.1-2. Kiess, C. C., C. H. Corliss, and H. K. Kiess: *Astrophys. J.*, **132**: 221 (1960).

R 17.1-3. Herzberg, G.: *Astrophys. J.*, **115**: 337 (1952).

Section 17.2. The observations of σ Arietis and their interpretation are given in:

R 17.2-1. Baum, W. A., and A. D. Code: *Astron. J.*, **58** : 108 (1953).

Section 17.3. A discussion of the composition of Jupiter's atmosphere, with many useful references, is:

R 17.3-1. Öpik, E. J.: *Icarus*, **1** : 200 (1962).

Section 17.4. The basic reference on the radiation temperature of Jupiter is:

R 17.4-1. Menzel, D. H., W. W. Coblentz, and C. O. Lampland: *Astrophys. J.*, **63** : 177 (1926).

Section 17.5. Some discussion of models of Jupiter's atmosphere is found in R 17.1-1.

Section 17.6. A good review paper, without references, is found in an account of a conference on Jupiter:

R 17.6-1. Wildt, R., H. J. Smith, E. E. Salpeter, and A. G. W. Cameron: *Phys. Today*, **16**(5) : 19 (1963).

An account of the source of the decimeter radiation from Jupiter can be found in:

R 17.6-2. Field, G. B.: *J. Geophys. Res.*, **64** : 1169 (1959).

A review of Jupiter's radio radiation is given in:

R 17.6-3. Smith, A. G.: *Science*, **134** : 587 (1961).

Section 17.7. See R 17.1-1 and R 17.1-3.

Atmospheres of the terrestrial planets

A discussion of the atmospheres of Earth, Mars, and Venus should contain a systematic development of the basic theory with a subsequent application to the cases at hand. This type of development is difficult to achieve because of the extreme imbalance in our states of knowledge concerning the various planetary atmospheres. Our knowledge of the terrestrial atmosphere, and especially the upper atmosphere, has increased tremendously in the last decade, but no corresponding large-scale advance has occurred in our knowledge of the atmospheres of Mars and Venus.

Hence, our procedure will be to sketch the general properties of the terrestrial atmosphere as a prototype and then to discuss briefly the atmospheres of Mars and Venus. We do not dwell on these latter atmospheres, because our state of knowledge is somewhat incomplete. For example, the major constituent of the terrestrial atmosphere is N_2, but the major constituent of the atmospheres of Mars and Venus is not definitely established. Mercury and Pluto are sometimes considered terrestrial planets; we do not discuss the atmospheres of Mercury and Pluto, since almost nothing is known about them.

18.1 ATMOSPHERIC NOMENCLATURE

The principal parts of the atmosphere are shown schematically in Fig. 18.1-1. The troposphere is the region of temperature decrease between the ground level and the tropopause (meaning the upper boundary of the troposphere). The height of the tropopause depends on latitude, and it varies from 7 km at high latitudes to some 18 km at the equator. The

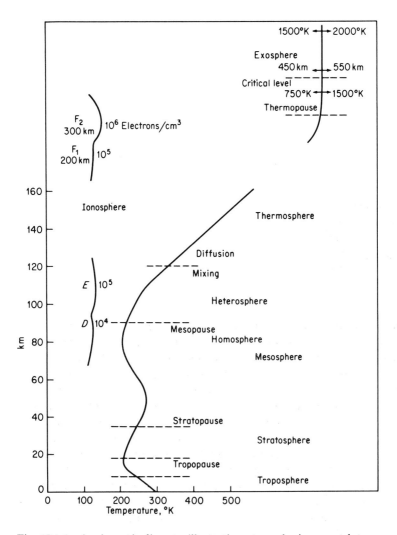

Fig. 18.1-1   A schematic diagram illustrating atmospheric nomenclature. (*After M. Nicolet in R* 18.1-1.)

stratosphere is often taken to be the nearly isothermal region above the tropopause, but some definitions differ on this point. The stratopause varies in height with place and time, and in low latitudes there is often almost no isothermal region above the tropopause. In this case the tropopause and the stratopause coincide.

The mesopause designates the level (between 85 and 95 km) at which the principal temperature minimum occurs. The region between the stratopause and the mesopause is the mesosphere, where it is possible to study chemical reactions and day-to-day variations. The thermosphere is the region of increasing temperature extending upward from the mesosphere. The outermost region of the atmosphere is the exosphere (Sec. 18.7). The so-called critical level or base of the exosphere can be taken as coincident with the thermopause.

We refer to the region of appreciable electron and ion content as the ionosphere, which begins at some 60 km and extends to the highest parts of the atmosphere. The region where chemical reactions are important can be called the chemosphere. Note that these various regions are not necessarily mutually exclusive.

Lastly, we consider the question of chemical composition. The region of homogeneous chemical composition is called the homosphere, and the homopause is at essentially the same height as the mesopause. Above this, we have the heterosphere, where the composition (influenced by mixing, diffusion, photodissociation, photoionization, and recombination) changes with height.

18.2 BASIC RELATIONS

If the atmosphere is in hydrostatic equilibrium,

$$dP = -g\rho \, dh \tag{1}$$

where P is the pressure, g is the acceleration of gravity, ρ is the density, and h is the height in the atmosphere. We also have the perfect-gas law,

$$P = NkT = \frac{\rho k T}{\mu m_H} \tag{2}$$

where N is the number concentration, T is the temperature, μ is the mean molecular weight, m_H is the mass of the hydrogen atom, and k is Boltzmann's constant. The density can be written as

$$\rho = \sum_j N_j m_j \equiv Nm \tag{3}$$

where N_j and m_j are the concentrations and masses of the various constituent gases. Combining these equations, we have

$$\frac{dP}{P} = \frac{dN}{N} + \frac{dT}{T} = -\frac{dh}{H} \tag{4}$$

where the local scale height is given by

$$H = \frac{kT}{mg} = \frac{kT}{\mu m_H g} \tag{5}$$

For an isothermal atmosphere, and a constant H, the scale height gives the vertical distance over which the density changes by a factor of e^{-1} [see Eq. (17.2-5)]. For regions of complete mixing, the proportions of the various gases are constant. Taking a representative constant value for the acceleration of gravity, we find

$$\frac{dT}{T} = \frac{dH}{H} \tag{6}$$

and thus

$$\frac{dN}{N} = -\frac{dH + dh}{H} \tag{7}$$

We may measure P as a function of height and determine H as a function of height through Eq. (18.2-4). Then we have the temperature and concentration distribution from Eqs. (18.2-6) and (18.2-7).

At a sufficiently great height, the atmosphere is not mixed and may be in diffusive equilibrium. In this case,

$$P = P_1 + P_2 + \cdots = \sum_j P_j \tag{8}$$

and

$$\frac{dP_j}{P_j} = -\frac{dh}{H_j} \tag{9}$$

The mean scale height is then given by

$$H^{-1} = \sum_j \frac{N_j}{NH_j} \tag{10}$$

Here it is evident that we cannot make much progress without first determining the ratios of the major constituents for at least one specific height. The total number of atoms per unit column (a column with cross-sectional area of 1 cm^2) above a specific height h_0 is given by

$$\mathfrak{N}(h_0) = \int_{h_0}^{\infty} N(h) \, dh \tag{11}$$

From Eq. (18.2-7), we have

$$-N\,dh = NH\left(\frac{dN}{N} + \frac{dH}{H}\right) = H\,dN + N\,dH \qquad (12)$$

and thus

$$\mathfrak{N}(h_0) = \int_{\infty}^{h_0} d(NH) = N(h_0)H(h_0) - N(\infty)H(\infty) \qquad (13)$$

Under most circumstances, $N(\infty)H(\infty)$, which is proportional to the pressure at infinity, is quite negligible, and we have the usual result

$$\mathfrak{N}(h_0) = N(h_0)H(h_0) \qquad (14)$$

This result is independent of the temperature distribution but depends on the assumption of a constant gravity and mean molecular weight.

A model of the temperature distribution and the density distribution of the principal constituents of the Earth's atmosphere is given in Figs. 18.11-1 and 18.11-2.

18.3 THE ATMOSPHERE BELOW THE MESOPAUSE

The atmosphere below 90 km—below the mesopause—is well mixed and homogeneous. Here the mean molecular weight does not depart significantly from the surface value, $\mu = 28.97$ g/mol. The principal constituents (by mass at sea level) are molecular nitrogen (N_2, 75.51 per cent), molecular oxygen (O_2, 23.15 per cent), argon (Ar, 1.28 per cent), and carbon dioxide (CO_2, 0.046 per cent). Minor constituents are Ne, He, CH_4, H_2O, Kr, N_2O, H_2, CO, O_3, Xe, and NO_2. The atmosphere below 30 km involves the weather, biochemical considerations, and the interaction of the atmosphere with the land areas and the oceans.

The region between 30 and 90 km involves the problem of the chemistry of an oxygen-nitrogen atmosphere with minor constituents. The concentrations of minor constituents are also interesting, particularly so the products related to water vapor. These constituents influence, for example, the night-sky Lyman-α problem and the emission of the nightglow OH bands. Note that the calculations of the abundances of minor constituents related to water vapor are very uncertain.

18.4 THE UPPER ATMOSPHERE

As we move upward from the mesopause, the dissociation of O_2 which began at 40 km (leading to ozone formation) becomes more important, and nearly all oxygen is in the atomic form. Above 200 km (i.e., in the F_2 region), oxygen becomes ionized and O^+ is the main ionic constituent. Nitrogen does not become dissociated appreciably at any height. The upper atmosphere is the seat of the auroral emissions and many of the airglow emissions (Sec. 18.10). The upper atmosphere contains several ionized regions which will be discussed separately in the next section. The temperature increases with altitude in this region; the general run of the temperature is discussed in Sec. 18.6.

In this part of the Earth's atmosphere one encounters the change-over from complete mixing to diffusive equilibrium, thought to begin near 120 km. Above this point and below the critical level, each species follows its own scale height. Above the critical level (550 km), exospheric theory must be used (Sec. 18.7). In the higher parts of the exosphere, neutral hydrogen, protons, and electrons are the major constituents. The protons originate at lower levels through charge exchange of neutral hydrogen with ionized atomic oxygen, viz.,

$$H + O^+ \rightarrow O + H^+ \tag{1}$$

The electrons and protons exist in substantial numbers out to several Earth radii and constitute the "whistler medium" (see Sec. 18.9). The concentrations and temperatures in the upper atmosphere are known to undergo variations daily, yearly, and through the solar cycle. A discussion of these phenomena is outside the scope of this chapter.

18.5 THE IONOSPHERE

The small amounts of ionization in the upper atmosphere are important in our daily lives, because they control radio communication. The ionosphere is important to atmospheric structure, because it is a region of deposition of solar radiant energy.

Description

The D region occurs near the 90-km level with a maximum electron concentration $N_e^{(max)}$ of 1.5×10^4 per cm^3 at noon; it is absent at night. The primary ionization occurs through the action of Lyman-α on NO, and electrons attach themselves to O and O_2. Some ionization can occur through the action of X rays shorter than 10 A on all constituents. Recombination can occur, for example, by mutual neutralization,

$$O^- + X^+ \rightarrow O + X \tag{1}$$

The relative rates of the ionization and recombination processes determine the electron and ion concentrations.

The E layer is found near the 110-km level with an $N_e^{(max)}$ at noon of 1.5×10^5 per cm^3. At night, the electron concentration drops below 10^4 per cm^3. Here all major constituents are ionized mainly by ultrasoft X rays in the wavelength 10 to 100 A. Patches of additional ionization can be caused by meteors or by particle bombardment. The recombination

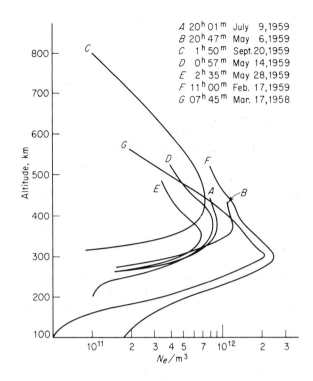

Fig. 18.5-1   Sample electron density measurements made
from rockets. [*From J. S. Nisbet and S. A. Bowhill, J.
Geophys. Res.*, **65**: 2597 (1960).]

can occur through dissociative recombination of O_2 and other elements,
e.g.,

$$O_2^+ + e \rightarrow O + O \quad \text{or} \quad NO^+ + e \rightarrow N + O \tag{2}$$

Dissociative recombination is also the primary means of recombination in the F region, but the intermediate processes that produce the
molecular ions are important. The F_1 region is found near the 200-km
level with a noon concentration of 2.5×10^5 electrons/cm^3. Ionization
occurs from the action of the Lyman continuum and the helium emission
lines on O (and perhaps N_2). The F_1 region is absent at night. The F_2
region is found near the 300-km level with a noon value of $N_e^{(max)} \approx 10^6$
per cm^3 and a night value $\approx 10^5$ per cm^3. The same processes that produce F_1 also produce F_2; a separate region is formed because of variations
with height in the rate of recombination.

The electron densities can be measured from above (using satellites,
so-called topside soundings) and below (ground-based) with ionospheric
soundings. This technique involves sending a train of pulses of varying
frequency and observing the time of return of the various frequencies.

Each frequency is reflected at the point in the ionized region where the transmitted frequency is equal to the local "plasma frequency," which is proportional to $N_e^{1/2}$ [see Eq. (5.3-27)].

Frequencies higher than the highest plasma frequency in the ionosphere are not reflected, but pass on through. The electron densities can also be measured by firing a rocket-borne radio transmitter through the ionized layer. An apparent Doppler shift (in addition to the real one) is introduced in the signal because of the varying index of refraction, which is a function of the electron density. Some sample measurements are shown in Fig. 18.5-1. As is easily noted by inspection of this figure, the various regions or layers that we have discussed are not very distinct. The concept of "layers" arose from the ionospheric sounding technique; minor deviations on the graphs could be interpreted in this fashion. The height and electron density of the ionized regions are quite variable; daily, seasonal, and solar-cycle variations are recognized (Fig. 18.5-1).

The basic theory of ionized layer formation, where ionization caused by solar radiation is balanced by processes of recombination, was worked out years ago by Chapman, Bradbury, and Mohler. The basic properties of the ionized layers can be understood in terms of these investigations.

Chapman layer

Consider an isothermal, plane-parallel atmosphere which is illuminated by monochromatic, ionizing radiation. The variation of the electron density due to ionization and recombination is taken to be given by

$$\frac{dN_e}{dt} = q - \alpha N_e^2 \tag{3}$$

where q is the ionization rate, αN_e^2 is the recombination rate, and α is the rate coefficient. Here N_e is taken as equal to the number of positive ions N_i.

The problem is to derive q. A light beam is diminished by passing through a layer of thickness dh at height h by

$$-dI = AI\, dm \tag{4}$$

where A is the absorption coefficient per unit mass. An isothermal, plane-parallel atmosphere has a density which varies as $\exp(-h/H)$, where H is the scale height. A beam that traverses the atmosphere at zenith angle χ travels a slant distance of $[-\sec \chi \cdot dh]$ in moving the vertical distance dh (valid for $\chi \lesssim 85°$). Hence, we may substitute for dm in Eq. (18.5-4) to obtain

$$dI = AI\rho_0 \exp\left(-\frac{h}{H}\right) \sec \chi\, dh \tag{5}$$

This equation can be rearranged to read

$$\int_{I_0}^{I} \frac{dI}{I} = \int_{\infty}^{h} A\rho_0 \cdot \sec \chi \exp\left(-\frac{h}{H}\right) dh \tag{6}$$

where I_0 is the intensity outside the Earth's atmosphere. An elementary integration yields

$$I = I_0 \exp\left[-(A\rho_0 H \sec \chi) \exp\left(-\frac{h}{H}\right)\right] \tag{7}$$

If β is the number of ions per cubic centimeter produced by the absorption of unit intensity from the incident beam, then

$$q = \frac{\beta}{\sec \chi} \frac{dI}{dh} \tag{8}$$

When Eqs. (18.5-8) and (18.5-7) are combined, we have

$$q(\chi,h) = \beta A I_0 \rho_0 \exp\left[-\frac{h}{H} - A\rho_0 H \sec \chi \exp\left(-\frac{h}{H}\right)\right] \tag{9}$$

The height of maximum ion production is obtained by setting $\partial q/\partial h = 0$ from Eq. (18.5-9). This yields

$$\exp\left(+\frac{h_{max}}{H}\right) = A\rho_0 H \sec \chi \tag{10}$$

Substituting Eq. (18.5-10) into (18.5-9) gives the rate of maximum ion production,

$$q_{max} = \beta A I_0 \rho_0 \exp\left(-\frac{h}{H} - 1\right) = \frac{\beta I_0}{He \sec \chi} \tag{11}$$

Now Eq. (18.5-9) can be rewritten in terms of h_{max} and q_{max} for vertical incidence which we denote by simply h_0 and q_0. Hence,

$$q(\chi,h) = q_0 \exp\left[\frac{h_0 + H - h}{H} - \sec \chi \exp\left(\frac{h_0 - h}{H}\right)\right] \tag{12}$$

Let

$$z = \frac{h - h_0}{H} \tag{13}$$

and Eq. (18.5-12) becomes

$$q(\chi,z) = q_0 \exp\left[1 - z - \sec \chi \exp\left(-z\right)\right] \tag{14}$$

For the case of quasi-equilibrium, Eq. (18.5-3) gives

$$q = \alpha N_e^2 \tag{15}$$

From the last two equations, we find

$$N_e = N_{e,0} \exp \left\{ \tfrac{1}{2}[1 - z - \sec \chi \exp (-z)] \right\} \tag{16}$$

where $N_{e,0} = (q_0/\alpha)^{1/2}$, which is the electron density at h_0. If the Sun is near the zenith (sec $\chi \approx 1$), Eq. (18.5-16) may be simplified by using the series expansion for the exponential to obtain

$$N_e = N_{e,0} \left(1 - \frac{z^2}{4} \right) \tag{17}$$

Here the electron distribution is parabolic with a maximum at h_0; such a region is called a simple Chapman region. The approximations used are valid within one scale height of the maximum ($-1 \leq z \leq 1$).

Equations (18.5-15) and (18.5-11) can be combined to give an estimate of the seasonal and daily variations of the electron density maximum. It is found that the maximum varies as $(\cos \chi)^{1/2}$.

This treatment gives some insight into the formation of ionized layers by the processes mentioned above. Equation (18.5-10) has a simple interpretation; for an isothermal atmosphere, Eqs. (18.5-4), (18.2-14), (17.2-5), and (18.5-4) can be compared, and we find that the maximum of the ionized layer occurs when the incident radiation has been reduced by a factor e^{-1}. In other words, the ionized layer associated with the emission at a particular wavelength occurs when the slant optical thickness is unity.

The principal uncertainty in the details consists in the form of the recombination law, taken here as αN_e^2. It is clear that other forms of the recombination law must be considered in detailed calculations as well as the effects of a nonisothermal atmosphere, diffusion, and a nonmonochromatic ionizing radiation.

18.6   THE TEMPERATURE DISTRIBUTION

While it is the main subject in this section, it should be realized that the temperature distribution determines the basic structure of an atmosphere of given mass and composition. The mass is determined by the interaction of the atmosphere with the sea and land and by exchange with the interplanetary space. The temperature, in turn, is determined by the amount and mode of energy deposition and loss. Heat is supplied to the atmosphere by solar radiation, both directly and from the surface; energy is lost via atmospheric emissions. We now consider the temperature structure in some detail.

The transport of heat in the troposphere occurs largely by convection from the ground, and hence we might expect that the temperature gradient follows the adiabatic lapse rate. This rate can be derived from the adiabatic relation for an ideal gas

$$P = A\rho^\gamma \tag{1}$$

and the perfect-gas law, Eq. (18.2-2). Here A is a constant and γ is the ratio of the specific heat at constant pressure to that at constant volume; that is, $\gamma = C_p/C_v$. Combining these two equations and differentiating yields

$$\frac{\partial T}{\partial h} = \frac{\mu m_H A}{k} (\gamma - 1) \rho^{(\gamma-2)} \frac{\partial \rho}{\partial h} \tag{2}$$

Differentiating the perfect-gas law and combining with the equation of hydrostatic equilibrium [Eq. (18.2-1)] gives

$$\frac{\partial \rho}{\partial h} = \frac{-g}{A\gamma} \frac{1}{\rho^{(\gamma-2)}} \tag{3}$$

Equations (18.6-2) and (18.6-3) yield

$$\frac{\partial T}{\partial h} = \frac{-\mu m_H}{k} \frac{g(\gamma - 1)}{\gamma} \tag{4}$$

The standard thermodynamic relation, $C_p - C_v = k/\mu m_H$, and the definition of γ reduce this expression to

$$\frac{\partial T}{\partial h} = - \frac{g}{C_p} \tag{5}$$

Equation (18.6-5) gives $-dT/dz$ of about $10°\mathrm{K/km}$. The observed lapse rate is usually between 5 and $8°\mathrm{K/km}$, and the departure from the adiabatic lapse rate is caused by the presence of water vapor. The observed rate can approach the adiabatic lapse rate on hot, dry days.

The troposphere stops and the stratosphere (isothermal region) begins because of heating caused by the absorption of infrared radiation by CO_2, H_2O, and O_3. The infrared radiation comes from the ground and from the atmosphere above and below the stratosphere. The temperature increases to a maximum in the mesosphere caused by ultraviolet absorption by ozone. Note that some authors define the stratosphere as extending up to the first temperature maximum. We do not follow this confusing convention. The region above the temperature maximum is heated largely by convection. Some insight into the mechanisms determining the temperature distribution can be obtained from the equation (see below) for the temperature distribution in the thermosphere.

The mechanism for heating the thermosphere is not entirely known. However, the lower thermosphere has a temperature gradient of some $6°\mathrm{K/km}$, and there is a downward flow of heat by conduction. The source of energy for the thermosphere may be simply the solar ultraviolet radiation or mechanical energy. Mechanical energy could be supplied, for example, by hydromagnetic waves generated by collisions of ionized gas clouds in the interplanetary medium with the outermost reaches of the geomagnetic field. The temperature profile in the higher parts of the thermosphere is rather uncertain.

If we assume that only photoionization and dissociation are important energy sources, the heat-budget equation can be written as

$$\frac{\partial}{\partial t}\left(\frac{3}{2}NkT\right) = \frac{\partial}{\partial h}\left(K\frac{\partial T}{\partial h}\right) + \frac{1}{2}[\pi F]\epsilon \alpha N(h)e^{-\tau/\mu} - R(h) \qquad (6)$$

where N is the density, k is Boltzmann's constant, T is the temperature, K is the thermal conductivity, $[\pi F]$ is the total solar flux in the relevant spectral region with the factor of $\frac{1}{2}$ allowing for heat flow on the nightside, ϵ is the fraction of the absorbed solar radiant energy which appears as heat, α is the total absorption coefficient for the relevant spectral region, $d\tau = -N\alpha\,dh$, $\mu = \cos\chi$ (where χ is the angular zenith distance), and $R(h)$ is the rate of thermal emission. Equation (18.6-6) can be integrated with the assumption of a steady state to yield

$$K\frac{dT}{dh} = \frac{1}{2}[\pi F]\epsilon\mu(1 - e^{-\tau/\mu}) - \int_h^\infty R(h)\,dh \qquad (7)$$

Physically, this equation states that the net downward heat flow at any point in the thermosphere is equal to the amount deposited above this point less the total amount which is lost through thermal radiation. Since the thermal loss term depends on the temperature, an iterative procedure must be adopted to solve Eq. (18.6-7) for the temperature T as a function of h.

In the terrestrial atmosphere, thermal emission (cooling) occurs in the mesosphere through CO_2 emission and in the thermosphere by a forbidden line of 0 I at 63 μ. The techniques described here can be used to obtain a temperature distribution for the terrestrial atmosphere, and this information is presented in Fig. 18.11-1.

In the exosphere, the temperature, defined in terms of the random motions, continually decreases, since the high-energy particles are more and more depleted by escape as one moves upward in the exosphere (Sec. 18.7).

18.7 THE EXOSPHERE AND THE NIGHT-SKY LYMAN-α RADIATION: OBSERVATIONS AND INTERPRETATION

One of the most important discoveries of rocket photometry and spectroscopy is the fact that the night sky when viewed from above 100 km is rather bright in the resonance line of neutral hydrogen, Lyman-α. The discussion of these observations properly belongs in Sec. 18.10; it is included here because of its great importance in the study of the terrestrial exosphere. This line lies at 1,216 A, and hence it is absorbed by molecular oxygen, O_2. It can only be observed from rockets higher than about 100 km above the Earth's surface (Fig. 7.2-1).

Lyman-α radiation was first observed in 1955. However, the intensity was much higher than expected, and all of the Lyman-α photon counters saturated quickly. A subsequent flight with a photometer in a tumbling rocket which scanned the entire sky both toward and away from the Earth gave the following information. The night sky was almost uniformly bright in the Lyman-α radiation with an intensity corresponding to an apparent emission rate of some $2,500R$. (This symbol is explained in the next paragraph.) When the photometer looked back at the Earth from some 120 km, it saw that about 42 per cent of the incoming radiation was reflected from the atmospheric layers below. Thus we say that the upper atmosphere at about 120 km has an albedo of about 42 per cent to this radiation. There was also a slight minimum in the antisolar direction.

The symbol R stands for a Rayleigh, which indicates that $4\pi I = 10^6$ photons/$(cm^2\ col)(sec)$. For the case when secondary scattering can be neglected,

$$4\pi I = \int_{\text{column}} \epsilon(r)\ dr \tag{1}$$

where $\epsilon(r)$ is the emission rate, in photons per cubic centimeter. This equation is easily derived for a photometer with a field of view of Ω steradians and photocathode area A looking into a plane-parallel stratified emitting atmosphere with an emission rate which is isotropic. From each cubic centimeter at distance r, the photometer receives $\epsilon(r)A/4\pi r^2$ photons. However, each distance r contributes Ωr^2 cm^3, and hence the total from distance r is $\epsilon(r)A\Omega/4\pi$. Since the intensity is in terms of unit area and solid angle, A and Ω drop out, and an integration over r (line of sight) gives Eq. (18.7-1) if the atmosphere is assumed to be optically thin.

The observed apparent emission rate of $2,500R$ is readily related to the number of hydrogen atoms per unit column that would have to be directly illuminated by solar Lyman-α to produce the diffuse, night-sky Lyman-α. If the function $\epsilon(r)$ in Eq. (18.7-1) is due to scattering in a uniformly illuminated column of atoms, we may write

$$4\pi I = \int_{\text{column}} N_H(r)g\ dr = gN_I \tag{2}$$

Here N_I is the column density of neutral hydrogen atoms and the number of photons scattered per second per atom is

$$g = [\pi F_\nu]\ \frac{\pi e^2}{m_e c}f \tag{3}$$

where $[\pi F_\nu]$ is the solar flux in photons per square centimeter per unit frequency interval and f is the f value or oscillator strength. Equation

(18.7-3) follows from Eq. (4.3-26). The quantity $[\pi F_\nu]$ is calculated from the measured flux in Lyman-α of about 6 ergs/(cm²)(sec) and the measured width of some 1 A (Sec. 7.3). Then, we find that approximately 1×10^{12} hydrogen atoms/(cm² col) are needed to produce the observed night-sky Lyman-α radiation by direct illumination. If secondary scatterings are involved, then 1×10^{12} atoms/(cm² col) is a lower limit.

The possibility of an interplanetary origin for the night-sky Lyman-α radiation was discussed and discarded in Sec. 8.5, even though we should remember the possibility of a small but significant contribution from neutral hydrogen moving at several hundred kilometers per second. Thus, it is necessary to turn our attention to models of the hydrogen distribution about the Earth. Two general types of model have been proposed. The first consists of a relatively thin shell of neutral hydrogen of substantial $(\tau \gtrsim 1)$ optical thickness close to the Earth $(r < 3R_\oplus)$. On this model multiple scattering is important; the fairly large densities needed on the night side may be obtainable through a fairly large diurnal variation in the hydrogen with a maximum on the night side. The second type of model envisions a cometlike distribution of neutral hydrogen with the bulk of the scattered radiation coming from hydrogen with $r > 5$ to $10R_\oplus$; here single scattering predominates and the escaping portion of neutral hydrogen is significant. The outer boundary of this cloud, the geocoma, is determined by charge exchange with solar protons.

To pursue this question, we need to consider the concept of a planetary exosphere. Sufficiently high in the atmosphere, collisions are so rare and the mean free path is so great that atoms may escape from an underlying layer of greater density. That a situation such as this must exist was realized over a hundred years ago. Atoms are injected into the exosphere from its base, the critical level. We shall consider that collisions are important enough to establish a maxwellian velocity distribution up to the critical level and that they are negligible beyond. Obviously, this is a simplified concept; nevertheless, it is a very useful one.

The height of the critical level h_c can be determined from the condition that a fraction $1/e$ of a group of fast particles moving upward at h_c will experience no collisions as they continue to ascend. If an atom of radius a moves through an atmosphere of similar particles, the effective cross section for scattering is $\pi(2a)^2$ or $4\pi a^2$. The probability of collision in traversing a region of thickness dh is then

$$4\pi a^2 N(h)\, dh \tag{4}$$

If, for simplicity, we consider the atmosphere to be isothermal,

$$N(h - h_c) = N(h_c)e^{-(h-h_c)/H} \tag{5}$$

then the density at the critical level is defined by the equation

$$1 = \int_{h_c}^{\infty} 4\pi a^2 N(h_c)e^{-(h-h_c)/H}\, dh \tag{6}$$

where H is the scale height. Note that the quantity on the right-hand side of the equation given above is essentially an "optical depth for collisions." Hence, when it has the value 1 (as in the above equation), an atom traveling upward has a probability $1/e$ of making a collision as required by our definition of the critical level. Thus, we find

$$N(h_c) = (4\pi a^2 H)^{-1} \tag{7}$$

Notice that this result states that at the critical level the mean free path for a particle moving rapidly in the horizontal direction equals the scale height H. For neutral atoms, a can be taken as the radius of an oxygen or nitrogen atom (about 1.5×10^{-8} cm) and T is about $1500°$K. This places the critical level at about 550 km. It is unlikely that this value is seriously in error. The critical level is higher for ions even without a magnetic field present because long-range interactions are important.

After fixing the temperature and density at the critical level, let us consider the kinds of particles in orbits expected in the exosphere:

1. Particles with less than the escape velocity which have come up to the level concerned on elliptic paths from the critical level; these are called the ballistic particles.

2. Particles with less than the escape velocity whose perigees lie above the critical level, called the trapped or satellite particles. These come about because there are still some collisions above the critical level which tend to populate these orbits. In any specific case, consideration must be given to the rates of injection and removal to determine the population in this group.

3. (a) Escaping particles whose perigees lie below the critical level. (b) Particles with velocities greater than the escape velocity that are being captured from space with resultant perigees below the critical level.

4. Particles with velocities greater than the escape velocity with perigees above the critical level.

In most practical cases, groups 3b and 4 are not present. As mentioned above, group 2 particles may or may not be present. With the various definitions and simplifications, the density distribution of each of these groups of particles can be calculated if the temperature and the density of the constituent can be specified at the critical level. Let us now consider the case of neutral hydrogen in the Earth's atmosphere.

There is very little "fossil," free hydrogen in the Earth's atmosphere, because the time of escape is very short when compared to the age of the Earth (Sec. 18.8). Free hydrogen in the terrestrial atmosphere is produced near the 80-km level by the photodissociation of methane and water vapor. This hydrogen diffuses upward into the higher altitudes until it reaches the critical level; then it is injected into the exosphere. Calculations concerning the production and diffusion of neutral hydrogen generally give

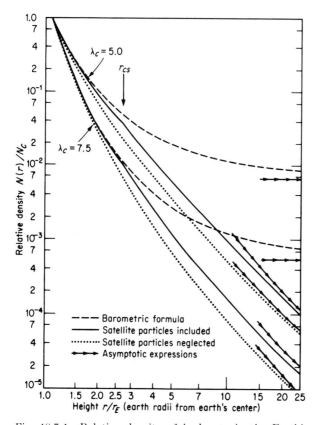

Fig. 18.7-1   Relative density of hydrogen in the Earth's
exosphere: the parameter $\lambda_c = GMm/kT_cR_c$, where the notation follows that of Sec. 18.8 and R_c is the geocentric distance
to the critical level, taken at 500-km altitude above the
surface. The values of λ_c of 5.0 and 7.5 correspond to
exospheric temperatures of 1407°K and 938°K, respectively.
All possible satellite particles are included out to the level
marked r_{cs}. (*Courtesy of J. W. Chamberlain, Kitt Peak
National Observatory, see also R 18.7-1.*)

number densities of hydrogen at the critical level of about 1×10^4 per cm³.
The distribution of neutral hydrogen in an exospheric model can now be
calculated (Fig. 18.7-1).

The results of exospheric calculations appear to support the geocoma
hypothesis, because substantial densities are found at large geocentric
distances. Densities of the correct order of magnitude to explain the
Lyman-α observations can be obtained, particularly if the cylindrical dis-
tortion by the solar wind is considered. Some radiation, of course, does
come from multiple scattering, but the amount is uncertain. Observations
of the night-sky Lyman-α with an atomic hydrogen absorption cell assign

a radiation temperature of some 8000°K, which agrees with the requirement of the 42 per cent albedo. If the observations are accepted, they
favor the geocoma hypothesis (if we also consider that the existence of
hot interplanetary hydrogen is improbable), since the lower exosphere
(responsible for this radiation on the multiple scattering hypothesis) is
at a temperature of 1000 to 1500°K. Hot hydrogen is easily produced by
charge exchange between geocoma particles and protons in the solar wind.

The situation is not at all settled and may be drastically revised
when additional data become available. We wish to emphasize that *all*
numerical data involved with this problem are very uncertain, a fact
which contributes greatly to the unsettled situation. In addition, we now
have observations which are spread over several years, and hence the
likelihood of a variation with the solar cycle must be considered.

18.8   ESCAPE OF PLANETARY ATMOSPHERES

The basic theory of the escape of particles from a planetary atmosphere
was given years ago by Jeans. From our discussion of planetary exo-
spheres, it is clear that the escape flux comes from group $3a$ particles
(i.e., escaping particles with perigees below the critical level).

Hence, at the critical level we simply count all particles whose velocity vector lies in the outbound hemisphere with magnitude equal to or
greater than the velocity of escape. Thus, the escape flux, assuming a
maxwellian velocity distribution, becomes

$$F_{esc} = \frac{2\pi N_c}{U^3 \pi^{3/2}} \int_{v_{esc}}^{\infty} \int_{0}^{\pi/2} e^{-v^2/U^2} v^3 \cos\theta \sin\theta \, d\theta \, dv \tag{1}$$

where N_c is the density of the escaping species at the critical level and
$U = (2kT/m)^{1/2}$, with m the mass of the escaping particles. Equation
(18.8-1) can be integrated to yield

$$F_{esc} = \frac{N_{0,i}U}{2\pi^{1/2}} \left(\frac{YR_0}{R_c} + 1 \right) e^{-Y} \tag{2}$$

where

$$Y = \frac{GmM}{kT_cR_0} = \left(\frac{V_{esc,0}}{U} \right)^2 \tag{3}$$

Here we write the escape flux in its historical form in terms of $N_{0,i}$, a fictitious density at the planet's surface (denoted by R_0). It has been assumed that the entire atmosphere is isothermal at the exospheric temperature T_c to write the density N_c at the height R_c of the critical level
in terms of $N_{0,i}$. This involves the use of the equation for hydrostatic
equilibrium of a spherical atmosphere which gives

$$N_c \exp\left(-\frac{GmM}{kTR_c} \right) = N_0 \exp\left(-\frac{GmM}{kTR_0} \right) \tag{4}$$

The total number of escaping particles L is then

$$
\begin{aligned}
L &= 4\pi R_c{}^2 F_{\text{esc}} \\
&= \frac{4\pi R_0{}^2 N_{0,i} U}{2\pi^{1/2}} e^{-Y} Y \left[\left(\frac{R_c}{R_0} \right) \left(1 + \frac{R_c}{Y R_0} \right) \right]
\end{aligned} \tag{5}
$$

Notice that R_c appears only in the term in brackets; usually $R_c \approx R_0$ and $Y \gg 1$. Hence, in the further discussion we neglect the term in brackets.

Somewhat more sophisticated analyses have been applied to the problem of planetary escape; however, these investigations show that the essential features are contained in Eq. (18.8-5), as long as diffusion is sufficiently rapid to permit the escape flux below the critical level. To determine an escape time during which the total number of particles in our isothermal atmosphere falls by e^{-1}, we divide the total number of particles by L. Hence,

$$
t_1 = \frac{2\pi^{1/2} H_{0,i} e^Y}{U Y} = \frac{\pi^{1/2} U e^Y}{g Y} \tag{6}
$$

Here, $H_{0,i}$ is the fictitious scale height in our isothermal atmosphere at the surface, and we have used Eq. (18.2-14).

Now we must allow for the fact that the total number of particles in a real atmosphere is usually different from the number in our fictitious, isothermal atmosphere. Thus, the time scale we seek is

$$
t_2 = t_1 B \tag{7}
$$

where

$$
B = \frac{N_0 H_0}{N_{0,i} H_{0,i}} = \frac{N_0 T_0}{N_{0,i} T_c} \tag{8}
$$

Again we have used Eq. (18.2-14).

The standard procedure is to assume that the atmosphere is mixed to a certain height and in diffusive equilibrium beyond (Sec. 18.4). For the terrestrial atmosphere, the changeover occurs at about 120 km, and hence we express the ratio $N_0/N_{0,i}$ as the product of N_0/N_{120} times $N_{120}/N_{0,i}$. This treatment assumes that the atmosphere is isothermal above 120 km at the exospheric temperature. This is likely to be an oversimplification, but the temperature in the atmosphere above 120 km is not known accurately. If the atmosphere is mixed to 120 km, then N_0/N_{120} is simply equal to the ratio of the total densities at these levels or [(3 × 10^{19} per cm³)/(5 × 10^{11} per cm³)] = 6 × 10^7. Also, $N_{120}/N_{0,i}$ can be computed from the usual isothermal formula [Eq. (17.2-5)]. Hence,

$$
B = 6 \times 10^7 \left(\frac{273}{T_c} \right) e^{-(120/H)} \tag{9}
$$

Table 18.8-1   Values of B [Eq. (18.2-9)] for the Earth

Element	Temperature, °K		
	500	1000	2000
H	2×10^7	1×10^7	8×10^6
He	1×10^7	9×10^6	6×10^6
O	3×10^5	2×10^6	3×10^6
N_2	1×10^5	3×10^5	1×10^6
Ar	4×10^2	5×10^4	5×10^5

where H is the scale height in kilometers computed for the species in question with the exospheric temperature T_c. Values of B for various species and values of T_c are given in Table 18.8-1. For Venus, Jupiter, and Saturn (included here because planetary escape was not considered in Chap. 17) we adopt $B = 1$, which is not grossly inconsistent with our knowledge concerning the atmospheres of these planets. The B values for Mars are taken to be the same as the values for Earth.

Finally, with the adopted values of B and Eqs. (18.8-7) and (18.8-6), we tabulate the various escape times for a variety of elements in the atmospheres of Venus, Earth, Mars, Jupiter, and Saturn in Table 18.8-2. The shorter times are not valid, because diffusion limits the escape (see R 18.8-2).

18.9   THE MAGNETOSPHERE

It has been known or suspected for centuries that a magnetic field is associated with the Earth. As measurements became available, various representations for the field were proposed; a simple and reasonably accurate approximation is the use of a centered dipole. Here we are interested only in the field above the Earth's surface.

A centered dipole of magnetic moment M has a magnetic field given by

$$B = \frac{M}{r^3} (1 + 3 \sin^2 \lambda_m)^{1/2} \tag{1}$$

where r is the geocentric distance and λ_m is the magnetic latitude. The components in the radial r and tangential λ directions are given by

$$B_r = - \frac{2M \sin \lambda_m}{r^3} \tag{2}$$

$$B_\lambda = \frac{M \cos \lambda_m}{r^3} \tag{3}$$

Table 18.8-2 Escape times t_2, in years, for several planets and exospheric temperatures*

Element	Earth			Mars			Venus		Jupiter	Saturn
	500°K	1000°K	2000°K	500°K	1000°K	2000°K	500°K	1000°K	130°K	100°K
H	1×10^8	8×10^4	3×10^3	7×10^3	3×10^3	2×10^3	6×10^{-1}	3×10^{-3}	10^{716}	10^{325}
He	3×10^{26}	4×10^{13}	3×10^7	4×10^6	2×10^4	2×10^3	5×10^{15}	8×10^4	10^{2870}	10^{1316}
O	7×10^{102}	4×10^{51}	8×10^{25}	2×10^{20}	6×10^{10}	1×10^6	8×10^{81}	4×10^{37}	—	—
N₂	3×10^{179}	1×10^{90}	7×10^{44}	4×10^{35}	5×10^{17}	2×10^9	7×10^{148}	7×10^{70}	—	—
Ar	4×10^{257}	1×10^{128}	6×10^{63}	9×10^{48}	6×10^{24}	5×10^{12}	8×10^{214}	2×10^{104}	—	—

* See the text for discussion.

The equation for a line of force follows from Eqs. (18.9-2) and (18.9-3) and the fact that the field is tangent to it; hence,

$$\frac{dr}{r\,d\lambda_m} = \frac{B_r}{B_\lambda} = -2\tan\lambda_m \tag{4}$$

or

$$r = r_1\cos^2\lambda_m \tag{5}$$

where r_1 is the distance to the line of force at the magnetic equator.

For the Earth, $M = 8 \times 10^{25}$ gauss-cm^3, corresponding to $B \approx \frac{1}{2}$ gauss on the Earth's surface. The axis of the centered dipole does not coincide with the Earth's axis of rotation; the North magnetic pole is at latitude 78° N, longitude 69° W, which corresponds to a position near Thule, Greenland. Thus the magnetic axis is inclined some 12° to the axis of rotation. We do not pursue the question of the origin of the terrestrial field here, although it may be related to planetary rotation (Sec. 15.7). Significant changes in the field in the past may be inferred from studies of fossil magnetism in rocks; the field may even have reversed polarity.

The type of magnetic field described by Eqs. (18.9-1) to (18.9-3) with the inverse-cube falloff is thought to hold at least to several Earth radii, but possible complications caused by a "ring current" of Van Allen belt particles should be noted. Near $10R_\oplus$ and close to the Sun-Earth line the regular magnetic field is terminated and an irregular or chaotic field is found. At about $14R_\oplus$ (still near the Sun-Earth line) a bow wave or shock front is found, and outside this one finds the essentially undisturbed interplanetary field. These features are shown in Fig. 18.9-1; note that the numbers given refer only to the sunward direction. The inner boundary can be called the magnetopause, and this boundary appears to be stable in the solar wind flow. The nature of the field between the two boundaries is quite uncertain. It is the outer boundary that has been called (in the literature) the geomagnetic cutoff and also the standoff distance.

The general location of the region of transition from the geomagnetic field to the interplanetary field can be calculated, because it basically must be determined by a pressure balance between the solar wind on the outside and the geomagnetic field on the inside. A simple picture is to assume that the solar wind particles are elastically reflected from the outer boundary of the magnetosphere, which is assumed to be sharp. Then,

$$\frac{B_c{}^2}{8\pi} = 2N_e m_\mathrm{H} w^2 \cos^2\theta \tag{6}$$

Here N_e is the interplanetary electron density, m_H is the mass of the hydrogen atom, w is the expansion velocity of the plasma, θ is the angle

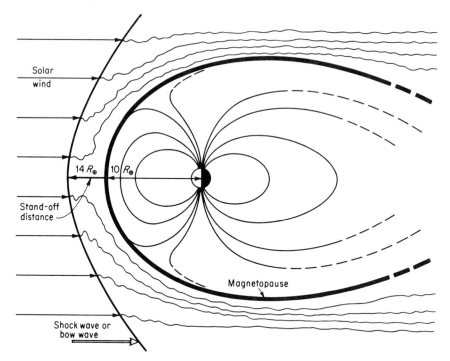

Fig. 18.9-1   Schematic diagram of the terrestrial magnetic field and its termination.

between the point on the boundary and the Sun-Earth line as seen from the center of the Earth, and B_c is the value of the magnetic field at the boundary.

In practice, the solution of this problem is rather difficult, since the problem is a free-boundary one in which the boundary itself must be determined. In addition, the boundary is determined by conditions at the boundary which are not preassigned. Finally, the detailed physical nature of the interaction between particles and fields at the boundary must be included.

Calculations which are available indicate that considerable compression of the geomagnetic field occurs on the sunward side. This compression amounts to a factor of 2.6; hence, the distance of the transition region on the Sun-Earth line can be obtained from Eqs. (18.9-1) and (18.9-6) by assuming a pressure balance; hence,

$$\frac{1}{8\pi}\left(\frac{2.6M}{r_c{}^3}\right)^2 = 2N_e m_H w^2 \tag{7}$$

or

$$r_c = \left[\frac{(2.6)^2 M^2}{16\pi N_e m_H w^2}\right]^{1/6}$$

For $N_e = 4$ per cm^3 and $w = 5 \times 10^7$ cm/sec, we find $r_c \approx 10R_\oplus$. The compression of the geomagnetic field increases the distance of the boundary by a factor of 1.37.

The existence of the bow wave or shock front makes possible a qualitative explanation of the discrepancy between the plasma probe results obtained from Mariner II and Explorer X mentioned in Sec. 8.4. Mariner II was far from any terrestrial influences, while Explorer X was apparently near the magnetopause and certainly within the shock front. The shock tends to thermalize the particles passing through it, and hence the temperature (in terms of random motions) is increased; this tends to decrease the velocity and increase the density. Qualitatively, all of these effects are found when comparing the Mariner II data with the Explorer X data. Hence, it is important to realize that the Explorer X measurements refer not to the interplanetary medium, but rather to the transition zone between the shock front and the magnetopause.

Whistlers

Lightning strokes provide a method of obtaining information concerning electron densities in the magnetosphere. Radio waves produced by lightning are channeled along the Earth's magnetic field between the northern and southern hemisphere. These waves are audio wavelengths, and they receive their name from their sound when reproduced over a loudspeaker. Multiple reflections from hemisphere to hemisphere are possible; this results in groups with equal spacing between individual whistlers. Whistlers with clicks originate in the same hemisphere as the observer and one detects a signal at 0 (the lightning stroke or click), 2, 4, 6, . . . trips over the path. If the lightning stroke originates in the opposite hemisphere, no click is usually heard, and the signal is detected after 1, 3, 5, 7, . . . trips along the path (Fig. 18.9-2).

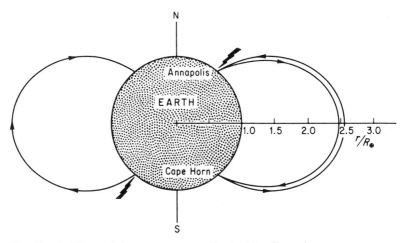

Fig. 18.9-2   The whistler geometry; see the text for discussion.

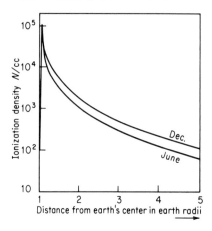

Fig. 18.9-3   The electron density in the whistler medium from 1955 to 1959. [*From R. L. Smith and R. A. Helliwell, J. Geophys. Res.*, **65**: 2583 (1960).]

Successive whistlers in a group have a rate of change of the pitch (frequency) which decreases from one whistler to the next. This delay is a function of the electron density and the magnetic field along the path. If the magnetic field is assumed, then whistlers yield information concerning the electron density. It must be possible to determine the true path of the whistler. This can be done with a so-called nose whistler, which consists of a rising and falling component on a record of frequency versus time; the two components join at the nose frequency. Electron densities derived from studies of nose whistlers are given in Fig. 18.9-3. The origin of the whistler medium is discussed in Sec. 18.4.

An annual variation of the electron density in the magnetosphere is clearly shown in Fig. 18.9-3. Some workers have interpreted this result as indicating an annual variation in the environment of the Earth as it moves along its orbit.

The Van Allen belts

One of the most entertaining results of rocket and satellite investigations has been the discovery by Van Allen and his associates of two zones of radiation which surround our planet. They can be detected with satellite-borne Geiger tubes. The general location of these two belts has been established by numerous rocket and satellite probes; the approximate location is shown in Fig. 18.9-4. It was soon established that the source of the observed radiation must be charged particles (i.e., electrons and protons) trapped in the Earth's magnetic field. This possibility had been considered much earlier in other connections by Störmer and Alfvén. Let us now investigate how this trapping of charge particles can take place.

The basic equation of motion for a charged particle is

$$m \frac{d\mathbf{v}}{dt} = q(\mathbf{E} + \mathbf{v} \times \mathbf{B}) \tag{8}$$

where m = particle mass, g
   $\mathbf{v}$ = velocity, cm/sec
   q = charge, emu (charge on the electron = $-e/c$)
   $q\mathbf{E}$ = electrostatic force
   $\mathbf{E}$ = field strength, emu

and the magnetic force is $q\mathbf{v} \times \mathbf{B}$, where $\mathbf{B}$ is measured in gauss. The notation here is the same as in Sec. 6.2. For the case at hand, we may consider that $\mathbf{E}$ vanishes; the acceleration then becomes $(q/m)\mathbf{v} \times \mathbf{B}$. This acceleration is perpendicular to the velocity and thus does no work on the particle; hence, the scalar velocity v does not change. If $\mathbf{E}$ vanishes and $\mathbf{B}$ = const (space and time), then the particle must move in a circle of radius a if $\mathbf{v}$ is initially perpendicular to $\mathbf{B}$. In this case, the acceleration may be set equal to the centrifugal acceleration v^2/a to obtain

$$\frac{v}{a} = \omega_c = \frac{qB}{m} \tag{9}$$

where ω_c is the "cyclotron" frequency. If $\mathbf{v}$ is not initially perpendicular to $\mathbf{B}$, we must use the perpendicular component $v_\perp$, and a can be written as

$$a = \frac{v_\perp}{\omega_c} = \frac{v_\perp m}{qB} \tag{10}$$

The quantity a is called the radius of gyration. The magnetic field does not affect the component of velocity parallel to the magnetic field, $v_\parallel$. Hence, the general motion for the case of $\mathbf{E} = 0$ and $\mathbf{B}$ = const will be a

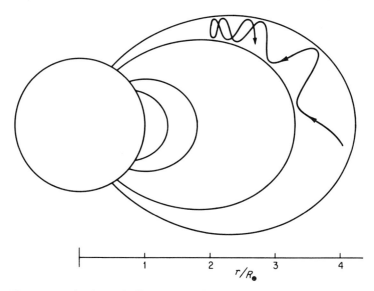

Fig. 18.9-4   A schematic diagram showing the inner and outer Van Allen belts and trapped particles.

helix of constant pitch around a line of force. The instantaneous center of gyration is called the guiding center of the particle.

If **B** varies slowly with position, the magnetic moment of a charged particle is nearly constant. The magnetic moment μ of a current I encircling an area S is IS. For the case considered above, $S = \pi a^2$ (a = radius of gyration), and I is simply the charge q times the number of gyrations per second. We have

$$\mu = \pi a^2 \frac{q\omega_c}{2\pi} \tag{11}$$

With expressions given above for a and ω_c, this last equation can be written as

$$\mu = \frac{mv_\perp{}^2}{2B} \tag{12}$$

From this expression, we see that the gyrating particles will tend to be reflected from regions of higher magnetic field. Suppose $v_\parallel$ takes the particle into a region of increasing magnetic field. Then $v_\perp$ must increase to keep μ constant, but it can increase only until it is equal to the total velocity, at which time $v_\parallel$ has fallen to zero. Thus, the particles are reflected back into a region of lower magnetic field. If θ_0 is the pitch angle at the point of injection and B_0 is the magnetic field at that point, the constancy of the magnetic moment implies

$$\frac{\sin^2 \theta}{B} = \frac{\sin^2 \theta_0}{B_0} \tag{13}$$

Reflection will occur when $\sin^2 \theta = 1$, and this occurs when

$$B = \frac{B_0}{\sin^2 \theta_0} \tag{14}$$

This kind of region may be called a magnetic mirror (Fig. 18.9-4). Regions similar to the simple example presented above occur around the Earth because of the nature of the dipole geomagnetic field (Fig. 18.9-4). These cusp-shaped regions are actually toroidal, because the particles drift longitudinally owing to the inhomogeneous magnetic field. For an electron, the drift is in the direction $\nabla \mathbf{B} \times \mathbf{B}$. Drifts can also be caused by gravitational and electric fields with components perpendicular to the magnetic field; in the latter case, the particle moves in the direction $\mathbf{E} \times \mathbf{B}$, a result which is independent of the sign of the particle's charge. These drifts (due to electric fields) are related to the Hall current, mentioned in Sec. 6.2. These simple examples explain the general shape of the Van Allen belts.

Let us consider the question of the origin of the Van Allen particles. Three general sources have been suggested:

1. The particles could be injected directly from the solar wind or plasma clouds.

2. The particles could be accelerated locally in the geomagnetic field.

3. The electrons could arise from β decay of neutrons. The neutrons would arise from collisions of primary cosmic-ray particles with nuclei of atmospheric nitrogen and oxygen.

There seems to be general agreement that sources 1 and 3 cannot alone supply the Van Allen particles. Thus, the choices available appear to be reduced to a mechanism involving acceleration in the geomagnetic field. This mechanism may be related to auroras. An acceptable mechanism should explain or be consistent with the fact that the inner belt appears to be stable with time, whereas the outer belt undergoes large variations, particularly during magnetic storms. Finally, it should be pointed out that the density of the Van Allen belts constitutes only a very small fraction of the density of the Earth's outer atmosphere.

Magnetic disturbances and solar-terrestrial relationships

The terrestrial magnetic field probably undergoes substantial changes with a fairly long time scale owing to causes originating within the Earth. Short time-scale variations are also measured with magnetometers; these appear to be of external origin and largely connected with the Sun and solar activity.

Smooth variations in the field are caused by the dynamo effect due to the motion of ionized material across the lines of force of the main field. These motions are tides (caused by the lunar and solar gravitational attraction) and atmospheric circulation due to solar heating. These smooth variations range from a few γ to a few tens of γ ($1\ \gamma = 10^{-5}$ gauss).

Major disturbances are called magnetic storms. A typical storm has a first phase which consists of a rise in the horizontal component of the field of a few tens of γ. After about an hour, the horizontal component begins a decrease to a strength some $10^2\ \gamma$ below normal. A minimum is reached after about a half day, and a time of the order of days is required for the return to normal. This decrease is the main phase, which may be associated with a ring current. Very large magnetic storms can have variations of $\sim\!10^3\ \gamma$. Variations can also occur in the form of a single excursion (either positive or negative) of $\sim\!10^2\ \gamma$ with a return to normal in a few hours. They are usually found near the auroral zones, and their appearance leads to the name *magnetic bay*.

The large magnetic storms seem to be associated with solar flares (discussed in Secs. 6.6 and 7.6). From the time between the flare and the onset of the magnetic storm a mean velocity of $\sim\!10^3$ km/sec has been derived. These large storms are also associated with solar radio emission (Sec. 7.6) and terrestrial aurora (Sec. 18.10).

The lesser magnetic storms are not easily associated with a particular solar phenomenon or area. The various indices used to describe the state of terrestrial magnetic agitation show a 27-day periodicity in the lesser storms; this fact led to the hypothesis of a region on the Sun which was magnetically active, the so-called M regions. These seem to be associated with unipolar magnetic regions of the Sun which appear to be at the locations of the extended coronal streamers (Sec. 6.8). This identification provides a reason for particle emission (presumed to cause the geomagnetic disturbance). The magnetic lines of force in the long coronal streamers appear to be radial for at least many solar radii near the Sun. Thus, it may well be easier for charged particles to escape from such a region than in the normal dipole (?) field where the field lines return to the Sun and are never very far from the surface.

Besides magnetic storms and auroras, solar-terrestrial relations include terrestrial effects of solar X-ray emission such as sudden ionosphere disturbances (SIDs) and radio fadeouts, and solar cosmic-ray emission such as polar cap absorption (PCAs).

18.10 RADIATION FROM PLANETARY ATMOSPHERES

Here we discuss radiation originating from local processes in planetary atmospheres and solar radiation scattered by planetary atmospheres. Emphasis is on those features which can be applied to Mars and Venus.

Auroras

The displays of aurora borealis and aurora australis have excited the imagination of men for many years. Considerable observational and theoretical effort has been devoted to the solution of the auroral problem, but essential understanding is yet to come.

For some time it was thought that auroras resulted from the direct action of high-energy solar particles which excited (through collisions with atmospheric constituents) the emissions we observe (primarily emission lines of N_2, N_2^+, and the forbidden lines of neutral oxygen, λ 5,577 and λ 6,300). It is very difficult for solar protons to penetrate the geomagnetic field and reach down to 100 km where auroras are observed. With the discovery of the Van Allen belts, a two-step process was imagined: Particles were trapped and stored in the outer radiation belt; at times of geomagnetic activity, particles are precipitated or "dumped" out of the ends of the radiation belt; the ends of the outer radiation belt coincide with the so-called auroral zones (located 23° from the geomagnetic poles), where the majority of auroras are observed. A suitable dumping mechanism does not seem to be available. This picture, based on long-term storage, is termed the "leaky bucket model." We note that the particles responsible for auroras are of higher flux and lower energy than the particles which constitute the Van Allen belts.

Some progress has been made from in situ observations made with satellites. These observations have confirmed the result known previously from spectroscopic analysis that the particles responsible for auroras are principally electrons; they seem to be *associated with* the outer radiation belt. From the measured particle densities and fluxes, it is established that the particles normally contained in a flux tube can supply the fluxes associated with auroras for only a few hours at most. In addition, the total energy in a flux tube can be computed and compared with energy (ergs per square centimeter) precipitated during auroras (computed from balloon observations of X rays or from optical observations). The amount of energy precipitated appears to be 1 to 2 orders of magnitude greater than that stored.

In view of the restrictions on the density of particles and their energies, it seems that particles (or alternatively, energy) must be constantly supplied to "aurora-producing" regions. It appears that the particles are injected into the geomagnetic field from a solar stream. They are then trapped and stored on a short-term basis, undergo magnetic reflections, and move toward the aurora-producing region, where they are accelerated and precipitated into the atmosphere to cause auroras. The radiation belts may well simply be a by-product of the auroral process. The acceleration mechanism is still obscure; perhaps the final answer is in terms of some kind of plasma instability.

Airglow

Here we briefly describe some of the processes leading to emission at discrete wavelengths in the terrestrial atmosphere. The situation as of 1961 is thoroughly covered in R 18.1-2.

The nightglow, or light of the night sky, probably arises from excitation by chemical reactions and recombination. It also properly includes solar radiation scattered by the distant atmosphere on the night side, such as the night-sky Lyman-α which was discussed in Sec. 18.7. There have been some reports of nightglow (or possibly auroral) emission from the night side of Venus. Subsequent observations have not confirmed the reality of this emission.

Considerable effort has been exerted in the study of the terrestrial twilight glow. This phenomenon occurs when sunset has already occurred on the ground but a part of the atmosphere is still sunlit. At present, these studies have little application to the atmosphere of other planets.

The study of the dayglow is growing in importance. This field will ultimately be essential to the study of the atmospheres of the other terrestrial planets. On Earth, we observe the dayglow from below the

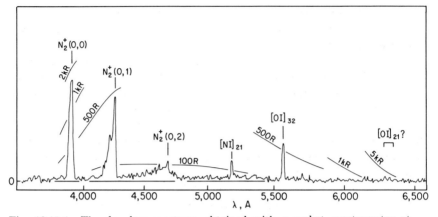

Fig. 18.10-1 The dayglow spectrum obtained with a rocket spectrometer at altitudes greater than 150 km. (*Courtesy of L. Wallace and R. A. Nidey, Kitt Peak National Observatory.*)

atmosphere, whereas, at least for some time, the dayglows of other planets will be observed from above.

The terrestrial dayglow arises from resonance scattering of solar radiation and through reactions beginning with a photoionization by incident solar radiation. The dayglow is difficult to observe from the ground (although some observations are possible) and rocket observations seem to be dictated. A spectral scan of the dayglow in the visible region obtained on a rocket flight is shown in Fig. 18.10-1.

Observations of dayglows on other planets will be hampered if appreciable continuous radiation is reflected upward by the atmosphere or the planetary surface. Hence, it may be advisable to seek emissions in the far ultraviolet, where little continuous radiation is expected. This would correspond to observations of scattered Lyman-α radiation on the day side of the Earth looking down, for example. Hydrogen may not be abundant on Mars or Venus, but it has been suggested that atomic oxygen could be abundant on Mars; and this could lead to an observable dayglow in the 1,302- to 1,306-A resonance multiplet. It should be emphasized that the radiative transfer techniques developed in Sec. 4.1 are applicable to the study of planetary emissions. These techniques are illustrated below in connection with the formation of weak absorption lines in planetary spectra. Numerous applications of the techniques of radiative transfer to discrete terrestrial emissions (including the dayglow) are found in R 18.1-2.

Transfer techniques and continuous radiation

Continuous radiation arises from the scattering of sunlight by dust particles and molecules. This problem includes the blue color and polarization of the day sky. Such problems are amenable to treatment by using the radiative transfer techniques. Studies of continuum radiation of other planets (such as the center-to-limb variation) can yield some information concerning the phase function of scattering [see Eq. (4.1-9)]. It is necessary to take account of radiation reflected from the surface. In fact, the transfer problem of a plane-parallel atmosphere illuminated from above by a parallel flux and from below by radiation reflected from the surface is called the planetary problem.

Here we illustrate the use of the transfer techniques by considering the formation of weak absorption lines in planetary spectra. Often the line profile is computed by assuming that there is pure absorption and that the incident beam traverses the atmosphere, is reflected at the surface, and passes back out of the atmosphere to the observer. Here the absorption is just twice the slant opacity, or in transfer notion (Sec. 4.1).

$$I = I_0 e^{-2(\tau_1/\mu)} \tag{1}$$

Unfortunately, Eq. (18.10-1) is valid only when all outbound radiation is reflected at the surface and when scattering is unimportant.

Consider now an infinite scattering atmosphere in which one finds an absorbing constituent which absorbs only near one frequency. Let σ be the scattering coefficient and K_ν the absorption coefficient; then the single scattering albedo (which gives the ratio of the amount of radiation scattered to the total amount removed from the beam) is

$$\tilde{\omega}_\nu = \frac{\sigma}{\sigma + K_\nu} \tag{2}$$

Obviously $\tilde{\omega}_\nu$ varies across the line and is 1 in the continuum. Here we consider that $\tilde{\omega}_\nu \approx 1$ always, and we adopt the monochromatic approximation (no redistribution of photons in frequency). For an infinite atmosphere illuminated by an incident flux $[\pi F]$, the reflected intensity is given by

$$I = \frac{\mu_0}{\mu + \mu_0} H_{\tilde{\omega}}(\mu) H_{\tilde{\omega}}(\mu_0) \frac{\tilde{\omega}_\nu F}{4} \tag{3}$$

This is just Equation (4.1-56), where we have included the subscript $\tilde{\omega}$ to emphasize that the H functions are a function of the albedo. Now, the desired quantity is

$$R_\nu = \frac{I_c - I_\nu}{I_c} \tag{4}$$

where I_c is the intensity in the continuum and I_ν is the intensity in the line. With Eq. (18.10-3) we have

$$R_\nu = 1 - \frac{H_{\tilde{\omega}}(\mu) H_{\tilde{\omega}}(\mu_0)}{H_1(\mu) H_1(\mu_0)} \tag{5}$$

where $H_1(\mu)$ denotes the H functions with $\tilde{\omega}_\nu = 1$. In the study of the H functions, it is found, for $\tilde{\omega}_\nu \approx 1$,

$$H_{\tilde{\omega}}(\mu) = \frac{H_1(\mu)}{1 + \mu[3(1 - \tilde{\omega}_\nu)]^{\frac{1}{2}}} \tag{6}$$

Substituting Eq. (18.10-6) into Eq. (18.10-5) and considering that $1 \gg \mu[3(1 - \tilde{\omega}_\nu)]^{\frac{1}{2}}$ gives

$$R_\nu = (\mu + \mu_0)[3(1 - \tilde{\omega}_\nu)]^{\frac{1}{2}} \tag{7}$$

Combining this last equation with Eq. (18.10-2) and recalling that $\sigma \gg K_\nu$ yields

$$R_\nu = 3^{\frac{1}{2}}(\mu + \mu_0)\left(\frac{K_\nu}{\sigma}\right)^{\frac{1}{2}} \tag{8}$$

Thus for weak lines, the absorption goes as the square root of the absorption coefficient.

It is often more convenient to compute the equivalent width,

$$W_\nu = \int R_\nu \, d\nu \tag{9}$$

For the interpretation of the CO_2 bands of Venus, the oscillator strengths are assumed to be equal, and hence the absorption coefficient is proportional to the population of the lower rotational level N_J involved in the transition. Thus,

$$W_\nu(J) = \text{const } N_J^{\frac{1}{2}} \tag{10}$$

From the equivalent widths in a band, we can derive the relative populations of the various rotational levels. If a Boltzmann distribution is assumed, a temperature appropriate to the region of reflection can be derived.

This concludes our example of the application of the techniques of radiative transfer to the study of planetary atmospheres.

18.11   MARS

The atmosphere of Mars is much rarer but otherwise somewhat similar to the Earth's. The atmosphere is transparent to visible radiation, and the surface gravity is not greatly different.

Composition

The only constituents of the Martian atmosphere which are definitely established are CO_2 and H_2O. If the pressure broadening is considered, one finds that CO_2 is some 2.2 per cent of the Martian atmosphere by volume; on the other hand, a curve of growth analysis gives some 20 per cent. The amount of H_2O is very small. Upper limits have been established spectroscopically for O_2, O_3, N_2O, CH_4, C_2H_2, C_2H_6, NH_3, N_2O_4, and CO; these species cannot be the major constituent of the Martian atmosphere. Escape times for H and He (Sec. 18.8) are very short, a fact which makes it unlikely that either of these elements is the major constituent. The choices invariably narrow down to N_2 and Ar, with N_2 being chosen by terrestrial analogy. It should be noted that this is an unproven assumption.

Structure

The thermocouple measurements give a temperature of some 270°K, which we take to be the temperature of the Martian atmosphere near the surface (Sec. 16.4). The scale height [Eq. (18.2-5)] can be computed for N_2; it is 21 km, or about two and a half times the terrestrial value. This means that the densities in the upper atmosphere of Mars are greater than those at the same altitude in the terrestrial atmosphere even though the terrestrial atmosphere has a higher density at the surface. This fact also means that various atmospheric layers, the mesopause, and the critical level are formed higher in the atmosphere.

The temperature distribution can be deduced by using the principles outlined in Sec. 18.6. The constituents in the atmosphere which are active in determining the temperature distribution are assumed to be CO_2 and CO. Other models are available which involve H_2O; some water was expected in the Martian atmosphere before its detection spectroscopically because the polar caps are thought to be hoar frost.

The adiabatic lapse rate for dry N_2 at the Martian surface is $-3.7°K/km$. The tropopause is placed at 8.5 km. The mesosphere extends from 8.5 km to some 130 km. There is no hot mesosphere on Mars owing to the lack of O_3. In fact, the energy loss in the infrared CO_2 bands keeps the temperature steadily decreasing up to the mesopause. Near the mesopause, CO_2 is dissociated into CO and O; in addition, this leads to a layer of O_2 near the mesopause. The thermal radiation of CO is rather efficient, and hence Mars has a fairly cool thermosphere and an exospheric temperature of 1100°K at the critical level height of 1,500 km. This temperature distribution is shown in Fig. 18.11-1 along with the terrestrial temperature distribution for comparison.

The available polarimetric and photometric data can be used to establish the pressure at the surface of Mars. With this information, our assumptions concerning the composition, and the temperature profile given in Fig. 18.11-1, the densities of the principal constituents can be computed. These are given in Fig. 18.11-2 along with the terrestrial values for comparison. However, these densities may be too high, since recent spectroscopic investigations find a surface pressure of 25 mb (some 2

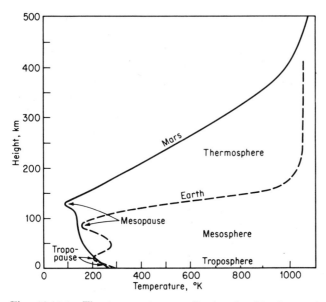

Fig. 18.11-1 The temperature profile in the Martian and terrestrial atmospheres. (*By J. W. Chamberlain in R* 18.6-1, *copyright* 1962 *by the University of Chicago, published by the University of Chicago Press.*)

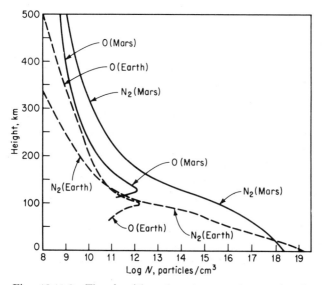

Fig. 18.11-2 The densities of major constituents in the Martian and terrestrial atmospheres. (*By J. W. Chamberlain in R* 18.6-1, *copyright* 1962 *by the University of Chicago, published by the University of Chicago Press.*)

per cent of the terrestrial value); the value used in the model given here is 85 mb at the surface.

The exospheric temperature of 1100°K allows the retention of atomic oxygen and opens the possibility of a substantial corona of neutral oxygen about Mars (analogous to the terrestrial hydrogen corona).

We reemphasize the tentative nature of models of the Martian atmosphere; the serious reader is referred to the literature for details and alternatives. Other effects such as the observed dust storms, blue haze, and seasonal changes in the polar caps may well be important in understanding the Martian atmosphere. These topics are discussed in Chap. 16.

Ionosphere

Rough estimates are available for the electron densities in the Martian ionospheric layers. The basic theory for the formation of ionospheric layers is given in Sec. 18.5.

The Martian E_1 probably exists near the mesopause with the photo-ionization of O_2 being balanced by dissociative recombination. The noon electron density is less than 10^5 per cm^3, and this layer disappears at night. An additional portion E_2 of the Martian E region results from ionization by X rays.

The Martian F layer arises from the photoionization of O (as does the terrestrial F layer). Recombination can occur through

$$O^+ + N_2 \rightarrow NO^+ + N \tag{1}$$

and

$$NO^+ + e \rightarrow N + O \tag{2}$$

At low altitudes, recombination is limited by Eq. (18.11-2), while Eq. (18.11-1) is the limiting process high in the atmosphere. For Mars, the rate of production of NO^+ by Eq. (18.11-1) is equal to its rate of destruction by Eq. (18.11-2) at some 700 km. This fixes the general area of the bifurcation into F_1 and F_2 regions. The F_1 region is analogous to the terrestrial case with its maximum N_e occurring near 320 km. The electron density is $\sim 10^5$ electrons/cm^3, and the Martian F_1 layer disappears at night. The F_2 region is above 700 km. The Martian F_2 layer is probably not as important as the terrestrial one, and it decays more rapidly at night.

Magnetosphere

No information concerning the magnitude or extent of the Martian magnetic field is available. General considerations concerning the origin of planetary magnetic field seem to depend on the rotation rate; hence, the magnetic field of Mars may be comparable to the Earth's Sec.15.7. The possibility of radiation belts has been considered.

18.12   VENUS

This planet is often called the sister planet of the Earth because of its proximity, size, and mass. We shall, however, see that the atmosphere is quite different.

Composition

The only definitely established constituent in the atmosphere of Venus is CO_2; there is weak evidence for small amounts of CO, and H_2O is probably absent. Upper limits of the abundance above the cloud tops are available for O_2, N_2O, NH_3, CH_2O, CH_4, C_2H_2, and C_2H_6.

The major constituent of the atmosphere of Venus is not known. The usual procedure is to assume some number ratio for CO_2/N_2 between 0.04 and 0.8. As on Mars, Ar could be important.

Structure

As we discussed in Sec. 18.10, the temperature associated with the CO_2 bands can be determined. This temperature (for bands near 8,000 A) is

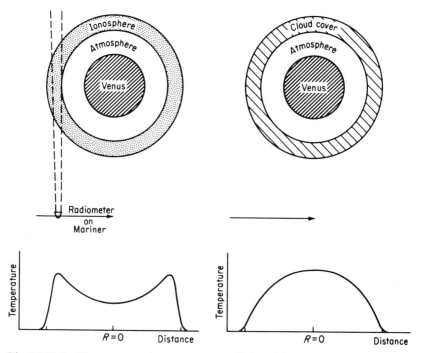

Fig. 18.12-1   The response of temperature vs. disk position expected for radiometer scans across Venus on the basis of the ionospheric model (left) and the hot-surface model (right). The Mariner II observations definitely favor the hot-surface model. (*See R* 18.12-3 *and R* 18.12-4.)

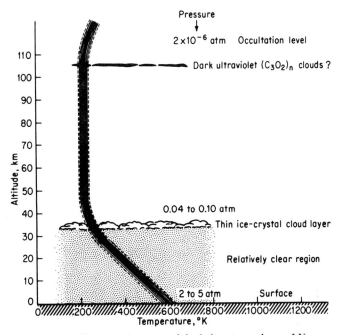

Fig. 18.12-2   The greenhouse model of the atmosphere of Venus. (*By W. W. Kellogg and C. Sagan in R* 18.11-1, *Courtesy of the National Academy of Sciences–National Research Council.*)

about 285° (but some interpretations give 300 to 400°K) and apparently refers to a region just below the cloud tops. However, radio measurements at 3 to 10 cm yield temperatures of approximately 600°K (see Fig. 16.3-3). Models that have been devised attribute the high-temperature radiation to the surface of Venus or to an ionosphere located at a height of ≈ 100 km. This issue appears to have been resolved with scans at 19-mm wavelength across the disk of Venus obtained from the Mariner II flyby. The response expected for the two cases is shown in Fig. 18.12-1; the Mariner II results confirm the existence of the hot surface. Allowing for absorption and the fact that the surface of Venus is not a perfect blackbody gives a preliminary estimate of the surface temperature of 700°K, in essential agreement with the earlier radio results.

Two models with rather similar temperature distributions are consistent with the observations. These are the greenhouse model and the aeolosphere model. On this latter model, the lower atmosphere is dusty and the surface is heated by hot, dry winds driven from high in the atmosphere. This model is related to the general question of atmospheric circulation, which is not well understood. The model also appears to encounter difficulties with the albedo and phase variation. The weight of opinion seems against the aeolosphere model, but the serious reader is reminded of the great uncertainties for *all* models.

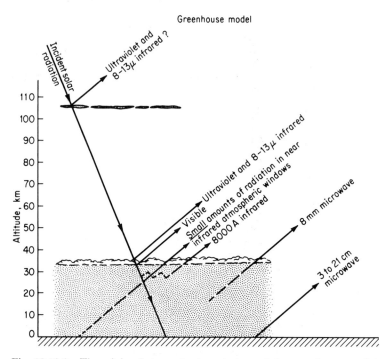

Fig. 18.12-3   The origin of atmospheric emissions of the greenhouse model. (*By W. W. Kellogg and C. Sagan in R 18.11-1, Courtesy of the National Academy of Sciences–National Research Council.*)

The greenhouse model seems to be growing in popularity. Here it is imagined that the atmosphere is relatively transparent to visible radiation, but that the atmosphere is opaque to the far-infrared thermal radiation from the surface. Substances such as H_2O and CO_2 could be effective in producing the greenhouse effect, but detailed calculations are difficult because of our basic lack of knowledge concerning the composition of the atmosphere below the cloud tops.

The dry adiabatic lapse rates for various mixtures of CO_2 and N_2 are usually close to $-10°K/km$. This gradient is assumed to hold from the surface to the cloud tops, which are taken to be at 230°K. Thus, the cloud layer is near 40 km. The atmosphere is taken to be isothermal from the main cloud layer up to a height of ≈ 100 km, which is near the occultation level and the level of the dark ultraviolet clouds. The temperature is thought to increase above 100 km. The greenhouse model for the temperature and related phenomena is shown in Fig. 18.12-2. The region of the various emissions in the atmosphere of Venus is shown in Fig. 18.12-3. The various types of clouds observed in the atmosphere of Venus are discussed in Chap. 16.

Little is known about the ionospheric layers of Venus or about the exosphere and related problems of atmospheric escape.

Magnetosphere

Some information concerning the magnetic field of Venus is available from Mariner II, which passed within 41,000 km of Venus and which carried charged-particle detectors and a magnetometer. No effect which could be definitely ascribed to Venus was detected. This result is obviously consistent with a magnetic moment M_v of zero. By considering various plausible models, an upper limit to the magnetic moment of Venus can be obtained in terms of the terrestrial magnetic moment; the result, albeit with considerable uncertainty, is $M_v/M_e \lesssim 0.1$. This result is of interest in itself, and also in terms of speculations concerning the interior of Venus. It is consistent with the idea that a slowly rotating planet would have a small magnetic field (Sec. 15.7).

BIBLIOGRAPHICAL NOTES

Section 18.1. The possible atmosphere of the planet Mercury is considered in R 18.11-2. For a discussion of atmospheric nomenclature, see:

R 18.1-1. Nicolet, M.: In "The Earth as a Planet," ed. G. P. Kuiper, pp. 644–712, The University of Chicago Press, Chicago, 1954.

R 18.1-2. Chamberlain, J. W.: "Physics of the Aurora and Airglow," Academic Press Inc., New York, 1961.

R 18.1-3. Mitra, S. K.: "The Upper Atmosphere," 2d ed., The Asiatic Society, Calcutta, 1952.

Section 18.2. See R 18.1-1 to R 18.1-3.

Section 18.3. See R 18.1-1 to R 18.1-3 and:

R 18.3-1. Bates, D. R.: In "The Earth as a Planet," ed. G. P. Kuiper, pp. 576–643, The University of Chicago Press, Chicago, 1954.

Section 18.4. See R 18.1-1 to R 18.1-3, R 18.3-1, R 18.5-1, and:

R 18.4-1. Ratcliffe, J. A. (ed.): "Physics of the Upper Atmosphere," Academic Press Inc., New York, 1960.

Section 18.5. See the references for Sec. 18.4. Sample measured electron densities and other results of experiments in space are presented in:

R 18.5-1. Rossi, B., and R. Jastrow: In "Science in Space," eds. L. V. Berkner and H. Odishaw, pp. 49–88, McGraw-Hill Book Company, New York, 1961.

Section 18.6. See R 18.1-1 to R 18.1-3 and:

R 18.6-1. Chamberlain, J. W.: *Astrophys. J.*, **136**: 582 (1962).

Section 18.7. A comprehensive review is given in:

R 18.7-1. Chamberlain, J. W.: *Planet. Space Sci.*, **11**: 901 (1963).

Section 18.8. The basic paper for planetary escape is:

R 18.8-1. Spitzer, L.: In "The Atmospheres of the Earth and Planets," ed. G. P. Kuiper, 2d ed., pp. 211–247, The University of Chicago Press, Chicago, 1952.

The limiting effect of diffusion is considered in:

R 18.8-2. Bates, D. R., and M. R. C. McDowell: *J. Atmos. Terrest. Phys.*, **11**: 200 (1957) and **16**: 393 (1959).

Section 18.9. The dipole field and various field representations are covered in R 18.1-2, which also covers the basic physics of trapped particles. The termination of the terrestrial field is reviewed in:

R 18.9-1. Hines, C. O.: *Science*, **141**: 130 (1963).

An introductory review of whistler studies is found in:

R 18.9-2. Helliwell, R. A., and M. G. Morgan: *Proc. IRE*, **47**: 200 (1959).

Models of the whistler medium and discussions of the annual variation (based on nose whistlers) are found in:

R 18.9-3. Smith, R. L.: *J. Geophys. Res.*, **66**: 3709 (1961).

R 18.9-4. Carpenter, D. L.: *J. Geophys. Res.*, **67**: 3345 (1962).

A review of the trapped-particle radiation belts with extensive references is given in:

R 18.9-5. Van Allen, J. A.: In "Science in Space," eds. L. V. Berkner and H. Odishaw, pp. 275–295, McGraw-Hill Book Company, New York, 1961.

Later measurements and discussions are found in:

R 18.9-6. O'Brien, B. J.: *Space Sci. Rev.*, **1**: 415 (1963).

R 18.9-7. Frank, L. A., J. A. Van Allen, and E. Macagno: *J. Geophys. Res.*, **68**: 3543 (1963).

Solar-terrestrial relationships and magnetic storms are discussed in R 18.1-2, R 18.1-3, and:

R 18.9-8. de Jager, C.: *Handbuch der Physik*, vol. 52, ed. S. Flügge, pp. 80–362, Springer-Verlag OHG, Berlin, 1959.

R 18.9-9. Kiepenheuer, K. O.: In "The Sun," ed. G. P. Kuiper, pp. 322–465, The University of Chicago Press, Chicago, 1953.

R 18.9-10. Ellison, M. A.: "The Sun and Its Influence," 2d ed., Routledge and Kegan Paul Ltd., London, 1959.

Section 18.10. The situation as of 1961 in auroral and airglow studies is thoroughly summarized in R 18.1-2. Discussions of auroral and particle precipitation based primarily on satellite observations are contained in:

R 18.10-1. Winckler, J. R., P. D. Bhavsar, and K. A. Anderson: *J. Geophys. Res.*, **67** : 3717 (1962).

R 18.10-2. O'Brien, B. J.: *J. Geophys. Res.*, **67** : 3687 (1962).

Progress (since R 18.1-2) in airglow physics is primarily in dayglow work, notably the detection of dayglow emissions from the ground and rocket observations. See:

R 18.10-3. Noxon, J. F., and R. M. Goody: *J. Atmos. Sci.*, **19** : 342 (1962).

R 18.10-4. Wallace, L. V. and R. A. Nidey: *J. Geophys. Res.*, **69** : 471 (1964).

Atmospheric emissions are discussed in:

R 18.10-5. Hunten, D. M.: *Appl. Opt.*, **3** : 167 (1964).

A review of dayglow physics is found in:

R 18.10-6. Chamberlain, J. W.: *Science*, **142** : 921 (1963).

Techniques of radiative transfer appropriate to planetary atmospheres are discussed in:

R 18.10-7. van de Hulst, H. C.: In "The Atmospheres of the Earth and Planets," ed. G. P. Kuiper, 2d ed., pp. 49–111, The University of Chicago Press, Chicago, 1952.

R 18.10-8. Chandrasekhar, S.: "Radiative Transfer," Dover Publications, Inc., New York, 1960.

R 18.10-9. Ambartsumyan, V. E.: "Theoretical Astrophysics," part VIII, Pergamon Press, New York, 1958.

R 18.10-10. van de Hulst, H. C., and W. M. Irvine: "La Physique des Planètes," pp. 78–98, Institute d'Astrophysique, Liége, 1963 (1962, Liége Astrophysical Colloquium).

The transfer problem worked in the text is from:

R 18.10-11. Chamberlain, J. W., and G. P. Kuiper: *Astrophys. J.*, **124** : 399 (1956).

Section 18.11. The model of the Martian atmosphere presented in the text is covered in R 18.6-1. See also:

R 18.11-1. Kellogg, W. W., and C. Sagan: "The Atmospheres of Mars and Venus," *Natl. Acad. Sci.-Natl. Res. Council, Publ.* 944, 1961.

R 18.11-2. Sagan, C., and W. W. Kellogg: *Ann. Rev. Astron. Astrophys.*, **1** : 235–266 (1963).

R 18.11-3. Kellogg, W. W.: "Space Age Astronomy," eds. A. J. Deutsch and W. B. Klemperer, pp. 425–429, Academic Press Inc., New York, 1962.

Extensive references are available in R 18.11-1 and R 18.11-2.

The detection of water vapor on Mars is reported in:

R 18.11-4. Spinrad, H., G. Münch, and L. D. Kaplan: *Astrophys. J.*, **137** : 1319 (1963).

The possibility of radiation belts is discussed in:

R 18.11-5. Singer, S. F.: In "Space Age Astronomy," eds. A. J. Deutsch and W. B. Klemperer, pp. 444–461, Academic Press Inc., New York, 1962.

Some thoughts on the magnetic fields of the planets are given in R 18.12-6 and:

R 18.11-6. Kern, J. W., and E. H. Vestine: *Space Sci. Rev.*, **2** : 136–171 (1963).

Section 18.12. The structure of the atmosphere of Venus is reviewed in R 18.11-1, R 18.11-2, and:

R 18.12-1. Sagan, C.: In "Space Age Astronomy," eds. A. J. Deutsch and W. B. Klemperer, pp. 430–443, Academic Press Inc., New York, 1962.

A thorough review of the spectrum of Venus complete to 1961 is:

R 18.12-2. Newkirk, G.: "The Spectrum of Venus: A Review," Unfortunately, this manuscript is not yet published.

The Mariner II microwave radiometer experiment is covered in:

R 18.12-3. Barath, F. T., A. H. Barrett, J. Copeland, D. E. Jones, and A. E. Lilley: *Science*, **139** : 908 (1963).

R 18.12-4. Barrett, A. H., and A. E. Lilley: *Sky and Telescope*, **52** : 192 (1963).

The Mariner II observations of charged particles and magnetic field in the vicinity of Venus are presented in:

R 18.12-5. Frank, L. A., J. A. Van Allen, and H. K. Hills: *Science*, **139** : 905 (1963).

R 18.12-6. Smith, E. J., L. Davis, P. J. Coleman, and C. P. Sonett: *Science*, **139** : 909 (1963).

See also R 18.11-6.

The Moon and other satellites

chapter

19

Among the many natural satellites of the solar system, the Moon is unusual and unique, not only because it is the only natural satellite of our Earth, but also because it is large in size relative to its planet. From elsewhere in the solar system, the Earth and Moon would have something of the appearance of a double planet. All of the other satellites are inconspicuous compared to their planets and are of relatively less interest as bodies of the solar system. Because of the importance of and recent intense interest in the Moon, most of this chapter is devoted to it.

19.1 MOTIONS OF THE MOON

The problem of the motions of the Moon in space is an exceedingly complicated one. The Earth-Moon system does not approximate the ideal two-body situation (Sec. 2.2) well. The reasons are (1) the importance of the perturbations on the system by the Sun, (2) the effects of the other

Table 19.1-1   Perturbations on the position of the lunar perigee*

Perturbation due to	Mean annual effect on perigee,''
The Sun	+146,426.92
Nonsphericity of the Earth	+6.41
The planets	+2.53
Mass of the Earth	−0.68
Nonsphericity of the Moon	+0.03
General relativity	+0.02
Net effect	+146,435.23

* After R 19.1-1.

planets, and (3) the nonsphericity of both the Earth and Moon. The relative importance of the various perturbations is illustrated in Table 19.1-1, which lists the effects of each on the location of perigee.

The methods of accounting for all of these effects on the Moon's motion were developed by E. W. Brown, whose publications on the "lunar theory" provide a comprehensive analysis of the problem. The predictions of the position of the Moon based on Brown's lunar theory are so accurate that they have enabled scientists to discover and measure slight changes in the rotational velocity of the Earth. The discrepancies, which amount to a few seconds of arc in a century, are explained as slight irregular changes in the length of the day.

The distance to the Moon is most accurately determined by radar methods; prior to 1957 scientists had to rely on the cruder method of optical triangulation. From radar measures published in 1959, a mean distance between the center of the Moon and the center of the Earth of 384,402 ± 1.5 km was calculated.

19.2   LUNAR SURFACE FEATURES

Because of the lack of any appreciable lunar atmosphere (Sec. 19.4), the surface of the Moon is easily observed in great detail from terrestrial observatories. The surface is clearly divided into two general types of terrain: dark, flat lands and bright, rough, mountainous areas (Fig. 19.2-1). Approximately 75 per cent of the entire surface is characterized by the rougher type of land. This estimate takes into account the Russian observations of the side of the Moon that perpetually faces away from the Earth.

Craters

The most striking and conspicuous lunar formations are the craters, some 300,000 of which larger than 1 km in diameter have been counted on the

Fig. 19.2-1   The full Moon, photographed by the Lick 36-in. refractor. South is at the top. (*Courtesy of Lick Observatory.*)

near side of the Moon alone. These objects consist of an enclosing circular wall, usually rising 1,000 m or so above the surrounding terrain, and a flat, relatively smooth floor, often depressed more than 1,000 m below the normal level of the lunar surface. The craters range in size from barely resolved objects a few hundred meters across to huge walled plains over 200 km in diameter (Fig. 19.2-2).

The origin of the lunar craters has long been a matter of controversy. By analogy with terrestrial craters, two possibilities are suggested: either they are impact craters, like terrestrial meteorite craters (Sec. 11.8), or they are volcanic objects. The only type of volcanic crater that is at all similar to the lunar formations is the type called *maars*, which are shallow, circular depressions with surrounding higher rims (Fig. 19.2-3). The arguments in favor of either a volcanic or an impact origin for the lunar craters deal primarily with the many important details and relationships which

Fig. 19.2-2   Three lunar craters just north of the Altai Mountains: Catharina (top), Cyrillus (middle), and Theophilus. Photographed with the Lick Observatory 120-in. reflector. (*Courtesy of Lick Observatory.*)

scientists have discovered in studying these objects. The primary features bearing on the controversy are outlined below.

1. Distribution. The statistical studies of the distribution of craters over the lunar surface have agreed fairly well that there is little or no significant departure from randomness. This is taken as an argument against the volcanic hypothesis, because terrestrial volcanoes are very nonrandomly distributed over the Earth.

2. Crater chains. In spite of the over-all random location of craters, there are found certain crater groups in which the craters are perfectly lined up in short chains containing five or so similar small ones. These have been used as evidence of a volcanic origin, since volcanic chains are common on the Earth because of the way in which vulcanism parallels

certain gross structural features of the Earth's crust. On the other hand, it has been pointed out that these crater chains might naturally be formed by streams of ejected material thrown out at the time of formation of a larger impact crater.

3. Central peaks. Many lunar craters contain conspicuous central peaks or groups of peaks (Figs. 19.2-2 and 19.2-4). These have been suggested to be similar to the cinder cones occasionally found in terrestrial maars. However, proponents of the impact hypothesis believe that such peaks could be formed by rebound of the material after impact.

4. Ray systems. Bright streaks that cast no shadows are found to emanate in radial systems from several conspicuous craters (Figs. 19.2-1 and 19.2-4). These often extend to considerable distances and cross over all kinds of terrain unimpeded. Their features strongly suggest that they were formed by radial ejection of material from the craters involved, though the suggestion has also been put forward that they represent loci of cracks in the lunar surface caused by impact. Whatever their nature, the ray systems could conceivably have been formed by either impact or volcanic explosion.

5. Filled-in craters. In the smoother portions of the lunar surface there are numerous craters in which only the top of the crater rim, or a portion of it, can be seen; the crater seems to be filled in by the lunar surface material (Fig. 19.2-4). It can readily be understood that volcanic lava flows might act in this way, though it is also conceivable that dust or meteoritic material might be responsible.

6. Schröter's law. The selenographer Schröter pointed out long ago that for most lunar craters the volume of the circular depression very nearly equals the volume of material in the crater wall. The impact hypothesis could very naturally explain this relationship.

7. Lack of erosion. Because there is no atmosphere, the lunar surface

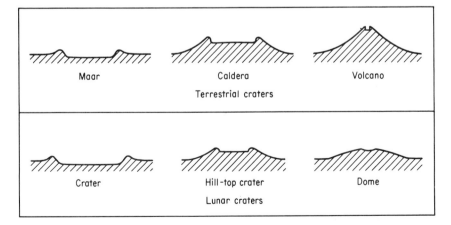

Fig. 19.2-3   Profiles of crater or craterlike formations on the Earth and on the Moon.

Fig. 19.2-4   The lunar craters Archimedes (right), Autolycus (top left), and Aristillus (bottom left). This remarkable photograph, taken with the Lick 120-in. reflector at its coudé focus, shows many features described in the text, including ray systems (around Aristillus), rills, ridges, filled-in craters, mountain chains, and innumerable tiny craters. The scale can be estimated by the crater Archimedes, which has a diameter of 80 km. (*Courtesy of Lick Observatory.*)

experiences little erosion, being affected only by solar and cosmic radiation of various sorts and temperature changes. Therefore, the argument is put forward that, since we know that many meteoritic and asteroidal bodies have undoubtedly (over the age of the solar system) collided with the Moon (the large terrestrial meteorite craters testify to this), then some, at least, of the lunar surface features must be the sites of these collisions.

8. Mountain-top craters and domes. Two somewhat similar features that cannot easily be explained by an impact phenomenon are the rounded mountain tops containing summit craters and the low smooth domes,

some of which also have central craters (Fig. 19.2-3). Both of these features are identifiable with similar terrestrial features of volcanic origin, and if the majority of the craters are impact phenomena, then these at least are probably volcanic.

9. Crater sizes. An empirical relationship has been found between the diameters and the depths of lunar craters, and this same law holds fairly well for terrestrial meteorite and nuclear bomb craters. The diameter D is related to the depth d (both in kilometer) by the relation

$$\log D = 0.108(\log d)^2 + 0.803 \log d + 0.62 \tag{1}$$

There is no proven answer yet to the question of the origin of the lunar craters, though the impact hypothesis is generally favored at the present. The available facts are numerous, and the use of modern astrophysical techniques (Sec. 19.3), as well as the imminent travel to and direct exploration of the Moon, promise an answer in the near future.

Maria

The large, dark, smooth areas on the Moon were originally thought of as seas and were therefore named maria. Of course they contain no water, and in fact they are not even perfectly smooth. In outline lunar maria are roughly circular or polygonal (Fig. 19.2-1), often with a surrounding ring of mountainous areas. Their surfaces, though relatively smooth, are dotted sparsely with small craters, ridges, and shallow valleys (Fig. 19.2-5).

The nearly circular shapes of maria have led to the suggestion that they were formed as giant impact craters by either asteroids or comets, perhaps very early in the history of the solar system. One explanation of the smooth surfaces of the maria is that they are covered with lava flows released by such an impact. Alternatively, it has been suggested that the maria are smooth because they are filled with a very thick dust layer made up of fine deposits from the higher elevations.

Mountains

In addition to crater walls and central peaks, there are many mountains covering much of the lunar landscape outside the maria. The mountains occur both as extensive ranges and as isolated peaks. Among the most conspicuous ranges are the Alps, the Apennines, and the recently discovered Soviet range. Heights of lunar mountains above their bases seldom reach values greater than 6,000 m, and most ranges have mean heights of less than 3,000 m. The slopes are generally not excessively steep; over-all slopes seldom reach 15° from the horizontal, though individual pitches may be considerably steeper than that. Measurements of the heights and slopes of lunar formations traditionally have been made

Fig. 19.2-5   The east border of the Mare Tranquillitatis, showing a portion of the remarkable Ariadaeus Rill (center right). Lick Observatory 120-in. reflector photograph. (*Courtesy of Lick Observatory.*)

by measuring the shadows of the formations. A height on the Moon can be determined from its shadow by a straightforward application of geometry.

Rills

Among the many puzzling and intriguing lunar features are the rills, shallow gorges which cut erratic paths through many parts of the lunar topography. Over 400 rills have been discovered and measured. The largest have lengths as great as 300 km and are some 5 km wide. Careful measures by the shadow method have shown them to be only a few hundred meters deep. Although there have been a number of hypothetical explanations of the rills, there is not yet any real understanding of their mode of origin. A remarkable example is the Ariadaeus Rill (Fig. 19.2-5).

Faults

Formations which may be related in origin to the rills are the long straight cliffs, the most famous example of which is the Straight Wall, 100 km in length. These cliffs may be fault faces similar to those of the Earth. Recent measures of the Straight Wall demonstrate that the differential height is about 200 m and that the slope of the cliff does not exceed 44°.

Valleys

Also apparently associated with rills are the occasional deep, linear mountain valleys. The largest is the Alpine Valley, which cuts a 150-km path through the lunar Alps. Some of the valleys have small ($\sim$10 km) block-like mountains at one end, and this has led to the hypothesis that the valleys are grooves cut by blocks of rock which ploughed through the area. Possibly, large chunks ejected from maria-producing impacts and projected nearly horizontally are responsible for the lunar valleys.

Ridges

Fairly common features on the smoother portions of the lunar surface are the low, rounded, snaking ridges. These rise to heights of a few hundred meters and are often as much as 20 km wide and 100 km long. Their wrinkled surfaces have suggested the possibility that they are edges of lava flows, but lack of any topological gradient across them seems to rule out this interpretation. The most commonly accepted view is that they were caused by compression of the lunar crust.

19.3 THE NATURE OF THE LUNAR SURFACE

The detailed nature of the surface of the Moon is very actively being investigated at the present time. The application of new techniques (radar, radio telescopes, infrared detectors, lasers, spacecraft) has opened the field to new types of analysis, new ideas, and new groups of scientists.

The way in which the Moon reflects electromagnetic radiation provides one of the clues to the nature of the reflecting surface material. The mean albedo of the Moon is very small; the visual Bond albedo for the entire disk has been set at 0.073. This implies a very dark surface material similar to the darker terrestrial rocks such as basalt. Individual areas on the Moon have various albedos differing considerably from this mean. Sample measured values are given in Table 19.3-1. In general, maria and crater floors have low values, whereas rays, crater walls, and mountainous areas have larger albedos.

The visual phase function of the Moon (Fig. 19.3-1) gives information on the coarseness of the surface material. The steepness of the decline of

Table 19.3-1   Albedos of several lunar formations*

Formation	Albedo
Floor of Grimaldi	0.061
Floor of Julius Caesar	0.074
Floor of Theophilus	0.088
Floor of Ptolemaeus	0.102
Rays of Copernicus	0.122
Wall of Hortensius	0.149
Wall of Copernicus	0.156
Central mountain of Aristarchus	0.183

* After Fessenkov.

brightness with phase angle is much greater than for a smooth, dull-surfaced sphere, and this indicates that there is considerable roughness to the surface on a scale larger than the wavelength of light; for much of the sunward surface must be in shadow on a small scale even at moderate phases. Another indication of this shadowing property is the fact that any individual point on the Moon is brightest at full Moon rather than at local noon, as would be the case for a smoother surface. The lack of limb darkening of the full Moon is a further demonstration of this fact.

A related observation is that of the reflectivity of the Moon by lunar radar echoes, which implies that the dielectric constant ϵ of the lunar surface material is approximately 1.5. Measures of the emissivity also imply a small value for the lunar dielectric constant. Rocks, glass, and other terrestrial materials have values of ϵ of between 3 and 10, but very porous samples (about 80 per cent porosity) of these materials can have values of ϵ as low as that of the Moon. This is further evidence that the surface is not smooth, but is rough and perhaps filamentary or porous.

Measures of the temperature of the Moon are also leading toward further understanding of the characteristics of the surface material.

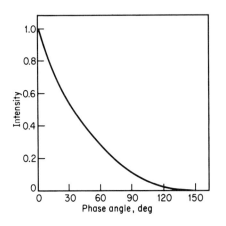

Fig. 19.3-1   Phase curve for the intensity of lunar visual light. (*After Russell.*)

Studies have been made of the variation of lunar temperature: (1) over the disk, (2) over the month, (3) during lunar eclipses, and (4) with different wavelengths. They have led to the following conclusions:

1. Infrared and microwave measurements of the temperature of the disk take advantage of the fact that at these wavelengths Eq. (3.1-2) can be used. If ξ is the angle between the point measured and the subsolar point, then the infrared results lead to the relation

$$T = 389°(\cos \xi)^{1/6} \tag{1}$$

For a smooth surface, it can easily be shown that the temperature should vary as $(\cos \xi)^{1/4}$. The variation observed is interpreted as indicative of a rough surface, though the details of interpretation have not yet been worked out.

2. The variation of temperature over the month, as measured by studying the variation with phase, is illustrated in Fig. 19.3-2. The measured curve can be understood in terms of the thermal conductivity K, the heat capacity c, and the density ρ of the lunar surface material as the shape of the curve is determined by the product of these three physical parameters. In cgs units, $(Kc\rho)^{1/2}$ (the thermal inertia) is found to be approximately 2×10^{-3} for the Moon, whereas it is $\sim 5 \times 10^{-2}$ for ordinary terrestrial rocks and $\sim 10^{-1}$ for terrestrial sands. Very fine dust in a vacuum, however, has a value of $(Kc\rho)^{1/2}$ near 10^{-3}, and so this measure suggests the presence of dust on the lunar surface. Microwave temperature measures show a smaller amplitude and a considerable phase lag with respect to the infrared measures. This is indicative that the microwave radiation comes from layers below the surface, and it suggests the possibility of establishing some of the properties of these layers. The phase lag gives some measure of the time of radiative transfer from the layers involved, and this can be related to the absorption coefficient of the material in a manner similar to that discussed in detail in Chap. 4. Results so far indicate absorption coefficients per unit mass ranging from 3 cm^2/g in the infrared to less than 10^{-2} cm^2/g at centimeter wavelengths.

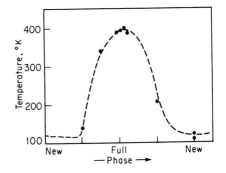

Fig. 19.3-2   Monthly variation of the temperature of the center of the Moon's disk. The dashed curve is a theoretical one for a surface having $(Kc\rho)^{1/2} = 2 \times 10^{-3}$. (*After Sinton.*)

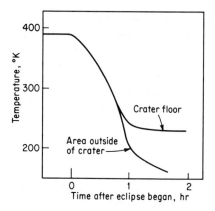

Fig. 19.3-3 Two temperature curves obtained during a lunar eclipse. The upper curve agrees well with a two-layer theoretical model of dust overlying solid rock. The lower curve agrees better with a model of a thick layer of dust or dustlike material. (*After Sinton.*)

Comparisons with laboratory measures for various materials have not yet been made for the wavelengths used.

3. Measures of temperatures of lunar features during lunar eclipses show very rapid declines, often as much as 200°/hr (Fig. 19.3-3). Theoretical temperature curves for various values of $(Kc\rho)^{\frac{1}{2}}$ have been compared with observed curves for a number of lunar areas. For the floors of craters, the observations imply two layers: a thin layer (∼0.5 mm) of dust overlying solid rock. Outside the craters there is recent evidence that the dust (or filaments; see below) is quite thick.

4. By comparing the lunar temperatures measured at widely differing wavelengths, it is possible to infer something regarding the homogeneity of the lunar surface layers, as well as to detect any possible heat from the interior. As yet, the data are too poor to do either with any degree of certainty.

Luminescence: The unimpeded incident solar radiation, especially in the X-ray region, may cause luminescence of portions of the lunar surface. The most promising method so far tried for detecting possible luminescence involves measurement of the depth of reflected solar absorption lines. Where luminescence exists, these lines will be anomalously shallow (Fig. 19.3-4). By scanning over a wide spectral region, an emission spectrum can be pieced together for any desired portion of the lunar surface. So far, results are very fragmentary and sometimes contradictory; nevertheless, this soon may be the most effective and efficient means of determining the chemical composition of the lunar surface.

Models: The current explanations of the measured properties of the lunar surface all hypothesize a finely porous or pillared framework of material. Three examples are the "fairy castle" model of Gold, the "cotton candy" model of Cudaback, and the "skeletal fuzz" model of Warren. The fairy castle model proposes that the surface is covered with fine dust which has gently sifted down to form delicate pillarlike formations resembling fingers or turrets. Laboratory experiments show that such structures could form under lunar conditions and that they conform with all

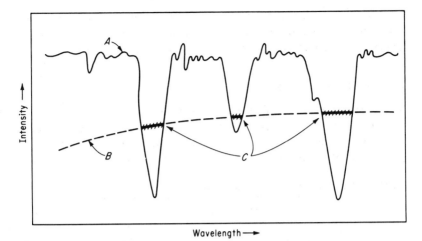

Fig. 19.3-4   Luminescence of the Moon detected in deep absorption lines of the reflected solar spectrum (A). If curve B is the luminescence spectrum of the Moon, the absorption lines are anomolously shallow (C).

the observed properties of the lunar surface. The "cotton candy" model suggests that molten filaments thrown out by the impact of meteorites are interwoven together to form a spongy, porous mass. The proposed "skeletal fuzz" is similarly filamentary; the randomly oriented linear filaments are either meshed together or are branching. No definite choice among these proposed models of the lunar surface can now be made because all satisfy the requirements imposed by the astrophysical observations.

19.4   THE LUNAR ATMOSPHERE

The small velocity of escape of the Moon (2.3 km/sec), combined with the high noon temperatures (389°K), argue against the possibility that the Moon can retain any atmosphere for very long, except perhaps one made up of very heavy gases (e.g., argon or xenon). Possibly gases are produced on the surface by volcanic escape or by meteoritic accretion. A possible volcanic eruption which may have released gases was observed in the crater Alphonsis in 1958. Nevertheless, all tests so far have shown that any atmosphere which may exist is too thin to be detected.

Optical methods of detection of a lunar atmosphere include photometry of stars being occulted by the Moon, polarimetry of lunar twilight, and photometry of the lunar cusps to detect any possible extension of them. The last-mentioned method seems the most sensitive optical test, and it has indicated that the lunar atmosphere is at least less than 10^{-9} that of the Earth, expressed in terms of density at the surface.

A more sensitive test at radio wavelengths attempted to detect the refraction of the Taurus A radio source (the Crab nebula) by any possible lunar ionosphere during a lunar occultation of this object. The upper limit placed by this test is 10^{-13} times the Earth's atmosphere.

19.5 OTHER SATELLITES

Table 19.5-1 is a compilation of physical data on the known satellites of the solar system. In general, the number of satellites that a planet has is related to the total planetary mass. The only planets that do not have known satellites are Mercury, Venus, and Pluto.

Table 19.5-1   Satellites of the solar system

Planet	Satellite	Mean distance from planet, km	Sidereal period of revolution	Radius, km	Mass ratio: satellite/ planet
Earth	Moon	384,402	$27^d7^h43^m$	1,738	0.0123
Mars	Phobos	9,350	$0^d7^h39^m$	8	
	Deimos	23,500	$1^d6^h17^m$	4	
Jupiter	V	181,500	$0^d11^h57^m$	100	
	Io	422,000	$1^d18^h27^m$	1,660	3.8×10^{-5}
	Europa	671,400	$3^d13^h14^m$	1,440	2.5×10^{-5}
	Ganymede	1,071,000	$7^d3^h43^m$	2,470	8.2×10^{-5}
	Callisto	1,884,000	$16^d16^h32^m$	2,340	5.1×10^{-5}
	VI	11,500,000	250^d	60	
	VII	11,750,000	260^d	20	
	X	11,750,000	260^d	10	
	XII	21,000,000	625^d	10	
	XI	22,500,000	692^d	12	
	VIII	23,500,000	739^d	20	
	IX	23,700,000	758^d	11	
Saturn	Mimas	185,700	$0^d22^h37^m$	260	6.7×10^{-8}
	Enceladus	238,200	$1^d8^h53^m$	300	1.5×10^{-7}
	Tethys	294,800	$1^d21^h18^m$	600	1.1×10^{-6}
	Dione	377,700	$2^d17^h41^m$	650	1.8×10^{-6}
	Rhea	527,500	$4^d12^h25^m$	900	4.0×10^{-6}
	Titan	1,223,000	$15^d22^h41^m$	2,500	2.5×10^{-4}
	Hyperion	1,484,000	$22^d6^h38^m$	200	
	Iapetus	3,563,000	$79^d7^h56^m$	650	2.5×10^{-6}
	Phoebe	12,950,000	550^d28^h	140	
Uranus	Miranda	130,100	$1^d24^m50^s$		
	Ariel	191,800	$2^d12^m29^s$	300	
	Umbrial	267,300	$4^d3^m28^s$	200	
	Titania	438,700	$8^d16^m56^s$	500	
	Oberon	586,600	$13^d11^m7^s$	400	
Neptune	Triton	353,600	$5^d21^h3^m$	2,200	1.3×10^{-3}
	Nereid	6,000,000	500^d	150	

There are very possibly more satellites than we have so far discovered. It is unlikely that any more satellites exist for the inner planets, but quite possibly Jupiter, Saturn, Uranus, and Neptune may possess undiscovered ones. The search for Jovian satellites extends to bodies as small as 20 km in diameter, so undiscovered objects must be smaller than this very small limit. The probability that Jupiter's small outer satellites have been captured from the asteroid belt (Sec. 19.7) makes it unlikely that Saturn, Uranus, or Neptune would have many similar satellites, both because of the smaller masses of those planets and because of their greater distance from the asteroid belt. For the other three Jovian planets there is no known satellite smaller than 280 km in diameter.

19.6 PHOBOS AND DEIMOS

Mars has two extremely faint satellites, discovered visually in 1877. Named Phobos and Deimos, these satellites are very close to the planet, with mean distances from the Martian surface of 6,000 and 20,150 km, respectively. Phobos has a period of only 7^h39^m, shorter by more than a factor of 3 than the Martian period of rotation. The result is that this satellite appears from the Martian surface to rise in the *west* and set in the *east*, at least twice each day. Deimos, on the other hand, has a period of $1^d6^m17^s$, nearly equal to the rotation period of the planet, so that it moves exceedingly slowly through the Martian sky. Both satellites are extremely small. By assuming an albedo for them, diameters can be calculated from their brightness; the best values so far give Phobos a diameter of 16 km and Deimos a diameter of 8 km.

19.7 THE SATELLITES OF JUPITER

Of the 12 satellites of Jupiter, by far the largest and most conspicuous are the four "Galilean satellites," discovered by Galileo and used by him as an argument (by analogy) for the Copernican model of the solar system. Roughly the size of our Moon, these satellites have measurable disks, and therefore it has been possible to derive radii and determine albedos for them directly. Presently accepted observations make the albedos of the first three Galilean satellites (Io, Europa, and Ganymede) about the same as that of Jupiter, but the fourth (Callisto) has an albedo less than half this value. When Callisto transits across the face of Jupiter, it is noticeable as a dark spot. Permanent markings have been detected for all satellites, and the evidence from observations of these suggests that their rotation periods and periods of revolution are equal, as for our Moon.

There is evidence that the Galilean satellites do not have atmospheres; this comes both from lack of lines or bands in their spectra and from observations of their phase effects, which, as for our Moon, indicate an atmosphereless, rough surface. Some evidence for the presence of frozen

H_2O on the surface of Europa and Ganymede has been found in the infrared spectra of these objects.

The four Galilean satellites are important in the history of science because they were the subject of the first demonstration that light has a finite velocity. The astronomer Roemer noted in 1675 that there were small irregularities in the times of eclipse of these satellites (their orbits are nearly in the plane of the planet's orbit, so that they suffer an eclipse with nearly every revolution). He found that these irregularities could be completely explained by assuming that light has a finite velocity, and therefore that eclipses are late when the Earth and Jupiter are on opposite sides of the Sun and early when they are on the same side of the Sun. If the size of the Earth's orbit had been better known in Roemer's time, he could have derived the velocity of light quite accurately from his observations.

The other Jovian satellites are all much smaller bodies, ranging in diameter from 200 km down to 20 km. The outer satellites have large eccentricities and high angles of inclination to the ecliptic. Three have retrograde motions. The suggestion has been made that these outer satellites might have originally been asteroids, captured at some time by a combination of perturbations by Jupiter and by the Sun. Calculations show that this is not impossible, and the orbits of the outer satellites are very unlike those of the inner ones, as would be the case if the capture hypothesis were correct.

19.8   SATELLITES OF SATURN, URANUS, AND NEPTUNE

Saturn's satellite Titan, largest of the satellites and possibly somewhat larger than the planet Mercury, is remarkable because it is the only satellite on which an atmosphere has been detected. Molecular bands of methane, as found for Saturn itself, are noticeable in Titan's spectrum.

For Saturn's satellites Mimas and Enceladus it has been found that masses computed from mutual perturbations of the satellites cannot be reconciled with diameters estimated from luminosities unless the albedo is assumed very high and density assumed very low, of the order of 1 g/cm^3. The satellite Iapetus varies in luminosity by a factor of 5, and it is not known whether it is irregularly shaped like an asteroid (Chap. 12) or whether its two hemispheres have extremely different albedos.

The satellites of Uranus and Neptune are difficult objects to study because of their great distance. Size estimates given in Table 19.5-1 are based on assumed albedos. The mass of Triton was computed from the perturbations on its motion caused by the equatorial bulge of Neptune.

19.9   THE RINGS OF SATURN

Also properly included among satellites are the numerous small bodies that make up Saturn's system of rings. This ring system, which makes

Saturn a remarkable object visually, remained a mystery long after first being seen by Galileo. It has the appearance of a large, extremely thin, flat circular sheet, lying centered on the planet and in the equatorial plane. Three rings have been distinguished; the outer or ring A is separated from the brightest ring, B, by a narrow gap called Cassini's division, after its discoverer. Interior to ring B is a very faint, semitransparent ring called the "crepe" ring.

The rings of Saturn are very large in extent. Ring A has a radius of 130,000 km and is 16,000 km wide. Cassini's division is approximately 5,000 km wide, and Ring B has a width of 25,000 km. The crepe ring is roughly 18,000 km wide and reaches to within 11,000 km of Saturn's equator. Since the rings are in the plane of the equator, inclined 27° to the plane of Saturn's orbit, we occasionally see them edge-on, at which times they virtually disappear. Their thickness, judged from measures made at such times, must be less than 1 km.

Although it was conjectured at one time that the rings might be liquid or solid sheets of material, it was shown more than a hundred years ago that this would be impossible. In 1850 Roche demonstrated that a liquid satellite that close to the planet would be unstable because of the way in which gravitational forces due to the planet would be spread out over a large solid angle. Maxwell demonstrated nine years later that a ring made up of small particles, each in its own independent orbit, would be stable under such conditions, whereas a solid or liquid ring would not be.

There are many demonstrations of the particle nature of the rings. Figure (19.9-1) shows one of them, in which the tilt of the lines in the spectrum of the rings shows that the velocity is not uniform for the rings, but varies with radius, decreasing outward. These velocities are found to follow Kepler's law. Another demonstration is presented when a star is occulted by the rings. The star, if bright enough, remains dimly visible

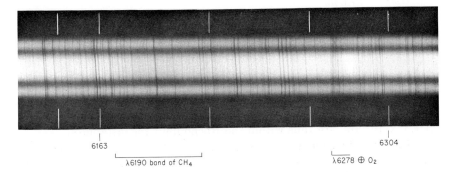

6163

λ6190 band of CH₄   λ6278 ⊕ O₂   6304

Fig. 19.9-1   Spectrum of Saturn and its rings, obtained at the coudé focus of the 120-in. telescope. The slope of the lines in the rings shows that the rings are not solid objects. The lines of the CH₄ band are absent on the rings. O₂ bands from the Earth's atmosphere are conspicuous by their lack of slope. (*Courtesy of Lick Observatory.*)

as it passes behind rings A and B, reaching its normal brightness in Cassini's division. Behind ring C it is very little dimmed.

The phase variations of the brightness of the rings permit certain important physical parameters to be derived. Whereas the planet's variations with phase are small, as for Jupiter or Venus, the rings show a striking maximum luminosity at full phase, with a rapid diminution with increasing phase angle. Detailed photoelectric observations, such as made recently in South Africa by Franklin, permit an interpretation of this effect in terms of mutual shadowing of the ring particles; space densities and particle sizes can be determined. The latest results indicate that the particles are primarily only a few meters in size. Apparently we see in Saturn's rings the material that might have made up a close satellite, but which, because of being inside Roche's limit, never was able to coalesce into a single body.

The Roche limit for Saturn can be derived in a very simple way. Consider two particles of mass m and radius r, at a mean distance d from the center of Saturn. They are taken to be in mutual contact and aligned along a projected radius vector of Saturn, so that one is at distance $(d - r)$ and the other at distance $(d + r)$ from the planet. These particles can remain as a stable gravitational configuration as long as their mutual attractive force is greater than the difference in the forces on each by Saturn. Saturn's mass (M) exerts a force on the first particle of $GMm/(d - r)^2$ and on the second of $GMm/(d + r)^2$, the difference being

$$GMm\left[\frac{1}{(d - r)^2} - \frac{1}{(d + r)^2}\right] \approx GMm\,\frac{4r}{d^3}$$

The mutual gravitational attraction for the particles is $Gm^2/4r^2$ so that the stability criterion, Roche's limit, is

$$\frac{Gm^2}{4r^2} = \frac{4GMmr}{d^3}$$

or

$$d = \left(\frac{16Mr^3}{m}\right)^{\frac{1}{3}}$$

Taking the density of the particles to be approximately 1 gives a value of d of $\sim 1.5 \times 10^5$ km. The rings of Saturn, which extend to a distance of 1.3×10^5 km, are thus within the Roche limit for instability.

Cassini's division, as well as the several other gaps in the rings that have been seen by different observers, can be explained by perturbations due to the satellites. A ring particle located at Cassini's division would have a period just one-half that of the satellite Mimas, and its orbit would therefore be unstable. The gaps in Saturn's rings are closely analogous to the gaps in the asteroid belt (Chap. 12).

BIBLIOGRAPHICAL NOTES

Section 19.1. Comprehensive treatment of lunar motions is given in:

R 19.1-1. Brown, E. W.: "Tables of the Motion of the Moon," Yale University Press, New Haven, Conn. 1919.

R 19.1-2. Brouwer, D., and G.-I. Hori: In "Physics and Astronomy of the Moon," ed. Z. Kopal, pp. 1–25, Academic Press Inc., New York, 1962.

Section 19.2. Lunar surface features are discussed in:

R 19.2-1. Baldwin, R. B.: "The Face of the Moon," The University of Chicago Press, Chicago, 1949.

R 19.2-2. Beer, W., and J. Madler: "Der Mond," Schropp, Berlin, 1837.

R 19.2-3. Fielder, G.: "The Structure of the Moon's Surface," Pergamon Press, New York, 1961.

R 19.2-4. Firsoff, V. A.: "Strange World of the Moon," Basic Books, New York, 1959.

R 19.2-5. Kuiper, G.: "Photographic Lunar Atlas," The University of Chicago Press, 1960.

R 19.2-6. Shoemaker, E. M.: In "Physics and Astronomy of the Moon," ed. Z. Kopal, pp. 283–351, Academic Press Inc., New York, 1962.

Section 19.3. Astrophysical observations bearing on the nature of the lunar surface are discussed in various chapters of:

R 19.3-1. Kopal, Z. (ed.): "Physics and Astronomy of the Moon," Academic Press Inc., New York, 1962.

R 19.3-2. Kopal, Z. (ed.): "The Moon," Academic Press Inc., New York, 1962.

Section 19.4. The lunar atmosphere is reviewed in:

R 19.4-1. Costain, C. H., B. Elsmore, and G. R. Whitfield: *Monthly Notices Roy. Astron. Soc.*, **116**: 380 (1956).

R 19.4-2. Dollfus, A.: *Ann. Astrophys.*, **19**: 83 (1956).

R 19.4-3. Öpik, E. J.: *Planet. Space Sci.*, **9**: 211 (1962).

Sections 19.5 to 19.9. Other satellites are discussed in:

R 19.5-1. Kuiper, G. P., and B. M. Middlehurst (eds.): "Planets and Satellites," chaps. 8 and 18, The University of Chicago Press, Chicago, 1961.

Index

Barringer meteorite crater, 275, 277
Bediasite, 279, 281
Behr, A., 198, 200, 296
Bénard convection cell, 85
Berlage, H., cosmogony of, 3
Bessel-Bredichin theory, 17, 18, 228, 230, 235, 236
Bethe, H., carbon cycle, 35
Beyer, M., 223
Bickerton, A., cosmogony of, 3
Bielid meteor shower, 255, 303, 309
Biermann, L., 198
Billitonite, 279
Bipolar group, 146
Bipolar magnetic region, 146
Birkeland, K., cosmogony of, 3
Blackbody temperature, 366, 367
Blackwell, D. E., 202, 203, 294–298
Blanketing effect, 65
Blue clearing, 359
BMR (bipolar magnetic region), 146
Bode's law, 2
Böhm, K. H., 60
Böhm-Vitense, E., 60
Bolide, 303
Bolometer measure, 341
Boltzmann constant, 33
Boltzmann equation, 123
Boltzmann formula, 75
Bound-free transitions, 36
Bow wave, terrestrial, 399, 401
Bowen, I. S., 74
Bowhill, S. A., 395
Boxhole meteorite crater, 277
Bracewell, R. N., 114
Brahe, Tycho, 7
Bremmstrahlung, 133
Brenham meteorite crater, 277
Broadening mechanism, 69
Brouwer, D., 287
Brown, E. W., 422
Buffon, G., cosmogony of, 3
Bullen, R., 328
Butterfly diagram, 141

C

C region, 173
CA (see Center of activity)
Cabannes, J., 74

Callisto, 434, 435
Campo del Cielo meteorite crater, 277
Canals, Martian, 356
Carbon cycle, 35
  reaction rate, 36
Carbonaceous chondrite, 264
Cassini's division, 437, 438
Catharina, 424
Celestial mechanics, 7–22
Center of activity, 122, 170–173
  C region, 173
  coronal condensation, 173
  M region, 173
  magnetic region, 173
  UMR, 173
Center of mass, 12
Centrifugal acceleration, 9
Čerenkov radiation, 133
Ceres, 285, 286, 289
Chamberlain, J. W., 201, 203, 394, 412
Chamberlin, T., cosmogony of, 3
Chandrasekhar, S., 47, 50, 64
  principles of invariance, 50–55
Chandrasekhar mean, 59
Chapman, S., 198, 200, 201
Chapman region, 388
Charge exchange, 232
Chemical composition, of meteorites, 267
  solar, 38
Chemosphere, 381
Chinguetti meteorite, 274, 275
Chondrite, 264, 266, 268
  carbonaceous, 264
  enstatite, 264
Chondrule, 264, 266
Chromosphere of Sun, 90–99
  chromospheric network, 97
  figure, 99
  density, 95–97
  emission gradient, 94
  fine structure, 97–98
  flash spectrum, 91
  granulation, 97
  model of, 63
  network, 97, 99
  spectroheliograms, 97–99
  spicules, 90, 98
  transition zone, 99

F

G

Tauras A radio source, 434
Taurid meteor shower, 253, 257
Tektite, 277–282
  Australite, 279, 281
  Bediasite, 279, 281
  Billitonite, 279
  Empirite, 281
  Georgia tektite, 279
  Indochinite, 279, 281
  Ivory Coast tektite, 279
  Moldavite, 279, 281
  Philippinite, 279, 281
Temperature, adiabatic gradient, 32, 34, 80
  blackbody, 366, 367
  bolometer measure, 341
  of corona, 110–112
  infrared spectrophotometry, 341
  of Moon, 430–432
  of planet, 322, 326, 340, 341
  radio measurements, 341
  thermocouple measure, 341
Ter Haar, cosmogony of, 3
Terrestrial planets, 316, 317
Tethys, 434
Tharsis region, 358, 359
Theophilus, 424, 430
Thermal conductivity, 200
Thermal inertia, 353, 431
Thermocouple measure, 341
Thermodynamics, 75–77
Thermometric conductivity, 86
Thermosphere, 381, 389, 390
Thickness, optical, 46
Thompson scattering, 36, 105
Thoth system, 354, 355
Three-body problem, 15–18
Titan, 320, 434, 436
Titania, 434
Transfer, equation of, 45–47
Transient radiation, 190–194
Transition zone in solar chromosphere, 99
Transmission function, 53
Triton, 320, 434, 436
Trojan asteroids, 15, 287, 288
Tropopause, of Earth, 380
  Martian, 411
Troposphere, 380, 389

Tunguska meteorite "crater," 275, 277
Two-body problem, 12
Type I comet tail, 229–232
Type II comet tail, 230, 231
Type III comet tail, 230

U

Ultraviolet radiation, 180–184
Umbrial, 434
UMR, 173
Unipolar group, 146
Unsöld, A., 62, 63, 74
Uranus, atmosphere, 375, 376
  interior, 332, 333
Ursid meteor shower, 253

V

Van Allen belts, 399, 402–407
Van de Hulst, H. C., 100, 104, 294
Van der Waals broadening, 69
Venus, 346–350, 365
  atmosphere, 414–417
    aeolosphere model, 415
    composition, 414
    greenhouse model, 415
    structure, 414
  interior, 329
  ionosphere, 415
  magnetic field, 333
  magnetosphere, 417
  nightglow, 407
  photography, 339
  radio emission, 343
  radio measurement, 341
Vesta, 285, 286, 289
Virial theorem, 29
Voigt profile, 71
Von Weizäcker, cosmogony of, 3
Vredefort formation, 275

W

Wabar meteorite crater, 277
Wallace, L., 408
Walled plain on Moon, 423